Treat Yourself to a Better Sex Life

*There is but one salvation
for the tired soul:
love for another person.*

JOSE ORTEGA

Contents

4
Getting Down to Cases
244

xiii

Preface

This book was written with the hope that it will help many of its readers get more out of their sex lives in a fairly rapid, pleasant way, without the embarrassment, time, and expense associated with professional help.

In many cases involving sexual problems, a professional sex therapist might charge $2,000–$3,000 to provide essentially the same procedures that are contained in this book. For a broad range of sexual problems, *Treat Yourself To A Better Sex Life* will go as far as the reader has to go to get help, as well as to achieve greater sexual satisfaction. And for the cost of a few dollars, that's not bad.

The reason we believe this is that this book translates into everyday English principles and procedures of sex therapy that have been demonstrated in research to be effective. These principles and procedures come from two sources. The first is the field of behavior therapy, a field that has pioneered in the development of specific helping procedures applied to specific problems, including sexual problems. This is one of the fastest growing and most important (because of its effectiveness) fields in the area of psychotherapy and counseling. The second source is the work of practitioners and researchers in sex clinics (such as Masters and Johnson) who have developed a range of effective procedures for relieving sexual problems and for enhancing sexual pleasures. Both areas—behavior therapy and the specialized work of sex therapists—are highly compatible with each other. They are integrated in this book to the extent that proven principles underlie much of the information, exercises, and procedures that we present.

In essence, then, *Treat Yourself to a Better Sex Life* translates scientifically demonstrated helping procedures into a self-help guide in what we hope is a highly readable, pleasant, yet effective format.

Treat Yourself to a Better Sex Life describes in a systematic step-by-step fashion just what many licensed expert sex therapists would tell you about understanding and dealing with sexual problems. In fact, the book is organized that way: It begins with a discussion of the sexual problems that you might be experiencing and takes you all the way through a number of guidelines and instructions on how to overcome these problems and enhance your sex life.

The focus of the book is, in part, on understanding sexual problems as largely a product of learning experiences. They are, therefore, treatable by the directed learning experiences that are the core of this book. The main focus of *Treat Yourself to a Better Sex Life* is on practicality—what to do and how to do it.

In many ways, the format of this book is organized along the lines of one of the comprehensive sex programs that are offered by many sex therapists. The book moves you through the logical stages involving a general understanding of your own sexual behavior to an understanding of the treatment program and its basic concepts. Next, it shows you how to identify and pinpoint sexual problems and then tells you what to do about them.

We realize—as should the reader—that no book, not even this one, can successfully resolve all sexual problems. There are problems that do require the services of a trained sex therapist. Indeed, if you find that the programs in this book do not significantly affect your sexual problems, you should not hesitate to seek out professional help. There are a growing number of psychologists, ministers, social workers, and physicians who have had specific training in helping individuals and couples overcome problems in their sexual functioning. In the Epilogue at the end of this book, we discuss ways to go about selecting a competent, professional helper.

However, we believe that the programs in this book should be able to offer substantial help to many men and women with a wide range of sexual difficulties. We also hope that it can provide some ideas to help people who have no particular sexual problems simply get more out of their sexual relationships.

This book is focused in large part on relationships between males and females. However, we hope that our readers will not interpret this emphasis as a rejection of other sexual activities, such as same-sex relationships. Such activities are often experienced as pleasurable and fulfilling by many people, including those who have very satisfying heterosexual relationships. Indeed, although the book focuses on ways to improve one's heterosexual activities, many of the ideas presented can be applied to improving same-sex activities as well, whether or not one also engages in heterosexual activities.

HOW TO USE THIS BOOK

This book was written not only to be read, but to be *used*. In fact, we've tried to write and organize this book in a way that will prove most useful, as well as most enjoyable, to you. It is organized to flow from general introductory material to specific programs for helping you enhance your sex life.

There are four parts to the book.

Part 1 is titled "(Re)thinking About Sex." In this part, we have tried to give you some ideas regarding what this book is all about. We have presented some general guidelines for using the book, tried to expose some common myths about sexuality, and devoted a chapter to discussing love, sex, and commitment. Love and commitment are topics that we believe are essential in understanding sex.

Part 2 is called "When Things Go Wrong." Here we describe some of the common problems that people experience in their sex lives. We have separate chapters on men and women, and one on the common sexual problems of both men and women. The chapters in Part 2 are intended to give you a handle on the sex problems that you might be struggling with. We hope that this understanding will help you when you try the Treat Yourself program to overcome them.

Part 3 is called "Treat Yourself." Here we present in detail the various exercises that you will be using to Treat Yourself. The basic program—what you can expect—is described in

Chapter 7. Chapters after that teach you how to assess your sex life, how to develop better communication with your partner, and how to set up contracts with your partner or yourself to help you with your Treat Yourself Program. Other chapters describe the specific exercises you will be using: relaxation exercises, fantasy and self-stimulation exercises, and some very exciting and helpful exercises called Erotic Pleasure. We also give you a brief introduction in Chapter 12 to how your body (and your partner's body) works. The chapters in Part 3 are very important to the success of your Treat Yourself program. You'll be using all of them in every program, so we urge that you read these first, before you begin treating yourself.

Part 4 is titled "Getting Down to Cases." Here's where we put it all together. We describe specific programs for dealing with specific problems. In essence, we integrate the material from Parts 1, 2, and 3 into programs that deal with a number of specific problems. There are individual chapters dealing with problems of arousal, orgasm, and painful or difficult intercourse for women, and with ejaculation and erection problems of men. The last two chapters of the book describe programs for helping you to overcome your distaste for certain sexual activities, and for what to do when you find sex boring.

We have some specific recommendations as to how you should use this book. Start off by reading all the chapters in Parts 1, 2, and 3. This is important background material that will help you when you start your actual program. Then, read the chapter in Part 4 that deals with the problem you want to work on. You might do this reading with your partner, discussing it as you go.

Once you're ready to begin, try to follow as carefully as possible our guidelines. Make sure that you follow through with *practicing* the exercises. Just reading the book won't be enough. You'll really have to practice.

Programs like the ones we describe have been used to help literally thousands of people, and we've based the Treat Yourself programs on considerable research showing that they can be effective. They can really help you. Each program is composed of graduated steps through which you work slowly but surely toward your goal. The instructions will move you quickly enough so that you keep your interest, but slowly enough so that you don't get overwhelmed or too uncomfortable.

We are trying to accomplish two things. First, we want you to overcome your fears, anxieties, or inhibitions about sex. Second, we want you to be able to increase the sexual behaviors you want to increase—to enjoy yourself more, to be able to be turned on and to turn someone else on, and to find increasing joy and pleasure in sex.

ACKNOWLEDGMENTS

We have tried to incorporate into this book the most current and the soundest approaches to sexual behavior and problems. Much of this comes from our own clinical practice and from the experiences of our students and colleagues. We have been fortunate to have a number of sex educators and counselors in Hawaii, such as Jack Annon, Craig Robinson, Ron Pion, Milton Diamond, Wendell Ricketts, Pam Russell, Vincent De Feo, Larry Lister, and Susan Chandler. Many of their ideas have found their way into this book. We have also drawn from the research and writings of leaders in the field of work with sexual problems, such as William Masters, Virginia Johnson, Randy Sue Arnow, Joseph LoPiccolo, Lonnie Barbach, Bernie Zilbergeld, Linda Alperstein, Erwin Haeberle, and Helen Singer Kaplan. Much of the progress in understanding and providing effective help for sexual problems is a product of their efforts.

We were fortunate that our wives, Jean Gochros and Ursula Fischer, not only sustained us during the many months this manuscript was being prepared but offered their critical evaluation of its contents.

We have also been blessed with having secretaries like Diane Miller, Louise Young, Mary Lau, Mildred Frank, and Hisae Tachi. As with our previous books, they not only typed our manuscripts but confronted us regularly with problems in our syntax, grammar, and thinking.

We also want to thank Joe Murray and Lynne Lumsden, our friends at Prentice-Hall, for their enthusiastic encouragement of this enterprise. They made the whole process seem almost painless.

And finally, we'd like to tip our hats to each other. This is the fourth book we've written together. Each time we write a book, we fight and disagree on just about everything. We each have very different writing styles and work habits. Indeed, we are always a bit amazed (as are our families and friends) that our books ever get completed, somehow satisfying both of us. We're usually even still talking to each other when we're finished. But in the heat of writing, we both regularly swear that we will *never* again write a book together. However, inevitably one of us gets an idea for a worthwhile new project. And then . . .

PART

1

(Re)thinking About Sex

One

What Are You Getting Into?

It's hard to admit that there's something about sex that you may not know. It may even be harder to admit that something isn't working right in your sex life.

Men are supposed to know about sex and be good at it, practically from the cradle. And women either aren't supposed to care, if they're unliberated, or be even better at it than men if they *are* liberated. But many, many people *do* have sexual problems. Indeed, the famous sex researchers Masters and Johnson have estimated that up to 50 percent of American marriages have or may eventually develop sexual problems. Add to this the countless number of single people who may have even more complicated sex lives, and you have—to say the least—an awful lot of problems related to sex.

What do you do if you have a sexual problem?

You can go to a neighbor, a relative, or a friend. Sometimes that helps. But sometimes they are as misinformed, confused, and uptight as you are.

You can go to a minister, physician, hairdresser, or bartender. Sometimes that helps. But sometimes *they* are as misinformed, confused, and uptight as your neighbors, relatives, or friends.

You can go to a professional like a psychiatrist, psychologist, or social worker. Yet it is an unfortunate but true fact that most of these professional helpers have never had specific training in helping people with sexual problems. Many of them know as much, or as little, about sex as you do.

You can go to a specialized sex therapist. Sometimes that helps. But that's difficult to predict. It is not always easy to be sure whether they are going to be competent and effective. For example, no state even licenses sex therapists, and national certification by professional organizations is just beginning to be a reality. So it's not even clear what kind of help you'll be getting from a "sex therapist."

To compound the problem, sex therapy, even when available, can be fantastically expensive. A flat fee of $2,500 is quite common. Ironically, it is usually considerably cheaper to get effective psychiatric therapy for a suicidal depression than it is to get therapy by a specialist for sex problems.

But even if you can find competent sex therapists (and there aren't that many around), and even if you can afford their services, there are several reasons why you still may not want to do so.

1. Going for help with sex problems can be embarrassing and can get you very uptight, and either you or your partner may feel that it's not worth the embarrassment.

2. Many people don't want to label themselves or be labeled as "sick," which they feel may be a result of going to professionals for help.

3. Many people do not feel that their problem is big enough or complicated enough to justify or require the expense, time, and effort involved in getting formal therapy.

So you decide, in the good old American tradition, "I'll fix it myself—I'll get a book!" You go to the corner drugstore and discover that there is no shortage of books about sex. There are confessions of Congressional call girls, autobiographies and how-to-do-it books by ex-hookers, advice books by people who give you only a single letter for a name, enthusiastic directions from a happy-go-lucky physician you have seen on "The Tonight Show," and illustrated "cookbooks" of sexual positions.

But although many of these books contain some useful ideas for some people, they often just don't give people what they need, and reading them just leads to more frustration. In one book, the language is too technical and sterile and the suggestions sound more like surgical procedures than uninhibited enjoyment. Another book sounds wild but seems as if it were written for people with bodies and sexual appetites that may be at home among the young swingers in Greenwich Village, New York, or North Beach, San Francisco, but that are hardly appropriate for you. Even the models for the illustrations, with their beards, long hair, and fantastic bodies, seem unfamiliar: "That isn't *us!*" All too often, the popular sexual-self-help books contain a sexist point of view and have maintained myths and fallacies about sex and values harmful to effective, satisfying, and enjoyable sexual functioning.

And so your questions may still go unanswered, and the useful specific suggestions relevant to the common sexual problems of most men and women are hard to find.

It's for these reasons that we have written this book: (1) to provide a source of accurate information and guided systematic instructions to help you with your sexual problems, and (2) to enhance your sex life. These instructions are simple and, we hope, enjoyable. They are based on tested, effective, scientifically based procedures for the average man or woman who is experiencing difficulties in getting and giving pleasure in his or her sexual relationships.

Although this book does focus on physical activities, it takes into account the knowledge that sexual problems are more often a product of destructive learning—attitudes, anxieties, assumptions, and values about sex—than a matter of genital mechanics. Someone once said that the most important sex organ is the brain. Once a person who is experiencing sexual problems begins to unlearn the ideas that have blocked his or her sexual enjoyment, nature often will take its course and sexual joy will emerge.

But perhaps the best way to set the stage for this book, and to let you know what we hope to accomplish with it, is to give you a little bit of a sneak preview. Let's use our title—*Treat Yourself to a Better Sex Life*—as our guide.

TREAT . . .

Treat has two meanings, and both meanings are intended in this book:

1. *Treat* can mean to intentionally bring about a change in people's behavior. As related to sexuality, we believe—indeed, we have evidence to support a strong conviction—that

people's sexual behavior is *learned*. It is not preordained or born into you but is a product of countless experiences, thoughts, fantasies, and feelings we all have had as we were growing up and continue to have as adults. The results of these experiences include feeling good or bad about ourselves and our bodies, having pleasant or uncomfortable physical experiences, and being told, if we engage in specific sexual activities, that we're okay or not okay by our parents, friends, teachers, ministers, and others. These experiences taught us how to think, feel, and behave as sexual human beings. This includes the happy, good, successful, and rewarding things we have learned to do, think, and feel about sex. It also includes the sad, bad, unhappy, and devastating things we have learned to do, think, and feel.

This basic idea is one that does not come easily to many people. Many of us are convinced that our sexual feelings, thoughts, and behaviors are built into us and thus cannot be changed. This just isn't true. Whatever is learned can be unlearned. And, once again, most of our sexual problems come from harmful things we have learned about sex. There is ample evidence that people whose sexual problems have been treated in terms of this knowledge about how problems are learned have significantly changed their sexual behavior. You can too.

This book will show you how. We will translate into everyday language the latest scientific findings on how you can treat your own sex life most effectively. As we mentioned in the Preface, we will provide you with a number of suggestions, procedures, techniques, and exercises covering all forms of your sex life—from what you do in bed to sharing intimate thoughts and feelings with your partner. They are presented here in a way in which you can apply them simply and enjoyably in order to change and enhance your sex life.

2. *Treat* also means to give yourself pleasure. Many of us are brought up to feel that somehow we don't *deserve* to have sexual pleasure or that if something feels good it must be either bad for us or immoral. For some, sex is a ritual one goes through from time to time as a duty to one's partner. We don't agree with these attitudes. We believe that our body has the capacity to give us—and others—joy, and that it is good to learn to get what we can from this joy. To be sure, we shouldn't misuse it, or use it without compassion and responsibility. But we think that most of us know when we're really using sex without concern for our partner, and that we can go beyond that to really treating ourselves to what nature has given us to enjoy. So "treat" also means: Enjoy!

Our basic conviction in this book is that, if at all possible, it is better to change your sexual behavior *yourself*. We realize that this goes against the grain of some contemporary American values. We hear all too often that if something is wrong, *don't* try to fix it yourself; you'll only make it worse. Spend an extra couple of bucks and go to an *expert* (mechanic, repairman, plumber, physician, etc.) and he'll fix it for you fast and it will stay fixed.

That's fine, and often a good idea. But there are several drawbacks—and even hazards—to searching for an expert to fix up any sexual problems you may have:

□ There may be no experts around.

□ The "experts" may be incompetent, using techniques that are basically ineffective.

□ Experts cost a lot.

□ It can be awfully embarrassing.

□ It may not help.

Certainly, there are situations in which going to a competent professional helper may be preferable to doing it yourself, or alas, necessary. So in the Epilogue of this book, we will provide some guidelines for knowing when to go to and how to shop for a professional therapist. But generally we have found that the first and often best line of help is self-help, and that is what this book is all about. You know most about yourself, and you probably care most about what happens to you. So *you* do it. What we'll provide is a systematic way of going about it; we'll give you the tools.

Perhaps even more importantly, we know that treating yourself can work; for most sexual problems, you just don't *need* a professional. You're a skeptic? Read on; we'll try to prove it to you.

One final note on "yourself." This book is intended as a self-help book. But that doesn't mean that your partner is excluded. Although we will offer numerous suggestions for you to use even if you don't have a partner, you're far better off if you do.

Don't underestimate the importance of your partner in going through our procedures. He or she should be reading through this book with you and should be as involved as you. After all, if all goes well, your partner will get as much out of any improvements as you will. If your partner is a little reluctant to give it a try, remember that you've got nothing to lose and that you both have everything to gain.

Indeed, we hope that one of the benefits of your using this book will be not only understanding yourself (and others of your sex) better, but also better understanding about where your partner (and others of his or her sex) is coming from. It helps to understand the factors that can create problems, because that understanding can enhance your pleasures and the pleasures of those people with whom you will be sharing your bed. Remember: Understanding your partner and being able to enhance his or her pleasure is half of the way home toward enhancing your own pleasure.

. . . TO A BETTER . . .

Notice that we're not saying "the best" or even "a fantastic" sex life. We believe that searching for "the ultimate orgasm" or perfection in sexual technique often leads to trouble. Such a quest focuses people on their technique and on competence rather than on experiencing the enjoyment of what they're doing. Indeed, Masters and Johnson use the term *performance anxiety* to describe the common problems of people who are more concerned with *how* they are doing than with enjoying *what* they are doing. Often, the result is that they can neither do it nor enjoy it.

Furthermore, there *are* no general rules or measures of being "good at" sex. There need be no specific goals to aspire to other than better understanding and enjoying your own— and your partner's—unique sexuality. Each person is different in what he or she enjoys doing in bed. And we each change over time. The "test" of any sexual experience, if there is any, is the personal and sexual enjoyment of both of the people involved at a particular moment in time, and this has, or should have, little to do with the rules or expectations of anybody outside the room.

Thus, the purpose of this book is not to turn out competitors for some sexual olympics. Rather, if this book succeeds, it will help you to relax, to be less anxious, and to get more satisfaction and fun out of your own sexual relationships. Indeed, the "treatments" we'll describe can be applied to overcome various sex problems, but they may also be used to enhance your sex life and to make it better—even if you may not have a particular problem.

7

The little word *sex* means different things to different people. To some, it means gender (i.e., whether you're a male or a female); to some, it means voluptuousness; to some, it just means intercourse. To us, it means a variety of feelings and actions having to do with enjoying your body while enjoying someone else's and, at the same time, sensing and enjoying the relationship that exists between you.

The purpose of this book is to help the reader get more out of his or her sex life. By that, we mean more than just being expert at a mechanical physical act or, at the other extreme, immersing yourself in a vague, mystical aura of sexuality. Instead, we hope that the reader will become more familiar with his or her own and his or her partner's bodies, and that he or she will become more aware about how to give and receive sexual pleasure, both physically and emotionally. In other words, we think that the programs we'll describe in this book will help you feel better and will help you function sexually with more comfort, more confidence, and more enjoyment.

Of course, one's sexual life involves more than what we actually do in bed, although it certainly does include that. But it also involves how we feel about ourselves, how we feel about our sexuality, and how effectively we integrate sex into our lives. As we mentioned before, the most important sex organ is the brain. We hope this book will help you exercise that organ!

And there you have have it. We hope that this book will help you "Treat Yourself to a Better Sex Life." To enable you to do this, we have reviewed current research on approaches to sexual problems and have chosen those approaches that have proven most effective and are most adaptable to helping yourself.

Although what we present is based on the latest research findings on sex, we have tried to write the book in everyday language avoiding the technical information and jargon that often creeps into sex books. We feel that technical language should be kept to a minimum in the area of sex. The language of sex in everyday use, as well as in the privacy of the bedroom, is and should be simple and clear and even full of joy. We hope that this book reflects that orientation to sex.

Two

You've Got to Be Carefully Taught: Sexual Myths

Warning: This book is written by people—two of them. As such, we have our biases. We have tried to base this book on the best "facts" that we can find from contemporary sex research. However, we realize that most of what we read—and a lot of what we have written—is based on opinions—what we *think* is true rather than on fact (what *is* true).

That's not all bad as long as we know it's opinion.

The point is that much of your approach to sex is also based on *your* opinion and on the opinions of all those people who have influenced you—and not only on facts. It's important not to confuse the two. Opinion can, and often does, change—and that's fine. As we learn more facts, our opinions *should* change.

Unfortunately, many of the supposed "facts" we acquire as we are growing up stay with us and greatly influence our sexual ideas and behavior. This may be partly because they are stated with such authority by people whom we respect and believe (parents, teachers, and friends), and partly because no one around us gives us solid information to challenge the misinformation.

In this chapter, we will take a look at the nature and

sources of the more common harmful sexual myths and how they may have influenced you, and we'll try to present the facts that challenge the myths.

HOW SEXUAL ATTITUDES ARE BORN

Everybody has had an elaborate sex education. It's not necessarily the kind you get in public school or even the type some people get when they sit down with their mother or father for a long, uncomfortable session on the birds and the bees. Rather, it's the type we get from the way our parents touch us or *don't* touch us when we're children, the way they treated our and their own nudity, the way they show or don't show affection to each other, and the way they react to or ignore our questions or comments about sex.

And it's not only our parents. Many of our ideas and values about sex—as well as our information and misinformation—come from our same-age and same-sex friends. Our gangs, classmates, and neighborhood buddies are major molders of our sexual expression.

As adolescents, and even as adults, most of us are very eager to be accepted and respected by our friends. We are vulnerable to their rejection. We therefore study very carefully what it takes to win their approval. Even more carefully, we study what will bring about ridicule from them, and then we avoid doing or even saying those things that will get us "put down." For example, we watch who and what is laughed at in our friends' dirty jokes: small penises, promiscuous girls, virgins of either gender, homosexuals, and masturbators. As we join in the laughter, we make mental notes about what is expected of us.

Indeed, dirty jokes, as well as pornography, can have a profound effect on our development. Pornography and dirty jokes often provide us with the only clear, explicit models of what people are supposed to like and do sexually.

It's true that our parents and our ministers talk about sex to a greater or lesser extent. But generally, they are concerned with the *control* of sex (that is, what we're *not* supposed to do, think, or feel) rather than with the specific expression of sex (that is, exactly what we're *supposed* to do, and how). Rarely do growing boys and girls get direct, honest, positive information about exactly how one goes about making love. Indeed, only rarely do we see our parents even hugging and kissing, let alone showing any erotic interest in each other.

10

Despite all the talk about sex in movies and on television, those media teach and show virtually nothing about what goes on between real people when they make love. (The camera always pans away at crucial moments.) And our parents and teachers certainly don't want to give out this information. They are embarrassed, and they may not want to sound like they're endorsing those activities. Furthermore, we rarely ask direct questions of our parents or other possible sources of information because, after all, we think we are supposed to know. We think everyone else knows, and we don't want to show our stupidity.

So it's back to our gang, our classmates, their dirty jokes, and the lies (and occasional truths) our friends tell us about their own sexual experiences. The characters in the jokes and the pornographic heroes and heroines, later supplemented by the characters in popular novels, become the people we get our information and misinformation from and the people we measure our own bodies, feelings, and experiences against.

WHAT DO WE LEARN?

Given this hodgepodge of learning, it's a miracle that anyone ever develops a functional, satisfying sex life. Certainly most of our sources of information maintain our interest in sex and may even prod us into sexual activity. But although they provide the motivation, the direction they endorse for our sexual activity frequently provides us with destructive ideas of what sex is all about.

Chapters 4, 5, and 6 go into some detail about the common problems that are created by our faulty learning as we're growing up. Here, we'll talk briefly about some of the distorted ideas and common myths that are often at the core of our learning experiences.

What Men Learn

Most young men learn that sex is just about the most important thing in life. Having sex regularly and doing it well often become two major life goals. Men are also taught that sexual activity and performance are the criteria for evaluating their adequacy as men and human beings.

Many men are taught to think about women as bodies to be sought after. And the worth of a woman as both a sexual

11

object and as a human being is largely determined by her measurements and attractiveness. Men may also learn that although women play the game of not wanting sex, they really *do* want sex and it's the job of men to convince them of this. Indeed, a man's sexual worth can be measured by his success in this undertaking.

Men may learn that there are two kinds of women—those who are sexy and interested in sex, and those whom they will marry. They learn that it's their job to "get" a woman, turn her on, turn themselves on, be in charge of what goes on in bed, and bring both their partner and themselves to orgasm.

They learn that their sexuality is expressed mainly through their penises. Thus, big penises that get erect easily and stay erect indefinitely are essential for sex. And these penises should not ejaculate too soon nor take too long. In fact, ideally, erections and ejaculations should be very much under their owner's control. A good penis should behave like a well-trained dog—immediately responsive to its owner's commands. Sexual enjoyment without an erect penis or an orgasm is unthinkable.

Men also learn that intercourse is the one logical conclusion to any act of intimacy—intercourse is what it's all about. All this kissing, stroking, and hugging is really only a prelude to "the real thing."

There are also lots of things that many men *don't* learn. The absence of this learning can be just as harmful as some of the things they do learn. Gentleness, tenderness, vulnerability, and uncertainty are not considered basic male skills. They are rarely shown by men—and somehow they are often perceived as not being really quite masculine. Yet these behaviors are essential to warm, loving relationships.

What Women Learn

Women not only grow up with their share of myths, but many of these myths conflict with one another, leaving women unsure about just what to believe concerning sexuality.

Many of today's women were taught that a "good woman" is fairly passive, and uninterested in sex. Yet she should be attractive to men—so that she will eventually be lucky enough to get herself a husband. Being attractive involves having large breasts (but not too large), a trim figure, and a somewhat seductive approach to men. However, if she were to be *too* seductive or too interested in sex, then her desirability would evaporate. That might take away the challenge men want in catching her.

Men, women soon learn, want to be the aggressors and the seducers. Yet if a woman succumbs to the man's advances, she may well lose her marketability. So the popular expression "a man chases a woman until she catches him" became an accurate description of the game women often used to be taught. Indeed, long after a woman has been married, she, and perhaps her husband as well, may feel a need to maintain the charade of the man's seducing his wife each time he wants sex. She, being a good wife, usually complies, and she may even enjoy it if he's a particularly good lover. The idea was that it was a man's job to turn on and satisfy his sexual partner.

Today's woman often receives a somewhat different message. She is taught that a woman has a right, if not a responsibility, to assert herself as a person, and this includes asserting her sexuality. She can, and should, have as much sexual pleasure as her partner. This orientation, however, can pressure a woman to be as goal-oriented in the quest for orgasms as men are. Thus, some women may copy the worst features of some men by becoming so preoccupied with achieving orgasms that they fail to enjoy all the aspects of a sexual encounter.

TWELVE COMMON SEXUAL MYTHS

There are also many problems and myths associated with the changing sexual relationships between men and women. The most useful approach, we feel, is that both men and women share equal rights to sexual satisfaction. Partners also have equal responsibility for getting pleasure from their sexual activities and for helping to meet their partner's sexual needs. Good sex involves a mutual caring and a full participation— even if it is a mutual agreement that one partner will enjoy a passive role while the other enjoys an active role.

In order to achieve this mutual sharing, partners must learn each other's desires and needs and rid themselves, as much as possible, of the myths that so often interfere with sexual partners' enjoying each other.

In the rest of this chapter, we will present just a few examples of the most common myths that people are likely to have heard and, perhaps, to believe, and that may be interfering with your own sex life. Although many other myths will be discussed in later chapters, the twelve that follow are among the most common and long-lasting of the sexual myths; they serve well as examples of how people's beliefs can lead to sexual dissatisfaction. You may want to discuss each of these myths with your partner; you may also want to talk over the extent to which it may have influenced your sexual attitudes and behavior.

1. Sex Is Essentially Intercourse.

Close your eyes for a minute and think about sex. What do you see? If you're like most people, you will probably visualize two people having intercourse. That's a problem. Most of our learning has taught us that the goal of all physical intimacy—and the natural conclusion of all sexual activities—is intercourse. That's understandable when you stop to realize how important reproduction is, and that there is little doubt that intercourse *is* the most effective route to having children. But unless all you care about is getting pregnant, there is a great deal more to sex.

Perhaps we should stop and ask, "What is sex, anyway?" We believe that there are at least six aspects to how we express our sexuality.

SENSUALITY

Sensuality includes those activities that can give pleasure to our own and perhaps to our partner's body. The types of stimulation that turn a person on and give them erotic pleasure differ from person to person and from time to time. Vincent DeFeo of the University of Hawaii refers to many of these good feelings as the satisfaction of our skin hunger. When there is a partner, sensual desire will generally lead to intercourse—but it doesn't have to. The good feeling we get from orgasms will also usually result from intercourse. But, again, it doesn't have to. There are many types of sexual activities—which we will describe in detail in later chapters—that people enjoy in addition to intercourse.

INTIMACY

This aspect of sex involves the deep feelings we experience with a person whom we care for. These feelings may occur in the midst of a passionate sexual encounter, while holding hands at the movies, or from just thinking about someone we love. Feelings of intimacy are an important aspect of our sexuality. Without the capacity to have these emotional feelings, many people find their physical sexual activities lacking in satisfaction.

REPRODUCTION

Our sexuality obviously involves our capacity to create new life. Indeed, many men and women feel uncomfortable about sexual activities that do not have the potential for producing children. Some find the possibility of pregnancy resulting from a sexual encounter a powerful erotic stimulant.

IDENTITY

A significant aspect of our sexuality involves our feelings and expectations about ourselves and our sexual behavior as a result of our sexual identity. What we expect of ourselves and our partners based on being a man or a woman can have a great effect on our sexual activities. There are considerable differences over time and from place to place about what behaviors are expected of men and women and about how they should express their sexuality.

EROTIC CHOICE

No one would want to go to bed with everyone. Each of us selects the person or persons whom we are willing to go to bed with as a result of complicated learning experiences throughout our lives. We may choose our partner on the basis of whether they're men or women; of a certain age, race, or ethnic group; of intelligence; and/or of appearance. We may well have a number of other conditions for the partner we select—an important one, for example, may be whether we are married to the person.

SEXUALIZATION

Finally, we often experience or use our sexuality as a way of influencing the attitudes or behaviors of other people. Although these activities might include specific sexual acts, the purpose of the activities may not be arousal or sexual satisfaction. For example, sexual intercourse is often used to dominate, humiliate (in rape, for example), or barter with a sexual partner. Couples will often have sexual intercourse only because they believe the other partner expects it or because they consider it their duty. Often people will have intercourse to gain the affection—or even just the attention—of their partner. Sexual activities that are based on these reasons frequently prove unsatisfactory for one or both partners.

Thus a person's sexuality involves a great deal more than sexual intercourse. Each of these six aspects interacts with the

15

others. For example, a man may enjoy sexual activities only with a woman he loves. Or a woman may feel all right about sex and like a "real woman" only when she has intercourse that could lead to a desired pregnancy.

2. There Is Only One Right Way to Have Sex.

This myth is an extension of the idea that sex equals intercourse. This myth states that not only should all sexual contacts end in intercourse but that the best, if not the only, "natural" position is what is known as the "missionary position"—with the man above the woman. It is called the missionary position, by the way, because when the missionaries who came to Hawaii found that the Hawaiians enjoyed intercourse in a variety of positions, they were horrified and tried to convince them that the "man above" position was the only holy way to do it. Although this position is the most-often used by most Americans (but not in other cultures, incidentally), it is by no means either the only or the best position for everyone. Indeed, many women find that they have more freedom of sexual expression in other positions, such as the woman above or the side-by-side position. We'll talk more about positions in Chapter 20, but at this point we'll just say that there is no *right* or *best* sexual position other than that position which satisifes you and your partner at any particular time.

Another extension of the "sex equals intercourse" myth is that if it's not intercourse, it's not "normal." This refers not so much to what position you prefer but to other sexual activities, such as oral sex or anal sex (and the list probably could be extended indefinitely).

This is a complicated myth, since it revolves around the word *normal*. This is a word we consider to be confusing and dangerous. It is confusing because it has a number of interpretations. Something might be considered "normal" if (1) most people do it, (2) the *Bible* or religious authorities approve of it, or (3) well-known psychiatrists, psychologists, or physicians say it's okay. It is dangerous because many people either rigidly limit their sexual activities according to what they think is normal or, worse, go through considerable guilt and shame because they think what they do or would like to do is not normal.

We believe that *normal* can be a dirty word. It creates needless suffering and does not help people find a satisfying sex life. What most people do most of the time is not a useful guide for what you will find most fulfilling. Even morality, we believe, is a very private matter. And what some physician or psychologist said about sex fifty years ago is not the most useful or accurate guide for you today.

Indeed, most of the ideas about what is normal were based on the ancient idea that sex was really for making babies and that anything that was not closely related to that goal couldn't be very good. Thus, since you can't get pregnant or get anyone else pregnant through the mouth (oral sex), through the anus (anal sex), or by any means other than intercourse, all activities other than intercourse have been considered abnormal. The only "normal" activity was getting a penis into a vagina, which, coincidentally, is the best way to initiate a pregnancy.

So we suggest that you try to forget about what is "normal" and focus instead on what gives you and your partner pleasure and fulfillment. If oral sex or anal sex are what both you and your partner enjoy at times, and if both of you agree to it, you should feel perfectly free to enjoy yourselves that way. There will be no negative effects and you both may find a new freedom and excitement in your sexual activities. If you think one of these activities might be distasteful but you still want to try it, use the program in Chapter 19 to help yourself get started.

Our point here is not that you have to try every sexual activity under the sun in order to feel fulfilled. Rather, it is that, if both you and your partner want to, you can and you should feel free to try a particular sexual activity, unafraid that you will be doing something wrong or harmful to you or your partner.

3. You Should Have Neither Too Frequent Nor Too Infrequent Sex with Your Partner.

It's hard to say what "too frequent" or "too infrequent" sex is. The fear that couples who have sex too often will get burned out and bored with sex is unfounded. Indeed, couples who have an active and enjoyable sexual life at the beginning of their relationship are most likely to have a long, happy sex life. On the other hand, you don't *have* to have sex at any special rate to keep the pilot light going. The average statistics for the frequency of sexual intercourse are no guide for any couple. There are as many couples who have sex less frequently than the average as there are couples who have sex more frequently. Sex is not like Vitamin C: There is no federally determined recommended minimum daily requirement. It's purely a matter of what you and your partner want. However, if you and your partner are having trouble agreeing on how often you should have sex, review Chapters 9 and 10 for some guidelines on how to negotiate your differences so that you come up with a frequency that is satisfactory to both of you.

4. It Is Important for Both Partners to Have Orgasms at the Same Time.

We have no objections to you and your partner's having orgasms at the same time. If that's what you want to work toward, go ahead. But we would like you to be aware of a few things before you try.

The first is that it's extremely hard to do. Men and women have different types of bodily movements at the time of orgasm. In fact, these movements may even be incompatible. Therefore, one or both partners may lose a great deal during mutual orgasm since the motions of one might distract the other from enjoying his or her orgasm.

Second, becoming preoccupied with the timing of your orgasms can take away from the joy and spontaneity of your sexual activities. Let's face it, having an orgasm is very pleasurable, and it also is very nice to experience your partner's having one. But worrying about exactly when your partner's orgasm should take place (let alone trying to time it exactly with yours) means that neither of you will be able to concentrate just on feeling good—or on helping your partner feel good.

If the man's and the woman's orgasms occur at the same time, it may be too much for each of you to focus on both. In fact, it's a common occurrence to more or less black out a little bit while you're having an orgasm and become more or less unaware of what's going on around you—including your partner's orgasm. So it might be more enjoyable to have your and your partner's orgasms one after the other.

Finally, if the reason you want to have mutual orgasms is that you think most "really sexually satisfied" or "really happy" people do, forget it. Few do. We believe that the people who are most sexually satisfied are the people who can really enjoy their own sexuality and their orgasms—and their partner's sexuality and orgasms—no matter when they occur. These are people who will be the least preoccupied with timing and most concerned with helping themselves and their partner get pleasure from their sex lives.

5. Both Partners Should Have Orgasms Every Time They Have Sexual Contact.

Many people believe that both they and their partner should each have an orgasm each time they have sexual activities. This is fine if it happens. But being orgasm oriented can take away from the pleasure of other aspects of your sexual activities. Sex is more than just having orgasms. It is a process of sharing—sharing relationships, sharing physical pleasures, and, at times, having orgasms. As a matter of fact, women may have several orgasms or none at all during a sexual encounter. And as a man gets older, there are likely to be times when he doesn't have an orgasm. Neither partner should try to force the other into an orgasm or feel crushed if they themselves don't have one. If the partner who hasn't had an orgasm shows interest in going on to orgasm, you can help him or her by providing continued stimulation by hand, mouth, or whatever else gives pleasure. But don't feel that you or your partner has to have an orgasm if he or she or you are satisfied. Indeed, this pressure to have an orgasm can prevent you from enjoying sex at all.

6. Sexual Intercourse Is Dangerous During Pregnancy.

There are dozens of myths that have grown up about pregnancy—some of them have been supported in the past by medical ignorance. One of the most common is that intercourse during pregnancy will do harm to the baby.

Certainly some care must be used in intercourse during pregnancy, especially if it is a first pregnancy. From time to time, a pregnant woman may experience some general discomfort, often accompanied by nausea and a feeling of being bloated. When these sensations occur, the woman may be in no shape to get turned on or to have sex at all.

There are also unusual physical circumstances that may make it unwise to have intercourse at all during the early months of pregnancy. Some medical authorities believe that if a woman has had difficulties in the early stages of her pregnancy, she may have contractions during orgasm that could threaten the pregnancy. Even if this is true, the woman may still safely engage in sexual activities during her first three months of pregnancy as long as these activities don't lead to orgasm.

Figure 2-1.

With these exceptions, there are no medical reasons to avoid sexual relations during pregnancy. Indeed, many women find themselves very easily aroused in mid-pregnancy and very much enjoy their sexual activities (see Figure 2-1). Even in the last few weeks of pregnancy, sexual activities are safe as long as there is no unusual pain, bleeding, or broken membranes, and as long as the woman is comfortable and desires sexual activities. However, it's always wise to check with your physician.

Chapter 20 describes several positions, such as "the man behind," and "the woman above," that may be preferable to the "man above" position during the late stages of pregnancy. This may also be a good time to experiment with sexual activities that do not necessarily include intercourse, such as oral and manual stimulation of the sex organs, as described in Chapters 14 and 19.

7. Sexual Activity Should Be Avoided During Menstruation.

There is no physiological reason for discontinuing sexual activities during menstruation. Some people find it aesthetically unpleasant; others don't mind it at all. Some men associate bleeding with pain and therefore feel that they may be hurting their partner if they have intercourse while there is a vaginal discharge. However, intercourse is no more likely to cause pain during menstruation than at any other time. In fact, some women find that having orgasms may actually reduce the cramps that they experience during menstruation. If you want to have intercourse during menstruation but don't like the messiness, the woman can use a diaphragm to hold back the flow. Diaphragms for this as well as contraceptive purposes should be prescribed and fitted by a physician.

Again, if one or both partners prefer not to have intercourse during menstruation, there are other forms of mutual sexual pleasuring which we will be describing which may be enjoyed during this period in place of intercourse.

8. A Large Penis Is Essential to Arouse and Satisfy a Woman.

This phallic fallacy is one of the most common myths about males. It's also a particularly destructive one in that it creates unnecessary anxiety and sometimes even avoidance of sexual contact for men who are preoccupied with what they think are the shortcomings of their penises.

Men who agonize about the size of their penis should realize that the vagina accommodates just about all sizes of penises and that most women experience their greatest physical pleasure from direct and indirect stimulation of the clitoris and the outer inch or two of their vaginas, in which most of the nerve endings are located. Therefore, physiologically, anything over an inch or so of erect penis is surplus property. To be sure, some women prefer a big penis, just as some women (and men) prefer lots of things in their partners, like money, black or blond hair, brown or blue eyes, big breasts, and so forth. The majority of men and women choose their partners and enjoy them sexually for a combination of attributes.

Being preoccupied with your sex organs, or even with your partner's sex organs, works against your having an enjoyable sex life. You make love with another person, not with their sex organs.

We'll talk more about penises in Chapter 5.

9. Men and Women Who Have Passed the Age of Menopause Are No Longer Interested in or Capable of Much of a Sex Life.

This myth has been amply disproved by a number of researchers, as well as by millions of men and women, who have passed the age of menopause and still enjoy sexual activities. Both men and women are physically and psychologically capable of active and enjoyable sexual contact throughout their life spans. The only reasons that might make older people become sexually inactive are illness, the restrictive attitudes of people around them (such as those of their grown children, the staff at institutions for the aging, or their partners), and their discomfort in adjusting to the physiological changes that tend to occur as people get older.

These changes are not necessarily negative. Many people feel that they enjoy their sexual activities much more as the pressures of youth wear off. For example, as men get older, they may not have the same urgency for orgasm that they had when they were younger, and, indeed, they may have much better ejaculatory control than they had when they were much younger, so that they can sustain intercourse for longer periods.

Women may not have as much natural lubrication as they had when they were younger, and both partners may experience changed patterns of arousal and orgasm. At the end of Chapter 6 we'll discuss some of the common adaptations for and changes in sexual activities as people grow older. At this point, however, we'll only emphasize that there is no age limit for either men or women for enjoying erotic physical intimacy with another person. As long as you and your partner take care of yourselves, don't try to act twenty years old, and find pleasure and interest in your own and your partner's sexuality, you can keep going for a long time.

10. Sex Should Be Natural.

Saying that sex should be "natural" is like saying that all children should just do what's right. Neither sex nor children's behavior just happens. Now it's true that we do have a "natural" sex drive. But the way we use that drive, the sexual activities we enjoy, and the type of partners we get turned on by—all of this is learned.

Unfortunately, a good part of what we learn is negative. We're often taught what *not* to do, how *not* to think, and how *not* to feel, so that whatever we do, think, and feel turns out to be negative. We believe, in part, that most sexual problems are a result of the negative things we learn as we grow up and even of what we learn as adults.

Our point here is that people are not the same as dogs and cats. With those creatures, sex may be pretty "natural." But for people, sex is a process that involves our total beings—especially what we think and feel—and much of that is learned. The importance of all this lies in our belief that if

Treat Yourself to a Better Sex Life

DR. HARVEY L. GOCHROS

DR. JOEL FISCHER

PRENTICE
HALL
PRESS

New York London Toronto Sydney Tokyo

Prentice Hall Press
15 Columbus Circle
New York, New York 10023

Published in 1987 by Prentice Hall Press
Originally published by Prentice-Hall, Inc.

Library of Congress Cataloging-in-Publication Data

Gochros, Harvey L.
Treat yourself to a better sex life.

Bibliography: p.
Includes index.
1. Sex.   2. Sex instruction.   I. Fischer,
Joel, joint author.   II. Title.
HQ31.G686   301.41'8   79-18111
ISBN 0-13-930677-3 pbk.

Manufactured in the United States of America

15 14 13 12

problems are learned, they can be unlearned as well. If the things we've learned aren't working for us and aren't satisfying to us, then we can learn new and more fulfilling forms of sexual expression.

We'll probably never get to the point of being as "natural" as dogs and cats (even if we wanted to). But we believe we can—and should—take the effort to ensure that what we do learn frees us to use what does come naturally—our sex drive—in the most fulfilling ways possible.

11. Sex Shouldn't Be Planned; It Should Just Happen.

Almost everything we see in the movies and read in novels suggests that sex is a spontaneous event that the man and woman just "fall into" with plenty of passion and little or no preparation. Well, we don't deny that this can happen. We just doubt that it happens very often (except in the movies and in fiction). Indeed, one of the commonest myths of all is that people know instinctively how to please each other. This is despite the fact that people vary tremendously in what turns them on, and that even a given individual may change (and probably will change) over time with regard to what turns them on.

The facts are very much like those we described regarding the previous myth suggesting that sex should be "natural"— unhampered by what we learn. That is, some of the most enjoyable and fulfilling sex is sex that is born out of adequate planning: the skills we learn, the efforts we take, the situations and moods we get ourselves in. This ranges from the very basic skills and understanding that we develop about sexual activity as we grow up to the specific time and energy we take with our partners to ensure that both of us enjoy our sexual activities.

Now, you might be thinking that this sounds artificial or phony and that, somehow, you should just be able to "do it." If only that were true. The problem with this attitude, though, is that it could keep you from doing the things that you *can* do to reach the kind of sexual fulfillment you want. Sitting around waiting for it to "just happen" is a good guarantee that it won't.

And, of course, the very purpose of this book is to help you with the things that you *can* do to enhance your sex life. When it comes time to take steps toward enhancing your sexual pleasure, we'll provide you with a number of the ideas you'll need in order to be able to do just that.

12. If Your Sex Life Is Healthy, You Shouldn't Have to Masturbate.

One of the most common myths of all is that masturbation is somehow harmful (and reflects problems in a person's sexual relationships): If it doesn't cause you to become mentally ill, it will make you blind or make hair grow on the palm of your hand.

Well, we're here to tell you that it just isn't true. There is not a shred of any type of evidence—scientific or otherwise—to indicate that masturbation produces any harmful effects or that it in any way hampers sexual development. If it did, most men and a large percentage of women would be in mental institutions, receiving aid to the blind, or spending half their time shaving their hands.

Many parents, of course, fear for their child's health and sexual development if they somehow find out that the child masturbates. If you're one of those parents, we urge you to hold off on the criticism. Kids need a sexual outlet too, and all you can do is lay a guilt trip on your son or daughter if you bug him or her about masturbating.

Adults, too, can do with the same cautions about not being concerned if their partners masturbate. There are times when spouses or adult sexual partners find out that their partners masturbate. The reaction often runs from shock to feelings of rejection: "Why should he (or she) have to masturbate? Aren't I good enough for him (or her)?"

Well, we believe that masturbation can serve many needs—not only strictly sexual needs but needs for reducing tension as well. Many people masturbate regularly and also maintain satisfying (to them and their partners) sexual relationships. In fact, guided masturbation—or self-stimulation, as we call it—can be one of the best ways to enhance your sex life with your partner. It can make your sexual relationship with your partner even more fulfilling. If you don't believe us, read Chapter 13 before you make a final judgment.

A related myth is that if a person masturbates "too much," this could diminish his or her sexual potency over time. Actually, this myth usually applies mainly to men, since it is feared that men are capable of only a limited number of ejaculations in their lives. Thus, it is reasoned that men could masturbate or ejaculate themselves out of business by the time they reach midlife.

These myths too are false. Men have the capability for unlimited numbers of ejaculations well into old age. And ejaculations obtained through masturbation are exactly the same as those obtained through intercourse. The only effect of any

24

form of ejaculation on the male is a temporary inability to ejaculate again after the first ejaculation. (Women do not usually experience this problem when they have an orgasm because they have the potential for several orgasms in a row.) The period of time it takes to ejaculate again (or even to ejaculate in the first place) may increase with age, but this also can be a distinct advantage in that older men often can prolong the period of time that they can maintain intercourse longer than younger men.

If you're still bothered by all this (whether it's by the feeling that you want to masturbate or by the feeling that your partner shouldn't), you can try to talk it over with your partner. Use the communication guidelines we present in Chapter 9 to open the topic up. Because sex really is a unique experience for each person, maybe this will help you and your partner come to a little better understanding about what both of you want and expect from each other.

Actually, this chapter, in discussing twelve common sexual myths, has only scratched the surface of the many myths that often serve to keep us from a fulfilling sex life. However, a large part of this book, especially Parts 1 and 2, is devoted to taking the myths out of your sex life so that you can enjoy it to the fullest. We hope that as you read, you'll be able to see how and why certain beliefs are keeping you from enjoying your sexual life to the extent you want.

The most important thing to remember here, however, is that each person is a unique sexual human being and that there are few universal rules about what you must do in bed. It's up to you and your partner to design your sexual life. Don't let the myths of sex deprive you of your right to sexual satisfaction.

Three

Love, Sex, and Commitment

What are nice topics like love and commitment doing in a place like a sex book? Perhaps the following concerns that we often hear will suggest some of the reasons:

"How does he expect me to hop into bed and make passionate love with him when he hasn't shown me any loving all day long?"

"I really care for her, but I just don't know how to show it!"

"I love him and enjoy going to bed with him, but will it last?"

"I used to believe that you really had to love someone before it was okay to have sex with him. Now I'm not sure any more."

"He says that if I loved him, I'd go to bed with him. If that's all he cares about, does he really love me?"

These are typical comments from people who are concerned and confused about the relationship between love, sex, and commitment. Indeed, there often is more pain, anxiety, and confusion about love and commitment than there is about the sexual activities themselves. Many people who need and want love and commitment are afraid to truly love or commit themselves to another person. If they find either one, they may

26

not know how to handle it. Why is it that people have such a hard time with love and commitment?

In the minds of most Americans, love, sex, and commitment are almost inseparable. To many, sex without love or commitment is unthinkable ("What kind of person do you think I am, anyway?") or at least highly undesirable. There are, however, an increasing number of men and women who consider the connections between love, sex, and commitment to be far more flexible. Purely recreational sex—in which there may be no ongoing love or commitment involved—is not only all right for them but may be preferred. For many people, however, their sexual feelings and their feelings of love are very much related. Look at the words and phrases we use to describe sexual relations, for example: "making love"; "have you had any loving lately?"; "my lover."

But just what is the nature of the relationship between love, sex, and commitment? Just how necessary is love for the enjoyment of sex? Is sex really better within a committed relationship? If you don't know how to express love or if you feel uncomfortable doing so, can you learn to do so? Can you learn to love better just as you can learn to be a better lover?

These are questions commonly asked about love and commitment and they might well be considered by all people who want to enhance their enjoyment in sexual relationships. In this chapter, we'll look at the relationship between love, commitment, and sexual enjoyment and offer some suggestions for getting more out of one's "love life."

Our point of view is that love, sex, and commitment are three separate and different human experiences, and that many of our problems come from blurring the differences among the three. Each can exist without the other two. Each may enhance and each may detract from one or both of the others. We have already made a stab at exploring what sex is all about. Let's now consider each of the other two components of the threesome: commitment and love.

COMMITMENT

Now that we've agreed to talk about it, let's admit that *commitment* is a very vague term. It means different things to different people. Generally, it is taken to mean a shared responsibility accepted by two people for each other. It means that the two people have agreed to be concerned about the welfare of the other, and that each can "count on" the other.

Does that sound vague to you? Well, it does to many

people. The definition leaves as many questions unanswered as answered: How long does a commitment last?—a night or a lifetime? Does it necessarily mean marriage? Does commitment mean you can't love or have sex with someone besides your partner? Does it have to be mutual or can it be just one person in a relationship being committed while the other isn't? Does commitment make sense in our rapidly changing world?

Each one of these questions reflects the kind of problems that are common today in committed relationships. Such problems were not so common in our parents' days, or the generations before them. People knew what commitment meant then, or at least they said they did. Indeed, both sex and even love were considered secondary to commitment and everyone knew what commitment meant; it meant marriage. Sex and love were fine, but ideally, religiously, and even legally they were only within marriage.

That was for a good reason. Marriage was essential for a smooth-running society and for the purpose of producing children and raising them properly. Everything else, including love, and sex for pure enjoyment, was almost immaterial. A beautiful illustration of this is in the song "Do You Love Me?" from *Fiddler on the Roof*, in which Tevye for the first time asks Golda, his wife of twenty-five years, whether she loves him. Her first reaction to the question is bewilderment. What kind of question is that? She has fulfilled her responsibilities of her commitment, producing and raising "his" children, cleaning "his" house, and even meeting "his" sexual needs. Why talk about love now? Only after extensive questioning does she hesitatingly reveal that she "guesses" that she does love him. But the unspoken question is: Does it really matter?

Our attitudes about the relative importance of love and commitment have changed since the days of Tevye. Many people no longer consider love, commitment, and marriage as necessarily a logical sequence or all part of the same package. In fact, even people's ideas of how commitment develops in a relationship have gone through a major revolution in recent decades. In years past, the relationship was supposed to start slowly. "Good" relationships were supposed to mature slowly, like good wine. (People would ask, "after how many dates can you kiss good night?") But once a good relationship was established, a commitment was supposed to naturally evolve, one that would carry on forever.

More recent attitudes about the pace of relationships are quite different. Many people today feel that intimacy—with or without sex—can develop quite rapidly and need not last forever. The ending of a close relationship doesn't have to reflect something wrong with either partner but may be just the natural course of events in a relationship. Popular songs such as "Will You Still Love Me Tomorrow" and "I'm Not Saying That I Love You" reflect the acceptance of the idea that intimacy and *short-term* commitment may be quite different from long-term commitment. As one young student once commented to one of us, "The trouble with your generation is you just don't know how to say goodbye!"

What Are the Options for Commitment?

Today there are probably more options for forms of commitment than ever before. That doesn't mean that they all work. Many of the options in relationships create problems. Many of these problems are connected with jealousy and possessiveness.

There are many people to whom commitment and perhaps even love imply some degree of "ownership" of their partners. Perhaps this feeling of ownership reflects a person's interpretation of what commitment means, or it may reflect the person's insecurity about his or her ability to compete with other potential partners, or doubts about the degree of the partner's commitment to the person.

Indeed, one of the most common problems encountered in couples is a relationship in which one partner is more invested—or committed—in the relationship than the other. Obviously, such relationships make the more-committed partner quite vulnerable and much more insecure about the relationship. They also raise questions about the "ownership" of their partner.

The way a person expresses this ownership may involve anything from claiming exclusive rights to his or her partner's body to the expectation that the partner will hardly notice any other human being as a potential sexual partner or even as a close friend. Jealousy arises when a person thinks that his or her partner has violated this sexual or relationship taboo. Indeed, some may feel jealous if their partner just seems to like or spend too much time with another person.

There is considerable support in our society for long-term relationships with one other person and for the idea that the partners have exclusive rights to each other. But what is involved in this? How much freedom can and should exist for the partners in committed relationships? If one allows one's partner to have loving relationships with others, how much "love"

29

is permitted, how much time is allowed for these relationships, and to what extent can the partner enjoy the freedom of his or her body in these relationships?

These are complex questions that are difficult to answer and that can have complex effects on a relationship. It isn't surprising that many, if not most, individuals in committed relationships deal with them by not facing them directly with their partners, choosing to go along with a rigid agreement about their own rights or secretly cheating on this compact with resulting guilt.

Certainly there is a wide range of options that *can* work within the context of a committed relationship. A pattern that works well for one couple can be disastrous for another. Each couple has to decide what will work for and what is acceptable to them. Each should consider how he or she would feel about the partner's having various degrees of intimacy with other individuals—including sexual contact. Each partner might examine for himself or herself whether he or she can have sex with someone other than the partner and still maintain his or her love and commitment for that person. Such expectations, along with the couple's agreements between themselves, can change over time. Couples may find that agreements they had previously considered unthinkable become acceptable, or that agreements that had been comfortable in the past become more and more of a problem. Couples may, therefore, want to re-evaluate their commitment with each other from time to time.

We're certainly not advocating mass adultery or ill-considered "open marriages." Indeed, there are many relationships that couldn't tolerate or have no need for outside relationships. Intimate relationships with outside partners can be devastating and destructive to a relationship or simply something additional for the relationship.

There are various degrees of intimacy that are desired or needed by different individuals and that may be quite compatible for people in committed relationships. (Remember, outside intimate relationships do not necessarily have to involve sex. Even so, they may or may not be threatening to your relationship.) Each couple should honestly and realistically look at their feelings about their wishes and needs for intimacy with other people, and at least consider their options.

Possessiveness and jealousy do not have to be a part of committed relationships. But honesty about our feelings about sharing the people we love is an important consideration in any committed relationship.

Okay, so that's commitment. Well, how about love? As we'll see, that can be even more complicated.

WHAT IS THIS THING CALLED LOVE?

There are few words in our language that stir up so much emotion as the word *love*. We all respond to it. Most of us love love. We yearn for it, have experienced it, and have experienced great joy and perhaps great pain from it. Yet it is difficult to describe love, and, more particularly, how we have experienced it.

Perhaps the problem is that the one word *love* is used to cover so many different ideas: We may love ice cream, New York in June, our mothers, a good conversation, a person with whom we had a brief sexual encounter, and our spouse of twenty years. But do we "love" all these people, things, and activities with the same intensity? Of course not. What seems to be needed is a more specific language for love. One word just doesn't do it.

Even the beloved expression "I love you" can mean different things to different people. John Lee, a sociologist who studied the patterns of feelings and behaviors of people who said they loved someone, came up with a number of common forms of love. They may be described as: physical or erotic love; playful love, seen as a sort of game by the lovers; mellow love, a kind of peaceful and comfortable relationship; dizzying love, with high highs and bottomless lows; practical love, the carefully considered choice of a partner; the classical kind of love that requires nothing in return from the loved one; and various combinations of these.

Lee concluded that in order to have a mutually satisfying love relationship, it is important to "find a partner who shares the same approach to loving, the same definition of love." The more apart two people are in their patterns of loving, the more likely it is that there will be stress and problems in their relationship. How do you and your partner compare in your approaches to love?

The Myths of Love

As we can see from the above, the myth that there is just one form of true love just doesn't hold up when you look at the various ways in which people love each other. There are a number of other myths about love that have been disproved by recent research. In their excellent exploration of research on love in their book *A New Look at Love*, Elaine and William Walster challenge some of our most widely accepted ideas

31

about love. Here are just a few of the most common myths about love along with what research has found to be true:

Myth: Women are more romantic than men. They generally fall in love before the man with whom they're involved does, and they keep on loving him long after he has lost interest in her.

The Findings: Women tend to fall in love with a man *after* he has fallen in love with her. And if the love relationship ends, it's usually the woman who quits first.

Myth: The people who get the most loving are those who have good looks, great personalities, and lots of money.

The Findings: Actually, it's the most easy-going, relaxed people who are the most popular. Those who work the hardest at looking good and being Mr. or Ms. Congeniality often end up last.

Myth: Fascinating, exotic strangers usually end up with the most desirable mates.

The Findings: Most of us end up in relationships and marriages with the man or woman next door or at the next desk. Someone who is familiar to us, and perhaps somewhat like us, usually is more attractive, more comfortable to be with, and thus more desirable than the exotic stranger.

Myth: Although men might be initially attracted to easy-to-get women, they generally are turned off by them in the long run.

The Findings: Most men are attracted to women who seem unavailable or uninterested in most other men, *but* who are both interested and available to that particular man as an individual.

As the above sampling of myths suggests, our thinking about love is often confused by folklore. Some of this folklore has a profound effect on how we approach love relationships. Nowhere is the effect of the myths about how love *should* be experienced more obvious than in our ideas about romantic love.

The Hazards of Romantic Love

The relationship problems of many men and women come at least in part from the strange yet traditional way we tend to classify our potential sexual partners. First, there are the poten-

32

tial partners who are good-looking and sexy, who "turn us on," and with whom we want to go to bed. Then there are the others whom we choose to marry: nice, clean, responsible, respectable people with whom we want to have children.

All too often, our choices for those we marry, or at least those whom we seek out for long-lasting, deep relationships, are determined by traditions of romantic love. Now we don't want to be too critical of the romantic love that is the subject of so many beautiful songs, stories, and movies. But taking romantic love, which is great in fiction, too seriously can foul up an otherwise rewarding relationship.

Why is this so? Expectations for love based on romantic ideals demand a state of intense passion toward a partner who is seen as being almost perfect. There are also expectations that a permanent state of bliss will result from the relationship. A pretty idea, indeed, except that there are few perfect people and few permanently blissful relationships. Thus, many romantic expectations can be hazardous to the health of relationships. They can lead us to see those potential partners to whom we are attracted in unrealistically idealized, highly antiseptic, almost worshipful ways.

Furthermore, these romantic traditions lead us to believe that "real love" is possible with only one person who is meant to be the only one for us; without that person, life becomes meaningless. This idealistic approach leads us to some mixed-up ideas about sex in the relationship. For many people, "real love" is seen as nonphysical. Yet we are lead to believe that when (and only when) we are deeply and continually loved, sex is really okay. We are taught to believe that without this kind of love, sex is reduced to the level of animals and is worthy only of contempt.

The possible hazards of this unrealistic view of love and sex are obvious. It is the view of love that is still portrayed in books, in magazines, and on television, even in teenage-romance comic books. It therefore influences how many people believe they should feel about sex with a partner they love.

Few of us can live up to this romantic ideal for any length of time. The facts of life, commitment, marriage, and intimacy in a long-term relationship may make such a goal almost impossible to reach. Indeed, a sound long-term loving relationship is based not so much on romance but on an honest, benevolent acceptance and concern for each other and a realization that ongoing, nonstop passion is only possible in Hollywood movies.

Because our romantic hopes are often dashed by these realities, some people drop out of what could be rewarding, honest relationships in order to seek new romantic experiences elsewhere and repeat the cycle of romance, disappointment, and separation over and over again.

Has this romantic ideal affected you? Perhaps this checklist will help you to find out. Try to answer the following questions about yourself (your partner might want to try, too):

1. Do you expect to love your partner all the time, nonstop, and to be loved by your partner in the same way?
2. Do you allow yourself to recognize your partner's shortcomings and allow him or her to recognize yours without being defensive or devastated?
3. Do you worship your partner?
4. Can you tolerate your partner's enjoying other people and preferring to spend time by himself or by herself from time to time?
5. Can you tolerate the possibility that your partner has warm or loving relationships with other people?
6. Do you expect your sexual experiences to be ecstatic every time and are you disappointed when they are not?

If you answered "yes" to questions 1, 3 and 6 and "no" to the rest, then maybe you're one of the many people who may be over-romanticizing your relationships.

We believe that it *is* possible for you to be realistic in your appraisal of your partner and of the relationship and still have a close, loving bond. Sometimes, however, that takes work. It's often useful to sit down (lie down?) with your partner and take realistic stock of your relationship. You may want to talk openly about your mutual expectations and evaluations of each other to explore how accurate they are, and to discuss what, realistically, you would like to have changed.

We suggest that you focus on strengths rather than weaknesses. Try to emphasize with your partner those things you wish more of rather than focusing only on what you would like less of. Perhaps you would like to review the suggestions for communication given in Chapter 9, which should enhance your ability to express your feelings and needs to each other. Part of your discussion may revolve around the realistic and unrealistic self-expectations and the expectations you have of your partner as described in Chapters 4, 5, and 6.

Once you break through the unrealistic and sometimes impossible expectations that you may have developed, you may find it more possible to accept your partner and yourself as "just human beings." Then it will be more possible to find pleasure with each other *as you are*, and that includes your body, your personality, and your sexuality.

The key to pleasure in sexuality, love, and life in general is not to be preoccupied with longing for what you don't have (or what your partner doesn't have) but to make the most of what you do have. And that includes a realistic acceptance of your partner.

Some Ways of Expressing Love

"All right, I'm convinced. I love my partner realistically and not overly romantically. I *still* don't know how to show it!"

That's really not so surprising, considering how most of us are brought up to feel about the expression of love. Compared with people in many other cultures, Americans tend to be quite cold. If you don't believe this, ask someone who has traveled to southern Europe, South America, or Africa. Have them compare such social behaviors as how long people shake hands when they meet each other, how close they stand to each other when they talk, and how often they touch when they are with friends. We score low on all these counts. Why? If you recall, as we mentioned at the beginning of the chapter, many of us have been taught that sex, love, and commitment must go together. One of the results of this is that we are brought up with the feeling that closeness and physical contact are completely tied up with genital sex: "If you don't want to go to bed with me, don't touch me!"

> Lew and Barbara appeared at the sex counselor's office with Barbara complaining that Lew never showed her affection. Lew, however, stated that his wife always wanted sex, and he had gotten tired of it early in the marriage. "Barbara's always pawing me and wanting to go to bed. Enough is enough!" As the two, with the help of the counselor, began to discuss the situation in more depth, they realized that some basic misunderstandings had occurred. Early in the marriage, Barbara had felt very close to Lew and had frequently wanted to pet, hug, and stroke him. She had seen such gestures as expressions of affection. But, unable to separate physical expressions of love from sexual expectations, he had interpreted them as requests to head for the bedroom. And in turn, she had misinterpreted his retreat as lack of love.

It makes relationships better, then, if you can enjoy verbal and physical affection without always seeing in it a demand for sexual performance.

Some people have even connected affection that does not lead to sex with weakness. Many men in our society have been led to believe that "all that mushy stuff" is for girls. Boys or men who start talking about love and stroking people with-

35

out the goal of getting someone to bed are seen as sissies. Being strong (often the male ideal) and being affectionate may not go together in some people's minds. And although this attitude is changing rapidly, it still affects the behavior of many American men.

So it's quite possible that your partner does experience loving feelings just as you do but that he or she cannot suddenly snap out of a lifelong pattern of holding them in just because he or she is now involved in a deep relationship. Don't forget that our training starts early, with many parents becoming quite uncomfortable about (physically) stroking their children once they pass infancy. You generally have to experience doing something before you feel comfortable at it, and that includes loving! So it's no surprise that many couples complain about the discomfort (to say the least) that they experience when their partners go from apparent indifference to a passionate bid for the bed. Your partner may have been having loving thoughts all evening but hadn't felt comfortable enough to show it, or didn't know how to show it. Nevertheless, we can't be our partner's mindreaders, and we may want, we may even need, to have their loving.

Is it possible, then, to overcome the "never show your feelings" learning that may have been going on for years? Yes, it is. How? We are just beginning to find out. Although there has been a fair amount of research on sexual problems, sexual behavior, and sexual techniques, there has been very little research on love until fairly recently. Love is not taken very seriously by many researchers. But what we are beginning to find out is quite interesting and very useful as well.

Love, as you may have realized by now, is a tricky thing to study or to understand. It's even difficult to define it except as "a feeling you feel when you feel you're going to have a feeling you have never felt before!" Love can't be seen, measured, or counted. (Maybe *that* is why the researchers don't research it.) But the way in which people *express* love *can* be seen, measured, and counted, and what people *do* with their love, after all, is what matters the most. If we can figure out just *how* people show their love, then people who have difficulty in this area can just begin doing those things, or they can do them more often and perhaps learn to do them better. Remember that we can't expect the people we love to be mindreaders. They can't just "know" that we feel love for them. We have to show it.

The researchers who have studied love have found that people generally show their affection to other people in several ways. These are presented here for you to try out as ways to increase your expression of love to the people you really do love, so that they will *know* it.

Try some or all of the following to express your love:

1. Statements of love and appreciation for what your partner has given to you. For example, "You know, sometimes I just get a rush of loving for you and I want you to know how glad I am that you're my wife. Thanks, honey." Or, "It's fun to be around you!" Or, "Wow, I really enjoyed last night!" There's no getting around it; statements of appreciation and affection are often the most direct and clear messages we can give of our love, and who doesn't want to be loved? Remember also that the closer in time that a statement of appreciation is given to the event that is appreciated, the more likely it is that the event will be repeated.

2. Material expression of affection and appreciation. Sometimes words are just not enough. Giving gifts, such as flowers; taking the one you love out for dinner; or even making something that you know the other person appreciates can go a long way toward enhancing a relationship. Of course, *just* giving gifts is not enough, any more than any verbal expression of affection alone is enough, but when given along with other expressions of affection, gifts can mean a lot.

3. Nonmaterial expressions of affection and appreciation. The little (and sometimes big) things we do for each other can show a great deal of affection. We can make sure that people we love are comfortable, we can help them carry things, or we can see to it that the peanuts are passed to them when they are at the wrong end of the couch at a party. Even the old-fashioned common courtesies, such as opening the door for someone (as long as such behaviors are not simply sexist), can show that the other person is noticed and that he or she matters to us. Some people feel that they are hardly noticed except in bed. These nonmaterial expressions of affection and appreciation can show that we consider that person important, which raises his or her self-esteem. Incidentally, nonmaterial expressions of affection and appreciation can and probably should include making sure you give your partner the sexual positions, gestures, and touches that you have learned that he or she enjoys, even if you feel relatively neutral about them except for sensing the pleasure they give your partner.

4. Physical expressions of love. These need not be in any

way aimed only at turning your partner on, although they may sometimes have that effect. But each partner can, for no particular reason and from time to time, kiss, pat, hug, or stroke the other with no demand or expectation for sexual reactions or even for the other partner to do the same thing back. Most of us enjoy being touched, and we enjoy it most when we don't have to ask for it.

5. *Self-revelation*. One of the characteristics of a warm, loving relationship is a willingness to share secrets about ourselves and to respond with warmth and understanding to the secrets of the other person. This can include secrets about our behavior, our doubts, and our problems, even secrets about the mistakes we've made. As with all the aspects of love, this is a two-way street. We can reveal ourselves to our partner and enjoy the experience of revealing ourselves without disapproval; at the same time, we can take joy and satisfaction in caring for the other person despite what we have learned about their humanness. However, we should never let honesty turn into callous insensitivity—for example, by using what our partner has told us against him or her, or just by being negative or brutal with our honesty.

6. *Accepting, to a realistic point, the other's limitations.* This is perhaps a product of all of the above. But if we feel love, then we are inclined to know and accept our partner's less-desirable attributes, such as having a tendency to tell corny jokes, having a big nose, or being preoccupied with football.

Increasing the frequency or quality with which we engage in the above activities increases our feelings of love, our desire to be close to and to give joy to the other person. And the more we have these feelings, the easier and more spontaneous these expressions of love will become.

It's interesting to point out that many languages don't even have a word for love. That doesn't mean, of course, that the people who speak these languages don't *feel* what we call love. Instead, many of these people use words that indicate appreciation. Instead of saying, "I love you" spontaneously and for no particular reason, they say, "I appreciate what you do for me," and they say it often. One of the things we all want to believe is that we are appreciated and needed. When we feel that, we want to do more for the person who appreciates us. We want to be important to somebody else and we want to have somebody around who is important to us.

Regardless of what love means to us, and how we express

38

it, there is little doubt that loving and being loved is one of the most important parts of all our lives. Freud once stated that the two most important factors in mental health were feeling productive and feeling loved. George Bach in his book on loving, *Pairings*, states that love is even more important today than it was in the past. "What men and women seek from love today is no longer a romantic luxury; it is an essential of emotional survival. Less and less it is a hunt for the excitement of infatuation, or for the doubtful security of the marriage nest. More and more it is the hope of finding in intimate love something of personal validity, personal relevance, a confirmation of one's existence."

Maybe that is what love is all about.

HOW LOVE, SEX, AND COMMITMENT RELATE TO ONE ANOTHER

All right, we've taken a long look at commitment, and we've explored love, and we've certainly talked a lot about sex. The question remains: How are they are related to one another? Does one require the other two? Do love and marriage always go together, as the old song says, like a horse and carriage?

These are difficult questions to answer, and the answers certainly will vary from person to person. We believe, however, as we said at the beginning of this chapter, that love, commitment, and sex can each exist and be enjoyed by any particular person without the other two. On the other hand, each can enhance or each can detract from one or both of the others. For example, you can love someone, and, depending on your relationship and the circumstances, find that engaging in sex with him or her might add to *or* destroy that love.

How about the other way around? Can you enjoy sex without a loving commitment with your partner? Well, if we're talking about getting turned on and having an orgasm, the answer is obviously "yes." For most people, most of the time, the main reason for having sex is to have pleasurable feelings. Physically, pleasurable feelings can be had without any intense emotional involvement. Self-stimulation (masturbation), for instance, provides physical pleasure yet doesn't require a relationship with another person. A great many people enjoy sex with partners with whom they have no ongoing loving relationship; the degree of emotional attachment needed for enjoyment will vary from person to person and situation to situation. Indeed, there may be a form of commitment and mutual love even in a one-night sexual relationship.

You, for instance, would have lots of company if you enjoyed, as just plain "fun," a sexual experience with a prostitute or with a casual acquaintance who turns you on, just as a source of entertainment and physical pleasure. You also might enjoy a sexual experience with another person whom you know better, like, and have warm and loving feelings toward, at least during that sexual experience, even though those loving feelings are related to that experience alone and may or may not disappear sometime after orgasm. You might have another enjoyable sexual experience with someone for whom you have great affection but for whom you do not actually feel "love." Your "enjoyment" might be purely physical in one instance, or totally emotionally satisfying in another. That will depend on the situation, on the person, and on your mood. It might also depend on your own personal moral code: If you consider sex without love immoral, that could (but does not necessarily) make it impossible for you to find sex with a casual friend or someone you hardly know enjoyable. But a position on morality is for you, and you alone, to decide.

We might note, by the way, that for various reasons that we'll discuss in detail in later chapters, you could love your partner a lot, yet not enjoy a sexual relationship with him or her. You may even experience many problems in the sexual relationship. Or you could enjoy it emotionally but not physically. Sexual satisfaction may or may not have something to do with a couple's relationship and emotional commitment.

You can see that there are many possibilities here. Yet despite the "sexual revolution" and the undoubtedly greater sexual freedom that has made sex outside committed relationships much more possible today, there has been considerable consistency over the years in the opinion of the majority of Americans that sex is best when it involves two people who love each other. Further, for many people, loving feelings seem to make sexual activity more enjoyable. Helen Singer Kaplan, one of our country's leading sex therapists and writers, has said that love may be the only real aphrodisiac.

There is nothing mystical about the fact that loving feelings can enhance sexual enjoyment. When you love someone, you will probably act differently with him or her in bed from the way that you would if you were indifferent to or even if you disliked that person. We know that if you and your partner love each other, you may be more likely to be the following:

40

1. More open and spontaneous together because you trust each other.
2. More concerned about each other's pleasure and more eager to give enjoyment since you are each committed to the other's well-being.
3. More tolerant and patient with each other.

Some people, however, find the opposite to be true and find that they can be more sexually spontaneous and open with someone whom they might never see again than with a partner with whom they regularly live, eat, and sleep. There are men and women who feel comfortable asking a prostitute or casual acquaintance to fulfill those sexual desires they would never ask their spouses to fulfill. Such discomfort in making sexual requests may, of course, reflect difficulties in communication patterns with a spouse rather than any sexual limitations inherent in committed relationships. It may also reflect the tendency of some people to put those with whom they have a loving relationship on pedestals that raise them well above what some may consider their lowly erotic passions.

We have talked about the relationship between love and sex, and between commitment and sex, but how about between love and commitment? Certainly they seem compatible, at least on the surface. But not always.

There can be conflict even in the union between love and commitment. George Bach, for example, in his book *Pairings*, points out that although the majority of Americans give lip service to the overriding importance of love, they "actually make marriage the real goal of male–female relationships. Pushed . . . toward marriage, singles tend to test every contact with the opposite sex as a contact with a potential husband or wife. The chance for love disappears as men and women try to distort their perceptions of the other, of themselves, and of the relationship into good marriage bets. They dare not risk being authentic." One result of this phoniness in courting relationships, according to Bach, may be that few marriages involve true intimacy. Further, for singles, contacts with the opposite sex may be threatening as a result of their fear that their statements or actions may be interpreted as a step toward commitment. For their own protection, therefore, many singles keep their relationships sex-oriented, yet cool and distant.

Although this may be an overstated and grim view of the relationship between love and commitment, there is no doubt that love and commitment don't always go together. Many couples today feel that their love and mutual enjoyment do best when there is no firm, permanent commitment to each other. They stay together only as long as both get something out of it.

In sum, despite the romantic stories and songs that have so strongly influenced our attitudes, sex, love, and commitment are three valuable but separate experiences. That is not to say they can't occur together. They very often do, and they often bring great joy at such times. But it's important for each of us to think about how we feel about each of these in relation to the others, and how they affect our relationships.

There is no question that our ideas about and expectations from sex, love, and commitment are changing. New forms of commitment are evolving, and a new understanding of love and sex is emerging. No one knows how people will experience sex, love, and commitment a generation from now. But we believe that the only way each of us can survive these changes is through understanding our own needs and wishes and by open and honest sharing with those people who are important to us.

PART

2

When Things Go Wrong

Four

Common Problems of Women

Simone de Beauvoir once observed that many people think that there are two kinds of people: human beings and women. But when women start acting like human beings they are accused of trying to be "like men."

Indeed, many women as well as many men are confused about what's going on with women today, especially about the changes in the ways some women behave sexually. Some men do accuse women of trying to act like men when they get "too assertive" in bed. After all, isn't lust supposed to be a *male* emotion? What do women want, anyway?

Some women, of course, just like some men, are not quite sure what they *do* want. Some are not as "free-thinking" as men think they are. We would seem to be at a time when ideas and standards are changing, and this may be creating many of the problems women are encountering. In this chapter we will look at some of the changes and conflicts in the ways many women approach their sex lives and some of the common problems women run into. We also will offer an introduction to some of the suggestions you will find in later chapters about how you might deal with some of these problems if *you* have run into them.

THE EROTIC MADONNAS

At first glance, it would appear that Americans have just discovered female sexuality. All you have to do is watch the "Today" Show or Johnny Carson on TV or read *Cosmopolitan* or *Playgirl* magazine or a dozen books by sex therapists and researchers to appreciate the great interest we have developed in women's sexual responses, problems, and potentials.

Certainly there have been some real changes in people's recognition and acceptance of the fact that women are and have a right to be sexual beings. And there seems to be a change in how many women behave in bed and what they expect to get out of sex. For example, many women appear to be more sexually active, more willing to experiment with a variety of sexual activities, and more likely to have more orgasms more often than they did in the past.

Yes, women seem to have "come a long way." Well, at least some women in some ways. But these changes have not come about without stress and some problems. Old, traditional ideas about how men and women are supposed to behave sexually die hard, and many women still live in a twilight zone between personal freedom and equality with men on one side and "the good old ways" on the other. Their sexual behavior often reflects a tug-of-war between what they would *like* to do and what they think they *should* do.

How could it be otherwise? The messages that women receive about sex are mixed, often unclear, and just generally confusing. Most have been brought up to believe many of the following myths:

- □ "Good women" should not be too interested in sex.
- □ Lust is for men.
- □ Since men's and women's bodies are different, then their sexual needs, feelings, and desires are, and should be different.
- □ Enjoying sex is mainly for men.
- □ Female sexuality should be less intense and less important than male sexuality.
- □ Having sex is just one more duty for happily wedded wives.
- □ At best, sex can be a "gift" a wife gives her husband to express her affection and devotion.

Sure, another myth says, there are women who really enjoy sex. Everyone knows who *they* are. They were called "fast," "promiscuous," or even "nymphos." But, women were taught, no one would have any respect for them.

45

Virginity was a treasure to be protected and preserved until marriage. Then, suddenly, after the marriage vows, sex would not only be okay, but it would be deliriously fulfilling as well *if* you really loved your man.

These were the myths many women were taught as they were growing up.

But what messages do many women receive today?

- Sex is good, and all right for women, as well as men, married or not.
- Women not only can but should have orgasms—lots of them.
- If you don't enjoy sex fully, there is something very wrong with you, or, at least something wrong with the company you keep.
- If you are to be truly "free," sexual fulfillment is practically a responsibility to yourself if not to all of womanhood.

It's no wonder that with all of these very different kinds of beliefs, so few women feel completely comfortable with seeking and enjoying their sexual activities. Most women have spent years being educated about sex from parents, friends, their male partners, and the media. What they have learned has been full of contradictions:

- "Have a good time tonight dear, but be a good girl."
- "You're not just a sex object."
- "A nice girl sits with her legs crossed."
- "Boys won't respect you if you're easy."
- "Come on, what's wrong with a little kiss; it's not gonna hurt you."
- "Remember your reputation."
- "What are you so uptight about? *Everybody* does it."
- "Don't trust any man."
- "Give yourself fully to the man you love."
- "Be assertive."
- "You have to be a little seductive if you ever want to get a man."
- "All a man wants is your body."
- "What's wrong with a little fun?"
- "A man will chase you until you catch him."
- "You have a right to control your own body."
- "If you don't have orgasms, you're frigid."
- "Find yourself a good man, get married, have lots of children, and forget the rest."

And so it's no surprise that women can be rather confused with the different expectations of them. On one hand they have to be "good" women: pure and deserving of the blessing of motherhood and of respect by all around them. Yet there Is the growing expectation that to be personally fulfilled and to feel really human, women ought to actively enjoy sex. Many of the sex-related problems that we will discuss later in this chapter stem from this conflict. It isn't easy to be an erotic madonna.

The Man Leads; the Woman Follows

If you're old enough to remember the old-fashioned dances in which women and men actually held each other, you will probably also remember the first rule of these dances was that the man led and the woman followed. If the man led well, and the woman followed well, then they made beautiful music together. What was true on the dance floor was supposed to be true in bed. Men were, and to a certain extent still are, expected to be in charge of sex. Traditionally it has been men who tell women how to feel and how to behave sexually, whether they are the "experts" who write about female sexual response or the husbands who direct sexual activities in bed.

In fact, women have been taught that their sexuality can only really exist in response to a man's sexuality, and that all sexual behavior revolves around the penis.

Even the everyday words we use to refer to females are extensions of male terms. The word *woman*, for example, literally means "wife of man." And the labels we use to describe female sexuality were developed and popularized mainly by men, probably in part, at least, to control women's sexual expression. The word *frigid*, for example, is a destructive label that has no real meaning. Does it mean not béing able to have an orgasm during intercourse? The inability to have an orgasm from other forms of stimulation, such as self-stimulation? The inability to get turned on at all? Lack of interest in sex? Or perhaps experiencing pain or discomfort during intercourse? Most usually, the word is used to put a woman down for not being as interested or enthusiastic about sex as the man feels that she should be. Since no woman wants to risk being called "frigid," she might try to please her partner sexually, even if this means faking her own enjoyment, and thus try to live up to others' sexual expectations of her. Although we certainly know that it's perfectly all right to enjoy sex, it's also a woman's (or man's) right to *not* feel like having sex at any time without having to fear being labeled "frigid."

47

At the other extreme, another label that also is used to control women's sexual behavior is the word *nymphomaniac.* This term is used to control those women who run the risk of threatening men by being *more* interested in sex than they may be. The truth of the matter is that women seem to be capable of as much as or more sexual responsiveness than men. Certainly they are capable of having more orgasms in rapid succession than men. This really scares some men, and sometimes other women. So scared people resort to their labels: "nymphomaniac," "slut," "fast woman," "promiscuous," and so on, at one end of the spectrum, and "frigid," "inhibited," "old-fashioned," and "uptight" at the other.

Men obviously have tried to control female sexuality not only by words but also by deeds. Even the most common position in the United States for intercourse—the "missionary" position (man on top), which many people consider the only "normal" position—puts the women in a position in which the male is dominant and in control. This position gives the man considerable opportunity to move around, but essentially it keeps the woman pinned down and perhaps unable to do much except try to avoid suffocation. It is no wonder that some women who never use any other position rarely have orgasms.

Women are taught that a good man may be gentle and considerate and that he will or should take charge of the sexual activities. But not many women expect—or even feel comfortable with the idea—that their partner will be very concerned with their sexual needs. Somehow the woman's sexual satisfaction seems secondary. Many men and women assume that what is really important is that the man has his orgasm. If her needs are met (whatever *they* are), that will be a by-product of his taking care of his own needs.

Even women who are "experienced" are taught the importance of leading a man to believe that he's really in control. Indeed, each time she goes to bed with her partner, she's supposed to act as if it were her first time—as if he were introducing her to sex. This approach provides little opportunity for the woman to express her own wishes openly to the man. She's not even supposed to have any creative sexual ideas or any knowledge that doesn't come directly from him. Yet if a woman is to enjoy herself fully in sex, she must begin to assert herself and communicate her own needs and desires to her partner. In sex, unlike in ballroom dancing, you *both* have to lead and you *both* have to follow. This is not easy for some women because of what they have learned about men.

What Women Learn About Men

The hesitation that many women feel about plunging themselves into enjoying sex comes from an idea that they are carefully taught. Men *get something* from sex. They are supposed to be always after "it," they want "it," and when they get "it," they have "scored." Women, on the other hand, *lose something* from sex. They may lose their virginity, or their reputation. The only thing they may get, they are taught, is pregnant.

After all, it wasn't too long ago that women, as well as men, were taught that there are only two kinds of women: good ones and bad ones. A woman who tried to be "good" even when she got very turned-on was a "cockteaser" or a "prude." But she also knew that if she "gave in," she would run the risk of being a "slut." A difficult choice indeed.

It has fallen to women, probably because they're the ones who get pregnant, to uphold sexual morality. They must give the red and green lights on sex. If they're unmarried, it is they who are supposed to be responsible for their dates' behavior. Men are supposed to be sexually aggressive; they can get carried away. But the women are the ones who have to control them—even when these women would *like* to go on.

The conflicting messages of "It may be okay to want it, but there's something very wrong about giving in" may well influence a woman's later sexual development. She might learn to deal with this conflict by playing sexual games. Since it's crucial to be wanted by a man, you should do those things that make you wanted: look attractive and sexy, but not cheap. Be cute and seductive, but stop before you're considered too wild and get yourself into trouble. This push and pull is often a source of great conflict for women. But it's not the only source. In addition to what women learn about men and their relationship with them, they often pick up some pretty damaging ideas about their own bodies.

It's Dirty Down There

Although many women and men grow up with a certain amount of respect and even awe for the male sex organs, they both often share some discomfort about and even some disgust for the female sex organs. Perhaps because it is not as easy to see as the penis, the vagina has an aura of mystery about it. From a number of sources, many women learn that their vaginas are not only ugly, but are also dirty and smelly as well. They overhear the stories from teenage boys about "stinky fingers" and get careful instructions from their physical-education instructors about "female hygiene." "You've got to work hard to keep yourself clean down there!" Women are constantly frightened by advertisers into buying douches and vaginal-deodorant sprays and other chemical preparations to "cleanse" their vaginas. In fact, these products are unnecessary at best and, at worst, can be harmful to the vagina's natural chemical balance unless, of course, a physician has prescribed their use for a specific infection. What the advertisements for commercial vaginal preparations do is play into many women's fears that there is something about their hidden vaginas that they are supposed to worry about.

Many women are not comfortable with exploring their own vaginas and may think there is something a little strange with wanting to do so. It may never even occur to them to use a mirror to get a better view of their own vaginas (see Chapter 12). There is nothing ugly about a vagina, and there are lots of differences among them—just as there are in other parts of our bodies. You might as well become familiar with your own equipment.

MENSTRUATION

Both men and women also have been led to believe over the ages, even by their holy books, that menstruation, "the curse," is dirty and bad and that a woman should be avoided sexually during "that time of the month." In some cultures the woman was supposed to leave her husband during the times of her menstrual flow. Even today, tampons and sanitary pads are considered somewhat shameful and are marketed in camouflaged containers, not clearly or openly talked about in television ads, and hidden in the back of closets at home.

There is no scientific reason for any of these prejudices against the vagina or menstruation. The healthy vagina has fewer germs in it than the average person's mouth, and it has mechanisms built right into it for cleaning itself with just the assistance of regular washing with mild soap and water. And there is absolutely no danger to either the woman or the man from engaging in intercourse while she is menstruating. Many people do consider it unpleasant, and that's their choice. But it *is* a matter of choice, not one of health.

MASTURBATION

Another product of some women's negative attitudes about their sex organs is the discomfort with masturbation, or self-stimulation. Whereas most men grow up enjoying the pleasure they can give themselves from stimulating their own sex organs, women tend to grow up feeling that their sex organs are somehow off base and shouldn't be touched except for cleansing purposes. These same women, of course, are taught that they will be giving their husbands the supreme gift on their wedding night by letting them enjoy the dirty thing. Such a double message can be pretty confusing for anyone.

A major consequence of the taboos against women's touching themselves is that they are often left being strangers to their own sexual responses. Although many (but by no means all) men enter heterosexual relationships intimately familiar with their sex organs, with what feels good, and with what turns them on, women often haven't yet fully explored their own bodies. Not only have they learned to fear and have little affection for their sex organs, but compared with those of men, they're a lot harder to reach. Thus it can be difficult for a women to tell her partner what feels good to her when she doesn't know herself what feels good.

Many women have found that learning to stimulate their own bodies and give themselves pleasure is an important step in their sexual development. They find that it is an excellent supplement to sex with their partners and a totally satisfying activity on its own. Of course, self-stimulation can be embarrassing for a woman who feels uncomfortable with her body and her sexuality. So we will be suggesting some exercises later on in the book to make the process of self-stimulation easier and more pleasant.

There is one more factor that often contributes to the problems many women experience with sex: fear of pregnancy.

Men Have Fun; Women Have Babies

Although there are probably more similarities than differences between male and female sexuality, there is one often overlooked fact that very much separates men and women. Adult women have in their bodies at all times—up until the advent of menopause—a baby-making machine. Everytime a woman goes to bed with a man, she brings her machine with her. Sure, the man brings his baby-making equipment with him, too. But there's an important difference. Babies are manufactured and carried in the woman's body as a result of what may happen in sexual activity.

Women react to this fact in different ways. Some are very much aware of—even preoccupied with—getting pregnant, and they may indeed avoid or become distracted in sex because of the risk of pregnancy. On the other hand, many women and men will have sex only under circumstances that

51

could lead to an acceptable pregnancy. Indeed, several religions still support this attitude. It is not unusual for women with such an orientation to lose interest in sex and stop having sex entirely as soon as they reach menopause or have had their "quota" of babies.

At the other extreme are the many women, as well as men (including a great many adolescents), who ignore the risk of pregnancy and act as if "it couldn't happen to me." Some, as Constance Lindemann points out, fear the commitment to being sexual that deliberate use of birth control methods implies. Erotic madonnas don't have premeditated sex. These women—and girls—can only accept sex by accident, by impulse, or by giving in to a passionate partner. Only when they are swept away by the situation or by their partner does sex become okay. The constantly growing number of unwanted pregnancies are largely a product of this kind of self-deception.

Most women, however, are very much aware of the ever-present possibility of pregnancy. And often, with little help from their male partners and with different degrees of success, they try to keep their sexual activities separate from making babies except when they plan a pregnancy.

Certainly any attempt to improve your sex life must include some clear thinking with your partner about your plans for having or not having children. Although we're talking about this topic here in the chapter on women's problems, this is an issue that should be of equal concern to men. It's important for your partner to be involved in these decisions. It's also a good idea to check out your plans with your physician. He or she can help you choose birth-control methods that work (remember, withdrawal—removing the penis from the vagina just before ejaculation—has serious drawbacks as a contraceptive method), that are pleasing to you and your partner (try colored condoms; they're fun and don't look surgical like other condoms), and that you are likely to use (a diaphragm doesn't do any good in a dresser drawer). Modern technology has come up with quite a choice of contraceptives that work. Using methods that you and your partner trust and feel good about will allow you both to relax and enjoy yourself more in bed. You can even try making putting your contraceptives on as part of your lovemaking, an arousing activity in and of itself. Remember, the less you have to distract you—and fear of becoming pregnant can be a major distraction—the more likely you are to enjoy and give enjoyment in your sexual activities.

If you're not sure about what contraceptive (birth control) methods are available, speak with your physician or phone your local Planned Parenthood office. In addition, several of the readings listed in the back of this book contain information on birth control, particularly those listed in the section dealing with general information. One of the best chapters on contraception is in *Our Bodies, Ourselves*. Here it's listed under "Female Sexuality," but it covers both male and female contraceptive methods.

So far in this chapter, we've looked at some of the general problems that many women have in their sex lives. Often these problems show up in certain physical reactions—or lack of them—while women are trying to enjoy sexual activities. Let's look at some of these problems now, particularly problems in getting aroused and having orgasms, and problems with painful or difficult intercourse. The goal here is to help you understand what those problems really are all about and how they develop. Then, if you are bothered by any of these problems, you will be better able to use the Treat Yourself programs for them that are presented later in this book.

PROBLEMS IN AROUSAL AND HAVING ORGASMS

With all the current pressures and conflicting ideas of what women's sexuality ought to be (remember the Erotic Madonnas?) it is no wonder that so many women feel sexually unfulfilled. It may not have always been that way. Mary Jane Sherfey, a writer on female sexuality, believes that in the dawn of history women had insatiable sexual appetites and fully enjoyed their capacities to have orgasms. In fact, she believes that each woman may have been capable of sexually exhausting a sucession of men. According to Sherfey, men may have had to hold down women's sexual potential in order to create the family structure of one man–one woman, which they felt was needed for the survival of society. Over the centuries, Sherfey argues, women have had to pay the price of holding down their sexual feelings in order to preserve society and to avoid the anger of the sexually inferior male.

Whether or not Sherfey's ideas are right, there is little reason to question many sex researchers' observations that the majority of women are sexually "held back" and that this holding back is most visible in the large numbers of women who rarely, if ever, achieve orgasm, as well as in many others who do not feel aroused at all by sexual activities. Despite the sexual revolution, the women's movement, and the popularization of the works of such sexologists as Masters and Johnson, things haven't gotten that much better. Shere Hite's and Morton Hunt's Playboy Foundation studies in the 1970s on the orgasmic experiences of married women didn't find much difference from the reported results of much-earlier studies. At most, only about a half of married women achieve orgasm during intercourse most of the time.

One of the problems in dealing with female orgasms is the difficulty of even defining them. Freud and his followers helped to create a couple of generations of concern over vaginal versus clitoral orgasms. They felt, and many women believed, that penis-in-vagina sex was the only "healthy" way for a woman to get turned on. Somehow, getting too much, if any, direct satisfaction from the clitoris was considered sick. Vaginal enjoyment was fine; clitoral enjoyment was immature. These interpretations were connected with Freud's idea that all women felt cheated because they weren't equipped with penises. According to this theory, disturbed women showed their "penis envy" by becoming preoccupied with their clitorises. Even today, the major importance of the clitoris is generally downplayed. We teach our children that boys have penises and that girls have vaginas, not clitorises. How many girls, let alone boys, learned about the clitoris in high-school gym classes?

In the last twenty years, most sexologists and sex therapists moved from that orientation through a phase in which, supported by some of the feminists, the clitoris became the queen of sex. An even more recent perspective is the one in which the distinction between clitoral orgasm and vaginal orgasm is not considered that important. Masters and Johnson have pointed out that there is only one kind of orgasm, physiologically speaking, and that it involves the entire clitoral–vaginal system.

More recent research on women's orgasms suggests that it may not be that simple. There seems to be a considerable range of orgasmic responses that women experience, varying in intensity, in quality, and in the location in which they are experienced. In Shere Hite's study, some women reported a diffuse but strong orgasm, usually during intercourse, felt deep inside their bodies; it came and went slowly and was accompanied by strong emotional feelings. Other women reported that their orgasms were experienced more specifically in the genital area, and that these were sharper and more intense. Those women who had experienced both kinds of orgasms had no difficulty in telling one from the other.

In a further attempt to define the sometimes elusive female orgasm, Irving Singer found *three* kinds of orgasms, differentiated both by the sensations the woman experienced and by the type of stimulation that brought them about:

54

1. The *vulval or clitoral orgasm* can result from intercourse or from almost any kind of bodily stimulation, including self-stimulation, or even just a good fantasy. It is felt in the whole genital area.

2. The *uterine or vaginal orgasm* generally is achieved only in intercourse through thrusting of the penis. It may not particularly involve the clitoris at all. It requires the penis's making contact with and repeatedly thrusting against the cervix (the opening of the uterus). It is reported to be deeply satisfying. This type of orgasm reportedly can lead to great sexual satisfaction.

3. The *blended orgasm* is a type of orgasm that again requires deep thrusting of the penis and involves indirect stimulation of the clitoris. It results in profound vaginal contractions. It is called "blended" because it is reported to contain aspects of both the first two types of orgasms.

At this point you may be wondering why there is a need to label female orgasms. Good question. In the final analysis, it may not matter what brand of orgasm you have in order to enjoy your sexual activities. After all, very few men stop and wonder what kind of orgasms they have: whether an orgasm involves their testicles, or the shaft, head, or the coronal ridge of their penis. If they enjoy it and feel satisfied afterwards, that's good enough. The same would seem true of female orgasm. It's not what type you've had, and not even necessarily whether you've had an orgasm at all (many women, as well as men, very much enjoy sexual activities without orgasms), but how you feel as a result of your sexual activities.

This does not take away from the findings that many women, even married women, after decades of intercourse, are not enjoying their sexual contacts and that they feel deprived of orgasmic release and frustrated after sexual activities.

The reasons for their not having orgasms are not always clear. Certainly, all women are physiologically capable of sexual satisfaction. Even women who have had their clitorises surgically removed still report orgasms. So what's the problem?

Margaret Mead wrote, "The human female's capacity for orgasm is to be viewed as a potentiality that may or may not be developed by a given culture." It seems that our culture has been inconsistent in allowing women to have orgasms. As said earlier, women in our society are often brought up with shame, fear, guilt, and embarrassment about their sexuality. Essentially, they are taught that a good girl is an inhibited one. They are given little, if any, information or guidance about how to enjoy their bodies, let alone about menstruation and contraception. On top of that, they are taught to fear and distrust men sexually.

As a result, a sense of mystery, discomfort, and fear is the most common feeling that a woman learns to associate with sexual expression. She has learned that her vagina is dirty and that men's sexuality is dangerous and overpowering. She has a fear of losing control of her dignity from letting loose in bed. After years of hearing that sex is dirty and perhaps dangerous, she may be unable to let herself go and relax and thus become aroused.

Finally, because she does not even know her own needs and is embarrassed to talk about them even if she does know them, she has trouble talking to her partner about what she wants and needs for her sexual satisfaction. Most women who haven't had an orgasm from intercourse would still probably not be too comfortable asking their partner to rub their clitorises or vaginas with their hands, even after their partners have had their orgasms.

Any wonder why so many women experience difficulty in achieving orgasms or in getting aroused by sexual activities?

This is not to say that orgasmic or arousal problems are caused only by emotional factors. Much more often, there is probably a different cause as well. Several researchers have agreed that a major reason why so few women have orgasms regularly in intercourse is that they lack adequate stimulation. It has been shown that a woman can stimulate herself to orgasm in an average of less than four minutes, yet it takes the same woman an average of eight minutes of intercourse to attain orgasm. Many sexologists agree that the difference is probably not entirely psychological but that the stimulation from intercourse is often not very efficient. That is, her partner is not adequately exciting her. There seems to be a clear connection between the likelihood that a woman will have an orgasm and the amount of excitement and stimulation she receives during sexual activity.

Types of Problems with Arousal and Orgasm

There seems to be much more variation among women in their sexual responsiveness than there is among men. Masters and Johnson, for example, found that there was considerable difference in the patterns and number of successive orgasms women experience, as well as differences in their intensity. As we mentioned earlier, there seem to be differences even in the kinds and locations of orgasms women experience.

There is also a variety of problems experienced by women

56

that are related to orgasms. As in most things, sexologists have attempted to label the different problems and have then proceeded to disagree with each label. On the other hand, three of the problems that commonly are grouped together as "problems with orgasms" can be described as follows:

1. *Lack of sexual arousal.* This applies to women who, in varying degrees, just don't get turned on. Often, this is reflected in their not experiencing vaginal lubrication (becoming "wet") or not feeling a desire for sex in situations in which they would like to be turned on. Of course, there are considerable variations in this pattern. Some women find that they turn on to some people but not to others. Some turn on only under certain conditions (when the house is completely quiet, with the children asleep, or after two glasses of wine). Other women respond to manual or oral stimulation, or even to self-stimulation, but don't get aroused (or may even get turned off) by the approach of intercourse.

2. *Infrequent orgasms.* This refers to the problem of women who have had orgasms in the past, who have them from time to time, or who have them only under certain circumstances, but who wish they could have them more often or under different circumstances. They may have had orgasms with different partners, or only from self-stimulation, or only in certain positions.

3. *Absence of orgasms.* There are some women who may or may not be sexually excited by their partner, and who may or may not otherwise enjoy intercourse, but never, under any circumstances, have experienced orgasms.

As the women's movement has brought about a greater awareness of the problems of women, more and more women are expressing their concern about problems in the above areas. At the same time, sex therapists such as Masters and Johnson, Lonnie Barbach, Helen Singer Kaplan, and others have developed techniques to help women increase their level of arousal and achieve orgasm more readily with their partners. These procedures will be discussed in detail in Chapter 15.

PAINFUL AND DIFFICULT INTERCOURSE

It is not unusual for a woman to occasionally experience some tightness in the entrance to her vagina or to occasionally experience some pain or discomfort with intercourse. However,

57

if you experience intense spasms, tightness, or pain with any frequency, you should consult your physician (see Chapter 16). In the following pages we will describe these conditions and some of the possible causes of them.

Vaginal Muscle Spasms (Vaginismus)

Vaginismus (pronounced vah-gin-IS-mus) is the somewhat frightening-sounding name given to a condition in which the muscles around the entrance to the vagina close so tightly that intercourse becomes impossible. It is an involuntary spasm or reflex over which the woman has no control. Women who have this problem may or may not be otherwise sexually responsive, and they may or may not have positive relationships with their sexual partners. Women who experience vaginismus generally, but not always, report a fear of intercourse, or a history of painful intercourse, and they will often avoid all sexual activity.

Husbands of women with this problem may obviously become quite frustrated by their wives' inability to engage in intercourse, and they may also blame their wives for what they perceive as unresponsiveness or downright rejection. Helen Singer Kaplan reports that husbands of women with vaginismus often have difficulty in achieving erections in reaction to their wives' condition.

There are both possible physical and emotional causes for vaginismus. Many of the possible physical causes—involving vaginal pain—are described in the following section. For these, and for any other physical concern you might have regarding the physical health of your pelvic organs, we urge that you consult your physician (gynecologist). As you might suspect, though, the woman's fear of the pain that might be associated with intercourse then could lead to the involuntary muscle contractions (spasms) that prevent the painful process of intercourse from occurring. This is not unlike the way in which you might clench your teeth shut when a dentist's drill is poised for action. A vicious circle could be created when the male attempts to penetrate the tightly closed vagina; this creates even more pain.

There are also a number of social and emotional factors that could lead to these involuntary muscle contractions around the vagina. Most of these are associated with fear and anxiety about sex. Some women have had a very punitive or strict upbringing that leads them to believe that sexual intercourse—even with their husbands—is somehow evil or degrading. These women may come to feel guilty or plain scared about voluntarily engaging in sex. Thus, when the possibility of intercourse comes nearer, the fear leads to the vaginal spasms, making vaginal penetration very difficult or impossible.

A fear of becoming pregnant—which ordinarily can be handled through use of appropriate birth-control (contraceptive) measures—can also lead in some women to vaginal muscle spasms, thereby preventing intercourse.

Other women who may have had a relatively non-punitive upbringing about sex may nevertheless have had early frightening or traumatic experiences with intercourse. Some women perhaps have tried to have intercourse but failed because of a lack of lubrication. Others may have suffered from the trauma of being raped or being sexually molested in other ways. Still others may have been involved in incest (sexual relations with a relative), leading them to feel guilty or fearful about future sexual activities. Further, there are many, many cases in which a couple's first attempts at intercourse, or at new or different sexual techniques or positions, may be so unsuccessful or anxiety-producing that the woman becomes progressively more nervous about the next attempts, leading to vaginal spasms.

Thus, any intense, negative, or frightening experiences associated by a woman with intercourse could lead to this response. This is especially so if the woman fears that something "bad" will come from voluntarily engaging in intercourse.

Painful Intercourse

Painful intercourse is sort of a catch phrase that describes several potential problems that a woman may encounter. Also called *dyspareunia* (pronounced dis-pear-OOO-nee-ah), all of these problems have a common element: they all involve some sort of pain in or around the vagina during intercourse. The pain might be a deep aching, a momentary twinge, a sharp pain, or simply intense discomfort. The pain could also be any combination of these. But whatever it feels like, you know that it hurts.

There are several possible reasons for painful intercourse. Some of the most common of these involve the "procedures" that a couple use during intercourse. The male may be unsophisticated or clumsy in his attempts at intercourse. For example, the man may get carried away in his thrusting, thinking that he has to act like a pile driver in order to satisfy himself or his partner.

Very frequently, a couple proceeds to intercourse too rapidly, before the woman is adequately aroused. This then could lead to insufficient lubrication (wetness inside the vagina) so that the vaginal walls become irritated. We should mention that some women naturally lubricate more than others, and all women tend to lubricate less as they get older. This in no way necessarily reflects on their sexual responsiveness or their love for their partner.

Another set of very common reasons for painful intercourse has to do with infections and other disorders of the vagina and urinary tract. There are a whole range of common infections that women can get such as fungus and yeast infections (one study found that more than 30 percent of the women in the study had yeast infections). There are a number of skin disorders, too, that may lead to painful intercourse. Now, we want to be clear that we are not talking here about venereal diseases (V.D.) but about a whole range of problems whose causes may be unknown or unclear, and that may be no more unusual than the common cold, but any of which could produce painful intercourse for the woman.

Finally, in a very few cases (sex therapists hardly ever run into these), there could be some kind of disorder that has been present since birth or early childhood, involving the size or shape of the vagina, making intercourse painful or impossible.

Fortunately, as suggested above, for most problems involving painful intercourse, or the vaginal spasms described in the last section, there are relatively simple treatments that result in rapid improvement. These treatments will be described in Chapter 16. But there is one guideline that you should follow if you are suffering from any of these problems before you start your Treat Yourself program: See your physician first. He or she will be able to tell whether or not you have any of the physical problems described above (such as an infection), and if you do, prescribe the correct medication. If you have seen your physician and have received a clean bill of health and still have one of these problems, then you should begin the Treat Yourself program. Either way, through your physician or the Treat Yourself program, in most cases, you should be able to begin comfortable intercourse within a relatively short time.

BEYOND THE OLD WIVES'
(AND OLD HUSBANDS') TALES

We are just beginning to understand the nature and potentials of women's sexuality. Although there is still much left to learn, there is much we already know. We know, for instance, that once you overcome some of the traditional old wives' tales and the inhibitions they create, you can begin to learn about your *own* sexual responses. Then, you can begin to make the sexual choices that can bring you joy and fulfillment.

We believe that old wives' tales are potentially harmful whether they come from the conservative traditions that discouraged women from being sexual or from the tyranny of the supposedly sexually liberated who *demand* spectacular female sexual response. New rigid rules under the guise of liberation do not seem to us to be what liberation is all about. Each person has to be free to make his or her sexual choices without having to prove anything to anyone.

As a way of summarizing this chapter, let's look at some of the things we know about female sexuality and how you might use these ideas to treat yourself to a better sex life.

We know that there is certainly a wide range in women's sexual interests and desires. These are probably as broad or even broader than those of men. It's just that many women were taught not to have these feelings, or at least not to express them. Enjoy your feelings and desires. And you don't have to wait until your partner gives you the go-ahead sign. Women have just as much "right" to initiate—and enjoy—sexual activities as their partners do. Of course, your partner has the right to politely refuse. (As we'll note in the next chapter, men are beginning to learn that it's okay for them to say "no" too.) But many men welcome the growing trend of sharing the initiative in sexual relationships. They may well get turned on by their partners' choosing and fully participating in their sexual activities. There's always the chance, however, that your partner may not feel comfortable with your being sexually innovative or assertive. If that happens, you may have some negotiating to do. But that does not mean that there is anything wrong—or unfeminine—about your wanting particular sexual activities.

One of the more common ideas about female sexuality today relates to orgasms—that they are essential to a woman's and probably her partner's sexual enjoyment and thus are well worth working for. Everyone knows that orgasms are great. But they *need not be essential* to either you or your partner's sexual enjoyment every time you have sex. If you and/or your partner are convinced that they *are* essential, one or both of you will obviously not feel satisfied unless you do have one. However, as we keep saying, there are few hard and fast rules for what is "required" for sexual enjoyment. That's up to you. And remember, trying too hard to do *anything* can be self-defeating when it comes to sex. Having orgasms is a natural female response, just as it's a natural male response. The trick—for both women and men—is to not work at it, but to let it happen by ridding yourself of those learned inhibitions and patterns of behavior that get in the way of your having orgasms. Becoming preoccupied with orgasms may be the best way of guaranteeing that you *don't* have them.

On the other hand, orgasms don't just come out of nowhere. And a man doesn't "give" a woman an orgasm. You have to be a reasonably enthusiastic and active participant in your sexual activities. Find out—and do—what feels good, and things will probably work out just fine.

Now, that doesn't mean that there will be fireworks each time. Yes, there may be times when the orgasmic bells will ring loudly for you. But at other times sex may be just a mildly pleasant experience for you. That's just in the nature of sex and it's true for all of us. Don't expect too much from sex, and enjoy each experience for what it is.

And remember, despite the old wives' and old husbands' tales, there is no reason why each sexual activity has to climax with a penis in your vagina—unless your goal is to get pregnant. Both women and men are capable of enjoying sexual stimulation in a wide variety of ways. Certainly, as we've noted several times, the clitoris is a central location for erotic stimulation. Thus intercourse, at least in the standard man-on-top position, may not be the ideal way to stimulate your clitoris, since there is no direct contact between the penis and the clitoris in this position. Intercourse is a time-honored way to enjoy sex, and orgasms are exciting and tension-relieving. But you and your partner are the best judges of what will meet your individual and joint needs and wishes each time you have sex. And if you still feel unsatisfied if he has an orgasm and you haven't, you can, if you wish, ask him to bring you to orgasm with his hand, or by some other way of your choosing. It's no insult to him or to you.

That brings up a final point. Too many women feel that their own sexual needs or wishes are only legitimate if an "expert," usually a man, tells her that they are. Otherwise they often see their feelings as "abnormal" at worst or "silly" at best. Too much concern about expert opinion (that includes ours) can keep you from discovering yourself. You have a right and a need to make your own sexual choices. Only you can expand your sexual horizons and enrich your sexual life. We hope that this book will help you to do that more easily.

Five

Common Problems of Men

Now that the smoke has begun to clear from the revolution in female sexuality, we are beginning to see that the sexual fulfillment of men has also been impaired by common misinformation and by the distorted expectations of male sexual behavior.

Men have suffered in many ways from the stories they tell themselves about what men are supposed to be. Popular television, movies, and novels all tend to paint the same picture: A man is supposed to be a strong, competent, self-assured, intelligent leader. He has high goals for himself, and he strives constantly and diligently to achieve these goals—at almost any cost. And, of course, the cost is high—certainly in terms of health and also, perhaps, in terms of lost opportunities for a joyful life.

Nowhere are the pressures to '"be a man" as great as in the world of sex. A man's bed (or his partner's) is his main arena for his (your?) lifelong contest to prove his masculinity. If a man resents this contest or has difficulty meeting the demands of maleness, he is taught to keep quiet and put up with it.

Many men seem to need to "prove" their masculinity (whatever that is) over and over again. A sexual encounter is often seen as a contest that they either win or lose. In fact, there are many similarities between how men approach sex and how they approach sports.

The contests start early, largely from the pressure boys feel from their teammates—the other young men and teenagers who grew up with them. Each boy is eager to win the respect of his teammates—after all, he is panic stricken that he may be thrown off the team! The atmosphere of his relationship with other boys and young men is always permeated with competition and achievement. That's the way group status is achieved. A man's individuality and personhood are often sacrificed as he works at being a good team member. The way he shows his worth to his team is: First, he enters as many contests as he can, and second, he wins the contests—that is, he scores. Scoring means to get "it"—to have intercourse.

In the process of learning to play this game, he learns to see women as the opponents—members of a rival team he has to overcome with his superior skills. Of course, no one teaches him exactly what these skills are. After all, in order to be on the team, he ought to already know. But he does learn one thing early, and that is that in order to play the game well, the most important thing is to have the proper—no, the best—athletic equipment.

The Athletic Equipment

The adolescent learns early that the most important, central item in playing the all-important sexual game well is a major-league penis. Without a top-notch penis, he feels relegated to the bush leagues.

How does the growing sexual athlete learn to evaluate his athletic equipment? He has plenty of opportunities. He checks out his teammates' equipment in the locker room, showers, and at the urinals; he listens to countless dirty stories told by his teammates; and he surveys the specially selected equipment depicted in pornographic magazines and movies. Based on these observations, he concludes that a good penis has to be awe inspiring in size and as hard as steel. Although he doesn't realize this, his own penis looks smaller when looking at it from above (in essence, a foreshortened view), as opposed to seeing other penises straight on. Further, he rarely sees other erect penises, which are somewhat more similar in size than soft penises.

After all, the penises he hears about, the ones he sees in dirty books and movies, and even the ones described in popular novels by Harold Robbins, Mario Puzo, and others are always huge: They spring out of unzipped flies like charging stallions and are as militant as battering rams. The young man is well aware that his penis is indeed his principal weapon as he goes forth into combat with the female species. No one takes a bankrobber seriously if he shows up with a pop gun. Not only must the penis be gigantic, but it must always be ready. If you're going to be caught with your pants down, your penis had better be up.

Finally, the equipment must not only be big and hard, but it must be fully loaded and with proper release action. It should be capable of discharging copious amounts of ejaculate—but at the proper time. It shouldn't have a hair trigger because, unlike in most other sporting events, speed is not such a priority in sexual competitions.

Clearly, these are pretty heavy specifications for the sexual equipment. And, as might be expected, few people are fortunate enough to have them. Indeed, a recent *Forum* magazine survey of a thousand men found the men (with the exception of a small minority) very much dissatisfied with the quality or quantity of their equipment. Not only that, but many felt that their small or "average" penises were a drawback to their sexual value.

There is no getting around it: Penises do come in different sizes, and although the differences in size are not as great when you compare men with erections with men calmed down, there are some small penises and some genuinely mammoth ones. These differences can be important. They can certainly affect a man's self-image, and fear of revealing a relatively small penis to a potential partner has kept many a man from seeking sexual partners. And there are women who do prefer big penises; there are even some who downright insist upon them. Some prefer them for psychological reasons and some really enjoy being stuffed.

On the other hand, there are many women who couldn't care less or who hardly even notice the size of their partner's penis. Indeed, some women are physically uncomfortable with big penises. (Smaller penises are easier when it comes to oral sex.) Furthermore, many of a women's sensations from intercourse come from the clitoris and from the nerve endings that are mainly in the first couple of inches of the vagina. (Both are reachable by a finger or with a one- or two-inch erection. And, as we've said before and will say again, joy in sexual activities—for both women and men—comes in large part from the affection expressed between partners and from the stroking, fondling, touching, kissing, licking, nibbling, and hugging that goes on between lovers. If all your attention is on big penises' plunging in and out of deep vaginas, you probably wouldn't be reading this book in the first place.

Assuming that you have at least a stump, and considerably less than a baseball bat, you're adequately endowed to give and receive considerable pleasure. You may have to learn to live with the fact that you may never be invited to act in an X-rated movie. We all have our limitations.

The Other Team

While the young man is learning what's expected of him in his life-long contests, he's also learning what to expect from his potential contestants: women.

First of all, as in all combat, we are taught to dehumanize the opponents. We strip them of feelings, needs, and personality. They are bodies that are there to be conquered. Their value is measured by how good they will be as trophies: particularly by how attractive, big breasted, and slim waisted they are. Studies of descriptions of first sexual partners show considerable differences between what men and women report. Although women tend to describe their first sexual partners by such characteristics as type of employment and personality, men tend to describe their first sexual partners by their physical attributes, particularly in terms of how attractive they were. It's downright embarrassing for many men to be seen with a less-than-gorgeous woman.

In addition to assuming that physical attractiveness is the prime requisite of a sexual partner, many men have been taught to make certain assumptions about what women are "really like" sexually. In the first place, they are taught that, deep down, all women really want to be screwed and that therefore they should ignore a woman's obligatory protestations that she really doesn't want to. That's not to say that rape is condoned. Rather, a "real man" is supposed to press the issue to the point that a woman's "superficial resistances" come down. How about respect and concern for her expressed wishes? Nonsense. Remember: She's the competition. She's just playing her part of the game.

This is a rather bleak picture of the "war of the sexes." But to some degree, it pervades the sexual patterns of a good percentage of American men. Certainly, such an attitude toward women does not encourage the development of feelings of

66

partnership with women, let alone friendship. Is it any wonder, then, that so few men feel comfortable turning to their girlfriends and wives as the major source of information about how to enjoy their sexual time together more fully? Rather, they turn to their friends, to pornography, or even to sex-manual writers for help when the best help might be six inches away from them in bed.

So, one way or another, men acquire more or less willing partners for their sexual enjoyment. But often that's when the problems really begin. Trained as they were to play the sexual game well according to the rules of their team, they carry a set of expectations with them to bed. These expectations are widely accepted as universal truth, and yet the majority of sexual problems that men run into stem from these beliefs.

These beliefs have put considerable stress on men to "do well" in bed—to prove to their partners as well as to themselves that they are indeed "real men" (whatever that is). With such powerful expectations, the man feels that he's on trial each time he engages in sex. Each time he climbs into bed, he readies himself for another test. The preoccupation with "doing well" in bed, as if to pass some big test, inhibits a person's ability to be spontaneous and enjoy his or her sexual activities.

The Big Event

Because he has been taught so long and so well about what he is supposed to be like in bed, the man can hardly relax and enjoy himself, much less explore and meet the needs and desires of his partner. He spends his time with a mental checklist of doing well in bed:

- □ Penis up.
- □ Stimulation of partner begun.
- □ Partner being turned on.
- □ Deodorant in working condition.
- □ Weight well distributed.
- □ Ejaculate ready for firing on command.
- □ Foreplay concluded; ready for insertion of penis.
- □ Partner coming.
- □ Bombs away!

Throughout the endeavor, the man's behavior is very likely dictated not by his or his partner's expressed desires but by a set of rules he has learned over the years.

In his provocative book *Male Sexuality*, Bernie Zilbergeld

67

lists a series of widely held myths that tend to limit the enjoyment both men and their partners get out of sex:

THERE ARE FEELINGS THAT MEN EITHER
SHOULD NOT HAVE OR, IF THEY HAVE THEM,
THAT SHOULD BE KEPT WELL HIDDEN.

Until recently, the models for male sexual behavior—movie stars and characters in popular novels—were able to be jovial, angry, competitive, sullen. But never or hardly ever could we see a Burt Reynolds or a Clint Eastwood be weak or confused (unless temporarily, after being hit over the head by a gun butt), vulnerable, tender, or just generally sensitive. Yet these are the characteristics on which deep relationships—including sexual partnerships—are based. Perhaps with Woody Allen's and Richard Dreyfuss's becoming new models of acceptable behaviors, we'll see men be increasingly able to admit their gentler and more vulnerable selves to their partners and to themselves.

A MAN IS RESPONSIBLE FOR WHAT GOES ON IN SEX
AND WILL BE JUDGED ACCORDINGLY.

It has been said that there have been three eras in the evolution of ideas about a man's responsibility in sexual activities. Sex used to be something a man did *to* a woman. As men's consciousnesses were raised, they began to perceive that a man has a responsibility for his partner's satisfaction—so then sex was something he did *for* a woman. After all, a considerate man would do anything in his power to give his partner satisfaction and would thus get a feather in his hat or a notch in his pistol handle or whatever. Only now are men (and their partners) recognizing that sex is best done *with* a woman, each sharing in the giving and in the taking.

And this no longer means that a man must take the responsibility for what goes on. After all, why should he have the responsibility not only for turning his partner on and for giving her orgasms, but for getting himself turned on? Fantasy images and adolescent memories to the contrary, a man just doesn't get turned on automatically as soon as his partner says "okay." He may need or want some stimulation himself. Instant erections occur more often in novels than in real life. It's unrealistic for a man or his partner to expect him to be a self-starter. Sex should be a joint enterprise for the man and the woman. No longer is the man perceived as the conductor, with the woman's body as the orchestra. It takes two to tango. And the woman has an important, active role in bringing about and maintaining her partner's erection. The responsibility for a man's erection need not be exclusively on his own shoulders.

68

This doesn't mean that instead of just the man's being performance oriented, we now have both the man and the woman scurrying around trying to prove themselves by turning each other on. Such preoccupation with "doing it right" is bound to create anxiety, which is the archenemy of sexual enjoyment and even of just plain intimacy. Other than mutual satisfaction, there are no goals or quotas in enjoyable sex. The greater the pressure to perform well, the less the likelihood that either or both partners will enjoy their togetherness.

Thus, men have taken on too much responsibility for sex. Both partners are—partners. Neither is or can be solely responsible for what happens between them. They are partners who enjoy each other and who share each other's bodies, as well as sharing the decisions about how to use them.

Being "horny" is often considered the natural state of men. Our memories of our adolescent ever-present erections as well as the high team premiums placed on frequent sexual activity combine to make us believe that the ideal man is always ready and eager to engage in sex. His only legitimate complaint is that he doesn't get enough of it, whether from his girlfriends or, later, from his wife. Push the button and out springs the ever-ready sex tool.

But men are not machines. Nor are their penises machines. Our sexual responses come from a complex network of circumstances involving our constantly interacting mind and body. Only when everything works together in harmony (a situation no man can will) will a man get turned on and produce and perhaps sustain an erection.

Although men are able to accept (perhaps reluctantly) their partner's at least occasional lack of interest in sex, they expect more of themselves and are embarrassed and guilt ridden if "it" doesn't work. No wonder. Even Zorba the Greek stated that "the greatest sin is when a woman calls a man to her bed, and he does not go!"

Well, maybe that worked for Zorba, he was a very determined man. But no matter how hard a man works for it, there's no way that he can guarantee an erection whenever, wherever, or with whomever it is called for. In fact, the more effort a man puts into achieving this unachievable goal, the less likely it is that he'll get what he wants. You might as well accept the fact that sometimes it isn't going to get up. Men have the right to say no, and so have their penises.

PHYSICAL CONTACT IS JUST A PRELUDE TO INTERCOURSE.

Back in our adolescent model of sex, the only desirable physical goal was intercourse. Hugging, stroking, licking, and kissing were all just steps toward "getting it in." The heroes in novels, movies, and pornography rarely, if ever, just stopped with these activities. The scenes faded only after it was quite clear that intercourse was inevitable for the hero and heroine. Since we carry with us the idea that "getting it" is the goal and responsibility of every man, we assume that if we're going to touch, we're going to have intercourse. The result is frequently disastrous.

> David and Joanne had been married for several months. She sensed that he was beginning to shy away from her every time she touched him. She wondered if he was already losing interest in her. Finally, she worked up the courage to ask him what was going on. He replied that he was getting worn out having intercourse with her two or three times every day. Joanne replied that she certainly didn't require or even want intercourse as often as they had been having it the first few months. She wondered why he had been initiating it so often. "*I* initiate it?" David replied with surprise. "You're the one who keeps hugging and stroking me. I've begun to think that you're insatiable!" Joanne patiently explained that she enjoyed touching, kissing, stroking, and hugging David and by no means did that necessarily mean that she wanted to go to bed at that time.

David had to learn that it's okay for a man to receive and give affection without any expectation or demand for an erotic response. Incidentally, the implications for male-to-male relationships are obvious. Many men are afraid of expressing physical affection to their friends for fear that it would imply sexual feelings or—good God—that it would precipitate a turn-on. Physical affection is a wonderful thing that binds many relationships together, friends and relatives as well as sexual partners. It's a shame that many men avoid almost all physical contact with others for this reason or that they limit it only to those situations that will end up in sex.

Our preoccupation with "foreplay" reinforces the idea that the main event and only logical ending to a sexual encounter is intercourse. Indeed, the very concept of "foreplay" is too often a variety of things a man thinks he has to go through in order to get his partner ready for intercourse. We don't like or use the term *foreplay* because we believe that making these sexual activities secondary to intercourse tends to lessen their value.

Most men would respond to the above by saying, "Of course, isn't that what it's all about?" No, it isn't. The idea that sex and intercourse are the same is a common one and probably stems from the fact that the most effective and efficient way to make a woman pregnant is to place an erect penis in her vagina and thrust it in and out until ejaculation occurs. Since conception often was the major, if not the only, goal of sex in the past, intercourse became the thing to do if you wanted a baby. All our ideas about intercourse's being normal and all other activities' being somewhat perverted (unless, of course, they are part of "foreplay") come from our heritage of connecting intercourse with reproduction. But most sex today—even between married partners—is for reasons far removed from making babies.

There is no "right" way to enjoy another person's body. There is no "normal" place for our penises to be when we ejaculate. Certainly, intercourse is a mechanically and aesthetically great way to enjoy sex. But it is not the only way, and it is not even necessarily the best way for all people under all circumstances. There are many orifices (openings) and appendages (things that stick out on our body). Any combination of these things that gives pleasure to a couple and that is mutually consented to is just fine.

Limiting our choices to just getting a hard penis into a wet vagina as soon as the woman is ready adds to the performance anxiety of the man.

> Isabel asked Herb what strokes or caresses he liked while they were in bed. Herb thought for a minute and said that he didn't really know. "I'm so busy getting you, and I guess myself, ready for intercourse and wondering when you'll be ready and whether I'll be ready that I hardly notice what we're doing beforehand."

Not only does the orientation to intercourse-above-all diminish the options and pleasures for the man, but it tends to limit the possibilities for women, many of whom are even more stimulated by oral and manual contact than they are by the penetration of the penis. To insist that all women learn to get their sexual satisfaction exclusively from intercourse hardly seems reasonable or realistic. Again, there's no one right way for men or women to enjoy themselves in bed. It's up to each couple.

YOU CERTAINLY ALWAYS HAVE TO HAVE
AN ERECTION TO ENJOY SEX.

If your whole sexual life pivots on your penis, you may often be disappointed. If it doesn't get hard every time you want it to, or if it doesn't stay hard as long as you'd like it to, it's bound to get you angry, frustrated, and embarrassed, and your partner may well follow suit, and you'll both end up feeling miserable. There's much more to sex than meets the penis.

Generally speaking, if you're not preoccupied with your

71

penis and if things take their natural course, you will wind up with your penis getting hard. But if not, it's no catastrophe. There's plenty that you and your partner can do with each other in a sensual, warm, relaxed, even playful way. If an erection comes up, fine. If not, there's always next time. Your erection is bound to come back if you just forget about it. In the meanwhile, enjoy (and let your partner enjoy) whatever else you have—fingers, tongue, a whole body, and a personality.

GOOD SEX MUST BE PASSIONATE AND SHOULD PROCEED IN A STEADY PROGRESSION THAT MUST END IN AN ORGASM.

According to this idea, the tide of sex proceeds at an inevitable pace. There's no holding it back. Once passion overcomes one, there's no stopping it. That's a very romantic idea in novels. However, the all-consuming passionate "fuck" is a rare phenomenon in real life, and if one sets one's goals on it for all times, one is likely to be disappointed. Enjoyable sex takes many forms. As we noted earlier, the passion may well ebb and flow, and the whole thing might be legitimately postponed, interrupted, or even terminated for a really good television program. Leisurely, playful sex—with or without erections—can be just as satisfying and far less tiring than all-consuming passion each and every time. It doesn't have to be a very powerful experience, it certainly doesn't have to have its total focus on the genitals, and it doesn't have to end in orgasm.

Especially as a man gets older, he may not have an orgasm every time he engages in sexual activities. There are times when orgasms are a natural outcome of sexual activities—we all know about them. At other times, a man will have an orgasm only if he really works at it, but why need he try so hard? Folklore to the contrary, nothing serious usually happens if an orgasm isn't forthcoming. "Blue balls" (that is, pain in the scrotum that sometimes occurs when a man is aroused for a considerable time without orgasm) is relatively rare and doesn't last very long when it does occur. If it seems that an orgasm isn't likely to occur, quit while you're ahead. That way, you both can relax with each other with smiles on your faces. Orgasms (like erections and passionate sex) are great, but they are not essential for you or for your partner. There is still much satisfaction in a warm, low-passion-level encounter. Variety is the spice of sex.

However, there are some problems that are a major concern to the many men who experience them. In the following sections, we will discuss the most common of these, problems with erection and ejaculation.

PROBLEMS WITH ERECTIONS

With the sexual expectations and concerns with which many men grow up, it's almost astonishing that any of them ever get erections. We know that anxiety and tension can prevent erections. Many men experience this feeling, which effectively prevents them from getting hard.

We're not saying that all erection problems are psychological. Many men fail to get erections for physical reasons. The erectile system is a complex one involving subtle interactions of mind and body. If either is impaired, nothing happens.

There are many physical factors that can keep our erections dormant. Fatigue, overeating, and overdrinking are probably the most common culprits. But there are others. In fact, anything that interferes with the complex physiological processes of the blood vessels, muscles, and nervous system components of our sexual responses can effectively prevent erections.

Sometimes the factors that interfere with these systems come from surprising sources. For example, some commonly prescribed medications for high blood pressure and diabetes (as well as diabetes itself) can lead to physiological chain reactions that lead to problems in getting erect. Even some tranquilizers and antidepressants can affect the ability to have an erection. Fortunately, often an alternative drug taken at a lower dosage can erase the negative effects of the medication. If you have any questions about the effect of drugs you are taking on your sexual responses, get in touch with your doctor.

Of course, one of the most common drugs is alcohol. In small doses, alcohol is an effective relaxer and may even help sexual activities by reducing tension and inhibitions. But the heavy use of alcohol is a common cause of erection problems. In fact, in one recent study of 17,000 alcoholics, almost one in ten reported being totally unable to get an erection. Overuse of alcohol provokes the liver to actually destroy significant quantities of testosterone, the male hormone, which the body produces. Fortunately, going on the wagon will often enable the body to bring its hormone level back to working order.

Any physical condition that brings about a constant state of pain, such as arthritis, can also lead to erectile problems. Again, the relief of pain can bring back the sexual response.

If you have an alcohol problem; if you have an illness that provokes considerable pain; if you have diabetes, high blood pressure, or glandular disturbances; or if you are regularly taking tranquilizers or antidepressants and often have problems in getting erections, then you should go no further without seeing your doctor for a consultation. In fact if you have a sexual problem, a physical checkup is useful in order to rule out the possibility of a physical basis for your problem.

A good way to determine whether your erection problem is emotional or physical is to see whether you ever get erections in nondemanding situations. If you achieve erections easily when you masturbate or if you often have one in the morning upon waking, then chances are that your erection problems are not physical. If you never get erections under any circumstances (even while you're asleep), then there's a good chance that your problem is a physical one. You may benefit from medical help.

However, the vast majority of men who have problems with erections are in perfectly adequate physical health. In fact, almost every man from time to time doesn't get an erection when he wants one. It's just one of those things that no one can completely control, just as sometimes all of us lose our appetite for food or get constipated. It's just part of being an imperfect human animal. As we said earlier, the erectile process is a complicated one, and no one can *will* erections to occur.

Also, as we get older, many changes can subtly creep up on us in the way our penises work or don't work. As we age, it often takes longer for us to get an erection, or we may not be able to keep it as long, or we may need stimulation to maintain it. Our penises may not get as rock-hard as we remember them from our adolescence, even under the best of circumstances. That's just part of aging, but, considering the alternative to aging, it's not really that bad.

But there are men who with fair regularity don't achieve erections, and the reasons are frequently a question of the mind's overpowering the natural process of a physical response to an erotic situation. The emotional causes for erection problems are as varied as the people who experience them. Some Freudian-oriented therapists suggest that the problems stem from deep-seated anger or fear of a partner or that they come from even more complicated reasons.

But we believe that often there are less complex explanations for the majority of erection problems. Erections refuse to occur for a multitude of reasons. Often the man is simply just not turned on but is trying to initiate sex for some other reason. Most likely this is because, for one reason or another, he feels that it's expected of him in a particular situation.

Another set of reasons involves the myth that "real men" can get erections any time, under any circumstances, just by "willing them." In fact, and especially as men get older (it may be true for some adolescents), there is an increasing need for stimulation in order to achieve erections. This stimulation could, at times, be only fantasies. But at other times, overt physical stimulation, especially of the penis, is necessary. Indeed, in most circumstances, men need as much direct physical stimulation to achieve an erection as women need to lubricate and become turned on. Thus, as we'll suggest in Chapter 18, one of the first tasks that a man who is experiencing erection problems has is to check to see that his partner is adequately stimulating him.

Another common source of erection problems is the vicious-circle pattern. The cycle usually begins with a man's having done something or feeling something that just naturally inhibits a sexual response. He may come home from a hard day's work, irritable and preoccupied with the day's events. He may have had a couple too many beers (which dulls sensations and sexual response) or he may have eaten too much (which gets the body working on getting all that food digested rather than turning on). So what happens? Perhaps almost not thinking, he winds up in bed with his partner. He probably isn't even particularly turned on. But there he is and there she is, and so he thinks he might as well.

But nothing happens.

He tries; she tries. They poke, and stroke, and grunt, and groan. But nothing. He's getting worried. It's a matter of principle now. How dare it not get hard! And she tries, too, maybe because she's concerned about his concern, but also because his not getting an erection is certainly not a very good commentary on her sexiness.

So they keep at it, on and off all night. But still nothing. By now, it may no longer be the alcohol, or overeating, or tension on the job that's keeping it down. It's the preoccupation and worry about getting it up. And so nothing happens.

And the next day it's more of the same—and perhaps worse. Because now each partner is preparing for what the sex therapist Jack Annon has called "The Big Test." The husband is psyching himself up for trying again as soon as he gets home from work. Perhaps he retreats to the men's room at work from time to time to check out his equipment. Yep, it's there, and it seems to work on manual—but will it work on automatic?

Meanwhile, back at home, the wife is also preparing for "The Big Test." She remembers how horny he used to be ten years ago (when, incidentally, he was ten years younger). She is wondering whether she's lost her attractiveness to her husband. Doubts begin creeping into her head about his fidelity. She buys herself some new perfume, puts on her bikini, and waits poised at the door. He gets home from work, they swoop into each other's arms, fly into the bedroom, and . . .

You guessed it.

What our troubled couple forgot—and what many people forget in such situations—is the fact that our sex drives are natural functions, unless physical or emotional problems get in the way. The trick, of course, is to just "let it happen." Trying harder and harder to make it work, and panicking if it doesn't, just does not help. If we are hungry for a particular meal, we don't panic and think, "Oh, my God, I'll never be hungry again!" or if we're constipated, we don't panic and think, "I'll never again enjoy a normal bowel movement."

But, somehow, if our sexual apparatus doesn't work, we panic and think: "This is it; it's over; I'll never have another erection." Then, of course, you start calling yourself "impotent." The worst thing you can do is label yourself. As we discuss elsewhere, the sexual labels we give ourselves (and others) are worse than useless. Calling ourselves something can create and maintain our problems. Notice that we haven't used the word *impotent*. *Impotence* is an ugly word, and one that has very vague meanings (impotent when, where, under what conditions, and with whom?); and the minute we start telling ourselves that we *are* impotent, our minds start affecting our bodies and make it harder for us to get hard. So scrap the labels: Just look at what happens when, where, and with whom—and let it happen.

What usually works best, as we will discuss in more detail in Chapter 18, where we have the Treat Yourself programs to deal with erection problems, is to try to relax. If it doesn't happen, just enjoy what you (and your partner) have: fingers, tongues, bodies, and we hope, friendship. You don't absolutely *have* to have an erection (or an orgasm, for that matter) every time you want to be close to your partner. Let it be, and, believe it or not, if you relax, it is more likely than not that your erection will soon return.

PROBLEMS WITH EJACULATION AND ORGASM

Orgasm and ejaculation are often considered the same in men. They aren't. Although they usually occur at about the same time, they are two separate processes. Ejaculation involves the discharge of the seminal fluid from the penis, whereas orgasm involves the sudden pleasurable sensations and the release of tension that usually occurs in the genital area and elsewhere in the body as a result of sexual stimulation. One *can* occur without the other.

Furthermore, there are considerable variations in the patterns of orgasm and ejaculation among men. Indeed, you may experience a variety of patterns from time to time in your own sexual life.

Sometimes, particularly after a long buildup, the main source of pleasure is a powerful ejaculation. On the other hand, the sensations of orgasm may be felt for a long time, with the ejaculation experienced almost as an anticlimax. On other occasions, a man may experience a number of continued orgasmic sensations long after he has ejaculated. At still other times, a man may experience a pattern similar to the multiple orgasms of women—a series of fairly close-spaced "mini-orgasms," with ejaculation occurring with the last.

Although usually most men experience orgasm and ejaculation at about the same time, one may occur without the other. A man may ejaculate as a result of sexual stimulation but not experience the sensations of orgasm. Less frequently, a man may have an orgasm but not ejaculate. Occasional episodes in which a man has an orgasm without ejaculation or ejaculation without orgasm are no cause for concern.

We're just beginning to discover that, just like women, men have a variety of orgasms—with the added variety that different patterns of ejaculation can provide. There is no right way for a man to ejaculate or to have an orgasm. Some men tend to have extremely powerful physical reactions during their orgasms, moaning and groaning, contorting their faces and bodies as they come, and sometimes scaring their partners by their reactions. Other men may have very tranquil, quiet orgasms, leaving their partners wondering if the man has come at all. Most men probably experience a range of intensities between these extremes. As long as you're comfortable with your patterns and don't expect the earth-shattering orgasms described in some novels, you'll do fine.

Although, as we noted, orgasm and ejaculation involve two different processes, they almost always occur together. For the sake of simplicity, we'll just lump them together when we refer to ejaculation.

Ejaculations come at four different times: before you want them, when you want them, not as soon as you'd like them, or not at all. Problems with the timing of ejaculations is usually a result of lack of control.

Probably the most frequent problem men (especially young men) have with ejaculation control is having them before they're wanted. The term *premature ejaculation* is often attached to this situation. Like most labels, "premature ejaculation" is a misleading, confusing, and basically harmful phrase. After all, what is "premature" anyway? What are the criteria: What a man wants? What his partner wants? Some arbitrary length of time? A certain number of thrusts?

So let's not even attempt to define "premature." Let's just talk about problems in achieving adequate timing of ejaculation, or achieving a reasonable amount of control over when you come.

There's been a long-running debate about the "natural" length of time before ejaculation occurs. It's often pointed out that most other mammals ejaculate more rapidly than most men do. In 1948, when Alfred Kinsey, the noted sex researcher, first reported on male sexual response, he noted that 75 percent of the men he studied ejaculated within two minutes of putting their penises into their partners' vaginas. In contrast, more-recent studies have found the average length of time for intercourse before ejaculation occurs to be somewhat longer. Therefore, there's good reason to believe that there is some flexibility in the timing of ejaculation. Indeed, many men—particularly those with less formal education—and possibly their partners as well, may not perceive rapid ejaculation as any particular problem but rather as natural male functioning. A great many American males see no value in prolonging intercourse. After all, in almost every other test of male ability, speed is an asset, not a liability.

But certainly many men and their partners wish that they could be more flexible in their timing. Ejaculation before penetration can be disappointing, not to mention messy.

What causes such ejaculatory enthusiasm? No one knows for sure. Unlike erection problems, there doesn't seem to be any association with any clear-cut physical causes. It is certainly possible that there are basic physiological differences between men, with some having more rapid reflexes than others.

It is also possible that learning experiences as adolescents may condition some men to have very rapid ejaculations. For example, many adolescent boys rush through masturbation because they fear getting caught or because of the sense of guilt associated with the whole undertaking. Further, first experiences at intercourse for many adolescents and young men occur under hardly ideal circumstances. Because of cramped quarters (back seats of VWs are hardly conducive to extended lovemaking) or fear of being discovered, the goal often becomes to get one's "rocks off" as quickly as possible.

Only as we get older and can have sexual relations in more tranquil circumstances does extended intercourse become a goal as well as a possibility for many. Then, tension and anxiety regarding sex usually create the problem. For many men, the aging process itself slows down the ejaculatory response. Coming too fast is one of the few problems that tend to take care of themselves as we get older.

There are some people, however, who have a problem with inadequate ejaculatory control and would prefer not waiting around until they're fifty or so to work it out. For them, we recommend reading Chapter 17 for the Treat Yourself programs for ejaculation problems.

However, as men get older, they sometimes get upset that it takes too long to ejaculate. (Is no one ever satisfied?) Indeed, some older men may not come at all from time to time. The reasons are usually physiological (ejaculations do tend to take longer as men get older), but the negative reactions are psychological. Some men and their partners get upset about it, others just take it in their stride as one more slowing-down process among several. Some even find enjoyment in a less intense, more relaxed pattern of sexual activity and don't consider speedy ejaculation essential for enjoying themselves.

Occasionally, younger men experience difficulty with delayed ejaculation for no particular physiological reason. They may maintain their erections and continue their thrusting motions for a long time before they ejaculate, or they may not ejaculate at all. Indeed, out of embarrassment and fatigue, or out of the desire to reassure their partners, some men may pretend to have had an orgasm when they haven't. The reasons for delayed ejaculation or the inability to ejaculate at all are not always clear. It may simply be the result of having intercourse too soon after having ejaculated before, of being fatigued, or of having eaten or drunk too much. It may also be a result either of not being particularly turned on or of having feelings of discomfort, embarrassment, or guilt associated with sexual activities. If this is a problem for you, you will want to read Chapter 17.

Before we leave the subject of ejaculation, we want to repeat our belief that the most enjoyable sexual encounters are not goal oriented. Ejaculation can be a satisfying and natural climax to love-making. But if it becomes the only goal or even the major goal of a man, much of the joy of sexual contact may be lost for him as well as for his partner.

BEYOND ERECTIONS AND EJACULATION

Male sexuality goes much deeper than the proper functions of a man's sexual apparatus. The decade of the seventies has witnessed major changes in the way men—and women—perceive male sexuality. The many profound changes that have occurred

79

in our ideas and expectations of female sexuality have naturally had their impact on men.

The shift toward sexual equality in bed has not always been smooth. Men may indeed welcome the growing sexual assertiveness of women in general and of their partners in particular, and yet a man may sometimes feel uncomfortable or even threatened by his partner's changing expectations of him to accept or meet her needs. Similarly, some women may have mixed feelings about their partner's move from aggressive dominance to a more gentle sharing.

Still, most people welcome the growing balance and sexual equality of men and women in bed. Each sex will probably always exhibit its biological uniqueness in its sexual behavior. Yet the trend seems clear that both men and women will increasingly enjoy their shared humanness in the honesty of sexual intimacy.

Six

Common Problems of People

The two previous chapters have discussed some common sexual problems of women and men separately. However, the sexual problems of men and women are not separate. Each affects the other.

Most sexual problems involve both partners. As Masters and Johnson have repeatedly said, there's no such things as an uninvolved partner in a sexual problem. If you have a sexual problem, there's no way in which your partner will not be involved, whether it's his or her sexual fulfillment's being limited by your problem, or his or her having a role in developing and/or maintaining your problem in the first place.

For example, if a man has a problem achieving erections, part of the problem might be his fear of disappointing his partner or his fear of being ridiculed by his partner. Or he may have had the actual experience of being ridiculed by her. Similarly, a woman who rarely has orgasms may be inhibited about sex and therefore not let herself loose with her partner, or her sexual needs for stimulation may not have been met, or perhaps her needs are even resented by her partner.

Even if there are no specific problems, any individual who wants to get more enjoyment out of his or her sexual relationship needs his or her partner's full involvement and participation. Satisfying sexual relationships require the joint commitment and sharing of the two people involved.

For two people to fully enjoy their sexual relationship, there have to be four elements. The man must be able to accept the pleasure his partner gives him as well as to enjoy the process of giving her pleasure. At the same time, the woman must be able to enjoy the sensations she receives from the man while she also enjoys giving him pleasure. Indeed, the more pleasure someone receives from his or her partner, the more he or she will want to give pleasure in return. In other words: "Give to get."

Perhaps it would be logical to assume that when two people want to enjoy their sexual relationship, mutual satisfaction will be almost automatic. Unfortunately, it often doesn't happen that way. The willingness to "give to get" is important, but it is not enough. This chapter will consider some of the common feelings, attitudes, and behaviors that get in the way of two people's getting and giving sexual pleasure to each other. Later chapters will review what can be done to eliminate these barriers to sexual fulfillment. Once these barriers are removed, and once some basic ideas about sex are accepted and supplemented by a few skills that you can easily learn, the pleasures you get from your sex life can be increased considerably.

Frankly, our ancestors didn't need sex experts or manuals to enjoy sex—ancient murals and paintings present men and women deriving considerable pleasure from sex. Many of the contemporary sexual problems we are discussing in this book are products of destructive attitudes, myths, and misinformation that have built up in recent times to complicate and get in the way of our fulfilling our sexual potential. A major goal of our Treat Yourself approach is to have you "unlearn" the ideas and behaviors that get in the way of your and your partner's sexual enjoyment.

PROBLEMS INTERFERING WITH SATISFYING SEX

In the rest of this chapter, we will describe some of the common problems encountered by couples, problems that prevent them from enjoying each other. Specifically, these joint problems include (1) fear of sex, (2) discomfort with intimacy, (3) pressure to be sexual athletes, (4) lack of sexual knowledge, (5) lack of effective communication, (6) lack of consensus on sexual activities, and (7) problems with boring and distasteful sex. We'll conclude the chapter with some comments about the common sexual problems that couples encounter as they get older. In the chapters that follow, especially in Parts 3 and 4, we'll provide a number of Treat Yourself programs to help you overcome these problems. So, if you see yourself described in the following paragraphs, maybe you'll have a little better handle on your problem when you do start one of the Treat Yourself programs.

Fear of Sex

When you consider the ideas people learn about sex as they grow up, it's amazing that more adults aren't scared to death about sex. The messages many parents give their children about sex can be summed up in one word: *Don't*. The fears we grow up with are often vague, and these fears are supported by friends who talk about sex in hushed tones as if it were something terribly exciting but, at the same time, something terribly frightening.

Sex education, when it is provided in schools, often *adds* to the fear. Rarely is sex portrayed as something joyful. Indeed, there are often few details provided about what sex *is*. Rather, students cringe as they learn the sordid details of the many forms of venereal disease and the tragedy of unwanted pregnancies.

As we grow up, we are often taught to fear the opposite sex. Boys fear rejection from girls, and girls fear being overpowered and being "used" by a boy. Both fear that they won't meet the expectations of the other. The sexual experiences of adolescents and young adults are frequently carried out in an atmosphere of fear—fear of being "caught" by parents or others, fear of pregnancy, fear of V.D., fear of guilt, or even fear of the retribution of God.

Many of these fearful associations with sex may carry over into adulthood and are added to the fear of failure. Men may be concerned about their ability to achieve and maintain erections, about coming too soon, or, as they get older, about not coming at all. Women may be afraid of pain, of pregnancy, or of losing control of themselves.

To compound these problems, often each partner fears sharing his or her fears with his or her partner, perhaps because of a fear that the voicing of these complaints will sound foolish, or that they will embarrass their partners, or that they will somehow violate an unwritten rule that you don't talk about sex. Thus, each partner may live with one or more of those fears and hence fail to relax and enjoy his or her sexuality.

Discomfort with Intimacy

In Chapter 3, we discussed the interaction of love and sex. As we noted in that chapter, problems in sex are frequently a product of difficulties in the couple's relationship.

An enjoyable sexual relationship—even a sound marriage—may not require an intense, permanent state of rapture or even a permanent emotional commitment for the participants. It does require, however, good will toward each other and comfort in sharing intimacy. Problems arise when either partner has difficulty being warm and close with the other. If the relationship is such that one partner feels more love than the other, the sexual relationship will likely suffer.

Any attempts to improve sexual enjoyment require the cooperation of both partners. If either partner feels hostility, resentment, or contempt for the other, cooperation will not likely occur. Even if the partner who feels the hostility seems to be cooperating in bed, he or she still may be subtly sabotaging efforts to work on the sexual relationship.

Also, if either person feels that his or her partner is demanding more affection (either by word or deed) than he or she feels comfortable giving, then there may be a steady pulling apart rather than a coming together. The result may be a tug-of-war in which, eventually, intercourse is seen as a required proof of love rather than as a mutually satisfying activity. Inevitably, the sexual activity will be resented.

Although sexual fulfillment does not require a constant state of passion, it generally does require basic mutual respect and affection between the partners. Without respect and affection, no sex therapy—including our Treat Yourself programs—can be effective.

Pressure to Be Sexual Athletes

As we have just said, it is a mistake to feel that all it takes is love in order to have a good sex life. It is equally wrong to assume that all it takes is physical agility and learning a series of sexual skills.

It is not surprising that many people, young and old, develop this idea. Americans tend to be skill oriented. "If you're going to play a game, be the best and play it to win!" seems to be our motto. "Marriage manuals" often convey this approach. Many of these books emphasize the technical skills related to sexuality. Although they may often provide useful information and be in favor of variety in sexual expression, these books also tend to overemphasize the importance of sexual skill and dexterity. Often they seem to have as their ideal reader some super-human sexual demigod.

Preoccupation with the mechanical aspects of sexual activities can do more harm than good. This athletic approach glorifies the beautiful and perfectly functioning body. Despite the image in some sex manuals, there are people who enjoy— or would like to enjoy—sex who are not young, tightly muscled, physically well endowed, or even particularly good-looking. This image of the ideal love-maker only encourages needless feelings of inadequacy. Our concerns with techniques, positions, and orgasms, regardless of their importance, should not obscure the joys of the physical closeness and emotional satisfaction that can come from sex.

Winston Churchill was reported to have said that "rules are for the guidance of the wise and the obedience of fools." This would seem to apply to sex. Even our Treat Yourself programs are intended as guidance; they are not designed for obedience.

There is no set pattern for "ideal" sexual behavior, and there are few rules of the game. Sexual enjoyment comes not from athletic skills and rigidly following rules but from expressing spontaneity in sexual activities guided by the unique personalities, needs, capacities, and desires of a particular couple at a particular time.

The sexual athlete approach to sex leads to one of the most common obstacles to sexual satisfaction: performance anxiety. This anxiety arises from the concern that the person is doing his or her job in bed well and living up to the expectations of his or her partner and of all the sex experts (friends, movie heroes and heroines, and writers of sex books) to whom he or she has been exposed. This preoccupation encourages what Masters and Johnson have described as the "spectator role" in sexual behavior. That is, many people find that they cannot totally immerse themselves in their sexual activity with their partners; instead they look upon themselves as actors in a performance with their partners, preoccupied with how well they are doing, the timing of their orgasms, how long it will last, how their deodorant is holding up, and how well they will be evaluated by themselves and by their partners when they're done.

Friends, throw away the scripts, close the books, relax, and enjoy your imperfect bodies.

Lack of Sexual Knowledge

The current saturation of sexual material in newspapers, books, and movies and on television leads many people to the mistaken idea that everyone knows everything he or she needs to know about sex. They don't. And what the average person does learn about sex is often distorted by biases, his or her personal needs, and firmly entrenched attitudes going back to childhood.

The lack of sexual knowledge and misinformation about sex is made even worse by the preoccupation of many people to perform "normally" in sex. Although most people could not care less how many slices of white bread an average woman consumes each day or what the length of an average man's right index finger is, many people *are* concerned about the "right" frequency of intercourse and the average length of an erect penis. The fact that these vary considerably and that they tend to be irrelevant to sexual fulfillment is more important to know than the statistics themselves.

Many sexual relationships are limited by false perceptions of what does or "should" go on in sex in general and intercourse in particular. Sexual ideas and attitudes are deeply rooted in people's value systems and are therefore hard to change.

Having accurate information about sex can help sexual relationships. For example, many individuals endure needless problems because they do not know some or all of the following facts: Men as well as women have sexual anxieties and cannot be expected to always perform on command despite socially supported pretenses of super-masculinity; masturbation by men does not cause "insanity"; even when a woman has a sexual partner, occasional self-stimulation may be enjoyable and may enhance her general sexual response; women who enjoy clitoral stimulation are not neurotic; penis size is not related to either masculinity or the capacity for giving and receiving sexual satisfaction; sexual activity need not terminate at fifty or with chronic illnesses; many mentally competent, law-abiding citizens like using their mouths to stimulate their partners' genitals, sometimes to orgasm.

Lack of accurate information about contraception can also impede mutual sexual satisfaction. Despite advances in contraceptive technology, the risk of undesired pregnancy is still a major concern of many women and men. Sometimes the particular birth-control procedure used can have a significant effect on the marital sexual adjustment. Withdrawal (removal of the penis from the vagina just prior to ejaculation), for example, often interferes with sexual satisfaction and is not one of the most effective methods of contraception. Yet withdrawal is one of the most common forms of contraception and its use is often the result of lack of knowledge or biases regarding other contraceptive choices. Other contraceptives are often avoided because individuals mistakenly fear that the contraceptives would negatively affect sexual satisfaction. Other contraceptives are seen as a threat to masculine self-images. Still others are avoided because the woman is uncomfortable about touching her own body. Finally, contraception is often not used because one or both partners resist acknowledging "premeditated" sexual activity even when neither partner wants a pregnancy. As we mentioned earlier, many of these concerns about contraceptive methods can be handled by just one visit to your physician or by a call to your local Planned Parenthood office.

Lack of Effective Communication

Many people find it difficult to talk directly and honestly with their partners about their sexual desires, fears, and problems. Even where communication is satisfactory in most other areas in a relationship, communication about sex can be a problem, especially for those couples who went through their adolescence before the sexual revolution following World War II. They have been trained to perceive discussions about sex as being so private, so embarrassing, and so revealing that they hesitate to talk about their own feelings and wishes even with the person they have been married to for years.

Often the problem in communication is a result of not knowing which words to use or of being afraid of revealing some inadequacy and appearing ridiculous in the eyes of the partner. People may also fear that breaking an unspoken contract of not talking about sex will bring to light sexual problems or inadequacies that have been hidden by mutual consent and will thus create a threat to the balance of the relationship.

If all is going ideally in a sexual relationship and both partners are fully satisfied, then there is no real need to have extensive discussions about it except to find out whether it really is going well. However, if there are problems, then a lack of clear communication can prevent the establishment of reasonable mutual expectations between the partners and can diminish the chance for each partner to meet the other's needs as fully as possible.

For some couples, even the simple matter of explicitly indicating the desire to have sexual intercourse becomes a problem. A clear request from one partner and an equally clear acceptance or rejection from the other is sometimes exceedingly difficult for one or both partners. Perhaps the reason is a sense of "nothing ventured, nothing lost." Nonverbal cues in sex are frequently used and can be a pleasant and effective form of communication, but only as long as the cues are clearly understood by each partner.

Some suggestions for enhancing sexual communication are discussed in Chapter 9. If you have problems in communication with your partner, read it and have your partner read it. Then try to communicate.

Lack of Consensus on Sexual Activities

This problem is complicated by some of those already discussed in this chapter—the lack of knowledge about sex, and problems in communication.

There is no doubt that there has been increasing acceptance and knowledge about the many alternative routes people are capable of taking to have sexual pleasure: orgasms in or out of intercourse, different positions in intercourse, oral sex, and so on. However, this freedom of choice is often unevenly accepted by each partner. Religious teachings often specify— or are thought to specify—the limited types of sexual activities that are acceptable even in marriage. These ideas can be particularly destructive if they are not shared equally by both partners.

For reasons that may have to do with physiology or for other reasons we don't yet understand, people have differing appetites for sexual activity. Furthermore, most people vary in their sexual interest from time to time—some days they are constantly turned on; other days they couldn't care less. That's only being human. Unfortunately, sexual partners often don't respond with the same rhythms. When that happens, one or the other might have to make compromises in his or her sexual interests. This is usually easy if good will and affection exist. If not, one person or the other is going to feel rejected, and/or one or the other may proceed to engage the other in a power struggle that will hardly lead to mutual sexual enjoyment.

Ideally, when conflicting sexual desires are expressed, or when differing degrees of arousal are experienced, the couple will engage in a process of negotiation. This process is discussed in Chapters 9 and 10 and is also illustrated in Chapter 19.

Problems with Boring or Distasteful Sex

We know that we have said that sex should not be an athletic event in which the partners become preoccupied with virtuoso performances. But that doesn't mean that sex should be boring, or, on the other hand, that one partner should engage in sexual activities that turn that partner on but turn the other partner off.

Often, couples who experience the problems discussed earlier in this chapter—especially inadequate sexual knowledge, poor communication, and lack of consensus in sexual activities—find themselves falling into habitual, routine sexual activities. Even the best of partners may eventually become bored after years of exactly the same activity, in the same sequence, in the same positions, on the same bed. Boring sex is rarely very rewarding to either partner. Chapter 20 presents some Treat Yourself programs that couples can use to overcome boredom in their sexual relationships.

There is a considerable range in the sexual activities that people find appealing and stimulating, just as there is a range in what sexual activities people find unpleasant and even obnoxious. Again, there are no universal rules about what people should enjoy in sex or what people *shouldn't* like. Assuming that a couple mutually agrees to an activity and neither finds it unpleasant, then there is nothing wrong or "sick" about enjoying it.

Remember that most of our ideas about what is "right" in sex stem from our historical bias that sex is basically for reproduction. It's more than a coincidence that the basic accepted sexual activity—intercourse with the penis in the vagina—is also the most effective way to create a pregnancy. Therefore, anything that gets away from an erect penis's ejaculating into a vagina departs from many people's ideas about what is right. Oral and anal stimulation of the genitals are not likely to create a pregnancy—and you can't get someone pregnant from masturbation, unless, of course, the man has fantastic aim.

However, society has departed considerably from our reproductive bias, and we are increasingly separating out our reproductive and sexual behaviors. People are capable of enjoying sexual stimulation in many ways that have nothing to do with reproduction. If there are some sexual activities that you would like to try but are uncomfortable with because they seem distasteful, try the Treat Yourself program in Chapter 19.

That's not to say that all people should therefore learn to

enjoy all potentially erotic activities. Nonsense. That's as foolish as saying that everyone should learn to eat all foods that are potentially nourishing—like worms or pig's eyes. People are aesthetic creatures who have likes and dislikes, and that's their right. If one partner enjoys an activity that the other partner doesn't, that doesn't give the partner the right to force it on the other partner. Again, a situation such as this calls for negotiations between the partners.

SEX AND AGING

Too often, the model for ideal sexual functioning is the young adult. Certainly, the sexual heroes and heroines of most romantic movies, television programs, and novels are rarely portrayed as being much more than thirty. We are still a youth-oriented culture, relegating people much beyond thirty to second-class sexual citizenship. Sex is supposedly for the young.

When most older people think of their own ideal sex image, they usually think of the way they responded when they were teenagers or young adults. Many, therefore, perceive their current sexual functioning as well as their physical attractiveness (also highly prized in our society) as steadily deteriorating.

There are indeed physiological changes that occur as people age. Men take longer to get turned on; their erections may not always be as firm as they were in the good old days; they may take more stimulation to stay firm; they may take longer to ejaculate. Occasionally, they may not be able to ejaculate at all. Women tend to lubricate less and may find that intercourse results in more irritation to their vaginal walls. Not all these changes occur at the same rate for all people.

These changes need not be perceived as necessarily negative. Indeed, some couples find sex more enjoyable as they age because they don't have the same urgency for orgasm or preoccupation with erection. They can enjoy extended lovemaking and intercourse, especially if the woman supplements her natural lubrication with artificial lubricants (see Chapter 7). They may enjoy the sometimes more subtle elements of extended caressing and emotional contacts.

But there are many individuals who don't take aging kindly. Since sexual attractiveness, desirability, and performance are highly prized in young adulthood, any thought of losing them can create considerable anxiety. Thus a middle-age crisis may be precipitated, one in which the man or woman actively seeks confirmation of his or her sexual adequacy by intensive sexual activity, perhaps with a series of partners. Failures in these efforts only increase anxiety and may precipitate a vicious circle of even more attempts to confirm one's desirability and adequacy.

Others give up. A man who for the first time does not have or cannot keep an erection when he wants it may be so threatened by the event that he avoids future situations that could cause him new embarrassments and thus he may give up the opportunity for years of his own and his partner's sexual enjoyment.

Here again, knowledge of sexual matters is essential. For example, one man who noted that his wife didn't lubricate as much as she used to was erroneously convinced that she no longer loved him.

Sex researchers have consistently found that men and women are capable of enjoying their sexuality into their advanced years. But, as in every other facet of our lives, accommodations have to be made to the aging process. The couple may find that reversing the trend of decades and having sex in the morning after a good night's sleep may enable them to be more relaxed and yet energetic in their sexual activities. By the time that the couple are that age, the kids are out of the home at that time, so why not?

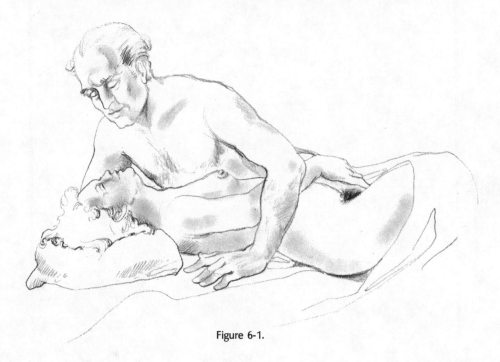

Figure 6-1.

One or both of the partners may not have an orgasm every time they make love. As long as that is accepted as a natural reflection of aging and not as a denial of adequacy, there is no harm done. Couples may indeed find pleasures in sex to which their youthful exuberance in earlier years had formerly blinded them.

There are certainly sexual activities that a person can enjoy by him- or herself. And there may well be some erotic and even communal pleasures in group sex. But sex in twos still seems to be the most satisfactory arrangement for most people. Each partner, of course, brings his or her own personality, needs, expectations, wishes, and fears to bed with him or her. But each brings the potential for joy for the other person. Together, they can create tension, discomfort, and disappointment. But with good will, affection, openness, and honesty, they can bring to each other the closeness, intimacy, and joy that sexual contact is capable of producing.

PART

3

Treat Yourself

Seven
The Basic Program

If you've read the first two parts of this book but feel a little frustrated because we haven't described some of the specific things you can do to treat yourself, well, there's a method to our madness. We really think that it's a good idea for you to try to grasp the "big picture" about sexuality. That is, we believe that focusing too much on one specific problem may encourage you to think of sex in a way that's too narrow. And the problem with that is that you and your partner may miss much of the joy and ecstasy that can come from viewing sex in all its guises—as a complex, deeply human, intimate, pleasurable experience in which all senses and all parts of the body can participate.

So we've tried to present sex in just that way. Sex that focuses on the genitals is certainly important, but it is not *all-*important.

But this is not to say that there aren't specific things you can do to help resolve sexual problems or to *enhance* your sexuality—to make it even better—whether you have problems or not. What we'd like to do in this chapter is get you ready for what is to come—the various programs for treating yourself. This chapter will present a review of the rest of the book; it will tell you pretty much what to expect and how to proceed. Each of the following chapters is introduced here. The purpose is to communicate the idea that the Treat Yourself programs are really not isolated grab bags of exercises but are actually a unified, integrated approach to do-it-yourself sex therapy. Thus, if you are suffering from a particular problem—say, the inability to maintain erections—and you turn only to that chapter to try to Treat Yourself, you may be missing the boat. The exercises in the chapters dealing with specific problems build on the material that will be presented in the chapters in this part of the book. Again, this is a systematic program, put together on the basis of years of research from the therapeutic experiences of numerous sex therapists and from the sexual experiences of thousands of people just like you. We've tried to omit unnecessary and irrelevant material and maintain only *what works*. But, for these programs to work, you've got to follow a few basic guidelines:

1. Read everything.
2. Don't ignore anything in the program.
3. *Practice* what you read.

GETTING READY

You may as well know right off that we're going to ask you to leave your orgasms and erections on the shelf, at least initially. If you're experiencing some problems in those areas, this will probably come as a relief. The idea here is that pushing yourself too quickly—trying too hard to perform—may be part of the problem. So, we'll ask you to cool it a little: Go slowly, enjoy the experiences, learn a little bit about yourself and your partner—what turns you both on—practice some simple exercises, and *don't move too quickly*. The orgasms and erections will come—if you follow some of these steps and if you let them come.

You might have to make an early decision about *where* you're going to practice the program. For example, if it's in your own home, can you ensure privacy? Are you sure that the kids won't burst in on you every time you and your partner are working together (enjoying yourselves)? This might call for rearranging your schedules for a couple of weeks (staying up a little later each night, leaving for work a little later, or coming home for lunch so that the two of you are together).

You might also want to consider what we've called "motel therapy." We know that it costs a little, but there's nothing like checking into a hotel or motel for a couple of days to practice these exercises. It may be a little expensive (save up your money and reward yourselves), but there'll be peace and quiet, and no one will interrupt you. Many people find this change of pace and scene so erotic and so pleasurable that their Treat Yourself programs are greatly enhanced.

Rome Wasn't Built in a Day

The key principle that we'll be using in all aspects of the program is: "Take small steps." We really mean it. Rome *wasn't* built in a day. And your sex problems won't be solved in a day. Don't go too fast. We'll get you there. But we want to be sure that the program works—all along the way. That's really the key to the success of these programs.

Now, we realize that sometimes this may be frustrating. You may really want to move more quickly. To some extent, this will be possible. We want to be flexible too. But we do urge you not to move ahead until you accomplish each step of the program. Let that be your guide. When you are successful at one step, then move ahead. Don't skip steps.

We also want you to avoid what we call "The Big Test"— pushing yourself to find out whether you really can do it and then getting upset and discouraged because you couldn't handle it. Don't worry: We'll push you pretty hard; but we'll be pretty careful that you're ready each time you move ahead.

Prevention as Well as Cure

Our major goal in this book is to help you with any of the sexual problems you might have. But we have another goal. We want to help you *prevent* the occurrence of new problems. We hope to accomplish this by illustrating clearly how sexual problems can get started, so that as we did in the first part of the book, you can avoid those situations that may produce problems. We hope to help you communicate about your sex life to your partner so that each of you can give and get what you want. And we hope to give you a variety of procedures to use so that if you do recognize that a problem is getting started, you can use the ideas in this book to nip it in the bud—deal with it before it really gets too bad. So, as you read through the book, keep prevention as well as cure in mind.

Check with Your Physician

One of the first steps you should take before starting a Treat Yourself program is to check your problem out with a physician. Although most sex problems do not have a physical cause, a small percentage of them do. For example, a number of different drugs—ranging from some sedatives to certain hormones and antihistamines to medications for a number of physical problems, such as high blood pressure, diabetes, and glaucoma—that your physician might be prescribing for you could play a role in the sex problem you are experiencing. So, if you are taking any type of medication at all, check with your physician to see whether it might have a side effect that could be producing a sexual problem. Don't just take yourself off the medication. You are probably using it for good reasons, and your physician may be able to prescribe other medications that would not have negative side effects.

Even if you're not using some medication, it's a good idea to consult with a physician before you start your Treat Yourself program. If there are any physical problems that could be affecting your sexual functioning, perhaps he can deal with them. If there are not, then you know that that's one less thing to worry about.

Check first with your family physician. You might also want to ask him to refer you to a urologist, a physician who specializes in problems involving the genital system, or for women, a gynecologist. Some urologists and a few gynecologists also have special training in dealing with sexual problems. Be frank about describing your problem. Try not to be embarrassed. We're sure that your physician won't be shocked; he or she has probably heard it all. If you feel that your physician hasn't heard you out completely, don't just get up and leave. Finish discussing the problem as thoroughly as you can, and specifically ask your physician to rule out any possible physical causes or to treat those that he or she might find.

Once all this is completed, you'll be ready to move ahead with your Treat Yourself program.

Practice Makes Perfect

We've mentioned this before, but it bears re-emphasizing. Read through the entire book—certainly, Parts 1, 2, and 3—before you start working on one of the specific problem areas described in Part 4. This reading will help you understand the program in general, give you the foundation for the

97

specific exercises in Part 4, and may possibly change the way you *think*.

But that's not enough. We don't believe that you can change the way you behave—what you actually *do* in a sexual relationship—unless you *practice* the exercises that we describe. So, once you've read about it, then get into it. Practice what we suggest—in the way we suggest. This will change your *behavior* in the directions you want it changed.

Taken together, these changes in thinking and behavior should affect your feelings. That is, once you are thinking and behaving in ways that are more positive for both you and your partner, you are bound to start *feeling* better—about yourself and about your partner. And, we wager, he or she will start feeling better about you.

These other goals—positive changes in your thinking, behavior, and feelings—are what this book is all about.

THE BASIC PROGRAM

The remainder of this chapter will provide you with an overview of the Treat Yourself program. The basic program—that part that applies to everybody—is presented here and in the other chapters in Part 3. Then, you can select one or more of the chapters in Part 4 to read, depending on your problem and your interests. But read this chapter, as well as the rest of Part 3, first.

The following are the basic dimensions of all Treat Yourself programs.

Defining Your Problem

One of the early steps in a Treat Yourself program is attempting to understand and clearly define your sexual situation. You will want to clearly define the problem—e.g., when and where it occurs—as well as understand a number of other factors about your sexual functioning, such as your sexual preferences (what you like and don't like), obstacles to solving the problems, areas of sexual functioning that you would like to enhance, and so on. It is important to understand as clearly as possible your own sexuality before you start making any changes. The understanding will give you the clues regarding where to start and what to change. In Chapter 8 we present a number of methods for helping you understand your own sexuality, pinpoint your sexual problem, and assess the circumstances that may be affecting it.

Communication

This is a book about sex. But we believe that there's no such thing as sex (or, at least, good sex) without communication. When we say communication, we mean the way you and your partner discuss (or don't discuss) your needs, feelings, desires, and wants with each other. Of course, there are numerous ways to communicate, including nonverbal methods (using gestures, touches, and body language). Although these are very important, a large part of our book deals with how you and your partner express yourselves to each other through your bodies. So we want to highlight the importance of how you communicate with each other with your *voices*.

There are several reasons for this. First and foremost, perhaps, is the fact that most of the exercises will call for you and your partner to *talk* to each other. This means several things: negotiating to agree on what, when, and where you will practice; expressing what you need or want at a given time; and telling your partner to stop or start some particular exercise that will help you overcome some problem. This kind of communication is basic to the success of your Treat Yourself program. It will also help you and your partner to get along better, because there are times during the program when one of you may have to sacrifice a little bit of pleasure in order to help the other, so that both of you can enjoy each other in the long run. In fact, we hope that you'll talk to your partner about your (and his or her) reactions to each exercise. Your feelings about the exercises are as important as the exercises themselves.

Second, we just have a belief that good communication is crucial to the success of any relationship. This means learning how to express affection, learning to say no without hurting the other person, and learning how to offer and accept constructive criticism. These are as important in a sexual relationship as they are in any kind of relationship.

Finally, communication is how you express encouragement and support for each other, both in general and while you are going through a Treat Yourself program. In fact, if anything, sex is an ultimate expression of intimacy between two people. That intimacy is established and maintained through communication skills—how you deal with each other.

In your Treat Yourself program, this support, encouragement, and intimacy are as necessary as any of the other exercises. Sometimes you or your partner might run into a good deal of frustration either at moving too slowly or at not being successful with a given exercise. These are the moments when being there—really being *with* the other person—counts for almost everything. A touch, a few soft words, and you and your partner will *know* that you're not alone.

Unfortunately, good communication skills don't come naturally. Whether good or bad, communication skills are learned. So, if you or your partner hasn't quite learned all of the necessary ingredients making up good, supportive communication, we'll try to help you. We'll provide a number of different exercises in Chapter 9 to help you practice your communication with each other, and we hope that these will enhance not only your sex life but other parts of your life as well.

Contracts: Agreements Between You and Your Partner

Each one of your Treat Yourself programs requires you to set up a contract between you and your partner. If you think this sounds a little corny, take a minute and think about it. How will you and your partner know what to work on? How will you and your partner agree on the conditions under which you'll work—like where and when and with what equipment? How will you and your partner know how far to go? The list could be carried on indefinitely.

The point is that each and every one of these has to be decided—and *agreed* upon—by both partners if the program is to be a success. Some aspects are trickier than others. For example, you and your partner may have to agree that you will go for a week without attempting intercourse. If it's not up front—clear and agreed to in advance—one or both of you may either forget or want to push ahead. So the contracts help you decide what you're going to work on. They provide a structure for your program, and they help the two of you to communicate about what you'll be doing. Don't ignore the contracts. Use them. Chapter 10 describes how to use contracts and provides an actual contract form that you can use for your Treat Yourself program.

By the way, for most of our programs, we'll provide some exercises for you to use even if you have no partner. These, too, require contracts—contracts you make with yourself. The contracts will help you structure your programs and will give you some goals to aim for.

Learning to Relax

One of the main things related to sexual problems is anxiety. You may be uncomfortable with sex in general, with certain kinds of sexual experience, with sexual experiences with certain people, or with the idea that you may not be able to do it "the right way." We're going to help you overcome your fears and anxieties related to sex. We'll do this in two ways.

The first way is to train you in methods of relaxing. This is a direct way of overcoming your fears, anxiety, and discomforts. This will be covered in Chapter 11. We'll provide you with several exercises that can help you learn to relax. In this way, we believe that you'll have a head start in coping with some of the anxieties that sexual situations might set up. We suggest that you read the chapter on relaxation and practice those exercises before you begin any of the programs in Part 4.

The second way of helping you relax is covered in the chapters in Part 4. Each chapter provides step-by-step instructions for gradually enhancing your sexual functioning in a nonthreatening situation. Thus, as you improve your sexual functioning and become more comfortable, the fears will gradually fall away.

Now we're not suggesting that you will become comfortable with everything about yourself and/or your partner. Nor are we suggesting that if some part of the program, or some aspect of sexual relations, is distasteful to you, we will provide foolproof ways of making this less distasteful. And most importantly, we're not trying to suggest that you *must* become less anxious about everything or that you don't have the right to find some aspects of sexual behavior distasteful. These options are always open to you; they are your right.

On the other hand, what we'd like to do is give you the *options* of changing what is distasteful or uncomfortable for you. Many of the exercises do just that. Whether or not you use them, of course, is up to you.

Getting in Touch with Your Body

It's probably possible to proceed with a Treat Yourself program without really knowing how everything works or where everything is (in or on your body, that is). But since we hope that reading and using this book will be somewhat of an enlightening experience, we'd like to add a little more to your enlightenment. Because so many people have grown up with sex education that didn't really describe basic body functions clearly or adequately (or may have had no real sex education whatsoever), we've prepared a brief introduction to the physiology of sex.

Chapter 12 will give you an idea of the anatomy of sex—the organs and muscles that are most important. We'll do this for males and for females. Then, we'll show you that there are many similarities between males and females in how their bodies function sexually. We'll provide a set of exercises for you to use—before you begin the specific programs in Part 4—that will help you strengthen your "sex muscles."

Study these chapters with two ideas in mind. The first is that you should understand how *your* body works. The second is that you should understand how your *partner's* body works.

By the way, because we believe that it's important to understand how your body functions doesn't mean that this is *all*-important. We still think that your brain is your most important sex organ.

Turning On

One of the commonest problems we've found is that people don't know how to use their fantasies to their own advantage. One of the best ways to turn on is to think about what you like—about whatever is really arousing to you. We'll help you to use these fantasies in Chapter 13, and we'll try first to illustrate how and why fantasies are as "normal" and useful as your morning cup of coffee.

Another area of sexual behavior that we are often told not to talk about—let alone practice—is masturbation, or self-stimulation. Most kids play with their genitals. Not only are they curious, but it also feels good. Yet, if we hear often enough that it's wrong, we stop—or we proceed only with guilt.

Not only do most kids practice self-stimulation, but almost all adults do so as well. Research reveals that most adults masturbate. So if you do but feel bad about it, try to relax. Chapter 13 will provide you with some self-stimulation programs. These are particularly important if you have no partner to help you with your Treat Yourself program.

Used together, fantasies and self-stimulation, plus a few other tricks, can really enhance your sexual arousal. The arousal exercises in Chapter 13 are very important to the success of your program. Make sure that you go over them before you proceed with the program.

Erotic Exercises: Getting in Touch with Your Partner's Body

Many of the specific programs in Part 4 are based on the exercises described in Chapter 14. These are erotic exercises—ways of learning to stimulate each other with a variety of senuous massage techniques. These exercises are also called "pleasuring" or "sensate focus."

The point of these exercises is to focus on the sensual pleasure that you and your partner can give and get without worrying about the performance demands of intercourse. By engaging in these exercises, you will be able to learn about your body and its reactions as well as about your partner's body and its reactions. You will also learn to offer and accept more and more sexual stimulation from your partner in an environment that offers both sensual pleasure and intimacy. And you will gradually learn to relax and become more comfortable in giving and getting sexual and sensual pleasure without being called upon to perform in ways that will place difficult demands on you.

We'll provide you with two specific sets of exercises. The first—*Erotic Pleasure 1*—will provide specific directions for pleasuring *without genital contact*. The second—*Erotic Pleasure 2*—will provide specific directions for pleasuring *with genital contact*. These exercises are meant to be done in sequence. Don't jump ahead to Erotic Pleasure 2 until you've completed all the requirements of Erotic Pleasure 1. As we said before, we'll move you ahead in small but steady steps when you're ready to move.

These exercises are the heart of all the Treat Yourself programs in Part 4. Do not undertake any of the programs without you and your partner's having read Chapter 14, which describes how to do the Erotic Pleasure exercises. Then you will see when to use the erotic exercises in the context of the specific program you're working on in Part 4.

Alone and with Partners

Most of the Treat Yourself programs involve exercises that you do with your partner. The basic reason for this is that the problems you have probably involve your sexual functioning with somebody else, and your problems will probably be resolved more readily if you practice with that person. That is, you will be able to move readily from beginning to end without any major breaks in the program.

On the other hand, we recognize that many people have no regular partners or have partners who may not be willing to cooperate. If you're one of these (and if, after you try enhancing your communication with your partner, it still doesn't work), we'll provide in each Treat Yourself program some exercises that you can practice in order to prepare yourself for sex with a partner. Of course, ultimately, someone else will be involved in your sexual functioning. The exercises we provide will get you ready for that encounter so that it will work more smoothly.

Positions

When you engage in sexual intercourse, you're going to be in one position or another. Now it's quite possible that much of the time until now you've used the same position—most likely, the one in which the man is on top. If so, and if this is what you and your partner prefer, go right ahead. There may be no reason on earth why you'd want to change now.

But we'd like to give you a few ideas about other positions; these will be described in Chapter 20. We present these ideas for a couple of reasons. Changing positions can add to the novelty of your sex life, maybe pep it up a little in case you're a little bored. So if you are bored, Chapter 20 will suggest a few ideas about how to make your sex life more interesting.

The second reason for knowing about these different positions is that some are better than others for different purposes. Different muscles are used in different positions. For example, if you are a male who is experiencing problems with rapid ejaculation—coming too quickly—you should know that the man-on-top position leads to the most rapid ejaculations. Hence, you and your partner might want to try a more relaxing position. Similarly, there are some situations in which the woman-on-top position is most conducive to the Treat Yourself program, because this gives the woman most control, not only allowing her to achieve stimulation in the way she wants, but allowing the man to relax and taking some of the performance pressure off him.

All of these positions will be described in Chapter 20. As you read through the programs in the other chapters in Part 4, you can see which position we recommend and then, after reading about it, give it a try.

Equipment

You've got all the equipment? Well, of course you do—at least the physical equipment. But there are times when additional equipment may be necessary to help you Treat Yourself. For starters, you may want to get yourself a vibrator and a lubricant.

VIBRATORS

Vibrators can be used for both men and women. They are soothing, relaxing, and sensual. They can play an especially important role in the Treat Yourself program for women who experience difficulty in achieving orgasm.

We understand that you might feel a little uncomfortable about coming to orgasm with a vibrator. It sounds unnatural. And, in fact, if you prefer not to, don't. But we've found using a vibrator to be one of the best ways of experiencing sexual arousal and orgasm. And, after all, you or your partner will be guiding the vibrator—it's really not just a machine doing something to you. Anyhow, if you or your partner feels kind of funny about the use of vibrators, talk about it. Try to get at the heart of what's bothering you.

If you do decide to go ahead with the use of a vibrator we suggest the kind called Prelude 3 (see Figure 7-1). This vibrator seems to be most conducive to arousal and orgasm. You can order the vibrator from Sensory Research Corporation, Dept. 78-016, 5 Lawrence Street, Bloomfield, New Jersey 07003. There are also vibrators very similar to the Prelude that you can pick up at any department store, so maybe you'd prefer to do a little shopping.

There are other types of vibrators available, such as the over-the-hand model (like the one barbers use) and the one that's shaped sort of like a thick pencil and is battery powered. Although we recommend the Prelude-type vibrator, which may be more successful because its vibrations are really concen-

Figure 7-1.

trated in the head of the vibrator, you still might want to take a look at the others.

LUBRICANTS

Perhaps the best lubrication is that which is natural, such as saliva, vaginal lubrication, and so on. But either you may not feel comfortable with these for all situations or you may not be able to use them (e.g., in prolonged manual stimulation of the penis). In these situations, we recommend the use of artificial lubricants. (We'll tell you when to use these in the chapters dealing with the specific exercises.) There are several readily available lubricants that you can purchase over the counter at almost any drugstore. One of the best and most widely available is called "K-Y Lubricating Jelly." Another is called "Lubrifax." Other oils and lotions can also be used, including salad oil, Oil of Olay, Neutrogena's "Lotion for Hands and Skin," Revlon's "Natural Honey," and Elizabeth Arden's "Hand and Body Lotion."

One of the best lubricants that we've come across is called Transi-Lube. This is a foaming lubricant that resembles natural lubricants, and it has been used successfully in a number of professional sex therapy programs. Some people call Transi-Lube fun foam (believe it or not, it's flavored). You can order Transi-Lube directly from the company by writing: Holland-Rantos, Co., Inc., Post Office Box 385, 865 Centennial Ave., Piscataway, New Jersey 08854.

We advise against using petroleum jelly ("Vaseline"). Because petroleum jelly is not water soluble, it is more conducive to holding in germs, and it can also cause some breakdown in rubber devices (e.g., condoms and diaphragms).

Although the lubricants we suggest above shouldn't cause any irritation, be sure to check. If irritation or a rash develops, discontinue use of the lubricant, wait until the rash disappears, and then try another one. Also, don't be embarrassed to buy these (or the vibrators) in the store. No one can read your mind as to how you're going to use either the vibrators or the lotions. Since they were all designed for other purposes, no one will know.

Exercises

Almost everything we suggest in this book that you should do is built around the use of specific exercises. This is so both in the material presented in Part 3 and in Part 4, the Treat Yourself programs. All of these exercises have certain dimensions in common.

106

STRUCTURE

The exercises provide a structure to help you focus on each aspect of the program. Each exercise tells you what to do and in what sequence. Try hard to develop and then to stay with a regular schedule.

COMMUNICATION

Each exercise calls for communication between you and your partner, not only in deciding how to proceed but also in providing each other with support and positive strokes. Further, each exercise calls for you to tell each other just what is pleasurable and what isn't.

GRADUATED STEPS

Each exercise proceeds in a step-by-step fashion, from a clearly defined beginning point that is relatively easily accomplished to a more complicated set of concluding exercises. Each is related to a specific objective that you should accomplish before moving to the next step. But each is intended to take your mind off your ultimate goal—what you eventually want to be like when your Treat Yourself program is over—so that you can function without the pressure of performing hanging over your head.

DISTRESS SIGNAL

There may be some part of any one of the exercises in this book that you find uncomfortable. If so, you must let your partner know, right away, before you become tense or resentful. We call this the "distress signal." It can be anything you want—a tap on the hand or a brief statement ("This is uncomfortable," etc.). Whatever you choose, both of you should agree in advance as to what the signal is, you should offer it as soon as you begin to feel uncomfortable, and you should try to do it without hostility or without putting your partner down ("I said, 'Cut it out, stupid!' "). When you or your partner uses the distress signal, you should try to remain in close physical contact, talk about the problem, and, at the same time, substitute another, more desirable activity. This might mean going back a couple of steps in the exercise to something you both were comfortable with, or perhaps moving to something else you like—say, gently stroking each other's back or lying in each other's arms for a couple of minutes.

BUILD IN REWARDS

When you finish specific steps in any of the exercises, or when you finish an entire exercise, it's important to give yourselves a special reward. Of course, just completing an exercise will bring plenty of rewards in and of itself. But if you build in a special reward system, not only will you be more motivated to work at and complete each exercise, but we think you'll have more fun. Although at first glance this may seem a little childish, we can assure you that it isn't. Let's face it: Our lives would be a lot more enjoyable if we always had something pleasant to look forward to. So, together with your partner, write up a list of nonsexual activities that you would enjoy doing together. These might be going to a movie, going out for a drink, playing a game you both enjoy, preparing a special snack together, or whatever you think would be a fun activity. Schedule these at regular intervals during your exercises. (There are specific places in the contracts provided in Chapter 10 in which you can indicate what your rewards will be and when and how you can get them.)

STARTING THE EXERCISES

For almost all of the exercises, there are a few basic guidelines we'd like you to follow when you start. As a matter of fact, just following through with these may produce not only relief from tension, but added enjoyment to the entire process as well. Remember, follow through with these points every time you start a program.

1. Stop trying to have intercourse. If you're having any problems, try to stop worrying about intercourse for awhile. Just follow the Treat Yourself program for your problem; we'll get you to (successful) intercourse soon enough.

2. Lock your door. If you're going to be following your program in your bedroom, put a lock on your door to keep the kids out. This will relieve your anxiety about their possibly coming in and seeing you. Believe us: The kids will be okay. If it is absolutely impossible for you to lock the door (when you think about it, it rarely is), schedule your Treat Yourself activities at some time during the day when the kids aren't around.

3. Do it on the floor. Well, we're only partly serious. But if you're concerned that the neighbors or the kids will hear your bed's squeaking, you can either put your mattress on the floor or pick up an inexpensive but thick rug to lie on when you're practicing on the floor.

4. Do it in the nude. One of our observations with many of our clients was that they rarely sleep in the nude. It can be far more stimulating to both of you than woolen pajamas or nightshirts. If for some reason you can't sleep all night in the nude, at least follow your Treat Yourself program with both of you in the nude.

These exercises are at the heart of your Treat Yourself program. Try to follow each one carefully. Try not to jump ahead and move too quickly. But if you find that some of them are boring or maybe not as stimulating as you'd like—well, make some small changes. Make the exercises as interesting and as enjoyable as you can within the framework we set out. This probably won't hurt—and it may even help—your program. We want to provide you with variety as well as structure, enjoyment and pleasure as well as specific accomplishments. We think that you can achieve both, using the exercises we've provided as guidelines for Treating Yourself.

Specific "Treat Yourself" Programs

At long last. The final part of the book describes the specific Treat Yourself programs. Each chapter focuses on a specific problem—erection and ejaculation problems in men, orgasm and painful or difficult intercourse problems in women, and, perhaps the most common problems of all, boring and distasteful sex—that is, attempting to enhance your sex life when other problems don't exist (or after they are treated).

There are specific step-by-step programs for each of these problems. But, as we've said before, these programs are based on the ideas and exercises in Part 3. So go through that Part first, preferably with your partner, so that you can discuss each chapter and exchange ideas about it. Then, go ahead and read the chapter dealing with the problem that you're concerned about. As you'll see, each Treat Yourself program calls for the use of exercises from Part 3—for example, the Erotic Pleasure exercises in Chapter 14—so these two parts of the book are intended to work hand in hand.

Now you should have an idea as to how the program as a whole works. We hope that with the help you receive from this book, you really will be able to overcome your sexual problems and enhance your sex life. So, take it a chapter at a time, one step at a time. Ready? Go!

Eight

Knowing Your Sexuality

There are many ways in which all men and women are alike sexually. Most of this book is about the common problems and potential joys we all share. However, this chapter is different. In this chapter, we will try to help you discover your uniqueness. Your sexuality is a very personal thing, something that has evolved over all the years you have lived and from the myriad of experiences and ideas you have encountered. From that complex web of events, you have developed all the sexual behaviors, wishes, disappointments, fantasies, problems, and joys that make you a unique human being. Only you know what these ideas and experiences are and how you have reacted to them. We don't. All we can do is provide you with an opportunity to define yourself—and any sexual problems you may be experiencing.

There are some very practical reasons for carrying out this inventory. Before you can start improving your sex life, you must discover where you're starting from. If there's anything that researchers in the field of interpersonal helping have learned about solving personal problems, it's this: The first and most important step in working on problems is to specify exactly what the problems are. If this book is going to be of any help to you, you're going to have to think about your experiences and about the feelings connected with your sexuality and try to pinpoint any difficulties or barriers that may be keeping you from a more rewarding sex life.

We're not saying that knowing what your problems are is enough to solve your problems. It is true that thinking about the barriers to your sexual fulfillment—and, especially, thinking about any faulty learning you may have had about sex—may help you to re-evaluate your ideas, some of which may stand in your way—or in your partner's way. Certainly our sexual self-inventory can be used as a focus for discussions with your partner to review your sexual needs, concerns, wishes, and experiences and to specify your mutual concerns and fears.

But perhaps even more important, this chapter will help you pinpoint the specific obstacles that you may be running up against and direct you to the specific procedures that can be of the most use to you. Once you have taken stock of yourself, you can then move on to setting the goals you hope to achieve through your self-help program.

And so, with this chapter you begin to take on the responsibility for improving your sex life. You begin by carefully going through the rest of this chapter, answering the questions, and filling out the checklists, which are intended to help you explore the basic aspects of your sexual experiences, attitudes, wishes, and behaviors.

The questions in this chapter were designed to probe widely and deeply into your sexual experiences and feelings, both past and present. If the questions provoke you into having new ideas about your present sex life, they will have served their purpose. Don't be shy about giving answers that stress your positives. Take stock of your strong points; it's as important as describing your problems.

We know that some of the questions may not exactly apply to you and that they may be difficult to answer clearly or even honestly. Do your best. The information asked for by some of the questions may lead to very embarrassing answers. There may be memories that you would prefer to forget and feelings that you would probably rather not admit to. You may have to look at these and ask yourself what they mean to you. Your discomfort may lead to a better understanding of your and your partner's sexual preferences, problems, and goals.

You may share or not share these answers with anyone you choose. Use your own judgment in sharing your answers with your partner. And, of course, your partner has a right to share or not share any of his or her answers with you. Using this questionnaire to facilitate communication between you and your partner is very desirable—as long as you do not use it to shock or hurt each other. Don't skip any answers that apply to you, and avoid glib, incomplete, or dishonest answers. They won't help.

There's no need to complete this questionnaire in one sitting. You can look it over and answer parts of it at different times, as the mood hits you. Feel free to change your answers as you review the questions over time. People do change, and so do their sexual behaviors, feelings, and wishes. The more you know yourself, the more this book will help you to achieve a more satisfying sexual life.

There is, of course, the possibility that this chapter will not reveal anything new to you and that it will not lead to pinpointing your problem. If that is the case, you may want to share your answers with your partner or with a friend and have him or her react to it. Or you may want to just put it aside and try it again at some other time. Further, it may be useful to review your responses from time to time in order for you to get a perspective on your development as a sexual human being.

We'll start with a quick look at whether you *do* have a problem and at what you identify as the characteristics of your sexual problem. Then we'll go back to helping you understand your sexual development; proceed to bring you up to date with a review of your current sexual activities, feelings, and wishes; and end with a survey of what you feel you need now in order to have a satisfying sex life. Throughout, we will explore your feelings toward your sexual partners and pay particular attention to giving your current sexual partner an opportunity to lend his or her perspective of you as a sexual partner.

DO YOU REALLY HAVE A PROBLEM?

We would hate to lose you as a reader, but we will take the risk by pointing out that you may not have the problem you think you have.

Some people who seem to enjoy their sexuality still feel that there's something missing. Often, they expect more from their sexual activity than it can possibly deliver. Sex has been oversold. We have even been led to believe that a really good sex life will solve many of your other problems. It will make an unhappy marriage happy, an ugly person beautiful, a lonely person loved. It can't.

112

Don't get us wrong. Sex is great. We wouldn't be writing books about it if we didn't think so. But it's only part of life, of marriage, of our humanness. A poor sexual adjustment *can* foul you up in other areas of your life. And certainly, sexual enjoyment can make us feel better when we're feeling lonely or going through personal hardships. But it doesn't *solve* these other problems, and its soothing effect can be shortlived.

So, think about it. How are you trying to use your sexuality:

□ To prove that you're an adequate man/woman?

□ To forget about pressures you're under?

□ To relieve depression?

□ To make you less anxious?

□ To relieve boredom?

□ To compete with other men or women?

□ To get someone to love you?

□ To dominate someone?

□ To express your anger toward your sex partner (or someone else)?

□ To carry out an obligation?

□ To get money or something else out of your partner?

To be sure, most of us engage in a sexual activity for some of these reasons from time to time—and often sex can accomplish some of these objectives. However, if any of these is your *major* reason for having sex, you're likely to feel unsatisfied and not able to accomplish your goals. And, frankly, if this is the case, your problem is not a sexual one, and your help won't be found in these pages. You may want to discuss your pattern with a professional counselor (see the Epilogue for suggestions on how to locate one).

Also, if you have become convinced that sex is supposed to be a spectacular event each and every time you get together with your partner, with instant erections, endless arousal, and four-star multiple orgasms, we can't help you. We'll try to help you give or get more enjoyment. But boundless ecstasy? Sorry.

And finally, if you are a woman and worry because you occasionally don't have an orgasm—despite your general enjoyment of sex—or if you are a man and occasionally don't get hard or stay hard when you want to—but you otherwise enjoy sex—your only problem may be having too many expectations of yourself. Welcome to the human race.

However, let's suppose that you do have a problem, that

you are not attempting to use sex to solve other problems, and that you would like to enjoy your sexuality more or even be more comfortable with what you are already doing. Then, the first step is an inventory of your feelings and activities and an exploration of any particular problem you are experiencing.

FOCUSING ON YOUR PROBLEM

All right, you have a problem, and you want to do something about it. The following pages are intended as a guide to pinpointing the problem and then understanding yourself as a sexual human being. Remember that this guide is intended to be *used*, not just read. We suggest that you first read it over. Then proceed to write out the answers to all the questions in a separate notebook. If you prefer, you can answer the questions into a tape recorder. If you have a partner, and he or she also goes through this inventory, don't discuss the questions or your answers with him or her until you complete each section.

If you already know specifically what your problem is, you can proceed to look at it from various angles, starting with defining it and then with exploring its history.

Pinpointing the Nature and History of Your Problem

1. What, specifically, do you think is your problem?

2. When does the problem occur? With whom? In any particular place or under any particular circumstances?

3. Who, besides you, is complaining about your problem? Does he or she see your problem the same way that you do?

4. When did the problem first occur? What were the circumstances? How old were you? Did it come on suddenly or at a specific time? What do you think brought it on?

5. What have been the results of your having this problem? What has happened to you or your partner because of it?

6. Has the problem changed over time? Has it gotten worse or better? When does it become worse, and when better?

7. Do you think that your sexual problem is in any way related to other aspects of your life? How?

8. What do you think caused the problem in the first place?

9. Have you tried to work on the problem yourself? Has it helped? If not, why do you think it didn't?

10. Have you ever tried to get help for the problem? From whom? When? What kind of treatment did you receive? Did it help? If not, why do you think it didn't?

11. Are you currently experiencing problems in other aspects of your life that may affect your sexual life?

12. Are you experiencing any physical illnesses that may have an effect on your sexual activities? Are you under medical treatment? Are you taking any medication that may have a bearing on your sexual adjustment? If you're not sure, check with your physician.

13. How do you hope your sex life and life in general will be improved if you are successful in treating yourself? Does your partner share your goals? (If you don't know, ask.)

Any Other Problems?

Besides the specific problems you have identified above, you may have other, more general problems or "complaints" about sex. The following questions should help you to get at them.

1. Are you getting what you want out of sex? If not, what are you missing?

2. How would you like to see your sex life changed?

3. Is your partner dissatisfied with you as a sexual partner? If so, what's his or her complaint? How do you react to his or her criticism? Do you think it's legitimate? What keeps you from doing something about it?

4. Do you feel that anxiety interferes with your sexual activities? (If so, we have a section on anxiety later in this chapter to help you look at the causes of your anxiety.)

5. Are you ashamed or uncomfortable about some part of your body? What do you think is wrong with it? How have your partners reacted to it? If you don't know, how do you *think* they react to it?

6. Do you feel that you're too hard on yourself and that you really aren't as bad as you sometimes make yourself out to be?

7. Do your sexual problems really reflect on some problems in your feelings toward your partners, your relationships with them, their expectations of you, or your expectations of them?

8. Are there other sexual activities you engage in or would like to engage in, such as self-stimulation or sexual attraction to people of your own sex? Do you have other sexual relationships that interfere in any way with your sexual relationship with your partner? Do you have any ideas about how you can resolve this conflict?

9. Do you have some difficulties in your feelings about love and sex? How does this affect you and/or your partner?

10. Do your sexual fantasies, either while having sex with your partner or at other times, interfere with your sexual relationship?

11. What fears do you have in connection with sex? How frequent and intense are they?

12. Do you and your partner have problems in balancing who gives and who receives pleasure when having sex?

13. Do you feel guilty about sex?

14. Are you bored with your sexual activities?

15. Do you find sex or aspects of it distasteful?

16. Do you have problems on those occasions when you want to tell your partner that you're not interested in sex? Do you have problems on those occasions when your partner tells you that he or she is not interested?

17. Do you and your partner have an unequal interest in sex? Do you have preferences for different sexual activities from those that he or she does?

18. Do you feel that you are "abnormal" in terms of your sexual interests or activities? Do you feel that your partner is "abnormal"? Does your partner think you're "abnormal"?

What About Your Good Points?

Often, people who read self-help books are too hard on themselves. It's just as important and often more productive to recognize and build on your good points and successes as it is to recognize your problems and limitations. Let's take stock of your positives (come on, you know you have them).

1. What do you like about your approach to sex?
2. What do you like about your appearance? What for?

3. What are the strong points about your personality? Are there ways in which you come across as warm and caring? To whom, and when?

4. What are your fantasies like? Can you enjoy them?

5. How skilled are you in knowing your own body?

6. What turns you on? What turns you off?

7. In which ways do you consider yourself as good as or better than most people sexually?

8. What do you like (love) about your partner's sexual behavior?

9. What aspects of your sex life do you enjoy?

10. Under what conditions do you relax and enjoy your sexuality?

EARLY SEXUAL EXPERIENCES

Now that you have had a chance to think about your problems and assets, it would be useful to step back and do a general inventory of yourself as a sexual human being.

In order to understand where you are, it is often useful to look at where you have come from. So let's start the review with your sexual history.

As you respond to the specific questions about your early sexuality, you might want to consider other things that were happening to you as you were growing up, such as the loss of a parent or frequent moves from town to town, which might have had an effect on your sexual development.

The way we express ourselves sexually is largely determined by our early sexual experiences and by what we were taught by our family and friends. Let's review your early sexual experiences.

EXPERIENCES WITH PARENTS

Our ideas about our own sexuality are partly based on what we observed in our parents. What kind of man was your father? How did he act toward you? What did he tell you, if anything, about sex? Did he ever talk to you about sex or give you any advice? What do you think he expected of you sexually? How about your mother? What kind of a woman was she? How did she act toward you? What do you think she expected of you as far as your sexual development goes? Did she ever talk to you about sex or give you any advice? What kind of relationship did your parents have? What kind of sex life do you think they had? Were they affectionate toward each other? Were they affectionate toward you? What did you (do you) feel you had to do—or not do—sexually in order to live up to their expectations? What kind of effect do you think they had on your sexual development?

EXPERIENCES WITH FRIENDS

Did you have close friends of the same sex? What were their attitudes toward masturbation, petting, and sexual activities with the opposite sex? What kind of dirty jokes did they tell? What did you feel you had to do to live up to their expectations?

Did you have friends of the opposite sex as you were growing up? Were you comfortable with them? Did you talk about or joke about sex with them as you were growing up? What effect do you think your friends had on your sexual development?

EXPERIENCES WITH EARLY CRUSHES

Who were the first people you were turned on to sexually? Was the first one an older person, a friend, a classmate, a teacher, a relative? Was the first one of your sex or of the opposite sex? Do you recall your feelings about these people? What were your reactions to them? How did you express your feelings? How did you feel about your feelings?

EARLY EXPERIENCES WITH YOUR BODY

As you were growing up, both as a child and throughout adolescence, how did you feel about your body and appearance? What concerns did you have about your body and your sexual organs? When did you really begin to understand how your body works sexually? How did you find out?

Women: Can you recall your first period? Were you prepared for it? How? By whom? What was your reaction to it? Can you recall your first orgasm? What was it like? How did it come about? What were your reactions, your feelings?

Men: Can you recall your first ejaculation? How did it occur: from a wet dream, from self-stimulation, from sex with another person? Were you prepared for it? How? By whom? What was your reaction to it?

EARLY EXPERIENCES WITH FANTASIES

What kinds of sexual fantasies and daydreams did you have as you were growing up? How did you feel about them? Did you feel that they were bad, or did you feel that they were

118

okay? Did they represent any misconceptions you had about sexual anatomy, physiology, or activities? Did you ever tell your fantasies to anyone? What was the reaction?

EARLY SEXUAL EXPERIENCES

Did you engage in sexual experiences during childhood and adolescence? What kind? How often did you stimulate yourself to orgasm? How did you feel about it? Did you have sexual experiences with others of your own sex (such as "circle jerks")? How did you feel about it? Did you have any sexual contacts with anyone of the opposite sex? How often? Under what circumstances? How did you feel about your partner(s)? How did they feel about you?

SUMMARY OF EARLY EXPERIENCES

Are you comfortable with your early sexual experiences or lack of them? How do you wish they might have been different? How would you want your children's sexual experiences to be different? What impact do you think your childhood and adolescent sexual experiences, attitudes, and the information you received had on you as a developing sexual human being?

Your First Sexual Experiences

Our first experiences with sex can have a profound effect on our future sexual adjustment. Despite the images of movies and French novels, initial sexual explorations are often awkward and messy. Learning how to enjoy sexual activities and give enjoyment to your partner takes practice. How was your first sexual experience? Where did it occur? Whom was it with? Was it planned or did it occur unexpectedly? What exactly did you do? Did you have an orgasm? Did your partner have an orgasm? How did your partner feel about it? How did you feel about each other after you were done? How do you feel about it now? Did you use a birth-control method?

Your First Long-lasting Sexual Relationship

Your first long-term relationship (if you've had one) was probably your first experience with combining sexual attraction and affection, along with some degree of commitment and mutual responsibility. It may have been one of many long-lasting relationships, or it may have been your one and only relationship, culminating in marriage. Regardless of which it was, it tested you out on your ability to get truly involved with a sexual partner.

Whom was your first relationship with? What did you expect from the relationship? What did you get? What problems did you run into? How did you attempt to resolve them? How was the sexual relationship? Did it change over time? How did it change? How did this relationship differ from ones you've had since then?

Did you live together? Were there problems in living together? Did you consider marriage? What advantages did you feel there would be from getting married? What disadvantages? Do you regret that the relationship ended—or didn't end?

YOUR PRESENT SITUATION

Let's move on to your current sexual feelings, attitudes, and behaviors. This will give you and your partner a chance to take an inventory of how you currently express yourself sexually—what you do and don't do, what you like and don't like.

On the following pages, we have listed a range of sexual activities. We have included some blank places for you to add any others you can think of. We want you and your partner to rate each of these activities according to (1) your estimation of how frequently you engage in the activity, (2) how frequently you and your partner would like to engage in each activity, and (3) how much you enjoy the activity. Fill out each of the lists separately. Stop after you complete each one and discuss it with your partner. Focus especially on any ratings that surprised you and on any items in which you and your partner's ratings are far apart. How do you feel about these differences? Are they okay? If not, what can you do about it? If you have no regular partner, go ahead and do it just for yourself.

Estimated Frequency of Activity

We'll start with rating roughly how often you have engaged in the following activities over the last few months when you and your partner have had sex. Use the following scale, putting the appropriate number in the space to the right of the item. For example, if you look at your partner's body about 50 percent of the time, you would put a "3" under your estimate.

120

1—Never occurs (0 percent of the time).

2—Rarely occurs (about 25 percent of the time).

3—Occurs fairly often (about 50 percent of the time).

4—Usually occurs (about 75 percent of the time).

5—Always occurs (100 percent of the time).

Activity	Your Estimate	Your Partner's Estimate
1. You look at your partner's nude body.	———	———
2. Your partner looks at your nude body.	———	———
3. You kiss your partner.	———	———
4. Your partner kisses you.	———	———
5. You stroke your partner's body.	———	———
6. Your partner strokes your body.	———	———
7. You stroke your partner's breasts and sexual organs (specify which and how; for example, firmly or gently, with fingers, lips, or palms of hands).	———	———
———————————————	———	———
8. Your partner strokes your breasts and sexual organs (specify which and how; for example, firmly or gently, with fingers, lips, or palms of hands).	———	———
———————————————	———	———
9. You talk warmly or sexily to each other.	———	———
10. You caress, lick, and/or suck your partner's breasts and sexual organs (specify which and how).	———	———
———————————————	———	———
11. Your partner caresses, licks, and/or sucks your breasts and sexual organs (specify which and how).	———	———
———————————————	———	———

121

12. You stimulate yourself by hand. ＿＿＿＿ ＿＿＿＿
13. Your partner stimulates him- or herself by hand. ＿＿＿＿ ＿＿＿＿
14. You hold or rub your body against your partner's body (specify how). ＿＿＿＿ ＿＿＿＿

＿＿＿＿＿＿＿＿＿＿＿＿＿＿＿＿ ＿＿＿＿ ＿＿＿＿

＿＿＿＿＿＿＿＿＿＿＿＿＿＿＿＿ ＿＿＿＿ ＿＿＿＿

15. Your partner holds and rubs his or her body against your body (specify how). ＿＿＿＿ ＿＿＿＿

＿＿＿＿＿＿＿＿＿＿＿＿＿＿＿＿ ＿＿＿＿ ＿＿＿＿

＿＿＿＿＿＿＿＿＿＿＿＿＿＿＿＿ ＿＿＿＿ ＿＿＿＿

16. You use your hands to bring your partner to orgasm. ＿＿＿＿ ＿＿＿＿
17. Your partner uses his or her hands to bring you to orgasm. ＿＿＿＿ ＿＿＿＿
18. You use your mouth to bring your partner to orgasm. ＿＿＿＿ ＿＿＿＿
19. Your partner uses his or her mouth to bring you to orgasm. ＿＿＿＿ ＿＿＿＿
20. You have intercourse to orgasm. ＿＿＿＿ ＿＿＿＿
21. You use the following positions for intercourse:
    a. Male above. ＿＿＿＿ ＿＿＿＿
    b. Female above. ＿＿＿＿ ＿＿＿＿
    c. On your sides, facing each other. ＿＿＿＿ ＿＿＿＿
    d. Rear entry. ＿＿＿＿ ＿＿＿＿
    e. Other positions (specify) ＿＿＿＿ ＿＿＿＿

＿＿＿＿＿＿＿＿＿＿＿＿＿＿＿＿ ＿＿＿＿ ＿＿＿＿

＿＿＿＿＿＿＿＿＿＿＿＿＿＿＿＿ ＿＿＿＿ ＿＿＿＿

22. Other sexual activities (specify). ＿＿＿＿ ＿＿＿＿

＿＿＿＿＿＿＿＿＿＿＿＿＿＿＿＿ ＿＿＿＿ ＿＿＿＿

＿＿＿＿＿＿＿＿＿＿＿＿＿＿＿＿ ＿＿＿＿ ＿＿＿＿

＿＿＿＿＿＿＿＿＿＿＿＿＿＿＿＿ ＿＿＿＿ ＿＿＿＿

＿＿＿＿＿＿＿＿＿＿＿＿＿＿＿＿ ＿＿＿＿ ＿＿＿＿

Frequency You and Your Partner Would Prefer

Now that you and your partner have indicated how often each of you *think* you engage in particular activities and have discussed any discrepancies in your estimates, you're ready to move on to exploring how often you wish the same activities would occur.

In order to avoid influencing each other, fill out the items separately, and cover up your answers until each of you has completed the form.

Go ahead and check how often you wish the following activities would occur.

Use the same scale you used before:

1—Wish it never occurred.

2—Would like it rarely (about 25 percent of the time).

3—Would like it fairly often (about 50 percent of the time).

4—Would like it to occur usually (about 75 percent of the time).

5—Would like it every time (100 percent of the time).

Activity	You Would Like It	Your Partner Would Like It
1. You look at your partner's nude body.	_____	_____
2. Your partner looks at your nude body.	_____	_____
3. You kiss your partner.	_____	_____
4. Your partner kisses you.	_____	_____
5. You stroke your partner's body.	_____	_____
6. Your partner strokes your body.	_____	_____
7. You stroke your partner's breasts and sexual organs (specify which and how; for example, firmly or gently, with fingers, lips, or palms of hands).	_____	_____
_____	_____	_____
8. Your partner strokes your breasts and sexual organs (specify which and how; for example, firmly or gently, with fingers, lips, or palms of hands).	_____	_____
_____	_____	_____
9. You talk warmly or sexily to each other.	_____	_____
10. You caress, lick, and/or suck your partner's breasts and sexual organs (specify which and how).	_____	_____

11. Your partner caresses, licks and/or sucks your breasts and sexual organs (specify which and how).

_____

_____

12. You stimulate yourself by hand.
13. Your partner stimulates him- or herself by hand.
14. You hold or rub your body against your partner's body (specify how).

_____

_____

15. Your partner holds and rubs his or her body against your body (specify how).

_____

_____

16. You use your hands to bring your partner to orgasm.
17. Your partner uses his or her hands to bring you to orgasm.
18. You use your mouth to bring your partner to orgasm.
19. Your partner uses his or her mouth to bring you to orgasm.
20. You have intercourse to orgasm.
21. You use the following positions for intercourse:
    a. Male above.
    b. Female above.
    c. On your sides, facing each other.
    d. Rear entry.
    e. Other positions (specify).

_____

_____

22. Other sexual activities (specify).

_____

_____

_____

_____

Enjoyment of Activities

Your partner's and your enjoyment of a particular sexual activity may be reflected by how often you do it. But not necessarily. As we said earlier, a lot of what we do is a result of what we think is expected of us and not necessarily of what we enjoy doing. So, our last checklist gives you and your partner a chance to think for a while about what you really like doing. This checklist, combined with the inventory on your conditions for good sex (which comes later in this chapter), should help to direct you away from your playing roles in bed and toward enjoying yourself more and giving more joy to your partner.

Again, you and your partner should fill out the checklist, covering up your answers. Then compare your answers, trying to negotiate your differences and relishing your similarities. Be as honest as you can. Use the following scale for your answers to rate the activities.

1—Don't like it at all; very unpleasant.

2—Dislike it somewhat; a little unpleasant.

3—Neutral; don't care one way or the other.

4—Like it somewhat; a little enjoyable.

5—Like it very much; very pleasant.

Activity	Your Rating	Your Partner's Rating
1. You look at your partner's nude body.	____	____
2. Your partner looks at your nude body.	____	____
3. You kiss your partner.	____	____
4. Your partner kisses you.	____	____
5. You stroke your partner's body.	____	____
6. Your partner strokes your body.	____	____
7. You stroke your partner's breasts and sexual organs (specify which and how; for example, firmly or gently, with fingers, lips, or palms of hands).	____	____
	____	____
8. Your partner strokes your breasts and sexual organs (specify which and how; for example, firmly or gently, with fingers, lips, or palms of hands).	____	____
	____	____

9. You talk warmly or sexily to each other. _____ _____
10. You caress, lick, and/or suck your partner's breasts and sexual organs (specify which and how). _____ _____

_____ _____ _____

_____ _____ _____

11. Your partner caresses, licks, and/or sucks your breasts and sexual organs (specify which and how). _____ _____

_____ _____ _____

_____ _____ _____

12. You stimulate yourself by hand. _____ _____
13. Your partner stimulates him- or herself by hand. _____ _____
14. You hold or rub your body against your partner's body (specify how). _____ _____

_____ _____ _____

_____ _____ _____

15. Your partner holds and rubs his or her body against your body (specify how). _____ _____

_____ _____ _____

_____ _____ _____

16. You use your hands to bring your partner to orgasm. _____ _____
17. Your partner uses his or her hands to bring you to orgasm. _____ _____
18. You use your mouth to bring your partner to orgasm. _____ _____
19. Your partner uses his or her mouth to bring you to orgasm. _____ _____
20. You have intercourse to orgasm. _____ _____
21. You use the following positions for intercourse:
    a. Male above. _____ _____
    b. Female above. _____ _____
    c. On your sides, facing each other. _____ _____
    d. Rear entry. _____ _____
    e. Other positions (specify). _____ _____

_____ _____ _____

_____ _____ _____

22. Other sexual activities (specify).

_____ _____ _____

_____ _____ _____

_____ _____ _____

_____ _____ _____

One final note about the use of these checklists. When you have filled them out, put them aside. Then, after you have followed some of the procedures recommended in Parts 3 and 4 of this book, take the scales out and you and your partner fill them out again. See if there have been any changes. If there have been changes, let's hope that they're in the direction that you and your partner have wanted.

Your Feelings About Your Body and Your Appearance

No matter how much we conceive of sex as an emotional and even spiritual experience, we come back to the fact that sex involves our bodies. And, as we will discuss in Chapter 12, most people are dissatisfied with at least some parts of their bodies. It's important, therefore, to remember that all kinds of bodies get involved in and enjoy sex: smooth bodies, wrinkled bodies, long bodies, short bodies, fat bodies, and skinny bodies. But a lot of us are plagued with the feeling that sex is only for beautiful bodies with outstanding "sexual equipment" and that, in some important ways, our bodies—or parts thereof—just don't qualify us for fully enjoying our sexuality.

Our motto for guidance regarding your physical appearance is: Change what you can, trim yourself down or build yourself up, and be aware of grooming and hygiene—but accept what cannot be changed and, believe it or not, there's a good chance that you can turn on your partner the way you are.

Let's check out how you feel about your body.

1. Overall, how do you feel about your appearance? Do you look attractive? Do you think that your partner considers you attractive?

2. How do you feel about your height and weight?

3. How's your posture? Do you slouch? Do you give the appearance of feeling comfortable with your body?

127

4. Our faces tell a great deal about ourselves. What do you think of your face? Does it look warm, friendly, attractive? Does it accurately portray your feelings to your partner?

5. (For women) Do you feel that you look feminine? How do you feel about the size, shape, and appearance of your breasts? How do you feel about the appearance of your vulva (your genitals)?

6. (For men) Do you feel that you look masculine? How do you feel about the size, shape, and appearance of your penis and your scrotum?

7. What impression do you think you give by the type and appearance of the clothes you wear? Do they make you more attractive or do they give the impression that you have something to hide?

8. Does the way you trim and comb your hair say something about you as a sexual person (casual, uptight, formal, youthful, etc.)?

9. People close to us smell us, just as we may smell them. Do you like the way you smell? Do you like the way your partner smells, including any genital odors? Have you ever discussed your or your partner's use or non-use of perfumes, deodorants, and so on with your partner? Have you asked whether they prefer your human smell rather than your covering it up with the smell of deodorants and perfumes? Have you told them how you feel about their smells?

10. People also tell a lot about us by our voices. How's yours? If you've never heard your own voice, get a tape recorder and record what you might say to your partner about sex, in or out of bed. Do the tone, volume, pitch, and general quality of your voice convey what you want to say about yourself? It's difficult to turn people on with either squeaks or roars. (You can change the way you sound if you want to: Use a tape recorder to practice.)

Your Feelings Toward Your Present Partner

Whether you've been with your partner a week or have been married to him or her for twenty years, it's practically impossible to separate your feelings toward him or her from the way you make love. In this section, we will give you a chance to explore your present relationship and its history.

1. When did you first meet your current partner? What was your first impression of him or her? What eventually im-

pressed you most about him or her initially? What were his or her first impressions of you? What turned him or her on to you? (If you don't know, ask your partner.)

2. How was he or she different from other people you dated or were close to? What was your first sexual experience with him or her like? How have your sexual feelings toward him or her changed over time?

3. What do you like most about your sexual experiences with your partner? What do you like least? What would you like to see changed in your sexual contacts with your partner?

4. Is there anything you would like your partner to do sexually that he or she doesn't do now? Is there anything your partner does with you sexually that you wish he or she wouldn't do? What?

5. How many of the items in this section have you talked over with him or her? How do you feel about discussing your sexual wishes, behaviors, and attitudes with him or her? What problems do you run into when you try to have an open, positive discussion of sex with him or her?

6. If you have tried discussing these matters with him or her and don't feel good about it, how come? What kinds of problems have you experienced in discussing sex with him or her? How have you tried to overcome these problems? (Chapter 9 will give you some guidelines and exercises to make it easier to talk about sex.)

7. How have your feelings toward your partner changed since you met him or her? Do you love him or her? Do you often wish you were involved with someone else?

8. Sometimes people blame their sexual relationship for creating problems in the rest of their relationship. However, often it's the other way around: Our sexual enjoyment is often dependent on how we get along with our partners outside of the bedroom. Are there problems in your relationship that you feel interfere with your sexual relationship? How have you tried to deal with them?

9. Do you share interests and friendship with your partner outside of sex?

Your Feelings About Your Fantasies

Your fantasies can play a very important role in your sex life. What we fantasize and when, and how important our fantasies become, can determine whether our fantasies are satisfying components of our daily sexual lives or a disruption to our "real" sex life (see Chapter 13). To help you take stock of your dream world of sex, answer the following questions:

1. What do you fantasize as you stimulate yourself when you're alone?

2. What do you fantasize or think about while you're having sex with your partner?

3. Do you have sexually oriented dreams? What are they about?

4. Do you feel guilty about your sexual fantasies? Why?

5. Are your fantasies related to your current partner? Do they make you feel better or worse about him or her? Do they make you want to have sex with him or her or make you less interested?

6. Would you sometimes or often prefer stimulating yourself in private than having sex with him or her? Why?

7. Have your sexual fantasies given you ideas of new sexual activities to try out with your sexual partner? Have you tried them out or discussed them with him or her?

8. Do any of your fantasies disturb you? Why?

9. Do you feel that it's all right to fantasize while having sex with someone other than your partner? Why or why not?

10. What would you like to know about your partner's sexual fantasies?

Your Feelings: Anxiety

The biggest and most common obstacle to sexual enjoyment is anxiety. High levels of tension and anxiety seriously interfere with the work of the nervous system in transmitting the sexy messages received through our senses to the rest of the body to get us turned on and ready for sex. Uncovering the sources of your anxiety may provide an important first step toward reducing it.

Here are some questions that might help to pinpoint your anxiety:

1. Do sexual activities generally make you anxious?

2. Are there particular situations in which sex makes you most uncomfortable—for example, with a particular partner, in a particular place, or at a particular time?

3. Do any of the following activities create particular anxiety for you?

- [ ] Not getting turned on (not getting erect or not lubricating).
- [ ] Getting turned on when your partner doesn't.
- [ ] Not getting turned on when your partner does.
- [ ] Stimulating yourself when you're alone.
- [ ] Stimulating yourself when you're with your partner.
- [ ] Oral sex.
- [ ] Anal sex.
- [ ] Certain positions in intercourse (if so, which ones?).
- [ ] Knowing that you want things from your partner, things that you're uncomfortable asking for.
- [ ] Being asked for certain things from your partner.
- [ ] Your partner or you don't have orgasms.
- [ ] Anything else?

4. Can you think of those sexual activities or circumstances around your sexual activities that seem to make you most relaxed?

5. Are there any particular sexual fantasies which make you anxious?

6. Are your anxieties in any way connected with fears of failure in sex or with concerns about disappointing your partner?

7. Can you remember any experiences in the past connected with sex which may be connected with your present discomfort?

8. Is there anything in particular about yourself that makes you anxious in sex, such as your overall appearance, the size, shape, or appearance of your sex organs or breasts, or your physical responses to getting turned on or not getting turned on?

9. Complete the following sentences as fast as you can, relating them to your sexual activities. Remember: Finish them with the words or phrases that first pop into your head.

I wish I could _____ .

I love it when _____ .

I'm afraid to _____ .

131

I get scared when _____.

I'm afraid I will _____.

I get uncomfortable when my partner _____.

I get uncomfortable when I _____.

I get embarrassed when I _____.

I get embarrassed when my partner _____.

I wish I didn't _____.

I wish my partner would _____.

I wish my partner wouldn't _____.

I'd love to be able to _____.

I'm afraid I will _____.

I'm afraid I won't _____.

I'm terrified of _____.

10. After putting your answers to the above questions together, what, if anything, have you learned about your anxiety connected with sex? Can you pinpoint when it occurs and under what conditions? Is there any way you can avoid those situations that make you anxious, or, better yet, is there any way you can reduce the amount of anxiety they cause you? Perhaps your partner can give you some ideas. It's also possible that talking over those things that make you anxious may help to reduce your anxiety. In Chapter 11, we provide a specific program for helping you to overcome your anxiety in sexual situations.

Your Conditions for Good Sex

Despite what you may think or what you have been taught, you have a right to establish conditions for having sex the way you want it. Not only do you have this right, but, in order to get your sexual responses in the best working order, you should try to come as close to your conditions as you and your partner can negotiate.

Conditions are any feelings, events, surroundings, characteristics, or behaviors of your partner that get you aroused or turned on and primed for an enjoyable sex experience. These conditions can be quite different from person to person, and they can change for you from time to time.

What are your conditions? Some of us are so used to responding to what is expected of us and conforming to the current sexual myths of how a man or woman is supposed to act about sex that we don't stop and evaluate what *our* conditions are for good sex. Stop and evaluate!

In order to do so, here are a few questions to help you determine your conditions:

1. Think back to those sexual experiences that you have enjoyed most. (If you've never had any good experiences, try to imagine some really enjoyable sexual experiences.) What was there about those encounters that most turned you on? Who was your partner? Where were you, and what was the situation? What did you and your partner do with each other? What parts or aspects of the encounter do you remember most vividly?

2. Next, think back to several sexual encounters that didn't turn out so well. (Come on, there must have been some. If you're one of the rare folks who have never had a sexual downer, try to imagine some really bad ones.) Whom were you with? How did you feel about your partner? Where were you, what were the circumstances, and what (specifically) did you do? In retrospect, what was there about these encounters that made them less than pleasant?

3. Now compare your best experiences with your worst ones. As specifically as possible, what were the most significant factors that separated the good experiences from the bad? List those factors that separate "good" sex from "bad" sex for you in your past experiences—or in your imagination.

Your list may well include items about your feelings toward your partner, your ability to turn on your partner, your ability to get really turned on yourself, your expectations and

133

respect for each other, the degree to which you were able to focus on the matters at hand instead of on other problems, the quality and comfort of the surroundings, your anxiety or lack of anxiety, fears about performance, your parents, pregnancy, and venereal disease.

4. Now work on the list, making the items as specific as possible. Then rewrite the list, placing the items in their order of importance with the most important item at the top of the list.

The list you now have ranks your conditions about sex. It's your list—no one else's—and, for the time being at least, it gives you some guidelines about what you need to have in order to have good sex.

5. Finally, a few more questions. Are you comfortable with your list? Do you think the items are reasonable? Do or can you have these conditions with your present partner? If some are missing, do you think you can work with your partner toward achieving more of these conditions?

PUTTING IT ALL TOGETHER

By now, you are probably exhausted from answering all of our questions. Perhaps you are wondering: What does it all mean? On the basis of all your answers, we would like you to try to put your sexual self together and discover what you have.

We hope that you will be able to come to some conclusions about what specific problems you have, about what led to them, about what may be maintaining them, and about what stands in the way of your having a more satisfying sex life. These answers should direct you to the chapters in this book that may give you direction in working on your problems. For example, if your problem is in the area of communication, you may want to focus on Chapter 9—"Let's Talk About Talking"—or if you find that everything seems fine, but you are bored with your current sexual activity, you would read Chapter 20. If your problem is in your relationship, then you may want to go back to Chapter 3.

As we said at the beginning of this chapter, we know that understanding what makes you tick sexually will not automatically improve your sex life. But getting a better perspective on how you got to be where you are and on what keeps you there as well as getting a clear understanding of what you and your partner want may be the most important steps in having a more enjoyable and fulfilling sex life.

Nine

Let's Talk About Talking

"If you really loved me, I wouldn't have to tell you what I want. . . . You'd know!"

This is one of the most often-heard complaints of sexual partners. It is based on the idea that people who "really" love each other are mindreaders—ever sensitive to each other's needs and wishes. They're not. And therein lies a basic problem.

Often, the wish that a sexual partner were a mindreader covers up the person's own discomfort and embarrassment about his or her sexual needs. The person is too embarrassed to ask for what he or she wants (or to tell what he or she doesn't want), so he or she simply expects that the partner should somehow know, and thus save him or her the embarrassment of telling the partner.

Sometimes, a person wishes that his or her sexual partner were a mindreader because he or she simply really doesn't know what he or she wants and hopes that the partner *will* know.

Unfortunately, no mere mortal can read someone else's mind or can really tell another person what he or she should enjoy. This is a process couples have to explore together and, perhaps most important, talk to each other about.

This chapter is intended to help you be more effective in talking to your partner about your sexual relationship and to explore what you want and need from each other and what you offer each other.

ROADBLOCKS TO OPEN COMMUNICATION ABOUT SEX

What should sexual partners tell and ask each other?

There was a fad not too many years ago that encouraged total "authenticity" and "honesty" between couples. If a couple is to really get it together—so the wisdom went— they've got to let it all hang loose and tell it like it is: Don't suppress it; express it.

A moving bit of philosophy, that, but one that probably did more harm than good. Total honesty, if that means saying everything to your partner on your mind, might get a lot off your chest, but it probably won't get what you want. It can also be needlessly harmful to your partner. *Open* communication is not the same as totally *honest* communication.

Open communication means deliberately telling your partner how you feel, what you want and don't want, and what you like and don't like about what you and your partner do in a positive, constructive, way. The intent of such communication is to bring you closer, increase the chances that you can get what you want from your partner, and give your partner what he or she wants.

What prevents people from communicating openly about sex?

First, most of us have grown up learning that it isn't nice to talk about sex. Maybe we can joke about it (even lie about it) with our friends, but we've had little experience in talking deliberately and directly about our sexual feelings, concerns, and wishes. "Nice ladies" don't talk about it, and "real men" don't have to.

People often have trouble deciding which words to use. They may know what they want or don't want, but they are not sure what to call it. Words like *fellatio* (stimulating the penis with the mouth) and *cunnilingus* (stimulating the clitoris with the lips and tongue) do not fall lightly from the tongue. (Many of us don't even know how to pronounce them.*) Yet, on the other hand, people often feel uncomfortable using the com-

*They're pronounced "cun-nah-LIN-gus" and "feh-LAY-shee-oh" or "fell-AH-shee-oh."

136

mon four-letter words—they sound dirty and make us feel that we are somehow lowering the dignity of our relationships by saying them. What a choice! We can sound as if we're in a doctor's office or up a dark alley—or not talk at all!

Even if we know and feel comfortable about the language, we are still often blocked by our feelings of guilt from telling our partners what we want. Somehow, we feel selfish for asking for what we want. Some people feel that they should take whatever they get with gratitude—that they shouldn't ask. Sex should be spontaneous, they believe, not directed.

Nonsense. We learn to walk, to talk, to drive a car—and to make love. We can't do any of these totally spontaneously—we learn them and we learn them best from partners. Joy in sex comes from both giving and receiving what each of you wants.

Okay, so you're convinced. But you're still uncomfortable about talking about sex with your partner. What can you do? That's why we're here. We know that it's uncomfortable, and we have some suggestions and exercises for you. But before we get to that, let's make one thing clear. It's all right for you to be uncomfortable. Your partner is probably uncomfortable too. Few things that are important come easily, especially talking about sex with someone you love. So try to get comfortable with your discomfort. You've had years of training to be uncomfortable about sex, and it's going to take a while for you to start getting comfortable with it. But if you want to get more out of—and put more into—your and your partner's sexual fulfillment, you've got to start thinking about what you want and letting your partner know about it. So take a deep breath, get uncomfortable, and let's go.

WHEN AND HOW TO SHARE

First of all, let's look at the times when it's *not* best to try to share your feelings and wishes about your sexual relationship. There are the times when you are angry at your partner. It may have nothing at all to do with your sexual relationship, but something has come up—whether it's her criticism of your mother, or his criticism of your new outfit—and you're angry. The temptation may be great to tell him or her what's on your mind and then throw in ". . . and furthermore, you were lousy in bed last night!" It's tempting to use sex in an argument. There are few places people are more vulnerable than in their sexuality, and it can hurt to hit them there. And moreover, when you're angry, about sex or about anything else, you are

137

in no frame of mind to work together on improving your mutual sexual enjoyment. So wait till things cool down.

We also suggest that you not bring the subject up late at night when your partner wants to get some sleep, or at any other time or place when you don't have the time or privacy to talk about your relationship in detail.

Not that you should have long, exhaustive discussions of your sexual relationship all the time. That can become tedious. The long talks are only to be held when they are necessary, when problems have accumulated, or on special occasions when you want a general review of how things are going. These discussions should be as casual and as relaxed as possible. Indeed, they can occur in the midst of making love. Certainly, stormy discourses are not desirable during intercourse, but brief comments, reactions, and even nonverbal suggestions via gestures can be very useful during love-making.

But when longer chats are desired, they should occur in places and times when you have privacy, when you have each other's attention (turn the T.V. off, please), and when the mood is appropriate for a positive discussion.

Choose a time when at least one (or, ideally, both) of you is feeling mellow toward the other—when you have had fun together and are more or less relaxed. As we suggested in Chapter 7, an excellent time and place for an initial comprehensive review of your sexual relationship would be during a brief (or extended) stay away from home—your self-directed motel therapy.

But if worse comes to worse—compromise on time, place, or circumstance. Some couples wait year after year for "the right moment." But the circumstances never seem quite right, so they keep putting it off until death does them part. Do it now.

HOW TO SAY WHAT YOU WANT
WITHOUT SCARING OFF YOUR PARTNER
OR YOURSELF

There you are—sitting facing each other with your coke/beer/ martini in hand, ready to have "the talk." You're wondering what's going to explode, what surprises are in store for you, what offense you will be charged with, and what counteroffense you can think up.

But that's not the way to improve things. No one is on trial. There's no blame to be trotted out. Instead, the session should be aimed at exploring how each of you can give more to the other, not at who can accumulate the biggest and best complaints against the other.

We know that it usually is much easier to get your partner to increase doing those things you like than to decrease doing those things you don't like. So before you sit down with your partner, think over your sexual relationship and decide:

1. What do you like that is already happening?
2. Is there anything that you do together that you would like more of, more often, or for longer periods of time?
3. Is there anything that you haven't been doing that you wish you did do?
4. Is there anything you're doing that you wish you were doing in a different way?
5. Is there anything you would like to see changed in terms of timing (that is, when you do what and for how long)?

While you're answering all these questions, you might focus on an even more general question: What do you want? More clitoral stimulation, more variety in positions, more time at this, less pressure at that? This will help you to feel more prepared for the actual discussions. You might even want to review your answers to the questionnaires in Chapter 8 in order to refresh your memory about some of your sexual likes and dislikes before you start your talks with your partner.

If you're kind of worried about how all of this might go, you might want to try practicing it by yourself first. Read through the rest of this chapter. Then pick any of the exercises that you feel unsure of. Find a quiet, comfortable place where you're pretty sure you won't be bothered. Try to imagine the scene as if you really were in it with your partner. Then, imagine yourself saying just what you would like to say to your partner. This will work even better if you practice saying all this out loud.

Evaluate how you felt about what you said. Did you feel nervous or uptight, or were you pretty comfortable? If you were kind of uptight, imagine the scene again and try saying the lines out loud a few more times. The first few times you try this out, imagine your partner responding very positively to your statements or request. Once you are completely comfortable with this type of rehearsal, you might even imagine your partner not responding positively, for example, turning down a request you make. Prepare some non-hostile statements for dealing with a negative response, just in case you get one. But remember, you do have a right to make your request (just as your partner has a right to turn you down). Try not to let a negative response make you feel bad or that you were wrong to ask. Once you've practiced by yourself through, it will be much easier for you to deal with in real life.

When you feel you've got the basic idea of this kind of rehearsal, you can change the scene you practice to deal with any number of types of situations. Practice making requests, practice receiving requests (some of which you want to do, some of which you don't), practice giving feedback to your partner on what you liked or didn't like, and practice receiving feedback. In fact, you can set up almost any situation you might run into in real life—from asking someone over for a drink to discussing some sexual activity—and rehearse it by yourself before it actually occurs.

Once you've finished rehearsing and are pretty confident that you can proceed without scaring off your partner or getting too uptight yourself, you're ready for the real thing: your talks.

Exercise 1: Setting the Ground Rules

Let's assume that you haven't had many positive experiences talking with your partner about sex. Therefore, we suggest that you start with a fairly structured system of talking with each other. The purpose of this system is to provide a pattern of communication that (1) reduces the chance that either of you will do damage to the other by what you say, and (2) increases the chance that each will hear—really hear—what the other has to say.

Since both you and your partner will have to agree to the ground rules before you proceed, it's important that you each read and agree to abide by what follows.

Here's the system:

1. Set aside approximately one half hour, no more than once a day, to talk about the topics we will suggest in the following exercises. Each day, work on each of the exercises in turn. Neither of you should try to coerce the other into going beyond the half hour unless you both want it.

2. Flip a coin and decide who will be the "first speaker."

3. The "first speaker" chooses one of the topics suggested in the following exercises and tells the other person how he or she feels about the topic. The first speaker's presentation should focus as much as possible on "I" comments—that is, statements that begin "I wish," "I feel," "I would pre-

140

fer," or "I am." He or she should avoid speaking for or describing the listener by using "we" or "you" statements like "we ought to," "you should," "you always want to," and so on.

4. While the first speaker is talking, the other person should listen attentively but should not interrupt for any reason except to ask the first speaker to repeat something that he or she didn't hear or to ask for specific examples of what the first speaker is talking about.

5. After the first speaker completes his or her statement, the second speaker then summarizes what he or she heard the first speaker say. This gives both of you the opportunity to check out how clearly one of you is communicating his or her message and how accurately the other is hearing it. Wait until the feedback is completed before you react to its accuracy, pointing out any significant omissions or alterations.

6. Now the second speaker has his or her turn to speak for five minutes. He or she can either react to the first speaker's comments or introduce another topic from the following exercises. In either case, remember the rules: stick to your own feelings and "I" comments, and don't interrupt except to ask for clarification of words you don't understand or can't hear and for specific examples. Again, the first speaker should try to repeat what the second speaker has said.

7. Continue taking turns for up to a half hour. After you're through, take a few minutes to discuss each exercise and decide on any modifications of the ground rules you both agree upon. You may, for example, agree to put off responding to each other's presentations until the next session, so that you will each have time to think it over. Also, if you seem to be accurate in hearing each other's comments, you can discontinue doing Step 5.

Exercise 2: Getting Comfortable with Your Discomfort

The first topic to discuss is your feelings about talking about sex with your partner. Use the format from Exercise 1 to answer the following questions. Both of you should take turns answering each question in turn. After both of you have responded to each question, you can spend a few minutes talking over your responses. But don't get bogged down on any one question.

> □ How comfortable or uncomfortable do you feel right now about talking over your sexual relationship with your partner?

141

- How do you feel about your previous attempts at discussing sex, both with your partner and with other people in the past?
- What problems have you encountered in trying to communicate your sexual feelings and wishes?
- What are your fears and hopes for the discussions?

Don't forget: If you feel that there is some humor in your discussion, recognize it. Humor—as long as it isn't hostile toward your partner—will make your discussions much easier.

Exercise 3: Choosing Your Words

When it comes to discussing sex, many people find themselves speechless. But if you are going to talk about sex with your partner, you will need to use clear, explicit language to make sure that you are getting your messages across. As we've pointed out, there are two vocabularies for describing sexual anatomy and activities. There's the proper technical vocabulary, and then there are the four-letter words.

The problem with the technical words is that they sound technical. Fellatio and cunnilingus don't *sound* like much fun. In fact, most technical words for sexual activities sound like diseases. On top of that, even if you know the words, how the heck do you pronounce them?

On the other hand, there are the four-letter words. They're clear, and some have a nice erotic flavor. But they are objectionable to or uncomfortable for many people. But that's all we have. Which are you going to use?

The purpose of this exercise is to determine which words you want to use and for you to get more comfortable with them.

Below is a list of words describing sexual anatomy and activities. The first thing we'll ask you to do is go over the list. Decide which words are most acceptable to you. There are no "right" words—just choose the words for each item that you want to use.

The best way to get over the resistance to using the words you have chosen is to repeat them over and over again, starting in the least embarrassing setting. So start by reading them out loud when you're alone. Say them clearly and at a normal volume. Repeat the words you are most uncomfortable with several times, first to yourself and then out loud.

Next, meet with your partner and, using the dialogue format from Exercise 1, discuss your feelings about sexual words and how you feel about using these words with your partner.

Finally, you and your partner can practice using the words with each other—read the words you like out loud. Repeat them several times each. Then put them in sentences, such as "I like to hold your boobs while we're screwing" or "I get real juicy while I'm stroking your cock." Come to some agreement with your partner about what words both of you would like to use in your sexual vocabulary.

Here's the list. We've started each category with the technical word. Feel free to add your own words to the list.

ANATOMY

Arousal	Buttocks	Erection	Hymen
Horny (men)	Ass	Boner	Cherry
Juicy (women)	Behind	Hard on	Maidenhead
Turned on (both)	Buns		
	Butt		
	Fanny		
	Keister		

Breasts	Clitoris	Menstruation
Bazooms	Clit	Curse
Busts	Button	Period
Bosoms		That time of the
Boobs		month
Tits		On the rag
Knockers		

Nocturnal Emission
Wet dreams

Orgasm and Ejaculation	Semen
Come	Come
Cream	Cream
Shoot	Jism
Get off	Load

Penis	Vagina and Vulva	Scrotum and Testicles
Cock	Beaver	Balls
Dick	Box	Nuts
Pecker	Cunt	Family jewels
Peter	Hole	
Prick	Mound	
Rod	Pussy	
Shaft	Snatch	
Tool		
Wang		
Yosh		

ACTIVITIES

Turning On	Fellatio (Mouth on penis)
Necking	Blow job
Petting	Blow
Make out	Frenching
Play around	Going down
	Sucking
	Giving head

Mutual Mouth-to-Genital Stimulation

69

Anal Intercourse (Penis in anus)	Masturbation (self-stimulation)
Cornhole	Beat off
Greek style	Jack off
Dog fashion	Jerk off
Buggery	Hand job
	Whack off

Analingus *(mouth to anus)*	*Sexual Intercourse or* *Coitus, Copulation*
Rimming	Ball Bang Fuck Screw Lay or get laid All the way Jive Getting nooky
Cunnilingus (Mouth to vulva and clitoris)	
Going down Eating out Muff diving	

Exercise 4: Reviewing Your Sexual Relationship

Now that you have some ground rules established, have gotten more comfortable with your discomfort, and have chosen a vocabulary, you are ready to move into discussing your sexual relationship. Use the ground rules from Exercise 1, with modifications on which you both agree. Discuss the following topics:

1. Begin by talking about how you feel about the good parts of your sexual relationship. (Come on now, there's probably a lot more right than wrong in your relationship.) It's important to recognize the positives and to build on them.

2. Next, share some of the ideas you have about how you can improve your *own* behavior in bed. Do you recognize any needs of your partner that are not being met? What more do you feel you can give your partner?

3. Now, take turns answering each of the following questions. (Try to stick to the ground rules from Exercise 1.) What would you like from your partner that you are not getting or not getting enough of? Are there things you wish your partner

145

would do more often, for a longer period of time, or in a different way? What, specifically, do you like about your sexual relationship? What would make you like it even more? Are there positions in intercourse or other forms of stimulation that you would like to use more often? Are there any problems in the timing of sex, events that lead up to it, or what happens after? Use the questionnaires in Chapter 8 as a basis for some of your discussion. You listed there many of the sexual activities that you like (and don't like). Emphasize the positives, that is, what you enjoy or *would* enjoy in your sexual activities. They're easier to accomplish.

4. Listen to your partner's requests. Then respond to them by letting your partner know whether his or her requests make sense to you. Are they news to you? How reasonable do you think they are—can you manage them? For each of you, take your time in telling your partner how you feel about his or her requests. Throughout this sharing, try to remember that you are going to get something out of giving your partner those things that he or she wants. The things that each of you ask from the other should be seen as requests to enhance your mutual joy, not as put-downs. Try to establish some procedures or signals you can use in your discussions in order to show your partner that you feel that your requests from each other are beginning to sound more like hostile put downs and so that they can be stopped.

5. If your requests run into an impasse, you may want to move into negotiations. We discuss how to go about negotiating differences in Chapter 10. You may also want to set up a contract with each other based on your discussion. (In Chapter 10, we discuss setting up contracts.)

Exercise 5: Reacting to the Treat Yourself Programs

This final exercise should be repeated regularly as you follow through the Treat Yourself programs in the remainder of this book. Each time you and your partner finish a chapter, or an exercise from one of the chapters, discuss what you got out of it. Take the time to listen to each other. Use the format from Exercise 1, with any modifications you both agree on. Here are some questions you can use to guide your discussions. What, if anything, did you learn that was new that relates to your own and your partner's sexual needs and feelings? What reactions did you have to the exercises? Did they help? Did they make you feel uncomfortable? Was there anything else that you or your partner could have done to make the exercise go more smoothly? How are you reacting to working on improving your sexual life?

This "reaction" period is crucial for evaluating how well your Treat Yourself program is going. But we believe that an evaluation period is equally important for any of your sexual activities. Sex should not just end with an orgasm. Spend some time after you complete your sexual activity just holding each other and talking about what you liked or enjoyed, or perhaps what you'd like to try next time. Laugh with each other. Many people never feel closer than during the period right after sex. Get all you can out of the experience by sharing it with your partner.

A FINAL WORD

The exercises in this chapter were designed to help you improve your sexual communication. We hope you understand that you don't have to use fancy technical words in order to communicate effectively. You don't have to use common four-letter words, either, if you don't want. In fact, you don't have to use *any* words. Sign language is fine. Facial expressions and gestures can get across many subtle messages. What matters is that you are able to communicate your feelings and wishes in such a way that your partner understands you. You get what you ask for.

Ten

Agreeing with Each Other: Goals and Contracts

George and Melveen were working on a "do-it-yourself sex program." The program was aimed at trying to help Melveen achieve orgasms during intercourse. George was getting a little frustrated because it seemed to him that things were moving too slowly. He loved Melveen a lot; that was no problem. But somehow it seemed to him that all the exercises that he and Melveen had been working on were going nowhere. At least, George didn't understand where they were going. And on top of it all, Melveen told him that they wouldn't be able to have intercourse for some time.

Poor George. It's hard to blame him for being upset. After all, it seems that George was really in the dark about what was going on. He didn't understand the sequence of exercises or the fact that they operated on a graduated step-by-step basis. He didn't understand that, in his and Melveen's situation, intercourse was delayed for some very important reasons, but that when they did try, it would result in greater satisfaction for both of them. In fact, it seems that George really wasn't all that clear about much of the program—where they were going, or how they were trying to get there.

Poor Melveen. With George's not being clear about what's happening and why, he's probably that much less willing to cooperate, and that makes everything more difficult for Melveen.

Let's look at this from a different angle. If George and Melveen were in two separate businesses and they wanted to complete a deal important to both of them, would they leave the terms of the deal vague? Would they be indefinite about what each business had to deliver, and about when and where? Would they be unclear about what the final product of the deal was supposed to be?

We doubt it—on all of these counts.

Now, we're not trying to suggest that Treat Yourself programs should be run the way a business is run, especially if that suggests to you that it should be run rigidly, or without warmth and affection. On the other hand, your Treat Yourself program is bound to be more successful if everything about it is as clear as it can be—to you and to your partner—and if you both agree *in advance* about what the program will consist of. A core set of guidelines for all the Treat Yourself programs, then, is:

1. Be clear.
2. Plan ahead.
3. Decide what you will work on.
4. Decide how often and where.
5. Meet the needs of both partners.
6. Negotiate with your partner.

GUIDELINES FOR SETTING UP A PROGRAM

Be Clear

You have a choice here, although we don't think it much of a choice. The choice is between being vague and nonspecific—both to yourself and to your partner—and being as clear as possible. As a general principle that cuts across the rest of the guidelines—from setting goals to negotiating—we urge you to be specific and clear. What you're after and the program you use to attain it will then not only be better understood and more concrete but you can be sure that you will bring about more cooperation from your partner.

Plan

Try not to spring any surprises, especially on your partner. Often the surprises are negative and make everyone concerned unhappy. ("Oh, no dear, we can't make love tonight. As a matter of fact, we may not be able to do it for a couple of weeks.")

There are at least a couple of ways in which you can ensure that you've planned if you're doing a Treat Yourself program. The first is: Read this entire book, or at least the first three parts, before you start the program. Also, read in advance the chapter describing your specific program. Do all of this with your partner; be sure that he or she has had the opportunity to do the reading, too. Then you'll both be prepared for what is to come.

Second—you guessed it—*communicate*. Discuss your problem and your program in advance with your partner. Follow the guidelines we suggested in Chapter 9. This way, your partner will know what to expect, and you will be aware of what he or she thinks and feels about what is coming.

Decide What You Will Work On

Can you imagine being all dressed up but having nowhere to go? This is exactly the sort of thing that will happen if you are not clear about what your goals are. It is important to have your program clearly and systematically established, but it's also important to be clear about what the goals of the program are. Obviously, if you and your partner aren't clear about what the goals are, you may not know when you get there.

What we urge you to do here is *be specific*. Establish what you want to accomplish in terms that are as clear as possible. Try to think of your goals in terms of the specific behaviors you want to change. Thus, rather than saying that your goal is to "feel better when you have sex," you might be as specific as this: "My goal is to have orgasms at least 75 percent of the time I have intercourse. At least half of those times, the orgasm should be during the time my partner's penis is inside my vagina."

If the above sounds a little *too* concrete, think of it this way. Neither you nor your partner will be unclear about what you want. There should be no disagreements between the two of you as to whether or not you've achieved what you agreed on. You'll know when you can finish the Treat Yourself program. And, if you find, at some time after your program is over, that you've fallen back below the goal you've set for yourself, then you can redo parts of the program to get you where you want to be.

Actually, there are two types of goals that you should set. The first one we might call your "ultimate" or "terminal" goal—what you want to achieve and the way you want yourself and your partner to be at the *end* of the program. The example we gave above on orgasms would illustrate that type of goal.

But there's also another type of goal—what might be called an "intermediate goal." As we've mentioned previously, we want you to think about your program in terms of small steps. This is because the ultimate goal is easier to reach if intermediate goals—steps on the way to achieving the ultimate goal—are set in advance. Each of these intermediate goals should be as specific as possible. These, too, should be established as specific behaviors. For example, one step in a program for helping a man delay his ejaculations in intercourse might be the intermediate goal of "masturbating for fifteen minutes without ejaculating." The point here is that these intermediate goals are not ends in themselves but graduated steps along the road to accomplishing the ultimate goal.

How, you might be wondering, am I going to know what goals to establish for myself? First, go through this book. After pinpointing what your problem is, and after reading the chapter particularly concerned with that problem, establish an ultimate goal. That is, put together what you know about the problem after reading the book with what you feel about it. Write down the way you want to be after the program is over. Whether it has to do with frequency of orgasms or with erections, state it as clearly as you can. Use specific behaviors in writing out your goal so that it will be as concrete as possible.

Things will be a little easier with intermediate goals. As you'll notice, in each of the Treat Yourself programs, specific steps are described. Each step has a specific goal associated with it; that is, we tell you just what you need to be doing in order to move to the next step. Or you can use these as your intermediate goals. If you would like to change any of these goals, we suggest changing them only in a more cautious direction. Thus, if the book suggests that the intermediate goal is to masturbate for fifteen minutes without ejaculating, we think that, if you are going to change this, you should do so by increasing the time to twenty minutes. This will then give you more (rather than less) practice with that specific step. Since each step in the Treat Yourself program is related to each other step, the goals we set are perhaps the minimum necessary in order to ensure successful accomplishment of the following step.

Decide How Often and Where

These are small details. But you'd be surprised how often small details can turn into big problems unless they're handled in advance. So decide how often per week you and your partner want to work on your program. This may be two to five times a week, depending on how you and your partner handle the negotiations. Decide how long each session should last. We suggest between thirty and sixty minutes. You might want to increase this somewhat if you're really enjoying yourselves, but try not to fall below thirty minutes per session. Decide in advance where you're going to work on the problem and at what time. This will save some possible hassles at the start of each session. If you want a little variety, you might want to vary the time and the place. But try to do this well in advance, and make changes only if both of you are in full agreement.

Now we don't want to make this whole process seem too concrete. But we are convinced that clarity in these matters really will enhance your program. Try to stick with what you decide for at least one week. Then, you might renegotiate any of these details at the start of the following week if you want to add to or cut down on any aspect of the program. (We'll discuss this in more detail in the section of this chapter that deals with contracting.)

Meet the Needs of Both Partners

It's your program and we really want you to succeed. And one of the best ways to ensure your success is to see that both you *and* your partner achieve some pleasure and satisfaction during each session. If you stay focused solely on your sexual needs to the exclusion of your partner's during the entire program, your partner is bound to become increasingly frustrated. Find out what he or she wants, and help your partner achieve it. We think that this is an important goal for each session. Thus, for example, when you and your partner finish a particular session focused on *your* needs, take a break and then focus on your *partner's* needs. Not only will this help motivate your partner to continue, but the fact that he or she will know that his or her needs are going to be met at the end of the session might be quite stimulating (and far more fun) for both of you.

152

Negotiate with Your Partner

This is the way everything we've discussed so far in this chapter comes together. Obviously, we believe strongly in the values of clear communication between people. Of course, this never comes automatically. If you feel that you and your partner don't communicate well and clearly, well, then, join the club. Few people are completely satisfied with the way they communicate with their partners. Most of us have plenty of room for improvement. All of us have to work on communication for it to get better. Again, it's just not something you and your partner should expect to do automatically, no matter how much you love each other. And poor communication doesn't necessarily mean at all that your partner doesn't love you. Communication is a skill, and, like any skill, it has to be learned. And you have to continue to work on it once you've learned the basics.

Since we've discussed communication in some detail in Chapter 9, we'd like to comment on only one aspect of communication in this chapter—the art of negotiation. Since this chapter deals with how you and your partner can come to agree with each other on your Treat Yourself program or on any aspect of your sex life, a crucial part of this agreement is using your communication skills to negotiate with your partner. Therefore, we'd like to outline briefly how you'd go about negotiating with your partner to make some changes in your sex life or to develop a Treat Yourself program.

1. Identify whom you're going to negotiate with. This may sound silly, but think about it. Especially in the event that you don't have a regular partner, this becomes particularly important. When you have a choice, try to select someone who will be supportive and cooperative and willing to participate. Of course, if the person has none of those attributes, then at the negotiation stage (rather than halfway through the program) is when to find out.

2. Be clear about what you want. Decide what you want in advance, when you're thinking about your own goals, desires, and needs. We'll discuss this process of determining goals in more detail a little later in the chapter.

3. Think about how your partner may feel. Before you even start negotiating, try to put yourself in your partner's shoes, if only for a few minutes. How do you think he or she feels about the problem? Try to get a good sense of what your partner feels and how he or she might react to you. This means that you will be prepared in advance to handle any of your partner's objections.

153

4. *Compromise.* Be prepared to give a little. This might mean having a "fall-back" position if you run into trouble in your negotiations. For example, if you want to increase the frequency of intercourse between you and your partner, you would want to take into account his or her wishes if they differ from yours. This might mean that you and your partner might eventually agree (with some flexibility, we hope) on a figure somewhere between what each of you wants. After all, negotiation means arranging for an agreement of terms by discussion, and the terms might not be exactly what either you or your partner wants.

5. *Set the stage.* We don't mean that you have to go into too much of a routine here. But if the topic is important to you, don't push it at the wrong time—for example, during an argument, when either you or your partner is tense about something, or when you can be easily interrupted. Pick a calm, quiet, comfortable, private, and friendly time and place. This will make things go much more smoothly.

6. *State your goals clearly and specifically.* When you finally do start the discussion, be clear and be specific. (This does not mean that you should be cold or distant.) Be sure that your partner understands how you feel about the current situation and what you would like to do about it. Also, be clear about intermediate or short-term goals and ultimate or long-term goals.

7. *Find out how your partner feels.* If he or she doesn't volunteer the information, make sure that you get it by asking questions. Find out about any reservations your partner might have, whether he or she feels put down, and whether he or she seems eager to agree or somewhat reluctant. If your partner appears reluctant, try to get at the source of the reluctance. If you don't explore all this in advance, you can almost be sure that some of the reservations will pop up again later during the program—when neither of you needs them.

8. *Don't blame.* It's pretty easy to get into this trap. Make sure that you don't. No matter who has the problem—at least on the surface—try not to start shooting off the guns about whose fault it is. Not only will this not help (you're both going to have to work on it anyhow), but it could destroy the program before it even starts.

9. *Give to get.* Make sure that you don't present the problem as a problem that exists only for you. It's likely that both of you will have to change some aspect of your behavior so that both of you can come to enjoy your sex lives together. Thus, negotiate out an agreement that clearly specifies what you will

do for your partner and what he or she will do for you. This mutual giving will ensure that each of you gets something that each of you wants out of the arrangement, and that both of you will increase your enjoyment.

10. *Formalize your agreement.* When you and your partner finally decide on a goal and on a program, put it in writing—don't leave it to the hazards of memory. Develop a contract. If you think that this makes the whole deal sound too formal and unlike the kind of arrangement you'd like with a sex partner, read ahead.

CONTRACTING

As you can see, there are really a number of things you have to consider when developing and following through on a Treat Yourself program. Make it easy on yourself, though. Don't subject yourself and your partner to unnecessary squabbles or differences. Put it in writing.

Two key principles in Treating Yourself are cooperation and mutual support. We want to be as sure as possible that this mutual support continues throughout the program. We've already discussed a number of guidelines that will help you in developing your program. Putting this in writing in the form of a contract is just the best way for making sure that these guidelines are followed.

As we've suggested before, contracts have numerous advantages. They help to structure the program for you and your partner so that you know what is coming and what is expected from each of you. Contracts provide clarity, both in terms of your goals and in terms of the specific steps and exercises in your program. Contracts can specify time limits, so that you and your partner will know that each step won't go on forever. Your contract can specify in which activities you and your partner will engage so that both of your needs are met and you're both rewarded. Contracts can even enhance openness and communication between you and your partner by requiring open discussion of what each of you wants and expects before it is written down.

Perhaps the most important characteristic of a contract is that it really sets up a commitment on your part and your partner's to follow through with the program. This is really an indispensable part of the Treat Yourself program. Like any other attempt to change behavior, whether you're trying it yourself

155

or using professional help, the commitment that one makes to the process is crucial in determining the result. Contracts help you to establish that commitment by setting it down clearly for you and your partner to see.

When we talk about contracts, we don't mean the typical sort of New Year's resolution that so many of us make ("This year, I will lose fifteen pounds"). Usually, these resolutions are, at best, goal statements and are often pretty vague. But, apart from being more clear and specific, contracts not only specify ultimate goals but describe intermediate goals, the steps taken to reach those goals, and all the details involved in those steps—including what, when, and where. Contracts can also specify, as we will illustrate later, rewards that you and your partner can give each other for finishing particular steps.

Our contracts are mutual. That is, the contracts you use should include the rewards and benefits for each party. Although the primary concern of a given program may be the problem of one person, reaching the ultimate goal means specifying what each will receive from the program.

Similarly, these contracts can be developed between partners or with oneself. There are obvious advantages to the use of contracts between two people; we've already described many of these. But, if your program basically involves your working alone, these contracts are also very important. In fact, the reasons for self-contracts are the same as those for mutual contracts. They establish a commitment to proceed, set a focus and a structure, describe specific steps and goals, and help to motivate you. So if you're doing it yourself, by all means, please don't ignore the use of these contracts. They are just as important for you alone as they would be if you were working with a partner.

Of course, contracts can be oral or written. We encourage you, though, to use written ones. This is because oral contracts too often lead to misinterpretation or to just plain forgetting. When it's in writing, you can't miss it. Provide a copy for you and one for your partner so that both of you can be sure about your agreement. If you do use an oral agreement, we suggest that it be limited to an initial agreement—say, to read this book and discuss it until a formal plan and specific goals can be agreed upon. Then, these goals should be put in writing.

Types of Contracts

There are several different types of contracts you might use during your Treat Yourself program. We will illustrate each of these so that you can copy them and use them in your own program. If you want to, you can make modifications in the contracts to better fit your needs. Just make sure that you negotiate these with your partner. We are presenting here some models for your use, and although we'll try to anticipate some of the details that cut across all of the programs, you will probably have to make changes in the wording to suit some of the individual needs of your own program.

Remember that all of these contracts should be negotiated between you and your partner. Remember, also, that they can be renegotiated if they turn out to be unsatisfactory. In fact, once you achieve a specific goal, the contracts will have to be rewritten in order to provide for the following step in the program. Finally, if you are at a step in your program that is not explicitly covered in one of these contracts, develop one yourself. Just be sure to include all of the basics: goals, steps, rewards, what you and your partner can expect to give and to get, location, time, and place.

The first contract we will present is a general-purpose contract. This form can be used to specify numerous dimensions of a Treat Yourself program, regardless of what the program is focused on. The next several contracts deal specifically with aspects of the Treat Yourself program that cut across most of the problem areas and that can be used in several different types of programs. The last is simply a scheduling form on which you and your partner, or you, can write down the schedule of sessions that you would like to follow.

GENERAL-PURPOSE CONTRACT

We've prepared a form that you can use to specify several dimensions of any program. This is called a General-Purpose Contract because it is not intended to deal with any specific part of your program. Instead, it can be used to clarify and structure just what it is you hope to accomplish (both the ultimate and the intermediate goals), how you're going to do it, and when and where you're going to do it.

You'll notice also that we have a place on the contract for you to indicate a "reward." We think that this adds an important dimension to your program, and that it can enhance your success. As we suggested in Chapter 7, if you're working with a partner, decide jointly on something you'd both like. Then, when you finish a session, when you finish a particular step, and/or when you finish a week of sessions, give yourselves the reward. This reward can be anything. It could be something sexual that is satisfying to both of you. It could be another type of activity that you both like—for example, going out to dinner or to a movie. It could even mean that both of you put some amount of money in a jar. Then, at the end of the week, when you finish your exercises, you can use that money to buy your-

157

selves something that you really want but that you probably wouldn't have purchased otherwise—some little luxury.

If you're working on a Treat Yourself program on your own, the same principle applies. Give yourself a reward when you finish a particular segment of your program.

Either way, be sure to use this reward system. It will enhance your motivation, make it all more fun, and even make it all more worth the effort.

GENERAL-PURPOSE CONTRACT

Participants: _____ and _____

Ultimate Goal: _____
_____
_____

Specific Treat Yourself Program: _____
_____

Specific Steps:
1. _____
                                    Achieved/Not Achieved
Goal for step 1: _____
2. _____
                                    Achieved/Not Achieved
Goal for step 2: _____
3. _____
                                    Achieved/Not Achieved
Goal for step 3: _____
4. _____
                                    Achieved/Not Achieved
Goal for step 4: _____

No. of sessions per week: _____ Location of sessions: _____
Length of each session: _____ Time period: _____
What you will do for your partner: _____
_____

Rewards:
1. After sessions: _____

2. After completion of steps: _____
_____

3. At end of week: _____
_____

Other specifics (e.g., how you will compromise; how you might re-negotiate; what to do if one partner can't fulfill terms of the contract, etc.):
_____
_____
_____

Agreed and Signed:

_____   _____
(You)   Date (Your partner)   Date

THE FIRST-STEP CONTRACT

In most of the Treat Yourself programs, you begin by trying to decrease the fears and anxieties associated with your sexual activity. This involves discussions, perhaps relaxation exercises (we will describe these in Chapter 11), and, above all else, the realization that you don't have to push yourself to perform. Thus, as a first step, you and your partner might establish a contract that you will not engage in any sexual activity; that you will practice relaxation exercises; that you will not even masturbate; and that, for purposes of closeness and to satisfy the "skin hunger" that you both might feel, you might lie together and hold each other, but not proceed any further. An example of this form of contract, which you can modify and write out to meet the specific needs of your situation, follows:

> We agree not to engage in any mutual sexual activity for the next seven days. During that period, Dave will practice relaxation exercises, using the method of deep muscle relaxation. Dave will do this every night from 8:00 to 8:30 in the family room. During this time, Molly agrees not to let the kids bother Dave. Molly also agrees to let Dave know if she plans to masturbate, and Dave agrees to encourage her to do this. At the end of the week, we agree to go out to Michel's (a restaurant) as a special reward.

THE "EROTIC PLEASURE" CONTRACT

All of your Treat Yourself programs involve some Erotic Pleasure exercises. These are described in detail in Chapter 14, so we needn't duplicate that discussion here. Briefly, Erotic Pleasure consists of a series of massage exercises to help relax you, to stimulate all of your senses, to enhance your sensuality, and to take your focus off genital sex as "the only form of sex." These exercises are divided into two types: "Erotic Pleasure 1," which specifically excludes genital contact, and "Erotic Pleasure 2," which culminates in manual and/or oral genital contact. Both of these exercises specifically rule out intercourse (that comes later).

A different contract should be used for each exercise. However, for purposes of illustration, we shall provide one model that can be used for both exercises; you can change the words around to modify the contract for the other technique. Note also that this contract contains a sentence that allows either or both partners to avoid any part of the exercise that is objectionable. We urge you, however, in the spirit of mutual cooperation, to try as much as you can before you decide you don't like it. Of course, before each contract is written up, you will be negotiating its contents. Be sure that you explore with each other what you feel about its provisions. If there are some activities that you're sure you won't like, simply exclude them specifically in the contract.

Following, then, is an example of the Erotic Pleasure contract:

> Morton and Jill agree to practice Erotic Pleasure 2 for a period of up to ten days. We will do this for a period of one hour, in bed, at night (after 10 o'clock). We agree to follow the exact steps as outlined in *Treat Yourself to a Better Sex Life*. However, if either of us dislikes one of these steps, we agree that we will not use it, and the other partner promises not to put down the one who dislikes the specific step. We will practice the technique until Morton can maintain an erection for at least fifteen minutes straight, and then for three sessions in a row when he can do that with Jill's help. We will have sessions at least every Monday, Wednesday, and Friday. We also agree to sleep in the nude and to hold each other for at least fifteen minutes before going to sleep. We will not attempt to engage in sexual intercourse during this period.

THE ALL-THE-WAY CONTRACT

When you have reached the point where your problem is under control, and you can achieve what you want to achieve *except* for intercourse (because you haven't tried yet), you're ready for your All-the-Way Contract. You can decide whether or not you're ready by reviewing the chapter dealing with your specific problem. If you meet the criteria for moving to the next stage (involving intercourse), then you know that you're right on the mark.

The All-the-Way Contract is an important one because it sets the conditions for, and the type of, intercourse. And with most sexual problems, this is the final step. You may tighten up or slip a little, but, if you've completed all the steps up to this one, with a little practice, you *will* make it.

There are several dimensions that you will want to include in this contract. You have to decide on the position; you have to decide on how much and what kind of movement (for example, the Treat Yourself program for ejaculation includes a step with the woman on top and no thrusting by either partner); you have to decide on variety and what to do after you're successful (for example, variations in position); and you even have to deal with what to do in the event that the attempt at intercourse isn't completely successful.

Don't rush this step, either in your contract or in your actual program. Take it easy, and you'll be successful. It takes time, it takes patience, but is it ever worth it.

Following is an example of an All-the-Way Contract that was used for a man who had been having difficulty in maintaining erections:

Jon and Marge agree to attempt intercourse beginning on Sunday. Marge will masturbate Jon until he has a firm erection. Then, Marge will get on top of Jon and insert his penis into her vagina. Marge will gently move up and down to maintain the erection. She will wait for approximately five minutes and then will remove herself and masturbate Jon until he has an orgasm. Following this, Jon will masturbate Marge until she has an orgasm. If Jon loses his erection before or during intercourse, Marge will stimulate him orally until he gets his erection back. We will try this for three nights in a row, in bed, and at the usual time of our session. If we are successful for three nights in a row, we will treat ourselves to a movie and dinner. Also, after three straight days of success, we will set up a new contract so that both of us can achieve orgasm during intercourse.

A contract that was used by a woman who had been experiencing problems with vaginal tightening (spasms) prior to orgasm started out as follows:

We agree to try intercourse with Harry on top. Harry agrees to penetrate slowly and carefully. If he can insert his penis all the way, he will do so, but he will not do any thrusting. Wilma will control the thrusting and let Harry know whether or not to continue. If no penetration or only partial penetration occurs, we agree to stop attempting intercourse for that session and to masturbate each other to orgasm.

A SCHEDULE

The last contract really helps you only to specify your schedule for engaging in your program. This is most frequently used along with one of the written contracts, since the General-Purpose Contract contains all of this information. Thus this supplements the written contracts in those cases in which all of these details are not spelled out, or if you want to see them in a clearer form. This contract includes a space in which you can note down whether or not you completed the session and how successful it was (just put a check in the space regarding whether or not it was not successful, particularly successful, or completely successful). This will allow you to monitor at a glance how well the program is going. This form can be extended to include as many days as you need.

We see these contracts as very crucial parts of all of the Treat Yourself programs. Don't move ahead without specifying in your contract exactly what you're moving toward and how you hope to get there. Use one of these contracts or some modification of one of them no matter what kind of a program you're involved in, even if it has something to do with changing the frequency or type of sexual activity and with trying something new.

161

SCHEDULE

Week	Day	Date	Location	Activity/step	Finished	Degree of Success			Reward Given
						Not successful	Completely successful	Partially successful	
1	Sunday Monday Tuesday Wednesday Thursday Friday Saturday								
2	Sunday Monday Tuesday Wednesday Thursday Friday Saturday								
3	Sunday Monday Tuesday Wednesday Thursday Friday Saturday								

Obviously, not all of the contracts you could possibly write are included here. This means that, in many situations, you'll have to write your own. Just go ahead and do it. Use these contracts as models, include the types of details we've suggested in these contracts, and write up a brief contract covering whatever other details are necessary for you to achieve your specific goals.

We hope that you won't see these contracts as a nuisance. We don't want these contracts to be seen as some goal in themselves, the master (or mistress) of your lives. But we do think that they can be used flexibly and creatively to enhance your Treat Yourself programs and, therefore, to enhance your sex lives.

Eleven

Forget Your Troubles, Come on Get Happy

You can learn to relax.

You're probably happy to hear that. But you're probably also wondering: "What does that have to do with sex?"

A good question. The answer is: Maybe everything; certainly a lot.

Being nervous, anxious, or fearful just doesn't go with good sex. All kinds of things can happen—if you're a man, you might not be able to get an erection or you may come too rapidly; if you're a woman, your vagina might tighten up or you may not be able to have an orgasm.

We've discussed this before, but, because of it's importance, it bears repeating: Sex and tension don't go together. Now the tension could be a result of any number of factors. You could be "a nervous person," that is, you kind of feel tense a lot of the time or repeatedly, at least, when you're in a certain kind of situation (e.g., meeting people, prior to sex, at work, and so on).

You could be experiencing what we call "performance anxiety." This means tightening up, feeling nervous, or worrying excessively because you want to be "good" in bed ("perform" well). You, of course, might not even be aware of this, but when you do think about it, this performance anxiety might be a key factor in your problem.

Another type of anxiety or tension could come as a result of specific, but temporary, situations—a bad day at work or at home; a spat with a friend, your spouse, or the kids; too many bills and not enough money; a particular deadline; and so on. Any of these could create enough tension to spoil your day, and, at least temporarily, ruin your sexual pleasure.

You can learn to overcome most, if not all, of these sources of tension by engaging in a few simple exercises. These exercises will help you become more relaxed, no matter what the reason for your tension. These exercises are intended to be used before you begin any of the specific programs for treating yourself that we describe in this book. The two areas—relaxation exercises and specific sex programs—go together. The relaxation exercises are intended as a direct attack on anxiety. The specific Treat Yourself programs are more of an "indirect" attack. That is, they help you to overcome your fears by leading you through a series of sexual exercises on a step-by-step basis. Thus tension related to each step along the way is reduced by practicing behavior (the sexual exercise) that is stronger than, and overcomes, the anxiety.

The exercises in this chapter are intended to help you overcome anxiety and tension in any situation, not just a sexual one. Thus, if you are experiencing fear, tension, or anxiety in regard to your relationships, your job, or your family, these exercises should help you to become more relaxed in those situations too.

The one guideline that we have here, is that in order for these exercises to be effective, they must be *practiced*. You can't just read about them and expect to feel more relaxed. Work on them and spend some time on them: You'll emerge as a more-relaxed person.

ARE YOU ANXIOUS?

Anxiety, tension, and fears (we're using the words interchangeably here even though there are technical differences) mean different things to different people. The one common dimension may just be that you usually know it when you've got it, although it may show up in a variety of ways. You can actually experience anxiety in one or both of two primary ways: the way your body acts (or reacts), and the way you think and feel.

You can usually tell most clearly that you're tense when your body acts up. Your heart may pound. Your mouth could get dry. Your stomach might feel all tied up in knots or as if it had "butterflies." You might break out in a cold sweat or feel dizzy. You might even throw up or have to urinate or move your bowels.

The second way that you might experience tension is in the way you think or feel. You might just sort of feel that something's wrong or you might feel a little uncertain—just subjectively feel a sense of foreboding. All these could be signs of tension. You might be thinking that you're not going to make it, that you won't be able to get an erection (performance anxiety), or that you're really not a capable or competent person. Any of these can produce tension or anxiety.

At any rate, the signs of tension and anxiety can show up in how you feel, in what you say, and in what your body does. If you're not really clear about whether you have tensions or anxieties, there's one more thing to check. Most people tend to *behave* in certain ways in order to deal with tension, either by avoiding the feared situation or by plunging into that situation in order to try to overpower the anxiety. For example, if you experience even some slight anxiety (which you might not even be totally aware of) about engaging in sexual activity, you may try to decrease that anxiety by avoiding sex. That will only make it more and more difficult and more tense when you do try it. Your anxiety could even turn into a full-blown phobia.

On the other hand, if you try to cope with the anxiety by forcing yourself into the feared situation, that might not work either. The fear or tension might be stronger than the potential relaxation produced by the sexual activity, and you could then have difficulty functioning in the way you want.

Now if you're not clear about how anxiety shows up in you or about the part it plays in affecting your sexual behavior, first, review the part of the questionnaire in Chapter 8 dealing with "Your Feelings: Anxiety." Then try the following exercises.

This exercise can be used to see whether or not you are relaxed right now. Find a private place and time without the likelihood of interruptions. Sit or lie down and focus your attention on any part of your body that seems to feel the tightest or the most tense. Don't relax it; just pay attention to it for several seconds. Now, in your thoughts, go through other parts of your body and compare them with the tense part and with one another—arms, shoulders, stomach, buttocks, back of the neck, head, legs, and feet. Are any as tense as the first part? Could any parts be more relaxed? Think about how those

166

tense parts of your body feel and how they would feel if they were relaxed.

Also, check your breathing. Are you breathing slowly or quickly? Are you taking deep breaths or superficial ones? What parts of your body are moving when you breathe? You might even want to take your pulse. Count the number of times your pulse beats per minute. (Use your second, third, and fourth fingers to feel for your pulse under your wrist.) Make a note of your pulse rate so that you can compare it later. If at any time it is much faster and you haven't just been exercising, the increased pulse rate could be a sign of increased anxiety.

The point of this exercise is simply to pay attention to different parts of your body in a way that you might not have before. Do this at different times, perhaps in different places. This will begin to give you an idea of how your body expresses anxiety. Since we'll be presenting exercises to reduce anxiety, getting an idea of how you feel *before* you do the exercises (e.g., tense parts of your body, pulse rate, tight or jittery stomach) will give you something to compare with *after* you complete them. You'll be able to evaluate how successful the program has been in reducing your anxiety.

Another way to evaluate your tension and anxiety that you can use to determine the success of the relaxation program is to use the following exercise: Comparing how you feel in one situation as opposed to another. Imagine a scale—or a long line on a continuum—ranging from 1 to 100, with 1 equaling complete relaxation and 100 equaling the most feared situation you can think of. The scale would be broken down into steps of, say, ten points, with each ten points representing an increase or decrease in the anxiety you might experience in a different situation. The scale could be illustrated thus:

Increases ——————→

Complete   ANXIETY   Peak

Relaxation ←————— Decreases   Anxiety

| 1 | 10 | 20 | 30 | 40 | 50 | 60 | 70 | 80 | 90 | 100 |

In order to find out what anxiety means to you, imagine the most fearful experience that you could ever think of—whatever is most horrible to you and what would produce the most tension you could even dream of. This would be 100 on the scale—peak anxiety. Then, think of a scene that would produce total calm—say, lying out on a beautiful beach in sunny Hawaii, listening to the breaking waves—or whatever else would be particularly relaxing. Consider this to be a 1 on the scale—complete relaxation. Now, compare the way you would experience the 1 with the 100 situation. How would you feel, what would your body be doing, what would you be thinking in the total calm versus the peak-anxiety situation? This will give you an idea of the way you tend to react in two completely different situations, one in which you're relaxed, the other in which you're extremely nervous.

Now think of other parts of your life that could produce tension: fighting with a spouse, a visit to the doctor or dentist, not finishing a project but having to present it to your boss or to your teacher, and so on. Think also of some relatively relaxing situations. Concentrate on how you would feel in those situations—whether your heart would be pounding, whether you'd be sweaty, whether you'd be telling yourself, "I hate this" or "I can't do this." Then put all of those on the scale, according to how much anxiety they produce (e.g., meeting someone new might be a 30, going to the dentist might be a 60, going to a friend's house for dinner might not be too bad, say, a 10). This will give you some basis for evaluating both how you feel and act in a variety of situations and, particularly, the different ways in which tension shows up in you.

Finally, turn to sex. Imagine the kinds of sexual situations you might find yourself in, imagine the kinds of activities you might engage in (or be asked to engage in), and imagine the partner or partners with whom you might have sex. (Use the questionnaire in Chapter 8 to help you list these situations and activities.) Think about how you would feel in those situations. Then rate them on the scale.

Take a look at your ratings of these sexual situations and activities. You should be able to get a sense of how you feel in each one, that is, whether you have physical reactions, racing thoughts, and so on. This will give you an idea of how tension and sexual behavior are related for you.

Second, you might be able to see which sexual activities are a problem for you because of anxiety. Although this scale is not intended as a precise scientific instrument, if you score any of your sexual activities higher than 25 or 30, then these might be areas that you want to work on—both by applying these relaxation procedures in those situations and by using one of the Treat Yourself programs.

If you have a regular sex partner, you might want to go through this exercise with him or her, with both of you rating yourselves. This would not only produce a greater understanding of each other but would also give you both the opportunity to communicate about what's going on with each of you.

Now you should have a clearer idea of how you experience anxiety and tension, and in what situations. The next step, of course, is learning what to do about it.

RELAX!

We are going to provide you with two proven methods for learning to relax. But before we do, there are a few things you might want to try that may help you relax in specific situations involving your sex life. If you've identified on the above scale some tensions related to sex, you might want to try one of these preliminary steps.

Talk About It

If you're feeling tense or uptight about a forthcoming sexual experience, and if you're comfortable enough with your partner, tell him or her about it. Let your partner know how you feel. This can have one or more of several effects. It might simply help you to discharge the tensions first by talking about it. It could start some communication going between you and your partner, possibly leading to a clarification of what each of you expects from the other. And talking about how you feel might lead to more support from your partner—physical and emotional—in a way that could help you relax right then and there. Use the questionnaire in Chapter 8, especially the part dealing with anxiety, as a basis for your discussion.

Exercise

If there are some situations, particularly temporary situations, in which you just *know* that you're going to be nervous, try exercise. The old joke about the man who does push-ups and takes a cold shower because sex is unavailable really isn't so farfetched. It can work. If you're feeling kind of tense, pick an exercise that's moderately strenuous—like swimming, jogging, bike riding, or, yes, even push-ups—and go to it. This kind of activity usually decreases anxiety, although you may have to exercise for quite a while (you be the judge) until you feel more relaxed. (Please: If you're over forty or haven't exercised in a long time, go slowly and be careful. You might even want to check with your doctor to see what he recommends about how much exercise you should engage in.)

Plan Moderating Activities

Many people have a hard time separating their work times from their fun times. If you've had a tough day at work, or at school, or with the kids, it's pretty easy to carry that over into your "fun time." And if your fun time involves sex, it's easy for that to get fouled up. So try planning some moderating activities—activities that will be a clear breakpoint between work and fun. This could be anything, including some of the physical activities we discussed above: watching TV, painting, reading, gardening, having a drink, or taking a shower. But whatever you choose, make sure that it's pleasing and relaxing to you. And make sure that you do it in a way that will clearly break up the period between work and play. You might even schedule these activities every day; if you do, you can always vary them so that you don't get bored.

Watch for High-Tension Situations

There may be certain situations that are going to produce extra pressure on you and hence make you feel more than usually anxious. These could be anything—related to work, friends, or school. But watch for these so that you can deal with them when they happen. In other words, these will be special times, and they may require special handling. If you just ignore them, they could just pop up later that day or night at a particularly inconvenient time. So use any of the methods described above or even combinations of them in order to deal with the tension.

Avoid Sex

This may seem like a pretty strange recommendation, since we've already said that avoiding a feared situation can often make the fear a little worse. And after all, isn't this book supposed to teach you how to enjoy—not avoid—sex?

Of course it is. And we think that you might be able to enjoy sex more if you don't force yourself into sexual activity when you feel particularly anxious or tense. If none of the above activities works, and you still feel uptight, that might just be the night on which you take a break. Be sure to discuss it openly with your partner so that he or she doesn't feel rejected.

Further, we're not talking about regular avoidance, just the once-in-a-while time when you are especially tense about something that's gone wrong during the day, and when the above suggestions don't work.

Finally, we don't mean avoiding sex if it's the sexual experience that's *producing* the problem. In that case, you will first need to use the relaxation exercises that we are about to describe and, second, possibly develop a complete Treat Yourself program to deal with the specific sexual problem.

If none of the above recommendations work for you, or if your anxiety or tension seems to be other than just a temporary reaction to some situation, then the relaxation exercises we are about to describe may be just what the doctor ordered.

Get Settled

There are two basic exercises we will teach you. The first might sound a little kooky to you, but it really isn't. It's a basic, simple meditation exercise developed by Herbert Benson, author of *The Relaxation Response*. Don't back off from this one because it sounds far out. It really works.

The second exercise is a deep muscle-relaxation exercise that you can use either along with, or instead of, the meditation exercise. It's kind of fun—and also very relaxing.

Both of the exercises have extensive research findings behind them showing that they are effective in helping people to relax.

Interestingly, you can use the same preliminary steps to get started for each of them. So, before you take the plunge, make sure that you've accomplished these steps.

1. *Find a quiet place.* Go to a place where there is no noise, or to one where there is as little noise as possible. It might be your bedroom; it might be somewhere outdoors (away from people); it might even be in a church or synagogue during the hours when there are no worship services. Make sure that there are no radios or TVs blaring. You want to turn off the world for a while.

2. *No distractions.* You might find a quiet place but still leave yourself open to distractions from the kids, the telephone (take it off the hook), from friends, and so on. Try to find a time when these distractions will be unlikely. If you want to practice at work, use the lunch hour, when no one is around.

3. *Get comfortable.* Find a position that is, first, "relaxing," and, second, that will allow you to remain in pretty much the same position for up to fifteen or twenty minutes. This

comfortable position is very important for both exercises. You want most of your muscles supported. If you're sitting in an easy chair but have no support for your head, you may be using your neck muscles unduly and creating a potential strain. Although lying down is okay, it wouldn't be our first choice. This is because lying down is far too conducive to falling asleep—and you do want to keep awake during the exercises. Some advanced practitioners of relaxation exercises use yoga positions—sitting in the cross-legged lotus position, sort of Indian style. If you're already into this, go ahead and use it. For those who are just getting started, you might want to stick with more-basic positions, and once you've got the whole process down pat, you can switch positions to any that you feel will produce more comfort.

4. *Learn to Breathe.* Well, of course, you already know how to breathe. You've been doing it for as long as you can remember, right? Obviously, breathing is a natural event, something you have little control over. Or do you?

We'd like to suggest to you that the way you breathe can really affect how relaxed you are, and that it can also have an effect on your sexual functioning. This is because breathing controls the flow of oxygen to the brain, and this can affect the way your body functions. Remember also that the way you're breathing can change when you become more or less relaxed.

The point here is that you can actually control your breathing and that you certainly can use the way you breathe to enhance your relaxation exercises.

BREATHING EXERCISE 1: COORDINATING BREATHING AND HEART RATE

Inhale and count the number of times your pulse beats up to the point at which you stop inhaling. Write it down. Although it might change, stick with this number. Then inhale once again, counting up to this number. Hold your breath for one half of the number. Then, exhale again to the number. Then, hold for one half the number. Repeat this for a few minutes. You should begin to feel some harmony between your pulse rate and your breathing. Continue this exercise until you do, but not for longer than nine or ten minutes as starters. You should begin to feel better all over.

BREATHING EXERCISE 2: DEEP ABDOMINAL BREATHING

Get into a comfortable position with all body parts supported. (For this exercise, lying flat on your back is a good position.) Close your eyes and begin to breathe slowly, inhaling through the nose and exhaling through the mouth. Put your hand on your lower abdomen (right below your navel) and focus on how your abdomen feels as you breathe. Use your abdominal muscles to push your hand up when you inhale and down when you exhale; push in with your hand to encourage yourself to exhale in a stronger way than you're used to. When you breathe out, push out with your breath, almost as if you were blowing. The point here is to exhale more strongly and fully than you're used to doing. Take your time and practice this inhalation–exhalation process ten to twelve times. This exercise will help you to relax, particularly in the pelvic area. (It's also a particularly healthy exercise, since most of us, during our waking hours at any rate, tend to exhale much too shallowly.)

BREATHING EXERCISE 3: NOSTRIL BREATHING

Get into a comfortable position. Place the forefinger of one hand on the side of one nostril and the thumb on the side of the other nostril. Push your forefinger to close that nostril and inhale through the other to a count of 7, breathing deeply with the abdomen and the chest. Then, close the nostril with your thumb and open up the nostril that had been covered with the forefinger. Breathe out through that nostril, again to a count of 7. Repeat this five times. Then, switch the pattern, inhaling through the nostril covered by the forefinger, exhaling through the nostril covered by the thumb. Do this five times as well. You can repeat this pattern two or three more times, remembering to always inhale through one nostril and exhale through the other. Remember to breathe in deeply and to exhale fully, as you did in the abdominal-breathing exercise. Now that you've changed your breathing pattern, you're ready to learn to meditate.

RELAXATION EXERCISE 1: MEDITATION

If the idea of meditation brings forth visions of exotic East Indian Yogis, well, you're partly right. But you certainly don't have to be a Yogi in order to master the art of this exercise. Anyone can do it, and millions have.

This exercise has been used to help people relax, control blood pressure, ease migraines, and control several other problems. We think that it has great potential benefit for helping people to enhance their sex lives.

Believe it or not, if you've been following along with the

exercises in this chapter, you're almost there. That's because this exercise is simply an extension of the guidelines we've already given you.

Here, then, is a way to teach yourself to relax, using the method developed by Herbert Benson. Follow through on all of the "Getting Settled" steps we outlined earlier:

1. Find a quiet place.
2. No distractions.
3. Sit in a comfortable position.
4. Close your eyes.

Now, a few additional steps.

5. *Use a mental device.* You want to shift away from externally oriented thoughts. A major problem in this exercise is that most people's minds tend to wander, especially when they're just staring, so you should select one word or phrase. This can be anything: the words *one, calm,* or *love,* the phrases "I relax" or "all is good," and so on. You will use this word or phrase by repeating it over and over again to break the train of distracting thoughts. Keep your eyes closed while you're repeating this word or phrase. Also, pay attention to your breathing.

6. *Adopt a passive attitude.* Try to ignore any distracting thoughts. Don't worry about how well you're doing. The distracting thoughts will occur. If they do, and if you're not using your "mental device" at the time, return to it. You'll get the hang of it.

7. *Relax all your muscles.* Just using your thoughts, start at your feet and go all the way up your body to your face, focusing on and attempting to relax one part of your body at a time. Just relax your muscles in your mind and they will become relaxed.

8. *Put it all together.* Once you're ready, having prepared through all the above steps, breathe deeply through your nose, using both nostrils. Focus on your breathing. As you exhale, use your mental device, either repeating it out loud or to yourself. Breathe in and then out, saying your word or phrase as you exhale. Continue to breathe in any easy, natural way, using your word or phrase for anywhere from ten to twenty minutes. When you've finished, sit quietly for a few minutes, first with your eyes closed, and then with your eyes open. Don't stand up right away.

There you have it: a truly effective relaxation program. Do it once every day—or twice, if you can. Don't worry about how well it's going: It will eventually work. Also, don't worry about the fact that you have lots of distracting thoughts. After you've practiced for a while, the thoughts will diminish. Also, try not to practice this exercise during the first two hours after eating; it could interfere with the total process.

After some practice, you should begin to notice a feeling of calm during and after the exercise, and you should become generally relaxed. Some people report a general sense of well-being, or even a sense of ecstasy. But whatever you feel, it's bound to feel good.

RELAXATION EXERCISE 2:
DEEP MUSCLE RELAXATION

A second series of exercises, one that has been shown by a great deal of research to be effective in producing relaxation, is called "deep muscle relaxation." Not only can you use this as part of the previous exercise, but you can use it by itself. In fact, one of the advantages of this exercise is that not only can it help to develop a general sense of relaxation (as does meditation), but it can be used to relax yourself in specific situations—for example, before a stressful interview, when you go to bed (in order to help you sleep), before a date, or before some expected sexual activity.

The basic principle involved in deep muscle relaxation is a simple one: alternately tensing and relaxing your muscles while focusing your attention on each muscle group.

In order to see how this works, try the following. When you next read the word *now* (not this time but the next), clench your right fist as tightly as you can. Hold it for five or ten seconds and concentrate on how it feels. Notice the tension in your fingers, your hand, and your forearm. When you see the word *relax*, quickly let your hand go limp, falling by your side. Concentrate on how it feels then; you'll probably experience some tingling in your hand and arm, which will diminish in a few seconds so that your hand and forearm feel more relaxed.

Ready to try it?

Now.

Clench your fist, hold it for five or ten seconds, and pay attention to how it feels.

Relax.

Let your hand go limp and hang down by your side, and concentrate on how it feels, on the tingly sensation. Not bad, eh?

Believe it or not, you've just gone through most of the process of the deep-muscle-relaxation exercise. Remember that the basic principle here is to contrast the tension with the relaxation while focusing on the sensations. Once the muscles have been tensed, they relax much more readily. Some other guidelines:

1. Repeat your practice with each muscle group (we'll describe these below) at least two and up to five times, until it is relaxed.

2. Focus on one muscle group at a time.

3. Tense each muscle group for five to seven seconds, then relax for approximately thirty seconds before you try it again. If you develop a cramp, shorten the time to three seconds and don't tense your muscles quite so hard.

4. Use one or two sessions per day, spending ten to twenty minutes per session. Don't worry about the number of muscle groups you complete during one session, but always end the session after you've finished at least one group.

5. Keep your eyes closed to help you concentrate on each muscle group.

6. At the start of each session, practice the muscle groups you've already completed.

7. When you've finished relaxing several individual muscle groups (e.g., hand, arm, shoulders), you can practice tensing and relaxing the whole area; just repeat the relaxation exercise once or twice, relaxing that entire area, following all of the above guidelines.

This last guideline (#7) gives you a clue as to how this exercise can be used to produce relaxation at any given moment. By the time you've finished practicing with the individual muscle groups and also with the area muscle groups, you will be able to apply this method to your entire body at once. That's right. The goal of this exercise is to tense up all your muscles (or at least several of the major groups, which we'll illustrate below) at once, and, after doing that once or twice, to achieve total body relaxation in just a couple of minutes.

When you're ready to begin this exercise, follow all the "Getting Settled" guidelines: Find a quiet place with no frustrations; get comfortable; take some deep breaths. Also, loosen your belt, take off your shoes, and, perhaps, take off your glasses. Let your arms hang limply by your sides.

176

There are really four major groups of muscles, each of which has several individual muscle groups. What you should do is begin with the first major muscle group, work through as many of the individual muscles as you can in the first session, and then either end the session or continue on into the next group, depending on how much time you want to spend.

The goal for each individual muscle group is complete relaxation and absence of tension. When you feel that, it's time to move to the next group.

We will present each of the muscle groups in order. With each individual group, do what we illustrated previously with the fist and forearm: Tense up for five to seven seconds, and then relax and concentrate on the sensations. When you've completed all the muscles in a major group, review what you've done by tensing all the muscles in that group for five to seven seconds, then relaxing for roughly thirty seconds, and then repeating. This should produce a real feeling of relaxation in each group.

Whenever you're ready, begin. Just follow along in the order described below:

Major Group 1: Hands, Arms, and Shoulders.

1. Right hand and forearm. Repeat the exercise we demonstrated.
2. Right Biceps. Flex biceps by bringing your right hand to your shoulder; tense the muscle, hold it . . . RELAX.
3. Right shoulder. Shrug as if you wanted to touch your shoulder to your right ear; hold, RELAX.
4. Left hand and forearm. (Repeat as for right hand, biceps, and shoulder.)
5. Left biceps. (Repeat as for right hand, biceps, and shoulder.)
6. Left shoulder. (Repeat as for right hand, biceps, and shoulder.)

Now, tense and relax all of the muscles in this major group: hands, biceps, shoulders. Hold . . . *relax.* Repeat once or twice.

Major Group 2: Head, Neck, and Face.

1. Forehead. Wrinkle your forehead as if it were in a frown, or lift your eyebrows as if you wanted to touch the top of your head.
2. Eyes. Close your eyes tightly.
3. Nose and cheeks. Wrinkle your nose; feel the muscles across the tops of your cheeks and lips.

4. Mouth. Draw the corners of your mouth back; feel the jaw muscles and the cheeks.
5. Chin and throat. Push your head forward to touch your chin to your chest.

Now, tense all the muscles in Major Group 2: forehead, eyes, nose, mouth, chin, and throat. Hold it for five to ten seconds, then *relax*. Sure it looks funny when you're all tensed up—but doesn't it feel good when you're through?

Major Group 3. Chest, Back, and Abdomen.

1. Chest. Take a deep breath, and hold it; tighten your chest muscles by squeezing your upper arms in to your sides.
2. Back. Take a deep breath and arch your back, pulling your shoulders up.
3. Abdomen. Suck your stomach in and tense the muscles—make it hard.

Now, tighten all the muscles in Major Group 3: chest, back, and abdomen. Hold; then *relax*.

Major Group 4. Buttocks, Legs, and Feet.

1. Buttocks. Tense these muscles; push your heels into the ground.
2. Right thigh. Lift your right leg until your foot is roughly eight to twelve inches in the air, tighten your thighs, hold it, and let your leg drop.
3. Right calf. Point your toe up toward your head and tense the calf.
4. Right foot. Because your foot can easily cramp, do this for only three seconds to begin with. Curl your toes toward the floor, tensing your arches.
5. Left thigh. (Repeat as for right thigh, calf, and foot.)
6. Left calf. (Repeat as for right thigh, calf, and foot.)
7. Left foot (Repeat as for right thigh, calf, and foot.)

Now, tighten all the muscles in this muscle group: buttocks, thighs, calves, and feet. Hold it . . . *relax*.

When you've completed all of the major muscle groups, you're ready to try complete muscle relaxation. Do this by tensing all the muscles in all the groups, holding for five to seven seconds, and then relaxing. Repeat once or twice. Pay attention to how you feel all over.

Ready?
Now.
Hold it.
Relax.

Go over your entire body: Look for muscles that might still be tense. Relax each part even more as you go over it. You will feel a deep sense of relaxation all over your body, a deep sense of calm. Just sit back for several minutes and relax. Enjoy it. Use these exercises—whenever you need to.

> Charles was never sure about whether he would be able to attain an erection. Although he was uncomfortable at first about doing this, he would spend a few minutes by himself before engaging in any sexual activity. During this time, he applied deep muscle relaxation just as we've described it here. He soon felt more relaxed and comfortable during his sexual activity, and he was able to achieve consistent erections.
>
> Martha's complaint involved vaginal spasms. She would tighten up so much that her husband wasn't able to penetrate. She engaged in a program of deep muscle relaxation that helped her relax considerably. But she wasn't able to have complete control of the spasms, so she used the muscle relaxation to prepare herself for a Treat Yourself program like the one described in Chapter 16. Within three weeks, the combination of relaxation training and the Treat Yourself program had completely eliminated the spasms.

Relaxation is a skill. You can learn it just the way you learn any skill. But, also like any other skill, you could lose it if you don't practice. We are convinced that this type of relaxation will be a tremendous boost in helping you to enhance your sex life. In fact, a few weeks of these relaxation exercises plus a Treat Yourself program might be all you need to overcome some specific sexual problem. But if you want to be sure that you can relax yourself in most situations after the Treat Yourself program is over, then we urge you not to stop practicing. The deep-muscle-relaxation program takes only a couple of minutes a day just to keep you in shape. The meditation program takes a little longer—say ten to twenty minutes. Either way, you have nothing to lose but your tension.

Twelve

Getting in Touch with Your Body

In many ways, every part of your body can be thought of as part of your sexual system. Just as one example, think of all the different ways you can be turned on—by touching yourself or being touched by others. You might get that very special feeling if your partner touches your ear lobe or gently strokes your thigh or the under part of your arm. You might be especially sensitive if your partner rubs your buttocks. And gentle playing with the genitals and the area around the genitals can be especially stimulating.

You've probably noticed throughout this book that we've said that we believe sexuality is an experience involving much more than intercourse, and more than genital stimulation. It is an emotional experience as well as a physical experience, and the physical part involves touching and stroking any part of your body and your partner's body that either of you enjoys, not just the genitals. Indeed, as we said earlier, we do not use the word *foreplay*. This is because "foreplay" seems to give the idea that the only goal of sex is intercourse, and that what you do before intercourse is only intended to prepare you for "the ultimate act."

We believe that this gives a distorted view of what sex is and can be. So we've tried to de-emphasize what we think is often the preoccupation with genitals and with intercourse that many people have. Instead, we've tried to illustrate the many ways in which sexuality can be expressed in ways that are fulfilling and satisfying to both partners.

On the other hand, we do realize that your genitals are—to say the least—important parts of your sexual equipment. And we also realize that it's pretty important for us to present some basic information so that you can have a clear idea of just how your genitals and other parts of your body function and how your partner's body functions. This will give you a well-rounded picture of the relationship between your body and your sexual functioning. Not only can we clear up any misconceptions about your own sexual functioning, but we can clear up any mistaken ideas you might have about how your partner's body works.

The way we'll do that in this chapter is to discuss briefly and illustrate both male and female sexual anatomy, the so-called "sex organs." Then, we'll illustrate just how your body works during sexual activity—what happens to you before, during, and after orgasm. (You might be surprised to see that males and females are quite similar in these respects.) We'll then give you a set of exercises that you can practice to help strengthen some very important "sex muscles." Finally, we'll take a brief look at your sexual anatomy in relation to your overall body and, particularly, to your thoughts and feelings about your body.

YOUR SEXUAL ANATOMY

Since many of our Treat Yourself programs refer to parts of your sexual anatomy, it seems to be a good idea to clarify just what parts of your body we're talking about. By "sexual anatomy," we are basically referring to the genital area, particularly the external genitals, because these tend to be more closely associated with sexual activity.

We realize that we've already said that your entire body is or can be part of your sexual system, and that it is unwise to focus only on the genitals when thinking about sex. So this probably seems like a bit of a contradiction. On the other hand, we don't want to *ignore* the genitals, either. Further, it has been our experience that many of the questions that

181

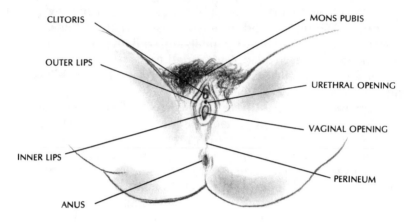

Figure 12-1.

people bring to us involve questions or misconceptions about the genitals. Of course, it would be impossible to do a really detailed presentation of general anatomy in this book, let alone to describe the physiology of sex. (For that, you can use some of the readings listed at the end of this book under the section dealing with general information.) But let's be sure that we all agree on what we're talking about when we do refer to specific parts of your sexual anatomy.

Females

Let's start with the external genitals. Take a look at Figure 12-1 and follow along as we describe the female sexual anatomy. If you are a woman, you might want to get a mirror and a flashlight, sit down and spread your legs, and then place the mirror so that, with the light from the flashlight shining on it, you can look into your own vaginal area and study it, as shown in Figure 12-2.

Together, the external genitals of the female are called the *vulva*. They include the most readily observable feature, the *mons pubis*, which is covered with hair in varying degrees, the outer and inner lips, the clitoris (pronounced with the emphasis on the first syllable), and the vaginal opening. Technically, the lips of the vagina are called *labia*. The outer lips, which are generally hairy after puberty (adolescence), vary in appearance from flat to bulging. The inner lips are located between the outer lips and are hairless and generally pink or dark looking. They might be large or small. These inner lips

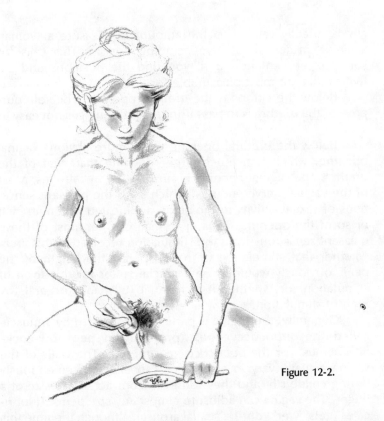

Figure 12-2.

enclose several structures: these are the clitoris, the urethral (urinary) opening, and the vaginal opening.

The *clitoris* is a key sexual organ. In fact, the only function known for the clitoris is to provide sexual pleasure. The clitoris is a small knob-like organ that contains thousands of nerve endings. It is extremely sensitive to the touch. The clitoris has a head (the glans, which is the exposed part of the clitoris) and a shaft (similar to that of the penis). Also like the penis, it becomes engorged (filled up) with blood and somewhat firmer during sexual excitement (the vaginal lips also fill up with blood during arousal).

The clitoris is covered by a small fold of skin. This fold, or hood, can be gently pulled back to expose the head of the clitoris, and each woman can decide whether or not she prefers stimulation with the hood pulled back or left in place, or whether she enjoys it both ways. The key point is that during sexual activity, a position should be found (whether in intercourse or in masturbation) that allows for the type of stimulation the woman wants. This is because clitoral stimulation usually is directly related to the amount of pleasure a woman achieves in sexual activity, including orgasm. This calls for some experimentation until you find the positions and activities that are most pleasurable for you.

Below the clitoris is the urethral opening. The sole purpose of the urethra is to pass urine. This opening is not easy to see.

Below the urethral opening is the more obvious vaginal opening, which is a much larger opening than that of the urethra. The vaginal opening is surrounded by muscles. Most of the vaginal nerve endings, which send the pleasant sensations of sexual activity to the brain, are located within an inch or so of the opening. Thus, a woman can get most of these pleasant sensations from the stimulation received in this area, whether that stimulation is from a penis (the length of the penis obviously wouldn't be a crucial factor for this form of stimulation) or whether it is manual (by hand) or oral (by mouth) stimulation.

Generally, the vagina is partially surrounded by a muscle called the *pubococcygeous* (pronounced pew-bow-cock-SIDG-ee-us), or the *pubococcygeal* muscle. The walls of the vagina actually vary in size. They can expand tremendously during childbirth, and they can even contract to the size of a finger. The vagina can adjust to almost any size penis. It lubricates (gets "wet") during sexual arousal, although the time this takes and the amount of lubrication vary a great deal.

It might be helpful here to briefly mention the *hymen*, a delicate membrane stretching across the vaginal opening. The hymen comes in many shapes and usually has one or more holes in it, whether the female has engaged in intercourse or not. The hymen may be so elastic that a penis might enter the vagina by stretching the hymen rather than breaking or tearing it. Thus, an intact hymen (or "cherry," as it is often called) is never proof of virginity; and one that is torn or broken does not necessarily indicate that a woman has had intercourse. Indeed, the hymen is often broken or torn in sporting activities long before intercourse is even attempted. If a woman is aroused and lubricating, there is likely to be little or no pain resulting from the hymen's being torn. Much of the pain, say, in a first intercourse attempt, may actually result from muscular tension, from clumsy attempts at penetration, or from an unlubricated vagina.

Between the vaginal opening and the *anus* is the area called the *perineum*. This area is surrounded by strong muscles, and the skin covering it is often erotically sensitive to stimulation.

184

Males

The primary external male sex organs are the penis and the scrotum. (The *testes*, or testicles, inside the scrotal sac, where sperm is manufactured, although outside of the body proper, are generally considered an internal sex organ.)

You might want to follow similar suggestions to those we made for the female. Use a mirror to examine your sexual anatomy, or look at Figure 12-3 and follow along as we describe the male sexual anatomy.

Like the female genital area, the area in the male above and around the penis is generally covered with hair in varying degrees after puberty. The penis, just like the clitoris, has a head, a shaft, and a hood. However, the hood (or prepuce or foreskin) is often surgically removed in a process called *circumcision*. There is no known difference in sexual functioning or pleasure with or without the foreskin.

The end of the penis is called the *glans* or *head*. This is the most sensitive part and contains numerous nerve endings. It is especially sensitive on the underside. Also particularly sensitive is the *corona* (or ridge or crown). At the tip of the penis is the urethral opening, through which both urine and *semen* pass. The semen, the fluid that males ejaculate, and the urine are manufactured in different parts of the body, but both leave the body through the same opening.

The shaft of the penis is generally hairless. When it is

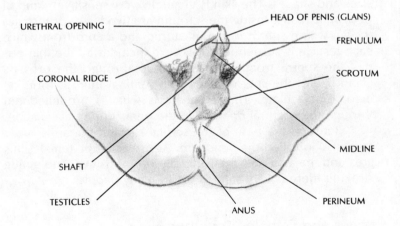

Figure 12-3.

185

flaccid (not erect), the penis hangs outside the body in a variety of positions. It might lean one way or the other or it might be slightly hooked. None of these variations is "abnormal."

The size of the penis varies from individual to individual. This is particularly so when it is flaccid or not erect; erect penises tend to be closer (but far from identical) in size to one another. Like every other part of the human body—including the female's vagina, the breasts of males and females, even our noses—these variations in size are as "normal" or as typical as could be. Indeed, what is most normal is the fact that there *are* variations. And these variations have nothing to do with masculinity, potency, or with the amount of satisfaction you can get from sexual activity.

The inside of the penis contains three cylinders made up of spongy tissue related to blood vessels. The lowermost of these cylinders contains a tube (the urethra) through which the urine and semen pass. With sexual excitement—either direct stimulation or thoughts—the spongy tissues in the cylinders fill up (are engorged) with blood. This is what brings the penis to erection. Despite the fact that this is often called a "boner," there is no bone in the human penis. Erection is purely a result of the filling up of the spongy tissues with blood. This process is called *vasocongestion*, a reaction that also occurs in the female when she is sexually aroused.

The scrotal sac is a pouch that contains several layers. It contains sweat glands and it also becomes lightly covered with hair at puberty. The scrotal sac—or bag—comes in all different sizes and shapes. The skin is generally very sensitive—kind of ticklish, actually. Inside the scrotum are two testes or testicles (balls), where sperm is manufactured and a cord from which each testicle is suspended. This cord includes a tube that carries the sperm from each testicle up through the prostate gland. Here, the sperm mixes with seminal fluid to form semen, or ejaculate. This ejaculate is what is propelled out through the urethral opening in the penis during ejaculation.

Between the base of the scrotal sac and the anus is the area of skin called the *perineum*. Again, as in the female, this area and the anal area are generally very sensitive, and gentle stroking there is very stimulating to many people.

Males and Females Together

One of the first things we learn as children is that boys and girls are "different." Well, as the French say, "Vive la difference!"

But the facts are that we are also very, very similar. In fact, it is likely that whatever differences in behavior there are between males and females are largely a result of what we learn as we grow up.

And although there are obvious physical differences between males and females (e.g., in the reproductive process), much of what we see on the surface as differences regarding sexual anatomy may not be so different after all. Indeed, much of male and female sexual anatomy is similar in origin and structure.

As we'll describe in the next section (and as we've already hinted at regarding vasocongestion, or filling up with blood), there are many similarities between males and females in the sexual-arousal process and in what goes on in our bodies during orgasm. Further, many of the physical structures of our bodies are homologous (similar): the glans or head of the penis and the clitoris, the outer lips (labia) of the female and the scrotal sac of the male, the urethral openings of both sexes, the perineum and anus of both sexes. Indeed, the fact is that both the external and internal sex organs of males and females are largely similar in origin and structure, although they may function differently for each sex.

It's important to remember these similarities, because knowing this may lead to increasing sensitivity between males and females as they engage in sexual activity. It may also clear up some of the mysteries and misconceptions between the sexes. And increased sensitivity and decreased misconceptions cannot help but lead to greater sexual satisfaction.

MAKING LOVE

In a general sense, all of us—male and female—respond in similar ways to sexual stimulation. There are actually far more differences between us as individuals in what turns us on than in how we respond to it.

Probably the commonest form of erotic stimulation is that which comes from touching. Although any given individual could be turned on by stimulating any particular part of his or her body, some parts seem to be more commonly sensitive. These are called *erogenous zones*. They generally include, in women, the clitoris and the labia or lips surrounding the outside of the vagina; in men, the head of the penis, particularly the underside; and, in both sexes, the anus and the perineum, the breasts, and the mouth—including the lips and the tongue-the ears, the buttocks, and the inner parts of the thighs.

Now, if you're not turned on by touching in all of these

areas, or if you have others that you find particularly arousing, that's okay too. Different strokes for different folks.

The point here, though, is that being aware of the zones that are stimulating for your partner (and that are stimulating for you) can really enhance your love-making. Finding out what turns each other on is an important clue to enhancing the joy of sex.

Of course, people can get turned on with all their senses. Certain odors, perfumes, and colognes, for example; sounds, such as a particular type of music; sights, such as certain articles of clothing; and fantasies and thoughts—all of these may be keys to enhancing your sexual pleasure when you can share them with a partner. Make your needs known—get them out on the table. Although there is no guarantee that your partner will always be willing or able to satisfy your every wish, good communication usually leads to an improved sex life.

Your Sexual-Response Cycle

As we mentioned before, people tend to respond in similar ways to sexual stimulation. That is, our bodies tend to react pretty much in the same ways. Although any given individual might differ on one or more of these dimensions—there are, of course, numerous variations—we'd like to describe briefly what happens to you and your body during sexual stimulation.

Much of the following material has been studied scientifically by Masters and Johnson, and has also been described by two sexologists, Drs. Herant Katchadourian and Donald Lunde. However, we won't go into all the physiological details of their research. Instead, we first will present a general description of some of the general characteristics, especially behaviors, that may occur during sexual activity. Then, we'll describe what actually happens to your body during sexual activity—the physiological changes during the so-called sexual-response cycle.

Remember: not everybody feels the same way. You, as an individual, might feel or act differently at any point along the line. But we think that it is helpful if you have an idea of some of the general patterns of response to sexual stimulation.

SOME GENERAL CHARACTERISTICS
OF SEXUAL RESPONSE
To begin at the beginning, once sexual stimulation starts (and what this stimulation is varies from person to person), a general sense of increased arousal (being "turned on") develops. This tends to be somewhat more gradual as one gets older. This preliminary stage is called Arousal.

There is a general increase in sexual tension as thoughts and feelings become focused on the sexual activity. This period can be quite pleasant in itself, and some people prefer to prolong it. Although most of the traditional sex manuals say that women take longer than men to become aroused, it is not really clear whether this is actually true for all or even most people. The most important principle here is: Be as clear as possible about how long it takes (and what you should do to help) your partner to turn on. Don't worry about how long it takes everybody else.

It's hard to describe all the variations in the way people react to sexual excitement. But there are some common patterns. When you are sexually excited, you may appear tense or tight all over. As excitement increases, you might reach out with your hands and feet as if to grasp something (such as a bed frame). There may be some involuntary muscle movement and even some pelvic thrusting.

It's likely that your skin will become flushed and that your mouth will feel kind of strange. For most people, there is an increase in salivation, although for others the mouth feels dry. There are likely to be some facial contortions; your heart may begin to pound and your breathing may become heavier.

We should note that these signs vary among different people and in the same person from time to time. In some, all of what we said is highly exaggerated; in others, few outward signs appear.

When this state of increased arousal reaches a point at which voluntary control is lost, orgasm is likely to occur. Orgasm is another experience that varies tremendously between people, and therefore it is difficult to describe in a way that covers every aspect for everybody. Any given individual's experience might be totally different from what another individual experiences, yet both experiences may be equally pleasurable and satisfying.

Of course, this is not to say that orgasms are the be-all and end-all of sex. They are not. A great deal of pleasure and fulfillment can be obtained sexually without the need for orgasm. Cravings for intimacy and for filling the need for "skin hunger"—to be held and touched by another person—as well as a range of other physical and emotional dimensions are needs that can be met without orgasms.

Orgasms are probably best described as a more or less explosive release of the tensions built up as a result of sexual stimulation and the excitement or pleasure that this stimulation produces. There is a push toward release that, after a certain point, the person feels helpless to stop.

Orgasms vary in individuals—from really explosive convulsions of the entire body to much more subtle movements and tension releases. Some general reactions might involve the body's becoming rigid, the legs' stretching out with the feet and toes twitching, facial contractions or grimacing, and some pulsing or throbbing of the genitals. The person might involuntarily grab at whatever is handy with his or her hands (be careful, don't scratch). You're likely to gasp for breath, and your whole body may twitch. At the point of climax, some people moan or mumble or loudly exhale. A variety of noises are quite common, ranging from gasping to laughing to crying.

In males, orgasm comes in two stages. The first is a sense that ejaculation is coming or is about to occur. This is called the point of *ejaculatory inevitability*, the point at which the male can no longer control the impending ejaculation. Incidentally, in males, ejaculation and orgasm are technically two different processes, although they usually occur together. Since women do not ejaculate, only the process of orgasm is similar in both sexes.

The second stage of orgasm in the male is an awareness of the contractions in the pelvic and genital area and of the fluid's (ejaculate) moving out under pressure.

In females, orgasm often begins with a feeling of almost being suspended. Sensations can usually be sensed in the clitoris, and these spread throughout the whole genital area. They can occur at varying levels of intensity, depending on the individual woman. The intense sensation changes to a feeling of warmth, often accompanied by involuntary pelvic thrusting and contractions. The whole experience is completed with a feeling of throbbing in the pelvic area.

For many years, there has been some controversy about the nature of female orgasm. As we noted in Chapter 4, recent research seems to suggest that there may be three types of orgasms. The first is called a "vulval orgasm" because it appears to involve the whole sexual area. This type of orgasm is most likely to occur from clitoral stimulation, manually, orally, or during intercourse. The second type of orgasm is called "uterine orgasm" and is said to mainly result from intercourse involving thrusting of the penis. The third type of orgasm is called the "blended orgasm" and is a combination of the other two.

On the other hand, some researchers believe that all of these types of orgasms may reflect different subjective experiencing of the same thing—orgasm. In fact, the "uterine orgasm" certainly cannot rule out direct or indirect stimulation of the clitoris prior to orgasm because of the thrusting of the male pelvic area against the woman's pelvic area. Hence, it seems reasonable, given the great sensitivity of the clitoris and the resulting satisfaction most women get from clitoral stimulation, to consider clitoral stimulation as a crucial part of the orgasmic process.

One thing can be said for certain: No matter what type of orgasm a woman experiences, none can be equated with more or less maturity, greater or lesser personality development, or more or less emotional "health." For every individual, it is her own personal sexual response and the degree to which she is satisfied with it that counts. In fact, maturity, personality development, and emotional health are not even issues for the woman who does not—or has not yet—experienced orgasm. Here, too, the major issue is the extent to which an individual is satisfied with her own sexual response, as well as the extent to which she wishes to change it.

Once the orgasm is over, the body gradually changes from sensations of tension to those of relaxation. In some people, this happens very quickly; in others, the changes come more gradually. You may feel a strong need to rest or sleep. Breathing and heart rate return to the way they were before sexual excitement began. The convulsions of the body become less intense and stop fairly rapidly. Your face is likely to change from a rather contorted expression to one of calm, perhaps with a slight smile on the lips. Many people simply laugh. Overall, the sensation is one of peace and comfort.

Other reactions vary. Some people may feel like urinating. Others want to go to sleep, to be left alone, or to be held. Some people feel hungry or thirsty. Others may like to talk, listen to music, or lie still with a feeling of contentment and warmth throughout their bodies.

Depending on a number of factors, this stage can last for only a few minutes to quite some time. For example, if one is tired prior to the sexual activity, one is likely to want to fall asleep at this point. Others may feel invigorated after a brief rest and may want to "do" something. Some may feel like continuing sexual activity, although this, too, varies with sexual appetite and, often, with age. For example, teenage males are much more likely than older males to be capable of more than one orgasm within a relatively brief period of time. This ability decreases considerably with increased age, however. Throughout their lives, females are often capable of multiple orgasms.

One of the most important parts of human sexual response occurs now—what some sex therapists call the Evaluation period. This is the period following sexual activity in which you react to and evaluate your sexual activity, especially how you feel about it. Was the experience pleasing for you, did it make you feel better about your partner, or do you have a "why did I do that" or "better I should have watched television" feeling? This evaluation period may occur immediately after sexual activity or may not occur until some time later. For some people, in fact, it may not occur at all. However, when it does occur, it generally involves more than how "expert" you or your partner was or how powerful your orgasm was. More likely, it will depend on your motivation for your sexual activity and how you feel about your sexual partner. In any case, it is this overall evaluation of your sexual activity that often plays an important part in determining how you feel about your sex life. If that overall evaluation is not too positive, you may want to take stock of what it is about your sexual activities that fails to make you feel good about them, and perhaps about yourself and your partner.

PHYSIOLOGICAL CHANGES

Along with the numerous changes in behavior such as we just described that might occur during sexual activity, there are a number of physiological changes—changes in your body—that also occur. Masters and Johnson have described these as four physiological phases of the sexual-response cycle: the Excitement Phase, the Plateau Phase, the Orgasm Phase, and the Resolution Phase. Males and females both tend to follow these generalized patterns, although there are some differences, which we shall describe. Much of what occurs in these phases can be understood in terms of two types of physiological mechanisms—the first is the swelling or engorgement of blood vessels and increased flow of blood into the tissues. The second is the increased muscular tension we described earlier.

It is important to remember that these are not lock-step phases that everyone goes through all the time in exactly the same way. In fact, many people go back and forth between phases, do not go "all the way" through the phases, or stay in one phase (for example, the Excitement phase) for a long time because it is particularly enjoyable. These merely are descriptions of what actually happens to your body (not your emotions) when you are in one of these phases. That is, they largely are automatic changes; you really can't control them. These are not steps that you have to go through in order to enjoy sex. But it might help to know what's going on in your and your partner's body so that you can recognize these changes when they do occur.

Excitement. Both sexes experience a hardening and erection of the nipples. Both sexes may experience a flushed skin,

192

although this is more common in females. Males develop an erection and, as the phase is prolonged, experience a tightening and elevation of the scrotal sac and the testicles. Females experience vaginal lubrication (the extent and speed of lubrication vary with age, occurring more slowly and less extensively with increasing age). The clitoris becomes firmer and enlarged. The inner part of the vagina expands and the inner and outer lips tend to swell and open up.

Plateau. This comes as a result of continuing sexual stimulation. For both sexes, heart rate and breathing will increase and blood pressure will rise. For males, the testicles will rise up even farther. The penis becomes fully erect. Fluid is gathering prior to ejaculation. The sensations here are said to be *premonitory* (giving warning) of ejaculation. The premonitory stage is very important because teaching the male to be aware of these sensations is a large part of the treatment for ejaculation problems, as we will describe in Chapter 17. A few drops of fluid may appear at the tip of the penis. This is not part of an ejaculation, but fluid that comes from the Cowpers gland, merely indicating increased sexual excitement. This fluid, however, may contain some living sperm, making withdrawal, even prior to ejaculation, somewhat risky as a birth-control method.

In females, the genital area is swollen with blood. The tissues in the outer third of the vagina swell or thicken. This is called the *orgasmic platform*. The inner lips change in color to a bright red or a deep wine color. The clitoris generally recedes under the clitoral hood.

Orgasm. Reactions from the previous stage are increased (heavy breathing, heart rate, etc.). There are contractions in the anus and, perhaps, involuntary sounds, grasping, and opening and closing of the mouth and eyes. There is a sensation of "letting go"—of release. Orgasm comes from the release of muscular tension. For males, the testicles have risen up toward the body and the semen begins to flow upward (the point of "ejaculatory inevitability"). Pelvic thrusting increases, and ejaculation results from contraction of muscles at the base of the penis. For females, the uterus and the walls of the vagina, especially the outer third (the orgasmic platform), rhythmically contract.

Resolution. Following orgasm, much of what was experienced previously reverses. The surplus blood leaves the genital area, heart and breathing rates slow down, and blood pressure

193

decreases. The erect penis and enlarged clitoris gradually decrease in size and the body begins to relax. Many people also experience moderate to heavy sweating.

A major difference between males and females occurs in the Resolution Phase. This is called the "Refractory Period"; it occurs only in the male. It refers to the fact that, after orgasm, males enter a resting stage before they can become sexually stimulated again—achieve erection and orgasm. The time necessary for this rest tends to increase with age and is nothing to worry about. Females do not have this refractory period, so they may be able to achieve multiple orgasms—orgasms coming one after another—with little or no resting period between.

As you can see, the sexual-response cycles of males and females tend for the most part to be very similar. In fact, the greatest differences in what actually takes place may be between individuals—no matter what their sex. As we noted above, these are only physical changes we described in the phases in this section. If we were to consider the total range of human sexual response—including feelings, behaviors, and physiological changes—we probably would expand these four phases to at least six that we've talked about: Arousal, Excitement, Plateau, Orgasm, Resolution, and Evaluation. And even these six phases will vary in how long or how intensely they occur in one or another person.

So don't be concerned if one or more of your reactions seem different from some of those we've described here. Try not to worry too much about what your physiological responses are. Most of those are automatic and out of your control anyway. We definitely don't want you to be preoccupied with these things to the exclusion of something far more important—enjoying yourself sexually and continuing to enhance your sex life.

EXERCISE YOUR SEX MUSCLES

There are certain sets of muscles in both males and females that are related to your sexual pleasure and that you can strengthen by some simple exercises. Like any muscle, these muscles need exercise. Strengthening them will give you better control over some important sexual functions. It may also increase blood flow to them and enhance sexual arousal and orgasm.

Actually, these exercises were originally developed by

Arnold Kegel to help women strengthen their pelvic muscles. But some creative sex therapists have been able to expand these exercises to produce benefits for men, also.

There are two sets of muscles involved in both females and males, although they have different degrees of importance for each sex. The two sets of muscles are called the *pubococcygeal* (we'll call them PC) and the *bulbocavernous* (BC) muscles.

In females, the PC muscles are the muscles that control the walls of the vagina. These muscles are important because you can increase your own pleasure during sexual activity by tightening and loosening them to enhance your experiencing of orgasm. Also, when you contract the muscles of your vaginal walls, you will create additional lubrication, just like that which would occur during the various phases of the sexual-response cycle.

The BC muscles in females are at the edge of the vagina. They are smaller than the PC muscles, and, in fact, these exercises will probably benefit the BC muscles to a lesser extent than they will the PCs. However, the BC muscles are important in certain situations in which the woman may experience spasms at the opening of the vagina during sexual arousal, thus making intercourse difficult. (This will be discussed in more detail in Chapter 16.)

In males, the BC muscles are at the root of the penis, inside the body and fairly close to the skin. You can feel them if you put your finger between the base of the scrotal sac and the anus. These muscles control the flow of semen, and therefore they are very important during ejaculation. The PC muscles in males are deeper inside the body and cannot be felt as readily by external pressure. The PC muscles help to control the flow of urine.

The relationship of the PC muscles to sexual pleasure in males may not be quite as directly related to sexual pleasure as it is in females, and the exercises are in an earlier stage of development for males so that their benefits are less clear. However, exercising these muscles may lead to increased control in ejaculation, to increased arousal, and, possibly, to more control of the penis during intercourse in a way that can be quite stimulating to the female.

Surprisingly, whether you are male or female, you can learn control of these muscles rather quickly. It takes a little concentration at first, but, with practice, you'll quickly get the idea.

Step 1. Just to get an idea of what muscles are involved, try this step first. Next time you have to urinate, try to stop and start the urine flow. It might even be better to attempt this exercise the first few times when you don't really have to urinate, because stopping the flow of urine can be uncomfortable. You might just *pretend* that you are stopping the flow of urine, just to feel how the muscles work. Do this one or two times, then empty your bladder. If you were able to stop and start your urine flow, you've got it made. You were using your sex muscles.

Step 2. Try this step again the next several times you have to urinate. Practice stopping and starting the urine flow two or three times, always being certain to empty the bladder after you've practiced stopping the flow two or three times. This "pulling back" that you feel when you stop the urine flow involves the very exercise you are now ready to practice when you are not urinating. If you are female, you will probably feel a slight tightening in the vagina. If you are male, you will probably feel a slight tightening between the testicles and the anus. Become aware of that feeling.

Step 3. Practice this pulling back or tightening and then the immediate release at least ten times in a row, anywhere from one to ten times a day. Because these muscles, like any others, tire when they are not in shape, start gradually and build up to ten times a day. You can do this at any time and in any place. You can be in public or at home, sitting or standing (while watching TV is a good time for regular practice). Only you will know what you're doing. For women, if you're not sure whether the walls of your vagina are actually tightening, it's easy to test. Insert one of your fingers into your vagina. You should be able to feel your muscles' tightening. If you don't, don't worry. Just keep practicing and you will be sure to gain control over your sex muscles. It may take a little practice, but these muscles will shape up. For men, in order to feel whether your muscles are actually contracting, put one finger on each side of the base of the penis (between the base of the scrotal sac and the anus) and you should be able to feel the strength and movement of the muscle.

Step 4. Once you can feel the muscles' tightening, try the exercise for six seconds in the following manner:

- □ Contract the muscles (count like this: "one thousand *one*").
- □ Hold (one thousand *two*).
- □ Hold (one thousand *three*).
- □ Hold (one thousand *four*).
- □ Give an extra squeeze (one thousand *five*).

196

□ Relax (one thousand *six*, or longer until completely relaxed).

When you're completely relaxed, go through this six-second set of exercises. Try to keep repeating the set five to ten times. If at first you can't hold for a count of five or six, start by holding to two or three, then build up gradually to the full five- or six-count exercise.

Step 5. Follow step 4, but now try to coordinate your breathing. Tighten the muscles while you're inhaling, hold it for a count of six, then exhale. For optimum benefits, practice twenty minutes in a row, twice a day. However, build up to this gradually. Start doing the exercise five to ten times per day. Add five sets every few days.

Step 6. Instead of holding the muscles to a count of six, tighten and relax them as quickly and as often as you can while counting to six. Start with five of these quick tighten–relax sets and work gradually up to 50 or so per set. Then, each day, you can alternate the slow with the quick exercises to add a little variety to your workout.

Step 7. Once you've practiced this to the extent that you are confident that the muscles are shaped up, cut down on the amount of times you do it per day. However, these muscles, like any others, need exercise. So continue to practice exercising your sex muscles from time to time, using eight to ten tightening–release sequences.

These exercises will not only help you gain more control over your sex muscles, but they are also likely to enhance the sensations that you experience during sexual activity. The time (just a few minutes a day) you spend at the start practicing this exercise is bound to pay off with increased enjoyment in sex, as well as with increased awareness of methods for controlling your own body. In addition, several of the programs that we will discuss in Part 4 will be using these exercises, so they definitely will come in handy when you Treat Yourself.

BODY IMAGE:
PUTTING IT ALL TOGETHER

Probably the most important fact that we could tell you about the human body has to do with the incredible range and variation in the way we look. As we mentioned before, the differences between people—the variations—are more common, typical, or "normal" than any single, idealized standard taken from *Playboy* or *Playgirl*. The range between individuals regarding parts of their body varies so much in size, shape, texture, and color that it would be impossible, and probably not helpful, to describe even such dimensions as "average" sizes or shapes.

On the other hand, we do realize that many people are concerned about the way they look, and the way they feel about how they look and how they want to look—their body image—can also affect the way they feel about themselves—their self-image. Hence, if you have a negative body image, you may also feel more negatively about yourself in general: Perhaps you feel that you're not as good a person as someone else who is perhaps a little more attractive, or has firmer breasts, or a larger penis.

Poppycock! Don't talk yourself into believing that. The fact is that a lot of what we think about our bodies is learned from comparisons with other people—often people who are glamorized in the movies and on TV. And since those comparisons are often with people whose special strengths may lie in attractiveness, they are grossly unrealistic. Further, purely physical comparisons tend to ignore the most important parts of people—their behaviors, their sensitivity, their caring and concern for others, their ideas and attitudes, and their personalities.

The truth is that most people are dissatisfied with some parts of their body. In some ways, this can be constructive. This dissatisfaction might lead us to take action to correct some problem—for example, using better grooming, losing weight, or exercising more to tone up muscles. All that is to the good.

But if this dissatisfaction is over areas that cannot be changed, then it could lead to problems in the way you feel about yourself and in the way you act toward others. In fact, it could lead to specific problems in sexual functioning—for example, the man who fears that his penis may be too small (too small to whom or for what?) becomes anxious about having intercourse with and being seen naked by a woman, which may lead to the development of erection problems.

So the first principle of body image is: Concentrate on what is positive about yourself—whether it's the texture of your skin, the color of your hair, or some other feature—and try to ignore or accept the fact that some parts of your body may never live up to your idealized image. In fact, we'd urge you to concentrate on what's best about yourself *as a person* and not dwell on what you perceive as negative, especially if it's something about your body that you just have no control over.

Review your answers to the questions in Chapter 8 regarding your feelings about your body and your appearance. Then try a series of body-image exercises:

1. Take a shower or bath. Rub soap all over your body, using your hands, not a wash cloth. Just relax and focus on your body.

2. Apply a lotion or oil all over your body. Focus on the way different parts feel to the touch. Which parts do you like to stroke and which ones don't you like to stroke? Which parts do you like to have stroked by others and which ones don't you like to have stroked by others?

3. Look at yourself closely in a full-length mirror. Examine all parts of your body closely from head to toe (use a hand-held mirror to see behind you in the full-length mirror.) Take different positions—sitting, standing, and so on. Move around a little. If you're a little uncomfortable with this exercise, start slowly. Just look at one part of your body the first day, two the next, and gradually increase the parts you look at until you can stand comfortably in front of a mirror, completely in the nude. If you're still a little uncomfortable, you might want to start this step by lying on a bed in a comfortable position, closing your eyes and relaxing. Then start thinking about each part of your body. Gradually explore all parts of your body with your hands. Examine each part of your body in detail in this way. Then, when you're ready and comfortable, begin to use the mirror to examine your body both visually and manually.

4. What parts of your body do you most associate with pleasure? How do you stimulate them?

5. What parts of your body do you like and dislike? Think about why. If there really is some part of your body that you're particularly worried about or that you may be having a problem with, speak to your doctor. He or she will be familiar with anatomy and physiology and, of course, with medicine and may be able to clear your problem up in no time. Try not to let your inhibitions stand in the way of talking to your physician. Believe us, your physician has seen every type, size, and shape of body you could imagine.

6. Now, think about what we described earlier—how did you learn those attitudes about body parts, and how constructive are they? Is this what you'd really like to believe or are you letting others influence you?

7. Is there anyone who likes you no matter how you look? Are there more people than just one who appreciate you for the way you are as a person?

8. Are there parts of your body that you especially like to have touched by your sex partner? Make a list of these and think about why you like them to be touched.

9. Are there parts of your body that you do not like to have touched by your partner? Make a list of these and think about why you don't like to be touched there. Does it have anything to do with what other people have told you is right and wrong?

10. Do something nice for yourself. Many of us have little things we do to make us feel better about our bodies or about ourselves in general. These may take only a short time or they may take quite a while. They may be sexual or nonsexual. They may have to do with eating, running, sitting, or relaxing. Make a list of these. Do one now. Do one or more of the others when you feel a little down.

Let's face it—nobody's perfect. We think that once you can acknowledge this to yourself, you're on the way to feeling better about your body and about your whole being. If there are parts of your body that you're not completely happy with, face up to it. You have a choice: Like yourself and accept yourself anyway, or hide away from sight—and maybe even from sex and from all the fulfillment that the combination of sex and relationship can bring.

We hope that you'll choose the first option. Get to know, appreciate, and accept your body. Learn to do the things that will make you feel better about yourself and you'll find it just that much easier to enhance the joy of an increasingly better sex life.

Thirteen

Turning Yourself On

Marion had a long bus ride every day from work to her home. She would use the time to read her newspaper or just gaze at the other people on the bus. Once in a while she would see a man on the bus who turned her on. She was particularly attracted to one of the bus drivers. Sometimes when this happened she would close her eyes and try to imagine what he would look like without his clothes on, and what it would be like to make love with him. From time to time she would get so turned on by this that she could hardly wait to get home and make love with her husband. On a few occasions when she got home first, she would simply go into the bedroom and stimulate herself to orgasm; when her husband got home, she was usually eager to go at it again with him.

Marion was obviously capable of a rich fantasy life and was also comfortable enjoying it. She also enjoyed stimulating herself to orgasm. Neither of these activities took away from her very satisfying sex life with her husband. Her fantasies about the bus driver were no threat to her love for her husband. In fact, in many ways, Marion's fantasy life and enjoyment from stimulating herself *added* to her sex life with her husband. How? The more Marion knew about and enjoyed her own sex-

201

ual responses, the more she could enjoy her sexual activities with her husband. What we fantasize in sex, and what we do when we stimulate ourselves, can tell us a great deal about what particular types of stimulation and ideas turn us on. In addition to enjoying our fantasies and self-stimulation in and of themselves, we can also translate what we learn about our turn-ons to improve our sexual activities with our partners.

And, since we have almost complete control over what we fantasize and how we stimulate ourselves, we can deliberately use these behaviors to overcome sexual problems with our partner. We'll discuss how to do this in almost all the Treat Yourself programs in Part 4 of this book.

However, before we discuss how to use your fantasies and self-stimulation, let's recognize that there are people who don't have sexual fantasies or stimulate themselves. In fact, there are those who feel that there is something wrong, immoral, or dirty about sexual fantasies and self-stimulation. Some people are particularly disturbed about women's enjoying these activities. Maybe, they think, it's all right for men to stimulate themselves and have sex fantasies, but "nice" women shouldn't. They should merely be responsive to what their male partners do with or to them.

We disagree. We believe that everyone—men and women—has the right to enjoy his or her own private thoughts and to take pleasure from his or her own body.

Further, although it *is* possible to enjoy sex by only responding to what your partner does to turn you on, usually you and your partner will enjoy your sexual activities more if you share responsibility for turning both yourself and your partner on. Your fantasies and self-stimulation patterns can help you learn how to get more aroused in your sexual activities with your partner.

Well, that's fine, you say, for people who feel comfortable with their fantasies and with self-stimulation. But what about those men and women who don't? And how about those who haven't stimulated themselves in years, or perhaps have never done it? And how about those people who aren't very creative in their self-stimulation or fantasy lives, or just don't fantasize very much? Fear not. Like most of our sexual behaviors, self-stimulation and fantasizing are learned. They are skills that we can work on and improve. The purpose of this chapter is to get you thinking more about your fantasies and your self-stimulation and to develop your skills in having better fantasies and more satisfying self-stimulation. We hope that you will then enjoy these activities more and also be able to use them effectively in overcoming some of the sexual problems we'll be discussing later in Part 4.

So let's talk first about developing your sexual fantasies. Then later in the chapter we'll discuss how to increase your enjoyment from self-stimulation.

USE YOUR HEAD: ENJOY YOUR FANTASIES

Getting turned on involves the complicated interaction of your mind and body. In fact, it isn't so much what happens to your body during sexual activity, but what you're thinking and feeling that really turns you on. Therefore, sexual fantasies can be an important source of sexual arousal to supplement what's going on with your body. And as you know, getting and staying aroused is not only pleasant but important for such physical reactions as getting and maintaining erections (for men); lubricating (for women); and having orgasms (for both).

We believe that there is nothing to be ashamed of or to feel guilty about in having sexual fantasies. Indeed, most men and women have sexual fantasies while having sex with their partners, as well as at other times.

The kinds of sexual fantasies people have are almost limitless, and the same person may have very different kinds of fantasies from time to time. These fantasies can be brief and simple—for example, just the fleeting memory of getting turned on at the sight of an attractive person earlier in the day. Or the fantasy can involve a long, detailed story with a large cast of characters and exotic settings. Your fantasies may include yourself, your partner, other people you know or have known, complete strangers, movie or television stars, celebrities, or characters out of fiction. You may be at the center of the action or you may be just an observer. In fact, your fantasies can include anything you want them to include, and they can be changed whenever you want to change them: from week to week or from moment to moment. Why not? After all, you are or can be the producer, director, the writer, casting director, photographer, star performer, and projectionist. It's your show.

Whatever your fantasies include, they can add a great deal to your sexual life. As we said, they can get and keep you aroused. They can suggest new activities to add variety to your "real" sex life and reduce your boredom with sex, if that's a problem. (We'll discuss in Chapter 20 the use of fantasies to avoid or reduce boredom.)

Fantasies can also lead the way to you and your partner experimenting with new sexual behaviors, such as new positions, settings, or activities. Of course, there are positions, settings, and activities that may seem just great in your fantasies but that just don't work out in real life. Perhaps they prove to be impractical, awkward, messy, or just downright uncomfortable. These fantasies may best be left in fantasyland. However, fantasies can often lead you and your partner to explore new and possibly rewarding sexual adventures.

At the very least, you and your partner can learn a lot about your sexual wishes from your fantasies. What you fantasize may be significant as well as how you portray yourself (and perhaps your partner) in the fantasy.

> While getting aroused with his wife, Collette, Cliff often fantasized about memories of an old girlfriend's performing oral sex on him. Once he was aroused, Cliff ceased to have fantasies, and he proceeded to orgasm through intercourse with Collette. Cliff felt embarrassed asking Collette to perform oral sex on him, and she had never offered. One day Cliff decided to tell Collette about his fantasies. When he did, Collette laughed and revealed, with some embarrassment, that she frequently had fantasies of doing "that" to Cliff but was always too "uptight" to suggest it.

Often, of course, as in Cliff's and Collette's situation, fantasies serve as attempts at fulfilling sexual wishes. Thus, the fantasies can lead you in directions you might enjoy in real life: seducing or being seduced; being more dominant or more submissive; enjoying activities that are a bit "offbeat" (although you are probably not the first person to think of them).

Problems in Using Fantasies

But, you may ask, aren't there hazards in using sexual fantasies? The answer—yes and no. There are people, for example, who have difficulty in accepting any erotic fantasies as a part of their sexuality. They may fear that sexual fantasies might do damage to their "real" sex lives, or they may believe that sexual fantasies are immoral, and these people feel guilty when they do occur. They may be concerned that fantasies that don't focus on their partners are anywhere from disloyal to unfaithful.

Actually, many happily married people are from time to time sexually attracted to other people and may from time to time fantasize about having sex with them. They would never dream of carrying out these fantasies in their real lives, but they *do* enjoy the fantasies. We don't believe that these or other kinds of fantasies either reflect a bad relationship or will bring about a breakdown in the relationship. They are just a product of our ability to enjoy the privacy of our thoughts.

There *are* situations, however, in which sexual fantasies *might* create problems. If any of these is true for you, then you may want to re-evaluate not only your sexual fantasies, but the problems they reflect as well. Sexual fantasies may be somewhat of a problem under the following conditions:

1. Your sexual fantasies occur so often and so intensely that you never seem to get anything done.

2. You find yourself getting turned off to your partner because your fantasies focus exclusively on partners or activities very different from and preferable to your own.

3. Your fantasies are of socially unacceptable or dangerous activities, such as sex with children or sex associated with violence, and you find yourself more and more wishing to carry out these fantasies in your real life.

4. Your fantasies are an attempt to compensate for lacks in your real sex life, and you find yourself using your fantasies to avoid working on your problems.

5. Your fantasies distract you so much that you do not pay attention to your partner's needs.

With the exception of these misuses of fantasy, you can relax and enjoy your fantasies as a pleasant diversion and as an important part of your sexuality.

Sharing Your Fantasies

All right, you have enjoyable fantasies, and as far as you can tell they are doing neither you nor your partner any harm. The next question might be: Should you tell your partner about them?

Certainly, you have a perfect right to keep all your thoughts and fantasies about sex to yourself. Indeed, one of the beauties of fantasies is that they *are* private and that nobody but you has to know what they are or when you have them.

However, if you have a partner, you may have a desire to share your fantasies with him or her. Of course, you have no right to insist that your partner share his or her fantasies with you. But sharing fantasies has its advantages. Doing so may help you to understand each other better and it may help to reduce any inhibitions you have in talking about sex. Further, as we have said before, discussing your fantasies may provide you both with ideas for improving your sexual relationship.

205

But sharing sexual fantasies may be a sensitive area for one or both of you. Hearing your partner's fantasies may create jealousy or feelings of inadequacy. After all, who can live up to a fantasy lover?

Because of the potential hazards involved, we suggest that before you go too far in telling each other about your fantasies, you might want to ask yourself a few questions: How secure is your relationship? How tolerant will your partner be of your having fantasies about someone else, or of activities he or she may not be comfortable about? Do your fantasies threaten sensitive areas of your partner's feelings of inadequacy, or of your own?

If you aren't sure how your partner will take sharing your fantasies, ask your partner. You might ask what he or she would like to know and can handle, as well as what he or she would just as soon *not* know. You should both be aware that there are hazards in opening up your private thoughts to another person—even to one whom you love and who loves you. But remember: There's a good chance that your partner has been having fantasies, too. If that's the case, you can play the game of "I'll tell you mine if you tell me yours."

If you both decide to share some or all of your fantasies, it might be best to start with those fantasies that involve each other. Or you might want to recall some of your childhood and adolescent fantasies. Such fantasies are usually less threatening than those involving other people in your current environment. See how that works before you tell about any more exotic fantasies or those involving your next-door neighbor or your partner's best friend.

Exercising Your Fantasies

Since the capacity to fantasize can be such an enjoyable part of your sex life (if it isn't already) it's worth developing. The exercises that follow should be helpful in developing your fantasy life. Again, you and your partner, if you have one, may both want to go through the exercises separately and, to the extent that you feel comfortable, share your experiences. If your partner chooses to do the exercises, don't discuss them until you both complete all of them.

EXERCISE 1: TAKING STOCK OF YOUR FANTASIES

This exercise is intended to help you to evaluate your present use of fantasies and how you feel about them. It might suggest some directions for you to take in enhancing your fantasies. Answer each of these questions on a piece of paper or into a tape recorder.

1. Do you have sexual fantasies? Have you ever? Have they changed over time? If so, how?

2. When do you tend to have your sexual fantasies? When you're stimulating yourself to orgasm? When you're first getting aroused in the presence of your partner? While you're having intercourse?

3. What effect do your fantasies have on your getting aroused? What do you fantasize or think about while you're having intercourse?

4. What have your recent favorite fantasies involved? Have they been very erotic? Who is in your fantasies? Where do they take place? What exactly are the participants in the fantasy doing?

5. Do your fantasies include your sexual partner? Do your fantasies reflect a wish that your partner do something in particular with you during your love-making, such as the use of particular positions in intercourse? Do these fantasies reflect any changes you would like to see in you or your partner's appearance or behavior?

6. Would you like to carry out any of these fantasized activities in your real life? If not, why not? If yes, why don't you?

7. Would you like to tell your partner about any of these fantasies? Why or why not?

8. Are you satisfied with your fantasies? Do any of them make you feel anxious or guilty? Why or why not?

Now read or listen to your answers. How do you evaluate your use of fantasies? What do you think you should do about it? Would you like to expand your repertoire of fantasies? If so, go on to the next exercise.

EXERCISE 2: WINDOW SHOPPING
FOR FANTASIES
Now that you have made an inventory of what your fantasies are like, let's see how you might improve them.

On the following pages we are going to describe categories of activities that may be arousing, along with some examples of each. On a separate sheet of paper or into a tape recorder, list those particular items in each category that you find particularly arousing. Later, we will give you practice in putting these together to form your own vivid and erotic fantasies.

If you have a partner, he or she might want to do the same on another sheet of paper or on a separate tape. Later you both can share whatever you care to from your lists.

Erotic Ideas. List those ideas that turn you on, such as group sex, watching someone else you know having sex; and/or particular memories of enjoyable past sexual encounters that were particularly exciting. Dominating (without hurting) your partner or being dominated may be particularly erotic for you. List your erotic ideas.

Erotic Places. Fantasies about sex in particular places can be a real turn-on. It might be back in the first place you had sex with someone you love, or the back seat of your old car. It can be somewhere exotic, like on a beach in Hawaii, in a fancy French hotel, or in the back seat of a chauffeur-driven Rolls-Royce. Or it can be somewhere unorthodox, like a public place, on a crowded long-distance bus, or in an elevator. What are some of your exotic, erotic places?

Erotic Times. Is there a particular time for sex that you consider particularly erotic? Late at night? Early in the morning? In the winter while the snow is falling? Just after a nice dinner? Quickly, during a coffee break? While you're both watching a football game? What time is it?

Erotic Sensations. Your five senses are capable of producing a spectrum of sensuous experiences that can enhance your erotic fantasies. What turns you on? A warm breeze over your back? Constantly changing colored lights? A windchime in the distance? The feeling of satin sheets? A light rain? The smell of incense? The smell of your partner's body? The sounds of his or her breathing? What sensual experiences turn you on?

Erotic Situations. Erotic fantasies often have plots. What situations turn you on? Seducing a partner? Getting seduced? Meeting someone at an airport? Having sex in the back of a gas station with an attendant? Under a table in a deserted restaurant with your waitress? Hiding on a spaceship and having sex with an astronaut during blastoff? Being dominated? Getting involved in a forbidden sexual activity in a place you shouldn't be and with someone you shouldn't be with? Having a group of people competing for your sexual attention and eagerly meeting every one of your sexual whims? Record your most erotic fantasy plots.

Erotic People. Finally, perhaps most important is the cast of characters you find erotic. What are the characteristics of the person or persons who turn you on? What are their personalities like: friendly, aloof, witty, intelligent, gentle, cruel, emotional? What are their physical characteristics? Tall, skinny, firm breasts, broad chest, narrow hips, dark complexion, big penis, blonde hair, winning smile, deep voice? Does any particular occupation turn you on—mailman, prostitute, construction worker, physician, schoolteacher, plumber, social worker, stenographer? What would you like to be doing in your fantasies? What would you like your partner to be doing? Last but not least, how would you picture your present partner in your fantasies?

Now check over your list. Sometimes we're rather uncomfortable about our fantasies and are embarrassed to admit them even to ourselves, so go back over your list and consider whether there's anything you conspicuously left out or anything else that you would like to add. This is a very personal and private list, and it should reflect your uniqueness.

In reviewing the list, ask yourself how you can use this information. In a minute we will get to putting these ingredients into a recipe for an enriched fantasy life. But you might also consider how you could apply this knowledge to your real life. Of course, many fantasies are not very practical to act out and might even be a disappointment if they were. However, if you have discovered that your list reveals that you would like having sex late at night in the shower with your partner whispering erotic comments in your ear as he or she shampoos your hair, why not try it?

EXERCISE 3: REVIEWING THE LITERATURE
This exercise will take some time, but it will, we hope, also be pleasurable and useful.

Although your best fantasies will be uniquely yours, you may have difficulty in creating your own erotic fantasies and may therefore want to draw on the experiences of others.

Movies and television programs can provide some fantasies for you. But censorship usually limits their erotic realism. Pornographic books are usually poorly written, and some people find most pornographic movies tasteless, not very stimulating, and in fact rather dull.

So, unless you'd like to try pornographic movies or books, we'll suggest that you concentrate on some popular, well-written novels. Obviously, not all erotic novels will turn on all readers, and not all parts of these novels are erotic.

But there are some good erotic books. Just to get you started, you might want to look through the following novels:

□ *Fear of Flying* by Erica Jong
□ *Delta of Venus* by Anaïs Nin
□ *Even Cowgirls Get The Blues* by Tom Robbins
□ *Lady Chatterly's Lover* by D. H. Lawrence
□ *The Other Side of Midnight* by Sidney Sheldon

You can add to the list almost any novel by Harold Robbins (if you don't find them objectionably sexist) or choose your (or your partner's) favorite books.

You can also review sex guides, such as *The Joy of Sex*, by Alex Comfort, *The Sensuous Woman* by "J" and *The Sensuous Man*, by "M," for particularly erotic scenes.

Finally, you may want to get one of the recent collection of actual sexual fantasies of men and women, such as *My Secret Garden*, by Nancy Friday, or *Secret Sex: Male Erotic Fantasies*, by Tom Anicar.

Take some time to look over these books. Skim the dull parts and underline the erotic passages, as you might have done when you were a teenager.

If you need more vivid illustrations than some of these books provide, you might want to look at some popular magazines, such as *Playboy* and *Playgirl* for pictures or stories that turn you on.

As you amass your collection of erotic scenes, make a note of the half dozen or so that most turn you on. Then, in turn, take each of these fantasies, close your eyes, relax, and think about it. Run through the scene in your head. Make any modification you choose to make it more erotic for you. Remember, it's your fantasy. Try to visualize the scene as vividly as you can—how it looks, sounds, feels, smells, and tastes. Practice focusing and concentrating on each element of the fantasy that you find particularly erotic.

EXERCISE 4: PUTTING YOUR FANTASIES TOGETHER

In the second exercise, you developed a list of components for your erotic fantasies. In Exercise 3 you checked out what was erotic for you in scenes from books. Now let's put them all together. Either sit down in a comfortable chair or lie in bed in a fairly darkened room. Close your eyes and get yourself relaxed, using the exercises you learned in Chapter 11.

Now proceed to construct a fantasy. First, think of one of the situations that you listed earlier. Where is it happening?

> I'm walking through the forest preserve with my wife. We sit down on a bed of pine needles in the middle of a small grove of trees. We begin to make love.

Try to vividly imagine the scene and the physical sensations you feel.

> I feel her stroking my thighs, with her finger tips brushing over my penis. I feel a warm breeze over my chest—I am shirtless. When she kisses me I taste her lips—it's a slightly sweet, pleas-

ant flavor. I hear the whistle of the breeze through the pine
needles.

What specifically is erotic about the fantasy?

There's the unexpected element of making it in the woods, high
above the ocean in the distance. I imagine hearing her moan
with pleasure as I enter her. We still have some of our clothes
on—I have to reach under her blouse to stroke her nipples.
Being partly dressed, being outdoors, and doing it in broad
daylight all really turn me on.

Practice each day with a different fantasy. Focus on what
most turns you on in the fantasies. Try to concentrate on the
erotic details; they will help you to get more involved with the
fantasy. If you are a woman and are fantasizing about genital
contact, ask yourself exactly how the penis feels inside of you
and what kind of friction and pressure you are experiencing
and where. What does your partner's body feel like against
your body? Is his body warm, heavy, moist?

If you're a man fantasizing intercourse, try to imagine the
position, how your body feels against your partner's body, how
your penis feels inside her vagina, its wetness and texture, and
the sensation in your testicles. All these details involving all
your senses—what you see, hear, feel, smell, and taste—will
enrich your fantasies.

Enhancing your ability to enjoy your fantasies is worth
your time and effort. It will help you, and perhaps your partner, to better understand your sexual wishes and needs, provide you with a readily available technique for increasing and
maintaining sexual arousal, and open new sexual horizons for
you to enjoy in the privacy of your imagination.

SELF-STIMULATION: A THOUSAND STROKES

Self-stimulation rubs many people the wrong way. Recent
studies show that most men and women, married, and single,
do it, but many somehow feel that it's not quite right.

Many sex "experts" communicate an "it's all right
but . . ." attitude about self-stimulation. Recognizing the
overwhelming weight of evidence, they agree that it won't hurt
you, but you really shouldn't do it too often anyway, and
ideally you should be doing other things instead. Sexual activities are still seen as only really being acceptable when they
are with an appropriate partner.

Some will quote—or more often misquote—the *Bible* to support their discomfort with self-stimulation. Others don't consider it manly or womanly. It is often dismissed as immature sexual behavior. Much of our rejection of self-stimulation is a leftover of our Puritan ethic. After all, it's not productive—it doesn't make babies or sanctify a relationship. It's just for—well—pleasure.

Even the most common word used for self-stimulation communicates our discomfort with it—*masturbation*. The word itself is a corruption of a Latin and a Greek root that, put together, literally means "to defile yourself with your hand." That doesn't sound like much fun. Indeed, the word sounds like an illness. *Masturbation* sounds like it belongs in the company of words like *meningitis* and *mononucleosis*. The Japanese have less-judgmental and more-pleasant names for the activity: *sensori* for men and *monsori* for women, meaning literally "a thousand strokes" and "ten thousand strokes," respectively.

We know of one sex therapist who prescribed self-stimulation for a woman who was having difficulty in achieving orgasm with her partner. The woman did her homework and joyfully reported considerable success at her next session. However, she said that there was one question that was troubling her: "Was I masturbating?" "Well," replied her therapist, who was very much aware of the power of sexual labels, "some people might call it that, but I consider it self-exploration." "Thank heavens," she replied. "I was afraid I was masturbating!"

We have chosen to call this activity *self-stimulation* in order to avoid all the negative connotations of masturbation that, many of us were taught, inevitably leads to blindness or, at least, to the growth of hair on one's hand.

We believe that self-stimulation is a harmless and pleasant experience in and of itself. In laboratory studies, sex researchers have found from such indicators as increased heart rate, changes in blood pressure, and measurements of muscle tension that for many men and women, orgasms from self-stimulation are more intense than those from intercourse. The most obvious reason for this difference is that when people are stimulating themselves, they needn't be simultaneously concerned with the needs or expectations of a partner. They are in complete control of their stimulation and not dependent on their partner's timing, changes in pressure, or movements. They know what sensations feel good to themselves and can give themselves accurate and immediate feedback of what they want.

Then how come people haven't given up intercourse? As

we have said numerous times in this book, there is, or can be, much more to sexual relationships than just genital stimulation and orgasm. The emotional and physical give-and-take of intercourse is likely to keep it popular for quite some time.

But the feedback you get from self-stimulation can teach you a great deal that can considerably enhance your lovemaking. In fact, in later chapters we will discuss how self-stimulation is used to work through some specific sexual problems.

The purpose of the exercises that follow is to guide your self-explorations in such a way as to learn more about your sensual reactions to various kinds of stimulation, and perhaps expand the range of stimulation that gets you aroused. If, in the process, you learn to enjoy self-stimulation or enjoy it more than you had in the past, consider it a fringe benefit.

Exercises for Women

There is considerably more variety in the ways in which women stimulate themselves than there is for men. These activities don't always lead to orgasm, and the woman may not even view them as self-stimulation, especially if the activity doesn't involve manual stimulation. Many women, for example, find that crossing their legs tightly together and applying rhythmic pressure to their vagina and clitoris creates a very pleasurable feeling. Others rub their genital area against their bed, a pillow, a stuffed animal, or their partner. Many women stimulate themselves by stroking or rubbing other parts of their bodies, such as their breasts and the insides of their thighs.

However, self-stimulation most often involves stroking the area around the vulva, especially around the clitoris and inner legs. Most frequently this includes rubbing or stroking the area just below the mons veneris (a fleshy pad, usually covered with hair, directly over your pubic bone [see the illustration in Chapter 12]). Recently many women have found the use of an electrical vibrator on the exterior sexual organs an excellent supplement to their fingertips and hand. Note that we said "exterior." Vibrators are meant to be used primarily for cliotral stimulation, with the woman experimenting to determine the best angles, degree of intensity, and exact locations for stimulation. Generally, the use of the vibrator is not intended to replace intercourse. However, each woman should explore the most pleasurable way to use her vibrator.

Men often think that when women stimulate themselves they use some form of penis substitute (candle, banana, sausage, etc.) for deep penetration of the vagina. Although this may be flattering to the male idea that a woman is dependent on intercourse or a close approximation of it for sexual satisfaction, this is not usually the case. Many women don't find deep penetration with a finger, vibrator, or a substitute penis as stimulating as other forms of stimulation. Deep penetration during self-stimulation is not used by many women, although some do find such stimulation highly satisfying.

Women, like men, find fantasy an excellent companion to self-stimulation. Some read erotic books, look at erotic pictures, recall past erotic experiences, or make up erotic scenes.

Although many women very much enjoy self-stimulation and engage in its regularly, there are many others who have had little experience with it or who find it unsatisfying. We are going to present some suggestions for you to get more out of your self-stimulation both as a pleasurable experience in itself and as a way of enhancing your sexual experiences with your partner.

The purposes of the following exercises are to get you used to your body, to find out what physical sensations turn you on, and to get you more comfortable with your whole body as a vehicle for sexual pleasure.

As we've said before, you may not be comfortable with the idea of stimulating yourself—it may violate what you've been taught. We're not saying that you have to take up self-stimulation as a full-time hobby. You may already enjoy self-stimulation, you may learn to in the future, or you may never want to. But many women do enjoy self-stimulation as one more form of sexual pleasure.

If it's at all appealing to you, go ahead and try it. We believe that pleasuring yourself is a very enjoyable—even beneficial—activity. We also believe that you have every right to enjoy your own body, including its capacity to feel good.

What we're going to have you do first is become more familiar with your body, especially your sexual organs. If you're already an expert in this area, fine—you may want to breeze through these exercises just to check yourself out. If you're a beginner, then take your time. There's no rush.

There are a few things to remember before you begin. You have a right to take the time to enjoy yourself. Most women want to be able to enjoy their own bodies more. You have to learn what works for you, and that's what these exercises are all about. Go through each of the steps in sequence, evaluating your experiences as you go. Don't overdo your sessions. We don't want you to get bored. Start with five- to fifteen-minute sessions, no more than a couple of times a day. Certainly, having satisfying orgasms from your exercises is a fitting reward for your efforts. But don't get discouraged or angry at yourself if it doesn't happen, at least right away. And if you *do* enjoy it, fine—that's supposedly what this is all about.

STEP 1

The first step is to prepare you for focused sessions by yourself in which your explore your body and give yourself pleasure. So for the first session, choose a time when you will be all alone in your house or apartment for at least an hour.

First, take a long, warm, leisurely shower or bath. Focus on the sensations as the water covers your body and as you spread soapsuds over yourself. While you are soaping yourself, focus on the sensations in both your hands and your body. Run your fingertips gently over your body. How does it feel? What strokes, angles, and pressures feel best? As you soap yourself, try to explore areas of your body you may not have previously explored: between your toes, behind your knees, your inner thighs.

As you explore yourself and as you look at yourself, think about how you feel about the parts of your body and what potential sensations each part possesses. How do your hands feel as they touch each part of your body?

When you feel that you have completed a total exploration of your entire body, rinse and dry off. Then spread body lotions or oils over your body as you focus on the experience you can give yourself.

Again, how do your hands feel as they stroke the rest of your body? As you stroke yourself, in a way, your body is stroking your fingertips—just as your partner's body sometimes strokes your hands as you caress him.

Don't rush; you've got a lot of exploring to do.

STEP 2

Lie down in your bed. Make sure that you're comfortable. You may want to prop yourself up on a pillow. Follow the relaxation exercises in Chapter 11 if you feel any tension. Now, stroke your body all over again slowly, but avoid your sex organs. Explore your thighs, your buttocks, your ribs, down to your toes. Recall what areas you found particularly stimulating in your shower or bath or from past experiences. Fully explore your breasts, not only the nipples but all around the surfaces of each breast. See if there is any difference in the feelings in each breast. Try different pressures, speeds, and touches. Use the palm of your hand, your fingertips, or perhaps both hands at once.

Each time you carry out these self-stimulation programs, start with parts of the body other than your sex organs. It is worthwhile to learn to enjoy your whole body. You already know (we hope) that your clitoris and vagina can give you pleasure. Now it's important to discover pleasure in other parts of your body. Later you may choose to stimulate these other parts at the same time or interchangeably with your sex organs.

STEP 3

Now take the time to explore the sensations in your sexual organs. Although there are various pleasurable areas, we will focus on clitoral stimulation. Locate your mons pubis. Let your hand rest on your mons while you fingers seek your clitoris. Feel the area where the top of your outer lips begin to open. The clitoris is just under this opening. Some women may have difficulty finding it. If this happens to you, just feel around until you find a particularly sensitive area. That's probably it.

If you exert a little more pressure and move your fingers around in a more or less circular pattern, your clitoris will probably respond by getting firmer (it happens in a way similar to the erection of a penis) and more sensitive. Eventually you will notice that it becomes a bean-sized bump. Some are smaller and some larger, but it doesn't seem to make much difference in terms of how pleasurable the sensations are.

If the bump doesn't appear or you don't sense an increase in sensitivity, don't worry—it's there. Every woman comes equipped with one. Just try to relax, go back to stroking the rest of your body, and come back to it later.

As you begin to get stimulated, you may notice other effects in addition to your clitoris's getting hard. You may start to breathe harder; your vagina probably will start lubricating; your nipples may get firm, as in Figure 13-1. If so, fantastic. Everything seems to be working fine. If not, give it more time.

As you get to know your clitoris better, you'll notice that it's a rather active organ that comes and goes as your level of arousal dictates. As you approach orgasm, your clitoris will seem to retract into your body and disappear. After orgasm it will come back and possibly disappear again after a while.

Try to be creative in the type of stimulation you use on your clitoris. Experiment with different strokes (circular, up and down, etc.), levels of intensity, and rhythms. You will probably find that some areas of your clitoris or surrounding areas are more sensitive than others. Many women discover that direct stimulation of the clitoris is actually unpleasant, and they enjoy rubbing or stroking the side or adjacent areas better. The best locations may also change as arousal increases or as orgasm approaches. You may find that some approaches are painful or irritating, or that others are boring.

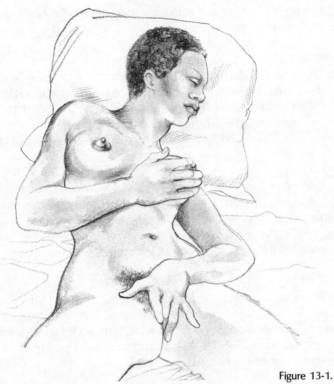

Figure 13-1.

Steps 4 through 9 are designed to enhance the pleasure you get from stimulating your clitoris. Check each of them out to see if it increases your arousal, does nothing for you, or even takes away from your pleasure. Then proceed accordingly.

STEP 4

Clitoral stimulation can be enhanced by exercising the muscles around the vagina. As you stroke yourself, rhythmically tighten and relax your pubococcygeus (PC) muscles, in the way we described in the last chapter. These are the same muscles you use to stop your urine flow. Also, rhythmically tighten and relax the muscles of your buttocks and anus, squeeze your thighs together, and try various combinations of these muscles to see which turn you on. Try various groups of muscles. You may find that arching your back, spreading your legs wide, stretching your leg muscles, or twisting your body in various directions adds to your stimulation. Body tension often speeds and increases the intensity of orgasm from any source of stimulation.

Also, try different positions—sitting or lying on your stomach, with your legs spread or close together. You may also

217

try standing up, sitting in a rocking chair, or bending over a tall object—whatever turns you on.

STEP 5

Try different lubricants. It's possible that your own body's lubricants are adequate. You may want to use saliva or put your finger into your vaginal lubrication. You may also want to try artificial lubricants. Anything that isn't irritating and you enjoy using is fine. (See Chapter 7 for suggestions on lubricants.)

STEP 6

Use your fantasies as we have discussed earlier in this chapter. You may want to fantasize that someone else is stroking you, lying next to you, talking to you, or engaging in any other erotic activity you developed while reading the "Use Your Head: Enjoy Your Fantasies" section of this chapter.

STEP 7

Try exaggerating your physical reactions as you turn yourself on. Stretch, squirm, arch your back, contort your face, moan and groan. Go on; no one's watching, so let your dramatic skills take over. This "role playing" will help you to experience more intense feelings.

STEP 8

You might want to increase the intensity or pace of your stroking and bring yourself to orgasm, or continue at a slower pace and just enjoy the sensations. Do what feels best to you. Focus here on the sensations and fantasies that arouse you the most.

STEP 9

Use other objects to stimulate yourself. Vibrators can be very stimulating and vibrate at a faster speed than the fastest-moving fingertips. Also, you may want to try various textures on your clitoral area, such as those of a piece of fur or of a feather. Use your creativity to see what turns you on.

STEP 10

Try anything else that turns you on, whether it's musical background, perfumes, incense, colored lights, or watching yourself in a mirror. If you want to reach orgasm but it doesn't come, don't worry. Relax and keep pleasuring yourself. It probably will come eventually. You can also try the program we describe in Chapter 15 if you feel that you have a problem in this area.

After you complete each of these exercises, evaluate what you learned about yourself from them. How can you apply this knowledge to sex with a partner?

Exercises for Men

There are few men who aren't old hands at self-stimulation. Almost all adolescents and young adult males do it, and the majority of married men also stimulate themselves from time to time. Yet despite the prevalence of this activity, many men believe that it is a necessary evil and feel uncomfortable about it. Men have been taught that it reflects some kind of inadequacy on their part—maybe it's all right for young boys and those who don't have access to a willing female, but "real men" shouldn't have to masturbate. After all, can you imagine Robert Redford or Arnold Schwarzenegger "needing" to stimulate themselves?

This ambivalent attitude toward masturbation leads to the characteristic "get it over quickly" approach to self-stimulation. The only goal is to have an orgasm and relieve tension. Little time or interest is taken in enjoying the wealth of erotic pleasure that can come from self-stimulation. Indeed, treating orgasm as the only goal of self-stimulation is often carried over to intercourse, in which case men don't fully enjoy the range of pleasure that they are capable of in addition to orgasms.

Again, we feel that there is much to enjoy in self-stimulation. There is nothing sick or unmasculine about it. Men and women in many cultures stimulate themselves to orgasm. Many people do it throughout their lives in addition to their activities with their partner. Some, both men and women, stimulate themselves while making love to their partners. We do not feel that it has to be either a substitute for or merely a supplement to sex with a partner. It is a separate activity with its own unique characteristic pleasures and advantages.

But beyond the pleasures that self-stimulation can give as an end in itself, it gives you an opportunity to explore the range of satisfaction your body can provide in addition to orgasm. You can then transfer this knowledge to enhance your lovemaking with a partner.

Furthermore, you can learn to overcome several problems associated with intercourse, such as ejaculating too quickly, through training yourself while stimulating yourself to orgasm. We discuss these uses of self-stimulation in Chapters 17 and 18.

But now, let's go through a series of exercises that we've designed to help you to get more out of self-stimulation, both as an end in itself and as a way of more fully enjoying sex with your partner.

STEP 1

Again, as with the exercises with women, you first have to relax. Men often associate self-stimulation with quickly releasing tension when they're uptight. Self-stimulation *is* a tension reliever. However, during the following exercises, we would like you to focus on the other, more leisurely pleasures of self-stimulation.

So give yourself plenty of time—and make sure that you'll have privacy.

Choose a time when you're as little preoccupied with other matters as you can be. Select a time of the day that best suits your mood.

Take a long shower or bath and explore your body. Many men are uncomfortable about enjoying or stimulating any part of their body except their penises or, perhaps, their scrotum during self-stimulation. Go ahead and find out what other parts of your body feel good as you soap yourself.

Continue the process as you dry yourself and then lie down in your bed. For the time being, keep clear of your penis. We'll get to that later. Particularly stroke such sensitive areas as your inner thighs, the area between your scrotum and your anus (the perineum), your buttocks, your stomach, and your nipples. Vary your strokes in speed and intensity—use your fingertips and the palms of one or both hands. Test out your creativity. What feels good?

Allow yourself at least a few minutes each time you stimulate yourself to enjoy parts of your body other than your penis. You may have some pleasant surprises.

STEP 2

You may have found yourself becoming aroused in Exercise 1. Fine. However, it may take some direct stimulation of your penis, and perhaps some erotic fantasies, to turn you on. That's fine, too. Whatever it takes to get you aroused, it's important for you to learn what does it. It is often a lack of knowledge about your own arousal patterns that leads to such common male problems as lack of arousal, coming too soon, and not coming at all.

In this exercise, you will focus on becoming even more familiar with your penis and with which sensations create the greatest arousal.

First of all, again try to relax, using some of the procedures from Chapter 11. Make sure that the room isn't too cold.

If you feel that a dark room is sexy, make it dark; if you find that you get more turned on if you look at your body and your penis, let there be light. If you have some music that tends to relax you or that you find sexy, put it on. If you find music distracting, keep it quiet. Part of the purpose of this exercise is to find out what kind of environment most turns you on. All these factors—and all your senses—have a role in arousal. Check them out.

Now start using the fantasies you developed while doing the exercises in the "Use Your Head: Enjoy Your Fantasies" section of this chapter. Perhaps it is memories of particularly erotic past experiences or an invented erotic situation. Perhaps it is suggested by erotic photographs, drawings, or literature. Vary your thoughts from time to time as you do this exercise to explore the range of fantasies that you find arousing.

Allow yourself at least several minutes at the beginning of each time you do this exercise to stroke parts of your body other than your penis. Recall which areas and which kinds of touching you discovered to be pleasurable from the previous step. Don't be in a rush to get to your penis. It won't run away. Remember, the focus is on learning leisurely, non-urgent pleasuring of your body.

STEP 3
In this step you will focus on "rediscovering" your penis. The purpose of this exercise is to pay greater attention to the sensations that your penis is capable of giving you and the types of stroking that bring these sensations about. Remember that for the sake of learning new things about yourself, the goal is *not* to have an orgasm. You probably already know how to do that. It isn't even necessary to get an erection. That's one of the nice things about self-stimulation: You don't have to do anything, for anybody. Sex with a partner requires consideration of her needs as well as your own. You don't have to do anything for anyone except yourself in this exercise.

You may be aroused from the things you did in step 2. Whether or not your penis is erect, begin to gently stroke it very slowly. Focus on the sensations you get from stroking various parts of your penis—the underside of the shaft, the top of the shaft, the area where your shaft meets your body, the coronal ridge, the head and the tip. Focus on the different sensations you receive from all these parts. Which do you like best? What kind of touch do you like best in each part—a brush of your fingertips or a firm grasp?

Remember, go slowly. Orgasm is not the goal. You can explore which lubricants feel best—or you may prefer no lubricants at all.

221

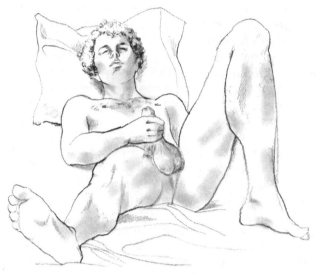

Figure 13-2.

Try various approaches to rubbing the length of your shaft. This is the most common way in which men bring themselves to orgasm. Try different strokes—firm and loose, varying the intensity of the stroke, different rhythms, circular motions, and different speeds—but no so fast as to propel yourself toward orgasm. You may want to try the hand other than the one you usually use, or going overhand instead of underhand, or using both hands. For an example, see Figure 13-2.

STEP 4
Try other forms of stimulation of your penis, including gentle tugging and moving it around in an arc as you stroke or rub it. Try lying on your stomach and rubbing your pelvic area in circular or up and down motions against the bed or a pillow.

STEP 5
Experiment with an electrical or battery-operated vibrator. You can try it on various parts of your penis, scrotum, and perineum. But be very careful here; use only the lightest touch or you could hurt yourself. In particular, the testicles are very sensitive. Also try various lubricants, unless you tend to reach orgasm too quickly. (Refer to Chapter 7 for our discussion of various kinds of lubricants.)

STEP 6
Try arching your back and tensing various groups of muscles, especially those in your buttocks and stomach. Test out

your pubococcygeus (PC) muscles (the ones you use when you deliberately cut off the flow of urine). You may even want to role play intense ecstacy, tossing your head from side to side and moaning and groaning.

While you are concentrating on your penis, simultaneously use your other hand to stroke other parts of your body, such as your nipples, scrotum, and the area between your scrotum and anus. Use your imagination—find out what feels good.

STEP 7

Continue all this for a good ten to fifteen minutes each time you do this exercise. But as soon as you feel yourself reaching orgasm, stop for a minute or two until you feel that the orgasm has been delayed. One of the purposes of this exercise is to extend the length of time you can stimulate yourself from arousal to orgasm.

Try to become acutely aware of the point during sexual stimulation when you feel that an ejaculation is on its way. That sensation is called the point of "ejaculatory inevitability," as we discussed in the previous chapter. Ejaculation usually occurs shortly after when the muscles in the base of the penis rhythmically contract and shoot the semen out of the penis. This process is involuntary and there is virtually nothing you can do to stop it once it starts. But you can learn to anticipate the point of ejaculatory inevitability and thus delay the process. You can do this by consciously trying to recognize the sensations that precede ejaculation, particularly the tensing of the muscles connected with ejaculation, as well as such other signs as increased heart rate and shallower breathing. Practice reducing the stimulation that would otherwise then lead to ejaculation. Once you master this skill, you—and your partner—will be able to get more enjoyment by extending an intense state of arousal. (We discuss this process in much more detail in Chapter 17.)

When you sense that you are reaching the point of ejaculatory inevitability while doing these exercises, stop all stroking and relax until the tension decreases. See how often you can bring yourself just to the brink and not spill over.

STEP 8

When you have spent ten or fifteen minutes on this step, bring yourself to orgasm if you wish. But try to do so in a leisurely way, with slow stroking and focusing your attention on the sensations—and fantasies—that accompany your orgasm.

STEP 9

Repeat this exercise (after the first session you can omit step 1 if you want) once or twice a day for five days to a week. At the end of that time try to write down on a piece of paper or dictate into a tape recorder what you have learned about your sexual responses. How do you think that your sexual activities with your partner can be modified to take advantage of what you have learned about your own sexual needs and patterns of response?

It is often quite embarrassing for men to admit or discuss with their partners their enjoyment of self-stimulation. But you may want to try this with your partner as a way of introducing some changes in your sexual activities. After all, if she wants to know why you stimulated yourself, you can blame it on us.

Some Additional Notes for Both Men and Women

You may want to get even more variety in your patterns of self-stimulation. Try stimulating yourself in a different room—when no one is around (or even if they are, if that's your thing). Try it in a shower, in front of a mirror, in a big armchair, or on a swing or in a rocking chair. Experiment with different kinds of music. Vary the time of day when you stimulate yourself—early in the morning, during coffee breaks at work (in appropriate places), late at night.

You may also find other objects besides your hands with which to stimulate yourself. Objects that have interesting textures may lure you on—leather, silk, velvet, or fur might be good to start with.

Remember, self-stimulation is useful for two purposes: (1) it is a means for both men and women to learn more about their sexual response and needs so that they can transfer their knowledge to their sexual activities with a partner; and (2) it can also be an enjoyable, uncomplicated experience in itself that need not interfere with sex with a partner.

COMBINING SELF-STIMULATION WITH FANTASIES

Combining specific erotic fantasies with self-stimulation is an excellent way of enhancing sexual activities with your partner. Go over your self-stimulation exercises as you fantasize what you can reasonably expect to do with your partner. Using self-stimulation for this purpose will help to prepare you in a relatively anxiety-free way to introduce desired changes in your sexual relationship. In fact, you can look on it as an undress rehearsal for sex with your partner.

First, bring yourself to orgasm using self-stimulation and your favorite erotic fantasies. Then, for several daily ten- to fifteen-minutes sessions, combine your self-stimulation explorations with fantasies that progressively approach your real-life situation, even if your fantasies are still somewhat idealized. Try to fantasize your doing something arousing with an "ideal" partner. As you approach orgasm, change your ideal partner into your real-life partner in your fantasy. In each successive session, switch over to your real partner earlier and earlier. At the same time, try to have your fantasized sex partner become more and more like your real partner in appearance and in any of his or her positive attributes. The purpose of this exercise is to build a bridge between your fantasy life and real sex life, with each enriching the other.

Finally, try to see to what extent you can combine your fantasies and self-stimulation into your love-making with your partner. There is nothing wrong with supplementing what your partner does to arouse you with your own stimulation from your fantasies as well as from your hands. You can also teach your partner to stimulate you the way *you* do it. It might embarrass you at first, and your partner may have his or her hang-ups about it, but if you gradually and gently try to build it into your sexual activities with your partner, and you both come to find it acceptable, this can add a lot of pleasure to your sexual activities.

Both fantasy and self-stimulation are important parts of your sex life—and they are almost completely under your control. Satisfying sexual relationships require that both partners assume responsibility for giving themselves and their partners pleasure. Much of this pleasure can come not just from your partner, but from your own hands and head as well.

Fourteen

Erotic Pleasure: Getting in Touch with Your Partner's Body

Almost all of the Treat Yourself programs involve erotic pleasure. That probably sounds pretty good, and indeed it is.

Erotic Pleasure is the name of two exercises that you will really enjoy. They are specifically designed to help you overcome any sexual problems that you might be experiencing and also to help you enhance your sex life, even if you feel that you don't have any sexual problems.

These exercises were developed by Masters and Johnson, who called them "sensate focus" or "pleasuring." The basic idea behind these exercises is that you and your partner will take a break from intercourse for a while and gently caress, play with, and learn to enjoy each other's body.

There are a number of reasons why these exercises are used and why they are necessary for the success of the Treat Yourself programs.

First, they get you away from the idea that sex means only intercourse. As we've mentioned before, sex is an experience that involves all of the bodily senses as well as the way you think and feel. The Erotic Pleasure exercises will help to reorient you away from a preoccupation with genital sex and toward the many pleasures that you can get from close encounters with your partner without worrying about having inter-

226

course. Erotic Pleasure will focus on your feelings and on the joy of sensuality as well as on "just sex."

Second, Erotic Pleasure will help you to relax and to feel less tense about what you have to accomplish sexually. One of the major causes of sexual problems is the feeling of pressure that one or both sexual partners may fail to perform. Not only will you not have to worry about erections and orgasms during Erotic Pleasure, but we will ask you specifically to try *not* to achieve them. The idea that it is your "duty" to perform can go out the window. Instead, we will ask only that you relax and enjoy yourself. In this way, it will be impossible to "fail." Thus, as you become involved in Erotic Pleasure, the fears and anxieties that you may have about the possibility of failing, or about not performing well enough, will gradually disappear.

Third, Erotic Pleasure will help you to become a better lover. This might sound a little contradictory because of our just mentioning that you don't have to worry about how good you are when you're doing Erotic Pleasure. But think of it this way. Although we want you to relax and first feel good about what you're doing with Erotic Pleasure, what you will be doing is learning different ways of pleasuring—turning on—your partner. Stroking, caressing, and perhaps tickling and teasing: All of these can be used to increase your partner's (and your) pleasure. So, in the long run, when you do use some of these Erotic Pleasure techniques just for the sake of enjoyment, your partner will be able to experience much fuller sexual pleasure.

Fourth, you will come to know your partner better; perhaps you will become more intimate with your partner. Indeed, the physical and personal closeness of Erotic Pleasure may introduce a new dimension to your relationship, particularly in your ability to feel close to and communicate with each other.

Finally, Erotic Pleasure exercises are just plain fun. They give you and your partner an opportunity to enjoy each other and to experience some really exciting and pleasurable physical sensations.

All in all, then, Erotic Pleasure is designed to decrease your anxiety, fears, and concerns about performing; to increase your physical pleasures, closeness, and intimacy with each other; and, generally, to enhance your sex life.

PRELIMINARY STEPS

For both of the Erotic Pleasure exercises, there are some general guidelines that you can follow in order to make sure that you get the most out of the exercises.

1. No Intercourse. This is really important. We want you to enjoy each other, relax, have fun, and *not worry* about how well you're going to do. Usually, the major concerns about sex involve intercourse. But in these exercises, all of those fears can be set aside. There *will* be plenty of physical contact, though.

2. No Orgasm. Again, although you probably will be really turned on while you're doing Erotic Pleasure, we want you to put off any concern about orgasms.

3. Contracts. When you begin either of the Erotic Pleasure exercises, use the contract we provided in Chapter 10. This will ensure that you both agree on what you're doing and on where you're going.

4. Communicate. Talk about what feels good. Let your partner know how he or she is doing. Use some of the suggestions in Chapter 9. Use your distress signal if you need it, whether it's because you're uncomfortable with what your partner is doing or because you're uncomfortable with what he or she wants you to do. Try to provide an alternative that would be more satisfying to you.

5. Build in a Reward. Just as we suggested in Chapter 10, give yourselves a reward when you've completed a particular step or when you've completed all the steps in one of the exercises.

6. Take Baths. Baths can be really sensuous experiences. Relax in the bath; just soak up the warmth from the water. We want you to feel good all over. When you dry off with a towel, you'll be tingly all over and ready to go. You'll also be clean and fresh, and we're sure that your partner will appreciate that. (By the way, if you don't like baths, go ahead and take a shower.) Once you get into the Erotic Pleasure exercises, if you and your partner feel like it, try bathing together. Enjoy the closeness that this can bring.

7. Read the Preceding Chapters so that you'll be familiar with all the parts of your partner's body.

8. Lie in the Nude. When you do the Erotic Pleasure exercises, both of you should be completely nude. This in itself can be a turn-on if you're not used to it. But it's necessary for this exercise because you will be stroking each other bodies. If you're not completely comfortable being nude in front of each other, start with a towel wrapped around you, and when you both feel comfortable and are lying together, you can remove the towel. Or, try starting out in the dark. Then, gradually add a soft light—even a flashlight—until you are both comfortable enough to look at each other when you're completely naked.

9. Decide on a Distress Signal. As we suggested in Chapter 7, pick some way that you both agree on to let your partner know if you get nervous. Don't hesitate to use it; we want to decrease, not increase, your anxiety.

10. The Right Time and Place. Choose a time and a place where you can be comfortable and relaxed and where you're not likely to be bothered. Don't lie in the living room if you expect the kids home any minute. On the other hand, if you know that you won't be interrupted, it may be a good idea to vary the places in which you attempt Erotic Pleasure—tonight the bedroom, tomorrow on the couch in the living room.

11. Follow the Steps. Try not to jump ahead with any of the steps. They are designed to move you slowly but surely toward the goal that you want to achieve—mutual happiness and enjoyment of sex. If you start to race ahead, this in itself may be a sign that you're too tense. Relax and enjoy each step. Spend thirty to forty-five minutes each day practicing Erotic Pleasure.

Most people really enjoy Erotic Pleasure, but some don't. Sometimes, they say things like "He (or she) doesn't know how to be gentle"; "We didn't have the time to practice"; "Why do I have to go through all of this?"; "This is boring"; and so on. If you start having problems with Erotic Pleasure, try to talk about it with your partner. Use the guidelines for communicating that we provided in Chapter 9. It might be that one of you is a little angry or hurt about something—maybe something that happened that day, maybe something from the past. Try to find out what is making Erotic Pleasure difficult for you.

It might also be that one of you is still pretty uncomfortable with any sexual activity, or that one of you still fears that he or she won't be able to perform well, even in Erotic Pleasure. In cases like these, please try to be understanding with your partner. A little encouragement and reassurance can go a long way.

Now you're about set. So, if you've done all of the above, you're ready for Erotic Pleasure 1.

EROTIC PLEASURE 1:
WITHOUT GENITAL CONTACT

With Erotic Pleasure 1, you and your partner will be stroking and pleasuring each other, learning what each of you likes in order to feel good and feel sensual. But during this exercise, you are

229

not to touch each other's genitals. If an erection or some other form of arousal develops, or even if one of you has an orgasm, well, fine. Don't worry about it. Just don't *try* to bring one or the other about. Continue with the exercise and complete the full half hour. Don't forget: If anything bothers you about the exercise, use your distress signal right away. Don't wait until the exercise is almost over or until you build up some resentment. If you get the feeling that your partner is uncomfortable—maybe he or she is giggling a little too much (or for that matter, tickling too much), or is somehow uneasy—talk about it. Try to get at what's bothering him or her. Then, try backing up a step or two in the exercises so that you can start with something that's a little less tension-producing. Also, at the end of each day's session, you might want to lie in each other's arms for a few minutes or longer. Just relax, say silly things, and enjoy.

STEP 1

Make sure that you've followed the preliminary steps described above. Develop Erotic Pleasure 1 contract as shown in Chapter 10. Specify steps and rewards. Decide which one of you is to be the "pleasurer" (the one who strokes the other) and the "pleasuree" (the one who receives the strokes). Make sure that each partner does both during each session. Both of you should give and both of you should get. When you're on the receiving end, all you have to do is relax and receive your partner's caresses. Get comfortable—stretch out in bed. Relax. Keep your eyes closed so that you can concentrate only on receiving pleasure. Keep track of the things your partner does that feel good; also, keep track of the parts of your body that really feel good when touched. Feel sensual. Be sensual.

The pleasurer's job is to give his or her partner pleasurable experiences and to help the partner learn what parts of his or her body can really feel good when they are touched. You can improvise with some of the suggestions we've provided. Do what you want to (but make no genital contact) to make your partner feel good.

Just for the sake of convenience, for the remainder of Erotic Pleasure 1, we'll consider the pleasurer to be the male and the pleasuree to be the female. In Erotic Pleasure 2, the female will be the pleasurer and the male the pleasuree. But remember that all of these exercises should be applied to both sexes.

STEP 2

Have the pleasuree lie on her stomach. Gently stroke—perhaps with the tips of your fingernails—her back from the base of the neck to the top of the buttocks. Just lightly stroke all over the back area. Don't rub too hard; don't tickle. Just do this gently. The pleasuree should be concentrating on how she feels and on what feels good. Continue this for a while, don't break the mood. Gradually move up to the base of the neck, the head, and the ears. Use a light, stroking motion. Don't be surprised if you see goose pimples. Enjoy them.

STEP 3

When you're ready, begin a light massage. Gently rub the shoulder muscles and those behind her neck, and then move down to the back and to the sides. Again, at this point, try not to tickle your partner, although you should be having fun. Move up and give a light scalp massage. (Remember that you've decided in advance how long the session will last. Be sure that each of you gets the chance to be pleasurer and pleasuree at each session. So, keep an eye on the time. If both of you really want to, you can let the session run a little longer).

STEP 4

Extend steps 1 and 2 to cover the waist, the buttocks, and down to the legs and feet. Start out the same way—a gentle, very light caressing, moving to a still gentle but somewhat firmer massage. There are several parts of the body that might be extremely sensitive. Slowly, gently, explore these. The inner parts of the thighs, the buttocks, behind the knee, even the ankle area and the toes—all of these areas may be specially sensitive. Gently stroke the entire leg, from the buttocks to the tops of the toes. Stroke each valley, each line of the body.

STEP 5

If you've come this far and haven't switched yet, this would be a good time to switch roles. After you've both been pleasured from head to toe while lying on your stomach, hold each other for a while. Talk about it. What areas really felt good? Did any of the areas make you feel uncomfortable? Learn about each other, with tenderness.

STEP 6

At your next session, you might want to begin with the back again. Sometimes it's a little easier to do this because you're both already familiar and comfortable with those steps. The next step is to have your partner turn over on her back. If she's a little uncomfortable with this, you can either place a towel over her or turn the lights down until she's more comfortable. Make sure that her eyes are closed so that she can concentrate more fully on her erotic pleasure. Begin by lightly stroking her head and face. Outline every feature with the tips of your fingers. Keep this up for a while—it is relaxing and very pleasurable.

STEP 7

Move down to the arms, the hands, and the fingers. Lightly caress these parts, one at a time, gently tracing the outline of the elbows. Tickles, doesn't it?

STEP 8

Move to the front of the shoulders, the chest, and the stomach, as in Figure 14-1. Again, gently caress those areas. Be sure, however, to skip the breasts and the nipples—for both males and females (this will come later). At this point, you want to highlight for your partner just how good it can feel when other parts of her body are stroked.

STEP 9

Now, gently massage these areas. It is most relaxing to lightly massage your partner's forehead and temples. Don't rub too hard. Also include arms, hands, and fingers. Try rubbing each finger separately. That usually feels pretty good. Gently massage the chest and shoulders, again avoiding the areas around the breasts. Be careful when you get to the abdomen,

Figure 14-1.

since too much pressure can be uncomfortable. Just use a light circular motion, using only enough pressure as needed to make her feel relaxed and comfortable.

STEP 10
Now, move slowly down to the hips. Gently trace the outline of your partner's hips—from side to front. Trace around the pubic area with your fingers. Again, skip the genital area completely. (Remember to use your distress signal if anything bothers you.)

STEP 11
Extend the exercise to include the front part of your partner's legs and feet. Lightly and gently, caress her inner thighs (pretty sensitive there, isn't it?), down her knees, her shins, her ankles, and the front parts of her feet.

STEP 12
Now, lightly massage the hips, moving down to include the front part of the legs, the feet, and the toes. Use a soft, gently probing, circular motion. Gently massage each toe separately.

STEP 13
Make sure that both of you are receiving equal time as pleasuree. Also, make sure that you are discussing what you are discovering about each other. Whether you do this during or after the session is up to you. Discuss your feelings about the exercise. In particular, let your partner know what he or she did to make you feel good. And don't forget the reward—when you finish a series of exercises, give each other the reward you agreed on.

STEP 14
Go through all of these exercises with the pleasuree's eyes open. It may make one or both of you uncomfortable at first, but give it a try. This will help you to feel even more relaxed with each other.

STEPS 15, 16, AND BEYOND
Try some variations. Use some lotions—for example, baby oil, hand lotion, or any lotion that either of you may like. Have these available right next to you so that you don't have to stop and get them.

Try telling your partner exactly what you like. You may even want to place your hand over your partner's and move it to an area that you especially want caressed.

Figure 14-2.

Try different positions. You've probably been operating with the pleasurer sitting up and the pleasuree lying down on her back or stomach. You might try lying on your side facing each other, gently stroking the exposed part of your partner's body. Try it with the pleasuree lying flat on his stomach with the pleasurer gently massaging his back, as in Figure 14-2.

Try different techniques. It might be delightful and quite sensuous, for example, to use a feather to stroke your partner lightly. One very sensuous technique is to gently run your lips along your partner's body, perhaps even licking with your tongue. If you're uncomfortable with that, you needn't try it (Chapter 18 presents some ideas on how you can overcome that distaste if you'd like to).

Above all else, be spontaneous. Once you've gone through these exercises, adapt them to suit your own needs. Explore together different ways of caressing and stroking that both of you find satisfying. Innovate.

Erotic Pleasure 1 can take anywhere from two or three days to a week. (This is assuming that you are following the guidelines about no genital contact, no performance pressure, and no attempts at orgasm.)

Let's review what you should have gotten out of it once you're finished. You should have learned about what parts of your body feel particularly good when stroked and about the ways in which you like them to be touched. You should have learned your partner's preferences. You should have learned how to communicate about what you like. We hope that you have learned that you don't have to engage in intercourse or touch the genitals in order to feel good and to enjoy your own as well as your partner's body. You've experienced a different kind of sexuality—one that's based on being and feeling sensual. And we hope very much that you feel closer to and more intimate with your partner.

EROTIC PLEASURE 2: WITH GENITAL CONTACT

Erotic Pleasure 2 is really an extension of Erotic Pleasure 1. Both exercises go together. Thus, we don't suggest jumping into Erotic Pleasure 2 without first having gone through Erotic Pleasure 1. In fact, it's a good idea to integrate the two. So, before you start genital contact, you should go through some nongenital stroking and touching.

But once you get to genital touching, we don't want you to stay fixed there so that all your sexual activity involves genitals (and eventually, intercourse). Nongenital and genital stroking are both part of a more important whole—total pleasure and joy in sex.

Even though Erotic Pleasure 2 involves genital touching, we still want you to try to avoid stimulating your partner to such a point that orgasm is inevitable. The point, here, is still to avoid trying to perform well—to have a long-lasting erection, to achieve orgasm, or to "succeed" in intercourse. You don't want or need those anxieties. Instead, the point is to illustrate the way nongenital and genital stroking can be experienced and enjoyed without any fears or preoccupations. We still want you to concentrate on how you feel about what your partner is doing and on the different techniques your partner can use to make you feel really sensual and sexually enjoyable. If you are the pleasurer (in this section, the female), we hope that you'll learn even more about what your partner likes and about how you can best enhance your partner's pleasure.

STEP 1
Follow all of the preliminary steps.

235

STEP 2

Write a contract between you and your partner according to the guidelines in Chapter 10. Be sure to specify the rewards you each want for completing the steps in this exercise.

STEP 3

You might want to take a bath or shower together. This in itself can be very arousing and very pleasurable. Either way, be fresh and clean before you start the exercise.

STEP 4

Go through the Erotic Pleasure 1 exercises. Get comfortable and relaxed, and allow yourself to really enjoy your partner's stroking. Use your lips to lightly brush and kiss nongenital areas. This can be a highly sensuous experience.

STEP 5

With the pleasuree lying on his back, gradually and gently move from stroking the shoulders and chest to very gentle stroking of the breasts. (For the first several steps of Erotic Pleasure, the pleasuree should keep his eyes closed, just relaxing and concentrating on his feelings.) Try moving your hand lightly all the way up from the navel across one breast, then repeat the movement with the other breast. Do the same thing, this time starting from the side and gently brushing across both breasts. Gradually focus more attention on the breast, but remember that the breasts can be particularly sensitive and that too much time spent and/or pressure on that area can be uncomfortable. Ask the pleasuree if it is enjoyable.

Go over the nipple very lightly. Play gently with the nipple and with the area around it (the areola). Watch your partner's nipple to see if it becomes erect (a sign of arousal). Caress it gently to help it become erect. At the same time, the pleasuree should concentrate on how it feels to have his breast stimulated in this way—and particularly on the sensations associated with an erect nipple. This may be a new experience for the male.

Now, begin to brush the breast area lightly with your lips, and, if you like, with your tongue. Gently kiss the nipple. If the pleasuree becomes uncomfortable, he should use the distress signal. Back off slightly to a type of touching or to a part of the body that doesn't produce anxiety, but continue physical contact, making sure that you both understand just what is producing the discomfort.

Once you've gotten this far, stimulate both breasts at the same time, first using your finger tips and then your mouth. If the pleasurer and the pleasuree are both comfortable with the idea, gently (very gently) kiss and then suck on one nipple and then on the other. Also, continue to stroke other parts of the body lightly and to get some feedback from the partner who is being pleasured as to what parts of his body he would like to have you stroke.

Don't forget to change roles and let the pleasurer become the pleasuree.

STEP 6

The next step involves genital stroking. With the pleasuree still on his back and his eyes closed, move down from the breast to stroke along the pelvic area, past the genitals, and along the thighs—especially the inner thighs. Don't just "attack" the genitals; gradually build up to it. The pleasuree should simply lie still and concentrate on the sensuous and sexual feelings. Since the focus will be on the genital area, it may be difficult at first for him to just lie still. Often, we associate stimulation of the genitals as a signal to attempt intercourse. But, in this exercise, neither intercourse nor orgasm is the goal. Instead, the goal is to learn to receive and give pleasure in a non-demand situation. For some of us, it may be even more difficult to receive than it is to give. But just try to relax and learn about the different types of touches and caresses that turn you on. If you feel tense or uncomfortable, use your distress signal.

6a. *Male as Pleasuree.* As you gently stroke the male's thighs, move slowly, even playfully, up to the genital area. With your finger tips, trace the area of skin around the genitals. Very gently and lightly, brush the penis, using just one or two fingers. Move down from the penis to the scrotal sac. Be careful, because the testes, within the scrotal sac, are very sensitive. Softly run your fingers over the scrotal sac. You can probably feel the testes under the skin.

At any point during this step, if either partner feels uncomfortable, he or she should use the distress signal. The pleasurer should go back to light stroking of an area that produces less discomfort, and the two of you should give feedback to each other. In fact, the pleasuree should be giving feedback during this whole period, because only he can express how the pleasuring feels; only he can relate to the pleasurer what feels good.

The whole idea here, though, is to move gradually and gently toward genital contact. Thus, the use of steps from Erotic Pleasure 1 should provide the lead-in to Erotic Pleasure 2 so that neither partner feels that the move is too fast.

Gently explore your partner's genitals with your hand,

237

Figure 14-3.

going from scrotal sac and testes to penis—the shaft, the coronal ridge, the head of the penis, and so on. As you're doing
this, take note of your own feelings about these parts of his
body. Notice also the differences between the nonerect and
the erect penis.

Play gently with the penis. Hold it in your hand and move
your hand lightly up and down the penis. The male may or may
not get an erection. (However, if he is completely relaxed and
enjoying the stimulation, it is likely that he will.) When you're
rubbing the penis (as in Figure 14-3), don't rub hard or in a
constant, rhythmic motion or he will have an orgasm. Lightly
play with the penis; then, perhaps, go back to another area
that he likes you to stroke; then, return to the penis. Keep this
up for a while, getting feedback as to how your partner feels. If
by chance he happens to come to orgasm, don't worry. This *is*
erotic pleasure, after all. But try not to use the same motion
next time; try to get some feedback so that you can prevent the
orgasm. The goal here, still, is for you to learn what your partner likes, for your partner to learn what he likes, and for both
of you to do it in an atmosphere free from concerns about
orgasms.

As far as grip goes, one good one is to use two hands, one
near the base of the penis, holding it steady or perhaps gently
fondling his scrotum, while the other hand makes a ring
around the penis with the thumb and the first and second

238

fingers or with the whole hand. Move your hand up and down slowly (later, when you want to bring him to orgasm, you can increase the speed and the pressure). Play with his entire penis; don't stay only with the head of the penis, which is the most sensitive part.

You'll probably note that the penis alternates between being erect and being soft. You'll probably also notice that it is possible to bring the penis back to erection by gentle rubbing. Don't be concerned if the male loses his erection. In fact, during the process of making love, erections do come and go, perhaps many times, and this signals no abnormality or loss of potency of the male or loss of attractiveness of the female.

Move from the penis down to the scrotal area; you might want to cup the scrotum in your hand, being very gentle because of the sensitivity of the testes. Trace a line with your fingertips from the base of the scrotum down to the anus. This (the perineum) is another very sensitive area; get feedback on how it feels to have you do that. Continue this kind of gentle play and gentle teasing—from genital to nongenital areas—until it is time to change places—from pleasurer to pleasuree.

6b. *Female as Pleasuree.* Have the pleasuree lie back and get comfortable, with her eyes closed. You, as pleasurer, should of course, get comfortable, too: You might lie on your side, supporting your head with your hand, or you might sit or kneel. Begin gently stroking some of the nongenital areas, particularly the ones that you know your partner likes. Gently fondle and stroke her breasts; tease the nipple until it is erect. If the female is comfortable with it, she can guide your hands to areas where she especially enjoys being touched.

Move down to the stomach, to the hips, and past the genitals to the inner thighs. Lightly stroke these areas, from the hips down to the toes. See if she has goose pimples. Check also for feedback and the possibility of the distress signal. Then, move your fingertips gently across the genital area, tracing your fingers through the pubic hair.

Gently touch the area outside of the vaginal opening (the major or outer lips). Trace your finger around this area, then drop down to the area of skin just below the vagina and to the inner tops of the thighs. Play back and forth between these areas for a while. You might also move back up to the stomach and gently massage the area around the navel.

Carefully and very gently spread first the outer lips and then the inner lips. Watch very carefully for your partner's possible distress signal. At the same time, be very careful to note your own reaction to your partner's genitals. Trace your

239

finger around this area, using a light circular motion. Gently—very gently—put the tip of one finger into the vaginal opening. Do not insert your finger all the way, as this might be uncomfortable, especially at first. Run the tip of your finger in and out of the vaginal opening two or three times. Don't forget to move away from this area so that you can pleasure other nongenital parts of the body.

Return to the genital area. After parting the lips, gently explore the area of skin over the clitoris. Move very softly and gently to the clitoris. Note that the clitoris has a tiny head and a shaft. The clitoris is extremely sensitive, so go lightly. (Check for distress signals.) Touch the clitoris gently, then move to another area, and then return to the clitoris. Even if your partner is not sending a distress signal, look at her face and body to see if she appears to be relaxed and to be enjoying the experience. If not, move to another area, and discuss this with her as you lightly massage her.

If all appears to be well, continue lightly running your fingers around the clitoral and vaginal areas. Many women find direct stimulation of the clitoris, because of its sensitivity, uncomfortable. You may want to try gently rubbing the sides of the clitoris (check this out with your partner).

Although you don't want to stimulate her to orgasm (we'll get to that later), perhaps the best position of your hand is with the flat of your hand over the vulva with your middle finger between the lips. Let the tip of your finger move in and out of the vagina, while your palm presses above the pubis.

Note whether your partner is aroused. You can tell this if the clitoris becomes firmer (it may even withdraw under the fold of skin that is over it).

Remember that the goal here is not to "overarouse" your partner to the point of orgasm. So, again, don't use the steady rhythmic motions that are more likely to produce high arousal. Use more of a gentle, teasing motion, moving back and forth between genital and nongenital areas. If your partner finds it stimulating, you may want to insert your finger more deeply into the vaginal entrance, moving it gently around the vaginal walls. If she is lubricating, this is a sign of arousal. Move playfully from the vaginal opening to other parts of the body.

The female, in the meantime, should be concentrating on her own pleasure. Don't feel that you're being selfish. You both have the opportunity to enjoy this exercise. Tell your partner what you like and what you don't like. Experience what it's like to be stimulated, to feel sensual, and to feel turned on—without having to worry about orgasms or anything else.

STEP 7

For both males and females, the next step, if you both agree, is to try oral–genital contact. For some people, this is an extremely sensual, sexy experience. For others, it is distasteful. If you or your partner finds it particularly distasteful, you can skip this step. However, if you would like to try oral–genital contact but are uncomfortable with it, try the exercises in Chapter 19 as a way of overcoming your discomfort.

If you do want to proceed with oral–genital contact, be sure that both of you are clean and fresh. Begin by using your mouth to stimulate other parts of your partner's body. Then slowly move down to the genital area. When the pleasuree is the male, the woman may want to softly kiss the penis or, with the tip of her tongue, lick the penile shaft. You may want to place the head of the penis in your mouth and gently move your mouth up and down once or twice. Try not to overdo this, since it could result in orgasm, and, at this point, you merely want to expose the male to the joys of this form of sensation.

With the male as pleasurer, he may want to lightly lick, with the tip of his tongue, the area around the major lips. Then, gently parting the lips with your fingers, let the tip of your tongue explore the entrance to the vagina and then dart up to tease the clitoris, perhaps lightly licking it. This can be extremely pleasurable to the female. Move back and forth from genital to nongenital areas.

In both cases, be sure to check carefully for distress signals and to move to less-threatening forms of pleasuring if this produces too much anxiety.

STEP 8

Up until now, the pleasuree has kept his or her eyes closed. At this point, when you are both very comfortable and relaxed with each other's bodies have the pleasuree open his or her eyes. At the beginning, this can produce some discomfort (probably, for both of you). If so, move to the part of the body that is the least threatening (with your eyes still open). Then, gradually expand the pleasuring and exploration until both of you are comfortable watching each other in the process.

STEP 9

If you've been pretty much staying in the same position up to now, try different positions—both of you on your sides; pleasuree sitting between the pleasurer's legs as he or she lies

Figure 14-4.

back down, as in Figure 14-4; the man behind the woman, supporting her with his arms and reaching around to stimulate her genital area.

STEP 10

Try this very erotic variation of Erotic Pleasure. Begin by ensuring that you have plenty of time and plenty of privacy. Embrace each other. Kiss and hold each other for a while, fully clothed. Gently rub each other's bodies through the clothing. Then, gently and erotically, undress each other. Find out if your partner likes to be undressed in a particular sequence. Stroke and kiss as you undress each other. When you're undressing your partner, gently stroke the skin of the parts of the body that you have just undressed. You may want to stroke parts of your partner's body through the clothing. Make this a highly sensuous experience.

Then, take a bath or shower together (or separately, if you're uncomfortable with this). Wash each other's backs first, then gently and slowly move to soap up other areas of the body. Luxuriate together. Rinse off and towel each other dry.

Then, move through the Erotic Pleasure exercises, first exercise 1 and then moving to exercise 2.

Talk about what you are experiencing. Give feedback to your partner. Ask your partner for guidance in his or her pleasuring of you, and be clear in telling your partner what you like when you are being pleasured.

If you want to repeat this step in the future, vary who

undresses whom first, what you wear, and possibly even the place and the time.

Pleasuring Yourself

If you do not have a partner for Erotic Pleasure, you can do most of these exercises yourself. Just follow the same guidelines that we've presented for Erotic Pleasure with a partner. The only difference is that your own fingers will do the walking. Explore and enjoy your own body, going from the actual making of a contract with yourself to Erotic Pleasure 1 to Erotic Pleasure 2. More-detailed ideas about self-exploration are presented in Chapter 13.

The whole purpose of Erotic Pleasure was to provide an accepting and understanding atmosphere between you and your partner and to help you relax, to teach you different ways of providing sensual and sexual pleasure to others, and to help you truly enjoy your own body, free from the concerns of performing the way you think you "have to." If you do feel comfortable now, and if you really can relax and just enjoy being touched, caressed, and stroked, then Erotic Pleasure has really worked for you.

As we've said, this is a basic step in all the Treat Yourself programs that are presented in Part 4. You are now ready to begin any one of the Treat Yourself programs to help you really enhance your sex life.

PART

4

Getting Down to Cases

Fifteen

Problems with Arousal and Orgasm

If you've ever been called "frigid" or if you even think of yourself as "frigid," then you have probably experienced a type of anguish that many people simply are unfamiliar with. You've probably felt guilty, angry, sick, abnormal, or depressed, or blamed yourself, or your partner—maybe all of these. Maybe you've even become obsessed about sex and tried to figure out what's wrong with you—why you can't be "like everybody else." You may even have been pushed to an extreme to try to overcome your problem—either by avoiding sex altogether so that you won't have to suffer anymore or possibly by making love with more and more people in order to finally find the one person who can "make you right."

Whatever way you've tried to handle it, you've probably suffered.

Part of the problem, we think, is the very term *frigid*. From now on, you can forget it. We're not going to use it, for a very good reason. Nobody's frigid!

Call It What It Is

We hope that this will be a relief for you and will not just produce a reaction of disbelief. Let's look at it this way: Frigidity is just a label. It's a vague term; it doesn't really describe a specific problem; and, most importantly, it has come to have a deprecating or disparaging connotation. It often leaves women feeling anxious, helpless, and hopeless. In other words, the term *frigidity* is meaningless and harmful.

The truth of the matter is that you may be experiencing one of a number of problems related either to sexual arousal or to having orgasms. As far as sexual arousal goes, you simply may not get very aroused at all. For example, you may feel very little, if any, sexual sensation or desire, despite physical stimulation, such as touching or stroking. You may not show signs of sexual excitement, such as lubrication of the vagina or hardening of the nipples, even during intercourse. You may not get mentally or emotionally turned on by sex, either. You may or may not enjoy the physical contact, you may feel neutral about sex, or you may feel that sex is duty.

Gail had a problem involving arousal.

Gail had been married to Dale for three years. During that period, they had made love only on the average of once or twice a month, and even that was decreasing. The problem was simple: Gail didn't like sex. At first, she tolerated it because that was her image of the way the "good wife" should be. But she used all kinds of little tricks to get out of it, ranging from fake headaches to "feeling too tired." But things increasingly began to go bad with her marriage, and she and Dale frequently found themselves fighting about sex. Dale would call her frigid, and she would scream and yell and blame Dale for being such a lousy lover.

Another set of problems involves orgasms (or the lack of them). This can have a wide range as well. For example, you may never have had an orgasm. Or, possibly, you were able to have orgasms at one point, but now you cannot. Or, you may be able to reach orgasm through self-stimulation, but not in intercourse. Some women are not even sure whether or not they've had an orgasm. They feel "wetness" in their vagina, and wonder, "Is this it?" Myrna's is a case in point.

Myrna was twenty-five years old, unmarried, and sexually active. In fact, she very much enjoyed sex—the feeling of closeness, of affection, the physical touching and stroking. However, she had never experienced an orgasm during intercourse—with her partner's penis in her vagina. She was able to reach orgasm when masturbating—every time—whether she used her hand or a vibrator. But she couldn't help wondering what was the matter with her.

So, you see, there may be all sorts of problems involved under the broad categories of arousal and orgasm. And it's particularly important for you to be clear about what your problem is so that you can be equally clear about what you have to do to treat yourself and to be sure that the problem is gone when you've finished.

There may be any number of different causes for these problems. As we suggested in Chapter 4, these can range from a lack of appropriate stimulation (a very common cause), to punitive sex education, to rough, negative, or traumatic early experiences with sex.

An increasing number of women are complaining about their lack of arousal or orgasms to the extent that these are the most commonly reported sex problems among women— perhaps the most frequently reported of all sex problems. So you are not alone. There is a long history of male-dominated society's forcing women to suppress their sexual desires and needs. But in recent years, this has been countered by the awareness of women about their sexual needs and rights: the rights to satisfying and fulfilling sexual experiences.

Now, despite the fact that there is not just one problem involving arousal and orgasm, many of the problems, with some exceptions, are treated in similar ways. The program that follows can be adapted to meet your own needs. For example, if your problem involves the inability to have an orgasm during intercourse, but you can have orgasms through masturbation, you obviously may not have to follow the parts of the program dealing with self-stimulation exercises. Many of these exercises, as we will show, can be done without a partner, whereas others do require the participation of a partner.

SOME PRELIMINARY STEPS

Be sure that you've read Parts 1, 2, and 3 of the book. Having done this will help you to understand your problem in more detail and will prepare you for the exercises to come. We also think that it's a particularly good idea to have your partner read these parts, as well as this chapter, so that he'll be prepared for his part of the program.

Pinpoint Your Problem

Go over the assessment steps in Chapter 8. Try to pinpoint the problem. Is it that you're not turned on at all to sex or that you are turned on only with certain people or at certain times? Is the problem that you have orgasms only at some times, or with some people, and not with others? Be clear about just what the problem is—from your own point of view, that is; how you experience it.

Also, review some of the material dealing with your attitudes and feelings about sex. How *do* you feel about sexual activity? Have you been taught that sex is dirty, that the only "proper" sex is that which is within a marital relationship for the purpose of having children, or that masturbation can lead to mental illness? Evaluate your own attitudes. Is it possible that some of the things that you've been taught by or heard from others have given you some negative ideas about sex—to the extent that you really can't enjoy it?

Once you've completed your assessment, you may already have some clues as to where the problem lies. If so, act on it; make the changes.

We'll make several suggestions of ways in which you can help yourself even before you start a formal Treat Yourself Program.

Communicate with Your Partner

If you have a regular, or even a semi-regular partner, try talking to him about your situation. If this is particularly awkward for you, use some of the communication guidelines we presented in Chapter 9. This may ease your burden considerably; it may even free you up enough so that the actual problem eases up. It also might give your partner a little insight into what you are going through. At the very least, open communication may prove to be a very motivating factor for your partner to become more involved in helping you through the program. Whatever you do, though, don't blame your partner (he'll probably just blame you right back), even if you think he is a clumsy lover. It's better to use the soft approach and gradual guidance in order to make him a more stimulating lover. When we get to the actual program, we'll build in some exercises that will help you to do just that.

248

Think Positively

We don't mean to be too corny about this. It's not as if you could just think yourself out of the problem or, by a snap of your fingers, end the problem. But there are some things you really should know that might help:

1. Many people suffer from arousal or orgasm problems either because they won't allow themselves to experience pleasure or because they have a fear of letting go. We're going to provide a step-by-step program to help you do both. But, at this point, we do want you to think about it. What would happen if you did let go? What are you telling yourself? The point here is that it really is okay if you let go, if you allow yourself to experience sexual pleasure. We want you to realize that this problem is often a result of your being taught that sex is bad, and that letting go results in something bad happening to you. You may even think that it's not "ladylike" to *really* let go. Well, that just isn't so. The only thing that can happen to you is that you will feel better. You can't get hurt if you let go. You will feel more relaxed, more content, and more fulfilled.

2. Some women don't have orgasms because they believe that clitoral stimulation is wrong. They won't allow themselves or their partners to directly stimulate their clitorises. Because this is a major part of the orgasmic process, they are missing out on a key aspect of sexual experiencing. The clitoris's only function is to provide sexual pleasure. It's as natural as could be to use and enjoy clitoral stimulation. Don't pass this up.

3. Some women feel guilty or fearful about masturbation or about orgasm. This robs them of a good deal of sexual enjoyment. What we've said above goes here, too. Sex is for you to enjoy. We don't want you to get involved in any activities that would be harmful in any way. But if you've been taught to feel guilty about masturbating or to feel that you're a fallen woman if you allow yourself to reach orgasm—forget it. Or at least realize that no respectable expert on human sexuality believes that.

4. Some women are turned off—either to sex entirely or to having orgasms in particular—because of the pressures they feel to enjoy sex or have orgasms. In some cases, the male partner puts pressure on the female to have an orgasm, because if she doesn't, he feels that he's failed. This pressure to

perform then inhibits the female's sexual response. Another source of the pressure—although a more indirect one—is from the increasing recognition of the sexual rights of women. Some women turn this into the feeling that they must perform better in bed, and that they must have orgasms if they want to be "complete women." This pressure to have orgasms can be an inhibiting factor. So don't try to out-perform anyone. Move at your pace, relax, and don't let your partner or society in general put that kind of pressure on you. You'll really benefit in the long run if you can resist it. Related to this is the idea that when you are involved in sexual activity, try to stop thinking about whether "it" will happen. Focus instead on the pleasure you receive from (and give to) your partner at that particular moment. Try to stop being "an observer of yourself." Focus on how you can stay with pleasant physical sensations.

Be Sure That You're Not Having Orgasms

This, of course, sounds pretty strange. But you'd be surprised at the number of women who actually are experiencing orgasm but are not aware of it. If you are expecting rockets to explode and to see stars, it's possible that you are expecting too much. Remember that orgasms are experienced differently by different people: They may be extremely intense with some people and more "restrained" with others. In fact, different sexual experiences can produce different orgasmic experiences in the same people at different times. The popular literature that reports orgasms to be the most fantastic, incredible, satisfying, wonderful experiences in the world does little to prepare people for what to expect. For some people, orgasms may be just that. For others, they may be much more subdued. Review Chapter 12, particularly the part that describes the several phases of the sexual-response cycle. Check yourself out once more after reading that chapter. It's possible that you were expecting a little too much.

Change Your Situation

There are several conditions that you might change and thus bring more satisfaction to your sex life.

1. Make sure that you are relaxed and comfortable before you begin sexual activity. If you're particularly uptight when you start, there's a good chance that you will feel that way

when you finish. Make sure, also, that you are in a situation that is peaceful and relatively free from interruptions.

2. Use fantasies. Review Chapter 13. Make use of the material there to build more erotic fantasies into your sex life. There's nothing wrong with sexual fantasies. We *all* have them, although some of us fight a little harder to ignore them. Don't ignore them. Use them to increase your excitement and enjoyment when you're involved in sexual activity. Just about any fantasy that turns you on can help you to enjoy sex more.

3. Increase the stimulation you are receiving. One of the commonest—perhaps *the* commonest—reason for not having orgasms is the lack of proper stimulation. Once you've mastered the art of using your fantasies to enhance your sex life, then it's time to make sure that you are receiving the proper stimulation. Sometimes this merely involves having the stimulation last longer. For example, it may mean asking your partner to stimulate you manually or orally for a longer period of time before you try intercourse. It might mean asking your partner to try to hold off from having an ejaculation for a little longer or to continue thrusting after ejaculation until you reach orgasm.

Stimulation can also be increased by changing positions. This calls for more experimentation (see Chapter 20 for information on different positions). For example, the female-on-top position allows her more flexibility and control of movement so that she can both determine the most pleasing rhythm and also the best motion to increase pressure on the clitoral area. The male-on-top position also allows for pressure on the clitoral area, although this results more from the pressure of the pelvic structure than from the penis. No matter what position you choose, you should choose. Try different positions and find the ones that enhance your pleasure to the highest degree.

Exercise Your Sex Muscles

Review Chapter 12, "Getting in Touch with Your Body." In particular, do the exercises that will help you to strengthen your PC muscles (the muscles around the vaginal wall). This is a very important exercise for increasing your arousal and your orgasmic potential. When your PC muscles are toned up, you'll be able to control the stimulation you receive to a much greater degree. In fact, some women who either had never experienced orgasm or had experienced it irregularly reported having their first orgasms and more consistent orgasms after using this exercise. Once your PC muscles are in good shape—you'll be able to tell, because the exercises get easier and you'll probably experience clearer feelings in your vagina—you can continue practicing them, perhaps fewer times per day, for as long as you like. You can practice these exercises and enjoy the sensations anywhere; it's totally private.

Refrain from Sex

The noted sex therapist Jack Annon sometimes recommends that women who are experiencing a low level of arousal should temporarily refrain from engaging in sexual activity. During that period, the woman is to engage in other activities that she may have found arousing in the past, such as reading erotic books or magazines or viewing erotic movies with her partner. Then, the woman and her partner can engage in what Annon calls "dating sessions." Each partner in turn selects a social "date" that goes with a sexual "session." For example, you might arrange to have lunch or see a movie and then engage in some sexual activity. At first, the sexual activity might only be talking about sex. But you can gradually increase the intensity of the activity (although there should be a "date" between each session) until you are going home, to each other's place, or to a motel, for prolonged love-making. You can see how the excitement and anticipation would build up.

INCREASING AROUSAL AND ORGASMS: THE PROGRAM

If none of the above steps has worked for you, then we suggest that you begin a formal Treat Yourself program.

The basic strategy for helping you to respond more fully, to reach an aroused state, and to reach orgasms both through self-stimulation and in intercourse is a simple one. We will help you to get rid of some of your hang-ups about sex and, at the same time, to receive increased sexual stimulation. The stimulation will come from several sources: from yourself (from your hands and from your fantasies) and from your partner, and it will include the ways in which he touches you and the types of positions you use for intercourse.

As usual, we will use a series of exercises, organized in such a way to move you slowly but surely through the entire process, without putting on pressure for you to jump into activities that you're not ready for.

252

As you'll see, many of these exercises call for you to practice by yourself, without a partner—a very handy thing if you have no partner available. Later, if you want to be able to share your progress with your partner, or when you want to be able to have orgasms during intercourse, we'll move gradually into involving your partner.

These exercises have been used by thousands of people in sex-therapy clinics all across the country. There is a good deal of research showing their success. That, in fact, is why we're presenting them here for your use. But, although some women do achieve their goals within a few days, don't be discouraged if you take longer. It may be several weeks before you achieve what you want to achieve from this program. So don't jump ahead thinking that if you move to a more advanced step your progress will be faster. The advanced steps are built on the earlier steps, and until you can be sure you've reached the goals at each step, try not to push ahead.

Okay. Now you're ready.

Step 1: Do All the Preliminary Steps

Read through Parts 1, 2, and 3 of this book so that you're prepared for the exercises you'll be using in your program. Also, read this chapter through in advance so that there will be no surprises. If you will be working with a partner later in the program, read and discuss the program with him. Remember: no surprises.

Also, be sure that you've followed through on whichever of the preliminary steps is appropriate for your situation. Pinpoint the problem; fill out the questionnaire in Chapter 8; if you're involved with someone sexually now, be sure that you're receiving adequate stimulation; try changing the positions you use in intercourse; make sure that you're not shutting off erotic fantasies.

Set the scene for yourself. Be careful to see that you've set aside adequate time for your program (twenty to sixty minutes, four or five times a week) in a calm, quiet place where you won't be disturbed.

Step 2: Relax

Remember that we said that one primary goal of this program is to help you decrease some of your inhibitions about sex. Review Chapter 11, which deals with relaxation exercises. Think about sexual situations in which you either don't get turned on when you'd like to or don't have orgasms when you'd like to. Evaluate yourself on the anxiety scale in Chapter 11. If you're running up over 30 or 40 in relation to your thinking about sexual activities, then the relaxation exercises are particularly important.

For these exercises, we suggest the abdominal breathing, followed by the muscle-relaxation exercises. Practice these for twenty to thirty minutes the first week and as needed the second and third week until you are able to relax yourself fairly rapidly within just a few minutes.

Step 3: Use Contracts

Be sure to build in contracts at each major stage of your program. Review Chapter 10, which will provide you with the models. In fact, use a contract even if you're doing this exercise yourself (without a partner). It will increase your motivation and will give you a clear goal to shoot for. Also, be sure to build in rewards for yourself—from yourself as well as from your partner (negotiate his cooperation on this). Or negotiate mutual rewards from and for both of you. Finally, select a distress signal to be used when you involve your partner. Make sure that he understands why and how it is to be used.

Step 4: Pleasure Yourself

If you feel that you are rarely or never aroused, if you have never had an orgasm, or if your orgasms are rare or unpredictable, this is a very important step for you. If your problem is mainly that you cannot achieve orgasm during intercourse, you can skip this step and move to step 2. Actually, this step blends into the steps that follow in a way that leads eventually to working with a partner and to orgasm during intercourse.

Incidentally, if you are going to do this program with your partner, we strongly encourage him to begin a self-stimulation program of his own at the same time. Let him use Chapter 13 as his guide, but encourage him to follow roughly the same progression of steps that you are following, trying to move at roughly the same pace. This ought to help him provide some support to you as he experiences what you are experiencing.

The step consists of several sub-steps. We will teach you a mini-program for pleasuring yourself—for using self-stimulation to turn yourself on and then to achieve orgasm. This program has been developed by W. Charles Lobitz and Joseph LoPiccolo, who have used it with many women with great success. Now, if you're uncomfortable with the idea of self-stimulation, we promise to move slowly, in a way that will allow you to become more and more used to the parts and sensations of your own body. But don't skip this step just because it does involve touching yourself. Once you overcome the idea that it isn't wrong to know yourself and to feel good about knowing yourself, then you'll be that much more able to achieve what you want in a relationship in which sexual activity is involved. When you know what turns you on, you'll be able to help others turn you on.

Now, move pretty much at your own pace with these exercises. If you get too tense with one step, move back a step or two to an exercise that you can handle with more comfort. Repeat these several times; then move ahead.

1. Read Chapters 12 and 13. These will prepare you for this exercise.

2. It's just possible that you're really not in touch with your own body, including your sexual organs. So, you will want to increase your own body awareness. Tonight, when you shower or bathe, use your hands instead of a wash cloth. Luxuriate in the bathtub. When you're finished, rub yourself with oil. Now, look at yourself standing in the nude in front of a full-length mirror. Begin to appreciate your body. Dwell on the strengths of your body for a while. Just look at yourself from as many angles as you can. Use a small hand-held mirror to look at your back. Try to get comfortable looking at yourself in the nude.

3. Use the small hand-held mirror to examine your genitals. You can look at the illustrations in Chapter 12 to guide you.

4. Lightly run your hands over all the parts of your body, excluding the genitals. Get used to the idea of lightly stroking yourself.

5. Now, with the aid of the hand-held mirror, use your hands to explore your genital area. Do this both sitting and standing. The point of this is *not* to arouse yourself. Just relax, get familiar with the different parts of your sex organs, and try to increase your comfort with the idea of touching your own genitals. First, run your fingers lightly across the pubic hair. Then, use a little more pressure to lightly touch the skin under the hair. You can feel and see the outer lips. Part them so that the inner lips are exposed; then, inside those, notice the vaginal entrance, the urethral entrance, and, at the top, the clitoris. Look closely at your clitoris and touch it lightly. Notice that it moves when you touch it. Note also the different parts of the clitoris.

Gail was unsure of herself, especially about how she would react to the self-stimulation program. First, she and Dale negotiated an agreement to refrain from sexual contact until Gail was well into her Treat Yourself program. Then, Gail wrote a contract for herself, because she felt that it would give her something clear to aim for. She figured that she could just take it out and read it if at any point she was not certain about whether she should continue. In part, the contract read, "I will set aside thirty minutes five nights a week to practice the mini-program on self-stimulation. I will continue to practice even though I might be uncomfortable at first. If I do follow through all five nights, I will spend up to $10.00 this weekend on something just for myself that I otherwise would not have bought."

6. Focus, in your exploration, on the areas that are most sensitive. Don't spend all your time on one area, though, such as the clitoris, but on all of the areas that seem especially sensitive to you. Get used to lightly touching these areas.

7. At this point, you should be increasingly comfortable with your body and with your own touching of yourself. Now, begin to lightly stroke yourself in the genital area in the ways that you find most pleasurable. Begin lightly and use increasing pressure. This is part of a self-stimulation exercise that will help you to reach orgasm. Be sure that you've read Chapter 13; follow the guidelines there on self-stimulation. Just briefly, to review those: Relax and get yourself in a comfortable position. Rub your hand across the mons pubis, the firm area covered by hair at the top of the outer lips. Part the outer lips and stroke along the inside edges of these and of the inner lips. Gently move your finger in and out of the vaginal entrance. Take your time. Enjoy. Find the clitoris and play with it. Place it between two fingers and rub gently. You can change the pressure and the rhythm as it pleases you. Stroke the clitoris with one finger, back and forth and sideways. If direct stimulation is uncomfortable, stroke the sides of the clitoris, varying the pressure and the rhythm. Place your hand over the vaginal entrance and the clitoris, rubbing the entire area. You can also move back and forth to and from the clitoral area by placing your hand over the entire genital area and moving it in a circle across the pubic bone, down to the lips, and in to the clitoris and the vaginal entrance. Relax. Get lost in yourself. At the same time that you are stimulating yourself, use your other hand to lightly stroke other sensitive parts of your body. In particular, gently stroke your breasts; play with the nipples until they are erect. Remember that only you can know how you feel. Continue to vary the pressure and the rhythm in ways that turn you on. If you are uncomfortable, try to maintain the self-stimulation

exercise as long as you can and the discomfort will likely disappear. Otherwise, go back to the previous step until you are comfortable with proceeding. (Of course, in setting up a time and a place for this exercise, make sure that you won't be interrupted, so that you can concentrate completely on yourself. Don't feel guilty about it. It's your body. You might even take the phone off the hook.)

8. You may reach orgasm during the activities of the previous step. Don't back away from it. Let yourself go! You'll soon realize that it's nothing but pure pleasure. You won't lose control, have to move your bowels, or urinate; you'll just enjoy.

If you didn't reach orgasm, keep trying. Really. Use a little more pressure or a faster rhythm. Don't quit after a few minutes. This might be a good time to add lubrication so that you don't get irritated; lubrication can also add to your pleasure. Use any one of the several we recommended in Chapter 7. This is also the time to be using fantasies in the way we recommended in Chapter 13. Think of things that really turn you on. If you'd like, buy a sexy book or magazine and read it while you're stimulating yourself. Keep going until "something happens." Don't stop unless you're tired or aching.

9. If you haven't reached orgasm yet, use a vibrator, such as the one we described in Chapter 7. Don't hesitate on this, even if the idea seems somehow wrong to you. Remember that the vibrator should be seen simply as an extension of your hand. You control it. Put together the erotic reading material, the lubricating gel, and your erotic fantasies. Apply the vibrator gently at first, as we suggested in Chapter 13. Gradually, you can add pressure to the point that is most stimulating for you. Use the head of the vibrator in creative and stimulating ways. Keep applying pressure and don't get discouraged if you don't have an orgasm immediately. Let yourself go. Get into it. It may take up to forty-five minutes, or even an hour, and it may take repeated tries over a few days, but it will happen if you let it.

Gail even surprised herself at how well she was doing. She had not yet reached orgasm, but she was luxuriating in the new feelings she was experiencing. It was like a new freedom, a new self. She began to use the vibrator with some degree of concern. At first, it seemed so unnatural to her. But she soon got the hang of it. She started slowly, using the vibrator to gently massage the area around the genitals. Then she slowly moved the vibrator across the genitals, with particular pressure over the clitoral area. She increased the pressure directly on the clitoral area. The first day, she went for thirty minutes, then stopped. She had not reached orgasm. The next evening, she took a long, warm bath, relaxed, had a glass of wine, and went to her bedroom. She began to fantasize an activity with Dale that really turned her on. She applied the vibrator and within ten minutes, her whole pelvic area began to thrust almost uncontrollably. She let herself just go with it. She had her first orgasm. She was in ecstasy.

10. Some women may not be able to experience orgasm at that point, particularly if the woman is afraid to let loose or is afraid of losing control. If you are still not having orgasms, we want you to try to role-play one. No one will know; you're all alone. Now, we hope that you don't get the idea that for the rest of your life you have to go around faking orgasms in order to satisfy your partner. No. This one's for you, to loosen you up a little. We want you to really exaggerate what might happen during an orgasm. Imagine that you are having a tremendous, incredible, hard-to-control orgasm. Overdo it. Move your arms and legs about in an uncontrollable way. Moan, scream, shout. Scrunch up your face in all sorts of contortions. Practice the very behaviors you would engage in during orgasm. Thrust your pelvis, point your toes, tense your thigh muscles, throw your head back, tighten your vaginal muscles (PCs). Let go. Lose control.

Now relax. Think about it a minute. You're still okay, right? Nothing terrible happened to you.

Now, do it again. Think of all the possible types of orgasms there might be—from violent ones to controlled shudders, twitches, and moans. Act them all out.

Do this until you're no longer tense and embarrassed. If you can, do it in front of the mirror, also.

When you are comfortable with this, go back and repeat the last few steps of this exercise, using the vibrator if you need it.

Now that you can have orgasms, enjoy them. Spend as much time as you want pleasuring yourself. Don't rush immediately into intercourse; take your time. Make sure that you can have orgasms when you want them and on a consistent basis when you're alone. Then you'll be ready to involve your partner.

Step 5: Erotic Pleasure 1

Whether you've been able to achieve orgasms all along by yourself, or whether you've only just mastered the art with your self-stimulation program, you are ready to move to the next step—involving your partner. If you've just worked

258

through the mini-program in which you've been able to bring yourself to orgasm when you like, bring him in gently. Try not to belittle his sexual prowess and his inability to "give you" orgasms. In fact, it's a shared problem now, and you really do want his cooperation. On the other hand, there's no reason not to talk about what you've accomplished. You did it on your own—with a little help from a friend—and you *should* be proud.

Now, even though you'll be working on this program with a partner, we want you to be selfish. That's right. This program is for you. Of course, we hope you'll also give to him and use your skills to help him sexually. But primarily, this program is to increase your pleasure in sex, and that is nothing to feel guilty about. However, we're sure that as your enjoyment increases, so will his. In fact, you'll be able to provide him with far more pleasure as you become more satisfied. You both have a lot to gain from success—and absolutely nothing to lose.

Now, you have a choice here. Eventually, we want you to be able to demonstrate to your partner just what you accomplished in step 4—the self-stimulation program. If you want to move immediately to that, then you can skip ahead to step 7. But if you want to move more gradually, slowly increasing the intensity of his involvement—and this would be our recommendation—then stay with this step—Erotic Pleasure 1—and then move on to the next step, Erotic Pleasure 2. This will lead, in a much more natural and comfortable progression, up to step 7.

> Myrna was uncomfortable about involving a man in her program. In fact, she was kind of uncomfortable about even talking about "her problem." But she knew that eventually she would have to. She made sure that she tried as many of the preliminary guidelines as possible, but she was still not able to come to orgasm with her current boyfriend. Although she really enjoyed masturbating to orgasm, she still wanted to experience orgasm during intercourse. And the way to do that was to involve her friend. So she took the plunge. First, she reviewed Chapter 9 (communication). Then, one evening, after coming home from a movie with her boyfriend, she described what she wanted. To her surprise, her boyfriend was not only cooperative, but he was relieved as well. "I'm glad you trusted me enough to tell me," he said. They reviewed Parts 2 and 3 and this chapter of the book together. Then they developed their first contract—the Erotic Pleasure 1 Contract.

Make sure that you've reviewed Chapter 14 (Erotic Pleasure). Set a time and a place where you and your partner can be relaxed, comfortable, and secure. Close your eyes. Let your partner be the first pleasurer. Be selfish. Relax and enjoy the sensations. He should lightly stroke and caress you all over your body, excluding the breasts and genital areas. He can lie or sit next to you, or he can sit between your legs to stroke the inner parts of your thighs.

The purpose of this step, of course, is to help you and your partner come to trust each other, to learn about each other's bodies, and to learn how you can feel sensual without having to worry about achieving orgasms. This is an important part of the exercise. The goal is to take your mind off worrying about how well you're doing or how good "it" is going to be.

Once your partner is through pleasuring you, don't forget to give him his share of pleasuring. This is, after all, a mutual exercise.

Step 6. Erotic Pleasure 2

You can now add genital touching to your Erotic Pleasure exercise. Begin, of course, with nongenital pleasuring. Only gradually move toward genital touching. As we suggested in Chapter 14, first your partner should lightly stroke your breasts and play teasingly with them. Then, gradually, slowly, he can move down toward your genitals. Have him carefully follow the guidelines in Chapter 14. Essentially, these guidelines urge that he move slowly, gently, and carefully. This may be a new experience for you and him, and, like many new experiences, it could be a little scary. If you get very tense, so that the exercise is not pleasant, use your distress signal. Then go back and spend more time in Erotic Pleasure 1 until you are completely comfortable. Also, don't forget to pleasure your partner when you are finished as "pleasuree."

The goal here is to let yourself float along, as high as you want to be, and to enjoy yourself as much as you can, without worrying about orgasms. But at the same time, you want to feel increasingly loose and comfortable with your partner's stimulation of your genitals. Tell him what feels good (we hope he'll return the favor). Then enjoy the sensations. If you feel an orgasm approaching, although it may be difficult, gently move his hand away or ask him to move to another step. But you do want him to play gently with your clitoris and with the surrounding area so that you can experience the sensations without worrying about whether you'll have an orgasm.

One good position for this is the one that Masters and Johnson recommend—what they call a nondemand position.

Have your partner sit up against a wall or headboard with his legs spread. Then, you sit between his legs with your back up against his chest and your legs between his. This way, your partner will be easily able to reach around your body and stroke your breasts, your genitals, and the front of your body (see Figure 15-1). Another position would be for you to lie on your back with your legs spread. Then, your partner could sit between your legs, giving him easy access to the lower part of your body. Of course, change positions as you see fit. Whichever position you choose, give and get feedback as to how you are feeling about it.

Step 7. Show Your Partner How You Do It

The next step for you is a direct move into helping your partner stimulate you to orgasm. But first, you want your partner, by learning from your experience, to know how best to stimulate you. There's another goal to this exercise. You want to be increasingly comfortable with your sexuality in the presence of your partner. When you show arousal and orgasm in his pres-

Figure 15-2.

ence, you want to be comfortable with it, and he should be comfortable as well.

Essentially, what we want you to do is to demonstrate for your partner the way you've been bringing yourself to orgasm. Whether this is with your hand or with a vibrator, go ahead and show him.

Set the scene well. If you're pretty comfortable with the situation, you might just want to have both of you lie together on the bed, play together for a while using Erotic Pleasure 2 exercises, and then, when the time seems right, go ahead and use your own self-stimulation procedures to bring yourself to orgasm, as in Figure 15-2.

If you're less comfortable, take even more care in how you go about this. You might want the room dark the first two or three times, gradually increasing the amount of light. Or you may actually want to have your partner sit in the next room while you bring yourself to orgasm. Then, the next time, he could be in the same room, but on the other side of the room, not facing you, while you bring yourself to orgasm. Next, he could stay in the same place but only watch. Eventually, he should be able to lie next to you and hold you in his arms while you bring yourself to orgasm, as in Figure 15-3. (Incidentally, if your partner feels very turned on, you can help him out by bringing him to orgasm—if the two of you agree—either orally or manually.)

This is actually a very difficult step for many people to follow. It often seems to produce enough discomfort for some to want to abandon the sex program. Although we think this an important step, because it helps desensitize you or make you comfortable with your partner's presence while you are highly

Figure 15-3.

aroused, it is not an indispensable part of the program. Try it for a few nights. If you are just too uncomfortable, move on to the next step.

Step 8. Partner Brings You to Orgasm

The essence of this step is simple. Your partner should simply do to you what you've been doing for yourself. Whether it is by hand or by vibrator, your partner should now try bringing you to orgasm using the same methods you've been using.

As you can see, this step is an extension of both Erotic Pleasure 2 and the previous step. (If you skipped the previous step, just tell your partner how to do it.) In either case, you should begin by using Erotic Pleasure techniques. Get comfortable, play with each other's bodies, and begin genital touching, as in Figure 15-4. Gradually have your partner increase the intensity of his stroking. Guide his hand with your hand. Lose yourself in the pleasure of it. Let go. Let him bring you to orgasm.

Myrna decided that she was going to involve her boyfriend in every step of the Treat Yourself program. At first it was very difficult for her to bring herself to orgasm in front of him. But after the second night, she was able to do it while lying in his arms after a good deal of Erotic Pleasure. She stayed with that step for three more nights. The next night she and her partner used a modified version of the Erotic Pleasure Contract in which he agreed to use the same procedures Myrna had used to help her reach orgasm. By that time, Myrna was so comfortable in his presence that she reached orgasm the first time he used the techniques she had showed him.

Figure 15-4.

Step 9. Non-demand Intercourse

Once you've been able to reach orgasms fairly regularly through your own self-stimulation and your partner's use of similar techniques, you're ready for the next step—intercourse. It's quite possible that you've actually been ready for some time now—in fact, it may have been difficult for you to avoid intercourse because you may have wanted to "see what happens." But, as we've said many times, there really is a method to this apparent madness of moving one step at a time. We hope that you'll enjoy each step. Even more importantly, each step gets you ready for the next one. So, by now, you're ready.

What we mean by non-demand intercourse is that you won't both be madly, passionately thrusting to achieve orgasm, with all the pressures that that implies. Instead, you will gently and playfully caress each other as we suggest in Erotic Pleasure 2 until you are both thoroughly aroused. Then, when the male's penis is erect and you feel aroused—your nipples are erect, you're lubricating (if not, have the male use a lubricating gel on his penis), your breathing is heavier, and both of you have other signs of arousal—then you can move to intercourse.

We strongly recommend the woman-on-top position. Just gradually move from your partner's side to a position of sitting on him (although supporting much of your weight with your knees on the bed). Then, you can gently insert the tip of the penis in your vaginal entrance or slide back onto it.

Now, this exercise is for you. This is one time when you shouldn't be overly concerned about your partner's feelings. His turn will come. Once you've mounted, just rest for a moment in order to get, and enjoy, the feel of his penis in you. Then, slowly and gently, move up and down on his penis. Avoid intense thrusting. Experiment with different movements and motions so that you not only see how they feel but see which you enjoy most. This effect can really increase your arousal level.

Remember that you're not preoccupied with orgasm. You are just checking out and enjoying these different pleasurable sensations.

Both of you should try to give and get feedback during this step. We hope that your partner will be encouraging and supporting you while you're trying different motions and rhythms. If he becomes overstimulated and feels that ejaculation is imminent, he should signal you, and you can both rest. You can either remove yourself from his penis or let the penis remain inside of you without moving. If it does happen that he ejaculates, try not to get too upset. After all, you are the one who turned him on. Take a longer rest and try again later, or try again the following day, watching a little more carefully for signs of an approaching ejaculation.

While you're resting, you may either lie still in each other's arms, or he may continue to stimulate you by hand in order to maintain your arousal level.

We should also point out that it is quite likely that your partner may lose his erection one or more times during this exercise. That is common in any prolonged love-making. With a little reassurance from you and some additional manual or oral stimulation, he may be able to get his erection back again.

This exercise should be continued for up to an hour, until you are just plain tired out, or until you have an orgasm with his penis inserted in you. Actually, if you are following this exercise as we suggest, it is unlikely that you will achieve orgasm (although some people do), because you are not thrusting with sufficient and prolonged intensity. That, you'll be glad to know, comes next.

Step 10: Orgasm Through Intercourse

Now! The next step is to try intercourse in order to produce a high level of erotic arousal that will lead to orgasm. The sign that you are ready is if you reached a high level of arousal during the previous step. Only you can decide that, of course. Build this step in as an extension of previous steps. That is, try not to jump into bed with one of you leaping on top of the other, thrust a few times, and expect fireworks. Go at it tenderly, sensuously, erotically.

Again, set the scene so that it will be both relaxing and stimulating. You might want to bathe together, washing and gently stroking each other's bodies. Luxuriate in the warmth and the sensuous feelings. When you move to the next step, do so playfully. When you're in bed together, play with each other, stroking each other's most sensitive parts. Use manual and oral stimulation to the extent that you both enjoy it. Go through Erotic Pleasure 1 and 2. Move slowly and gently to the point of intercourse. You may want to use artificial lubricants if you are not well lubricated. These can also add to the erotic sensations. Your partner should pay particular attention to stimulation of the clitoral area in order to increase your arousal. If you find it particularly arousing, he can use a vibrator to stimulate you even more. Use whatever erotic fantasies turn you on.

When both you and your partner are very highly aroused, you can start intercourse. Talk about this beforehand with your partner. This is your program. You make the decision as to when you're ready. You should also make the decision as to which position to use. We suggest a single guideline for deciding on a position. Select the one with which you're most comfortable and the one you find most stimulating (we hope that they are one and the same). If you can't decide, we again suggest the woman-on-top position, or the rear-entry position. (Rear entry does not mean entry into the anus. It means, though, that the woman supports herself on her knees and elbows or arms while her partner enters her vagina from the rear. This has been called "doggie fashion." See Chapter 20 for a more detailed description of this position.) We recommend these positions because they allow the male easy access to the female's genitals so that he can continue to stimulate her with his hands while pelvic thrusting is proceeding.

On the other hand, the male-on-top position allows the male to put pressure on the female's clitoral area with his pubic bone (the bones just above the penis, which are covered by pubic hair), and this may provide the necessary stimulation. (By the way, if for some reason you object to your partner's continuing to stimulate your clitoris manually, at least make sure that his pubic bone is applying pressure to your clitoral area.)

The key point here is that the woman must receive adequate stimulation in order to reach orgasm. Once you are through with the Erotic Pleasure exercises prior to intercourse, and assuming that these have allowed the woman to become highly aroused, you should both be careful to ensure that this stimulation and the high level of arousal do not decrease. We hope that you'll both talk about it beforehand to make sure that you agree on what is required.

Once your partner's penis is inserted in your vagina, you should both thrust in ways that you, particularly, find most arousing. Again, *you* should control this to begin with. Use the techniques that *you* find most arousing. This may mean that you do most of the thrusting, that your partner does it, or that you use a combination.

Continue thrusting until you reach orgasm.

Now, this may sound like a pretty tall order, especially if you've never reached orgasm during intercourse. But keep these ideas in mind: You no longer are tense or uncomfortable about sex (if you ever were). You are highly aroused and the stimulation will continue during intercourse. You now know the techniques that produce the greatest stimulation during intercourse. You can and should use whatever fantasy you find most erotic in order to increase your arousal. (At a later stage, once you are reaching orgasm fairly consistently, you can begin switching your fantasies to thoughts about your partner, as we suggested in Chapter 13.) All of these conditions combined may produce what you're after.

Of course, there may be some problems. Your partner may come first. If so, try again later. You can use oral or manual stimulation to help your partner achieve another erection. Having already ejaculated once, he may be able to maintain his erection longer. If not, try again the following day, calling a brief rest when your partner feels that he is about to ejaculate.

Another possibility is that your partner may resent your focusing so much attention on your own pleasure (and we do want you to be selfish here, just for a while). But, if you prepare him for this, establish your contract, and discuss in detail the ways you will both ultimately benefit, then we hope that the sailing will be smoother. Keep checking with each other as to how it's going. In particular, we hope the male partner will be especially encouraging and supportive here.

Finally, one problem might be that you do not reach orgasm during this step. If you do, fine. Let go and enjoy it. We

267

know that it probably will be a highly rewarding experience in sexual pleasure for both of you. But if you don't, don't despair. In the first place, it takes most women several tries before they reach orgasm in this step. So try for several nights, perhaps taking a night or two off between each try in order to build up sexual tension. But try to relax each time. Don't focus on the fact that you must have an orgasm. Focus instead on your erotic fantasies and on the erotic sensations.

Second, if you don't reach orgasm here, there are several other things you can try. These are described in the next steps.

> Myrna and her boyfriend were really ready the first time that they tried to achieve orgasm during intercourse. They were excited—both emotionally and sexually. They wrote up their contract, part of which went as follows: "We will attempt intercourse with Myrna on top. Myrna will control the thrusting while Norm continues to stimulate her clitoral area with his hand. We promise not to be too disappointed if Myrna doesn't have an orgasm the first couple of times. But we will keep trying. In fact, every three nights of trying, whether or not Myrna reaches orgasm, we will go out to our favorite restaurant for a special late snack as a reward for trying."

> Myrna and Norm were smart. They were prepared for the worst. But they didn't need to. The first night, Myrna didn't reach orgasm because Norm was so excited that he ejaculated before Myrna could reach orgasm. They decided to wait a night and try again. The second night, after ten minutes of thrusting, Myrna reached orgasm. "It was great," she later said, "Believe me, it was really worth all the exercises and all the buildup."

Step 11: Role Play: Once More with Feeling

If you didn't reach orgasm in the previous step, we think that you'll be able to with the addition of this or one of the next steps.

Some women are still pretty uncomfortable about going through all the twitching, moaning, and other movements that may accompany orgasm. In other words, you may not want to feel that you're losing control, and you may lose arousal as the orgasm approaches. If this is you, try the role-play exercise again. As you play with each other's bodies and continue manual or oral stimulation, role-play an exaggerated orgasm, as we suggested in step 4. Remember: Do this in an exaggerated way, with all the screeching and moaning you like. Do this with your partner present. Have fun. Make a game out of it. Do this until you no longer feel inhibited in his presence. Then, go back to the previous step and try intercourse culminating in orgasm.

Step 12: The Bridge

If you still haven't reached orgasm, try what we call "the bridge." This is really an extension of step 10, wherein you tried to reach orgasm through intercourse and, in some cases, maintained manual stimulation. Well, this step is essentially the same thing, except that you'll be paying even more-careful attention to manual stimulation of the clitoris before and after penetration.

Move through your Erotic Pleasure 1 and 2 exercises. Wait, of course, until you are thoroughly aroused—as aroused as you think you could possibly be. Wait until just before you think you will have an orgasm. Then, help the male insert his penis while he continues clitoral stimulation with his hand. Use one of the lubricants we suggested in Chapter 7 if you need it. He may enter all the way or just partially. That isn't important as long as his penis is in the vaginal entrance and clitoral stimulation is continued. Orgasm could result almost immediately. Continue to practice this until you can consistently achieve orgasm in this manner. Then you can gradually move the time of insertion back to earlier points, while gradually decreasing the amount of manual stimulation and replacing it with thrusting and stimulation from the penis and pelvic bone.

If you can feel the orgasms coming while you are being stimulated manually or with the vibrator, ask your partner to stop. Now, you should thrust vigorously to bring on the orgasm through your own thrusting. If, at this point, you become less aroused, don't worry. Just try it again, perhaps starting your thrusting a little later. It may take several tries, but it really works for many women.

Also, in situations calling for prolonged stimulation, two things could happen to your partner. He may have his own orgasm, or he may lose his erection. Either one should be expected. If he has an orgasm, try to enjoy it, both of you. Just try again next time. If he loses his erection—a very natural reaction—just help him reach it again, using your own sensual techniques.

One of the best positions for the bridge is the side-by-side position (see Figure 15-5). This allows the male particularly easy access to your clitoral area. But, of course, other positions do the same, so you and your partner should experiment with different positions in order to find the one that is most suitable.

There are other variations of this that you might try.

One important one is to use a vibrator to stimulate the clitoris before and after penetration. This may be a little awkward at first, but you'll soon get the hang of it. Don't feel that

269

Figure 15-5.

it's bad or somehow wrong to do this. And we hope that the male won't feel hurt that he can't bring you to orgasm without a "machine." The goal of this is to eventually decrease the use of the vibrator to the point where you don't need it. But, even if you do continue to use the vibrator because of the excellent stimulation it provides, what's so wrong about that when you think about it? It should be your decision as to whether or not you continue using the vibrator. It's your pleasure and joy that are at stake. (But please be sensitive in dealing with each other when negotiating this.)

Another variation is the woman's continuing to stimulate her clitoris manually once her partner's penis is inserted. This can be a very effective source of stimulation (you yourself know best), and it works well for many women.

A third variation is not to wait until just before orgasm occurs but to have your partner insert his penis at an earlier point; then, more attention is paid to manual or vibrator stimulation until orgasm is reached. If it is successful, you can gradually replace the manual stimulation or vibrator with pelvic thrusting.

Gail had not reached orgasm during intercourse by using any of the conventional means. She was ready to give up. As a last resort, she agreed to allow Dale to continue to use the vibrator to stimulate her after he inserted his penis in her vagina. Nothing much happened the first two nights. But the third night, Gail decided to look at some erotic pictures before going to bed. She kept their images in her mind once Dale inserted his penis, all the while continuing to stimulate her clitoral area with their vibrator. It took almost twenty minutes of continuous stimulation with the vibrator until she felt the beginnings of the contractions. They built and built until finally, she climaxed with Dale's penis still inserted in her. She was so relaxed and so happy that she just lay back and cried. Dale couldn't help feeling a bit tearful himself.

•

Step 13: Help from Another Friend

One technique that has been found successful with women who don't reach orgasm through any of the previous steps is to use a combination of fantasy and an object that resembles a penis in size and shape. You might want to use the type of battery-operated pencil- or penis-shaped vibrator that is very inexpensive and is available at most drug and department stores (see Figure 15-6), or you may want to use an artificial penis, which can be purchased at an adult bookstore. The type of object you use is up to you. Do make sure that it is not dangerous (that it can't break in normal use) and that it is very clean.

1. In sessions by yourself, or with your partner present, if you're comfortable, get used to having the object (let's call it a dildo) in your vagina. Use gentle in and out movements of the dildo so that you'll know what it feels like. The idea here is not to bring yourself to orgasm (unless you want to, of course) but to familiarize yourself with these sensations.

Figure 15-6.

2. Once you're familiar with these sensations, use your self-stimulation program (step 4) to bring yourself to orgasm. Fantasize having intercourse with your partner, and just before you reach orgasm, insert the dildo (lubricated if necessary) and imagine that it is his penis inserted in your vagina.

3. Once you can do this consistently, bring your partner in to observe it so that both of you can come to feel comfortable with your reaching orgasm with the dildo inserted in your vagina. Begin to insert the dildo earlier and earlier when you are aroused. Also, allow your partner to gradually take over moving the dildo in and out. Tell him how to move it and guide his hand with your hands.

4. The next step is simple. Instead of using the dildo, replace it with your partner's erect penis (obviously, after you and he have completed Erotic Pleasure so that you're both aroused). First, insert his penis and get used to the idea of its movement within you. Don't worry about orgasm at this point. Next, fantasize intercourse with your partner while you are stimulating each other manually, and as you become highly aroused, have him insert his penis in your vagina and proceed with thrusting until you reach orgasm. Third, and finally, have him insert his penis earlier in the process and continue thrusting until you reach orgasm. Repeat this procedure several times. You will probably want to move slowly through this step, introducing your partner into the process as gradually as you need to in order to ensure your own comfort. Also, be sure that you are both prepared by signing a mutual contract, so that each of you is aware of the steps in the process and of the ultimate goals. Then, let it happen. If you do, it probably will.

We hope that you now are able to attain a sense of sexual and personal satisfaction that you may not have experienced before. But we also hope that now that you have achieved it, you won't lose it. The ways to be sure of maintaining what you've been able to achieve are these:

1. Continue to move slowly and sensuously during your sexual activity. Don't jump into bed, move right into intercourse, and expect that special feeling to occur every time. (It might for a few people, or even for you some of the time. It probably won't for most people most of the time.) You need, and you deserve, a gradual prolonged buildup of stimulation. Proceed almost as you would during this program—through a period of Erotic Pleasure, varied as you like it—in order to ensure high levels of arousal before intercourse.

2. Remember to be sure that you continue to receive

adequate stimulation, especially of the clitoris, during intercourse. This is something that you and your partner both have a responsibility to arrange.

3. Both you and your partner should talk about how you feel about each step in the program, and about how you feel about each other as you both progress toward your goal. The communication and relationship part of these exercises and your feelings about them are as important as the exercises themselves. Also, if there are any problems, you may be able to head them off before they become too set. It's even possible that your partner may resent part of the program or may be upset with some of the changes in you. Many of these problems can be headed off by frank communication between the two of you. In fact, we hope that you'll be able to build this into your relationship from now on. Your communication with your partner shouldn't stop when the formal program ends.

4. Try also to remember, despite the emphasis of this chapter, that there really is much more to sex than just genitals, or even orgasms. Part of the success of this program involves the interrelatedness of the whole variety of sensual, emotional, and sexual parts of your being. Indeed, there are many times when many of your needs can be met just by lying close to and holding your partner. Sexual pleasure can be enhanced by increasing not only the intensity of the sexual relationship but also the intimacy of the personal relationships.

You can experience a joy in sex that you've never experienced before. It requires time, patience, effort, and a lot of mutual understanding. But you'll know that it's worth it when you find new heights of pleasure, and when you and your partner find a new joy and intimacy.

Sixteen

Painful and Difficult Intercourse for Women

Rita was plenty nervous about her wedding night. Although she and Oscar were deeply in love and had been engaged for six months, they had never attempted intercourse. They had come pretty close, with some heavy "making out," but they had both agreed that they would wait until after they were married to go "all the way." Rita was preoccupied the whole day with thoughts of that night. After the wedding ceremony and party were over, Rita at last found herself alone with Oscar. Rita went into the bathroom to undress and when she came out, Oscar was already in bed. At once excited, scared, and unsure, Rita joined him. They kissed and stroked each other passionately. Finally, they tried intercourse. Oscar attempted to penetrate Rita and found that he could not. As he said later, "It was like pushing my penis against a stone wall; I couldn't even find the entrance to her vagina." Rita started to cry; Oscar was so upset that he just stormed out of the room.

Rita and Oscar have come up against an extremely frustrating and disturbing problem. If not treated quickly, it can lead to problems in the relationship between two sex partners, including hostility, blaming, feelings of being inferior, and lots of name-calling.

But the truth of the matter is that this is one of the easiest to treat of all the sexual complaints. Sex therapists consistently claim very high rates of success for this problem. So, if this is a problem from which you or your partner is suffering, take heart. Help can be found.

There are actually two problems associated with painful or difficult intercourse. The first is called *dyspareunia* (pronounced dis-pear-OOO-nee-ah). What this means is simply pain during sex, especially vaginal pain. The second is called *vaginismus* (pronounced vah-gin-IS-mus). Essentially, vaginismus refers to an involuntary tightening of the muscles at the entrance of the vagina so that penetration of the vagina is difficult or impossible. You might want to review Chapter 4 once again for some of the possible causes of this problem.

Although women sometimes experience both vaginal pain and muscle spasm at the same time, we'll discuss each separately in order to provide clearer guidelines for you to Treat Yourself.

PAINFUL INTERCOURSE

There are several different types of vaginal pain a woman might experience during intercourse. The woman might experience a burning or tearing sensation. The pain might be experienced as a dull ache. The pain might be present only during intercourse, or it might last for a long while after. Finally, even the location of the pain might differ—from pain at the vaginal opening to pain in the vaginal walls to "deep" (internal) pain.

These are important distinctions, because the type and location of the pain could provide specific clues as to how the pain can be treated.

Actually, most cases of vaginal pain *can* be quickly treated. Here are the steps you can follow to ensure that just about any pain or discomfort you are experiencing is taken care of:

1. Follow the assessment guidelines presented in Chapter 8. Pinpoint where, when, how often, and with whom the pain occurs. It's important to do this whether you treat the problem yourself or get outside help.

2. See a doctor. For some people, this is a very difficult or uncomfortable step itself. But this is one of those situations in which a doctor's help can really be important. At best, the

doctor can rapidly cure the problem. At the least, he or she can rule out any illness or purely physical cause for the problem.

In the case of vaginal pain, the doctor you see should be a gynecologist, a specialist in the treatment of vaginal and pelvic problems. Try not to be embarrassed about seeing a gynecologist. He or she has the expertise you need in this instance, and you should be sure to make use of that expertise. If you don't have a regular gynecologist, ask a friend about her doctor, call your family physician and ask for a referral, or phone your local chapter of the American Medical Association and ask them to give you the name of a good gynecologist.

The doctor will probably do at least three things. He or she will check to see if there is a bacterial or other type of infection and, if there is one, prescribe antibiotics. The doctor will check to see if there are any cuts or slight tears in the vagina and will prescribe the appropriate treatment if one is found. Finally, the doctor will examine the general condition of the pelvis and pelvic region in order to ensure your general physical health.

Seeing a doctor is a prerequisite to any Treat Yourself program for vaginal pain. If, after seeing the doctor, you receive a clean bill of health but still experience pain, try the following steps.

3. Check to see that you are adequately lubricated during intercourse. Lack of adequate lubrication can easily cause irritation from the rubbing of the penis against the vaginal wall or entrance. There are two parts to this. Make sure that you and your partner are taking adequate time before he attempts entry. If you feel that might be the problem, discuss it with him and try to reach an agreement that he will wait until you are more aroused.

The second part is a little simpler. Make sure that you and your partner are using an adequate amount of a lubricant, such as "K-Y Lubricating Jelly" or "Transi-Lube." This will reduce the friction caused by the penis's moving in and out.

4. Check for allergic reactions. Some women are allergic to or develop reactions to specific lubricants; to the type of condom their partner is using (especially if it is lubricated) or even to the diaphragm they are using; feminine-hygiene deodorants or douches; some material in their clothing (e.g., their panties); a particular type of toilet paper; and so on. Check to see which and how many of the above you use. Then, one at a time, change or remove them from your use. (If you change everything at once and the pain goes away, you won't know which of the above you were reacting to.)

5. Use the sex-muscle exercises described in Chapter 14.

One of the possible causes of painful intercourse is weakness in the vaginal walls. The exercises we presented in Chapter 14 to tone up the pubococcygeal muscles (PC) will strengthen the muscles around the vaginal wall and help reduce or eliminate pain. So, if you are still experiencing some pain after you've gone through all of the above steps, strengthen your sex muscles. Just follow the steps described in Chapter 14.

If you go through the above steps, being especially sure to see your doctor, you are likely to be able to eliminate the pain you're experiencing.

DIFFICULT INTERCOURSE (VAGINAL SPASMS)

The problems involved in difficult intercourse due to spasms (vaginismus), what Rita was suffering from, are somewhat different from those involved with painful intercourse. As we mentioned earlier, difficult intercourse essentially involves the inability of the man to insert his erect penis in the woman's vagina. In some situations, the woman has trouble inserting anything in her vagina, including tampons.

Generally, this problem is a result of vaginal spasms— involuntary muscular contractions, usually of the muscles at the vaginal entrance. Often, the vagina simply closes up, although urine and the menstrual flow can pass through. If there is any pain, it is often a result of the spasms, although, as we note below, other causes should not automatically be ruled out.

There are any number of reasons why this problem comes about. In a few cases, physical illness could be responsible. In most cases, though, the reasons are related to the woman's fears and anxieties about sexual activity. The fears could be a result of negative (or no) sex education, some traumatic experience like rape, a history of incest or rough sexual handling, or other less specific but nevertheless important fears or feelings or repugnance about sexual activity.

The treatment is, as you'll see, relatively simple. Basically, we will help you to overcome your fears about sex and, at the same time, help you to deal directly with the problem of the muscular spasms.

Preliminary Steps

Before you start your Treat Yourself program, you will want to be sure that you've covered several preliminary steps.

1. Don't ignore the problem. It probably won't go away by itself. If you ignore it, you may be condemning yourself and your partner to an existence without some of the real pleasures in life. As Rita and Oscar found out and as you can too, you can have a perfectly enjoyable sex life by facing up to this problem and by doing something about it.

2. Pinpoint your problem. Be clear about when, how often, and with whom it occurs. Review Chapter 8 for guidelines on assessing your problem.

3. See a doctor. Just as with painful intercourse, there may be some physical cause that the doctor can treat. Certainly, you want to rule out the possibility that any physical condition or infection may be related to the problem. Again, see a gynecologist for this.

4. If there are no physical problems, try the following. Check to see that your arousal level is adequate. In some instances, the woman's vagina cannot be penetrated because there is little or no lubrication. As with the situation involving painful intercourse, this might mean that you and your partner could discuss the situation, go slower during love-making, and be sure that you are using an adequate amount of an artificial lubricant such as "K-Y Lubricating Jelly" or "Transi-Lube."

5. Take a break from attempting intercourse. During the period of your Treat Yourself program, avoid getting involved in any sexual situation other than those we suggest here. This will take some of the pressure off and will possibly ease some of your fear of penetration. Also, it means that you and your partner won't get involved in arguments and mutual blaming about whose "fault" it is.

6. Talk it over with your partner. You and your partner can read the parts of this book (including Chapter 4) that deal with the kind of problem you're experiencing. Then, in a quiet, nonpunitive atmosphere, discuss the program. Both of you should know right now that this program can really work.

7. Use contracts. In order to ensure that you both understand exactly what will happen, make sure that you use contracts to state your goals and your activities. For example, right at the start of their Treat Yourself program, Rita and Oscar wrote the following contract, based on the First-Step Contract described in Chapter 10:

> We agree to suspend all attempts at intercourse for the next month or until we complete the appropriate Treat Yourself program. We also agree to go out for dinner every Saturday night as our reward for following the program faithfully that week.

The Program

As we noted above, the two basic goals of this program are to overcome any fears or disgust the woman feels about sexual activity, and also to eliminate the vaginal spasms. In fact, when specifying your goals for this program, you can be quite specific: to be able to have a penis inserted in your vagina without any feelings of pain or any unwanted muscular contractions. There are a series of very simple steps that you can follow in order to accomplish both of these goals. Although eventually you will want to involve your partner, you can proceed by yourself through many of the steps involved in this program.

STEP 1: RELAX

Learning to relax is particularly important in order to overcome vaginismus. For this problem, we recommend the deep-muscle-relaxation program described in Chapter 11. Start out with the deep-abdominal-breathing exercise. This will help you to relax, especially in the pelvic area. Then move to the deep-muscle-relaxation exercise. Learning this may take a few days or up to two weeks. But keep practicing until you've really got it. You can use this not only during the Treat Yourself program but also before you actually attempt intercourse with your partner. Use the scale we presented in Chapter 11 to rate your anxiety. On that 1 to 100 scale, how do you rate when you think about sexual activity? Continue to use the scale to assess whether you become less anxious when you think about sex as you go through the program.

STEP 2: EXERCISE YOUR SEX MUSCLES

Remember the exercises near the end of Chapter 12? These were specifically designed to help you tone up the vaginal muscles. Although these exercises aren't guaranteed to cure vaginismus, they certainly can help you to develop some control over these muscles. Follow the specific steps described in Chapter 12. Practice every day for a week. You can do this exercise during the same period of time that you're training yourself in deep muscle relaxation. These sex-muscle exercises not only can help relax the vaginal muscles but they can also help to increase lubrication, which will eventually permit easier insertion.

STEP 3: INSERTION EXERCISE 1

Keep evaluating yourself on the anxiety scale. When you begin to feel more relaxed, especially when you think about sex, then you're ready to try the insertion exercise.

This exercise is done by yourself, in the quiet and comfort of your own bedroom or bathroom. There are several steps involved, but they are all related to the basic procedure—learning that you can easily insert something into your own vagina. We teach you to do this on a slow and careful and step-by-step basis, working at your own pace. You'll be surprised at how easy this will be for you.

> Rita was nervous about the insertion exercises. She wanted to make sure that she would follow through, so she developed a special contract with herself. "I will follow through with the insertion exercises every night this week, and when I am finished at, the end of the week, I will buy myself that pair of straight-leg jeans that I've been dying to get."

1. Select a calm and peaceful time and place where you can practice without being disturbed.

2. Do your abdominal-breathing exercises and your deep-muscle-relaxation exercises.

3. Sit in a comfortable position, perhaps with your knees bent and legs spread apart. Place your hand gently over the genital area, covering the vulva. Just hold your hand there for two minutes. Okay. Remove your hand, take a few deep breaths, and relax. Do this five or six more times, and that's it for the first day. How do you feel? Evaluate yourself on your anxiety scale.

4. The next day, follow steps 1, 2, and 3. While you are holding your hand over your vulva, gently put the tip of your index finger into the vaginal entrance, as illustrated in Figure 16-1. (Make sure that your fingernail is cut short and the edge well filed.) Don't move the fingertip around. Just hold it there for two minutes, then remove it. Again, breathe deeply and relax. Now, do this again five times. If you're having any trouble at all inserting your fingertip, have some lubricating gel available and use a liberal amount on it. This will make it much easier. Also, make sure that you are as relaxed as possible by continuing to use your breathing and muscle relaxation exercises while you're inserting your finger.

5. Repeat step 4 the next day.

6. The following day, go through steps 1 through 4. (Have lubricating gel available if you need it.) Today, try inserting your entire index finger into your vagina. Hold it there for about three minutes without moving it around. If you feel some muscle contractions, don't panic. Keep your finger there. After three minutes, remove it. Do this five or six more times. Believe it or not, you've almost got the problem licked. You are

Figure 16-1.

becoming increasingly able to tolerate an object's being in your vagina.

7. Repeat step 6 the next day. After you have inserted your finger, very slowly and gently move it around the vagina.

8. The next day, follow through with all of the previous steps. This time, however, insert two fingers into your vagina. If you care to, slowly move them around. If you feel especially tense or if you happen to have strong muscular contractions, go back to an earlier step in which you felt more comfortable. Evaluate yourself on your anxiety scale. How are you feeling about all this? If you are feeling very comfortable, you can even try inserting three fingers, although you might want to wait a day or two for this.

9. The following day, go through steps 1, 2, and 3. Instead of using your finger today, get a package of tampons from the drug store or grocery store. Take one of the tampons but *leave it in the container.* Try slowly inserting the container into your vagina. You can do this with the container dry or lubricated, although a lubricated container will be much easier to insert. Hold it there for three minutes. You may experience a little extra tension or perhaps some additional muscular contrac-

tions, but you won't feel any pain. (This is particularly important; by now you've gotten the idea that there need not be any pain associated with insertion of an object into your vagina.) But if you do feel a little tension, it will slowly go away, especially if you keep the tampon in your vagina. Do this exercise five or six more times and you will become increasingly comfortable. Evaluate yourself once again on your anxiety scale. By now, you should be increasingly relaxed.

10. Repeat the entire process the following day.

STEP 4: EROTIC PLEASURE 1

Up to this point, you've been working on this problem by yourself (and, we hope, with a lot of support and encouragement from your partner). But it's time to bring your partner in on the process. Be sure that you describe to him what you've been doing, and particularly be sure that he's read at least this chapter and Chapter 14 (the section on Erotic Pleasure).

> Rita was so excited by her success that she just couldn't wait to share her progress with Oscar. She also really couldn't wait to make love. But she knew that she shouldn't go too fast. She and Oscar wrote up a contract for Erotic Pleasure 1 and included a new special reward for themselves. They also agreed that Rita's distress signal would be "I'm uncomfortable."

Begin Erotic Pleasure 1. Be sure to use your distress signal if you begin to feel tense or anxious. Move slowly and leisurely and enjoy each other's bodies. Probably, you will both be very turned on at this point, but try to stick with those steps. Try this variation of Erotic Pleasure. Before you start the exercises, insert the tampon container and leave it there. This will help you to become used to the feeling of penetration, while, at the same time, you can relax and enjoy other forms of stimulation.

STEP 5: EROTIC PLEASURE 2

Continue into Erotic Pleasure 2. Write a new contract. Also, insert the container before the exercise begins. Since this steps involves touching the genitals, you may experience some initial anxiety, so use your distress signal if you need it.

There are certain variations of Erotic Pleasure that can make this exercise even more successful. Go through nongenital touching. You and your partner should discuss how genital touching will be accomplished. In this instance, you should do this slowly, perhaps even more gently than you would otherwise. When you are ready to begin genital touching, simply duplicate the steps that you worked on by yourself, only this

Figure 16-2.

time, have your partner insert his fingers. Begin with the tip of the finger, as in Figure 16-2. Then, the next day, have him insert the whole finger but with no movement. Follow this with two and, if it's comfortable, with three fingers, first with no movement and then with movement for up to fifteen minutes at a time (your tampon container, of course, should not be left in your vagina during this part of the exercise). Finally, after as many days as you need to go through this with comfort, your partner can insert the well-lubricated tampon container. At this point, you will probably realize just how good all of this can feel.

Incidentally, be sure that your partner receives his share of Erotic Pleasure from you. Although it is true that the main source of concern is overcoming your discomfort at having objects inserted in your vagina, he still deserves some physical and emotional attention too. At the very least, it will be very motivating for him to continue. If your partner becomes extremely stimulated during this period, you can help him have an orgasm either manually or orally, but you should try to maintain the prohibition against intercourse.

STEP 6: PENETRATION WITH THE PENIS—NO MOVEMENT

You are the one who will make the decision as to when you'd like to try intercourse. Think about these guidelines: (1) Do you feel comfortable with the tampon container in your vagina? (2) Do you feel comfortable with your partner's inserting his fingers in your vagina? (3) Are you relaxed and are you enjoying Erotic Pleasure 2? If the answer to all of these is yes, then you're ready to proceed.

Talk this over with your partner. Fill out an All-the-Way Contract, as we suggested in Chapter 10. This allows you to set up the specific conditions for intercourse. For example, you have two choices for intercourse positions in this step. We recommend the woman-on-top position, with her pretty much in a squatting position, supporting most of her weight on the bed with her knees. If you are not experienced with or are uncomfortable in this position, you can use the man-on-top position, and you can help to guide his penis with your hand.

You also want to be sure that the penis is well lubricated with lubricating gel and that you move very slowly through the exercise so that both partners are aroused. Also, if you begin to feel especially tense, use your distress signal and move back to an earlier step.

> Rita and Oscar were extremely eager to try intercourse. They wrote an All-the-Way Contract, as follows: "We agree to use Erotic Pleasure 2 exercises to turn each other on. Rita will lubricate Oscar's penis with gel. Then, when Rita decides, she will get on top of Oscar and insert his penis. Oscar agrees not to move at all while his penis is inside Rita—he will be still with no thrusting. After three minutes, Rita will gently remove Oscar's penis from her vagina and help him have an orgasm outside of the vagina."

Begin this step by using Erotic Pleasure 2. Enjoy each other's bodies. Luxuriate in the erotic feelings. Gradually, at a point when you're both aroused, and after lubricating the penis with lubricating gel, help him insert his penis into your vagina. Be sure that you do this after he's inserted two fingers into your vagina to help prepare you. Make sure that the male does not thrust with his penis (this technique is called "the quiet penis"). Do not move the penis all the way into the vagina unless you are completely ready. Take your time; you should also avoid thrusting. Most importantly, notice that he can penetrate you without your feeling any pain.

By the way, if he happens to have an orgasm while his penis is inserted in your vagina (for that matter, you may, too), try not to get upset. Let's put it this way: You turn him on.

284

On the other hand, though, the male may lose his erection. Assure him that this will only be temporary, and help him to achieve an erection with some additional manual stimulation of his penis.

There's a variation to this that you may want to try. Before you begin Erotic Pleasure 2, insert the tampon cylinder into your vagina and leave it there. Then, just before you insert his penis in your vagina, remove it and immediately insert his penis. This can help to prevent any spasm of the vaginal muscles.

Leave the penis inserted in the vagina for a few minutes; then, slowly withdraw it. You can practice this exercise a few times the first day, being sure to use Erotic Pleasure to arouse both of you each time. If you'd like to, you can continue this step for another day or two.

STEP 7: PENETRATION WITH THRUSTING

The next step, of course, is to build on the previous step, but this time, add thrusting. However, you should be the one who sets the pace. Let your own comfort be the guide as to who does most of the thrusting. If you're more comfortable with your partner's doing the thrusting, so be it.

Follow the same procedure as you did in the previous step. Insert the penis (continue to use heavy lubrication) as far into your vagina as you can while still feeling comfortable. Then, when you are ready, start a gentle, slow thrusting motion (or, if you've decided in advance that your partner will do the thrusting, tell him to go ahead). The first couple of times you try this, make sure that the thrusting is not overly vigorous. Take it easy—short, gentle movements in and out. You can gradually build up to the desired depth and speed of the thrusting.

STEP 8: TRY DIFFERENT POSITIONS

Well, you've done it. It is probably hard to believe, considering how hopeless you may have felt only just a short while ago. Now, all that you have left to do is to ensure that you can try intercourse in any position that you'd like to try and not have vaginal spasms.

Select whatever positions you'd like. Go through the process above. In other words, don't just jump into it—at least not right away. Make sure that you are both aroused, and precede intercourse with the insertion of two fingers into the vagina. Then, just enjoy the pleasure that you were missing before you began to Treat Yourself.

The treatment of vaginismus can be one of the simplest

and most successful forms of Treat Yourself programs. In fact, depending upon the individual, success could be achieved in a matter of days, or perhaps weeks. Remember to follow up on your success every so often with some of the "stretching" exercises that we've described—e.g., inserting two fingers into your vagina and moving them around is an especially important exercise. Remember that you'll be able to experience the joy that Oscar and Rita did. In fact, after completing her Treat Yourself program, Rita commented, "Sex was absolutely terrific when I finished treating myself. In fact, it seemed to me that I was much more excited and turned on when I finished than before I started. I sure know that I was a lot more comfortable with myself and with Oscar."

Seventeen

Ejaculation Problems

One of the most frustrating and agonizing of all sexual problems involves what might be called "lack of staying power." Commonly called "premature ejaculation" or "rapid ejaculation," when boiled down to basics, this problem involves ejaculations that, in the perceptions of either the man or the woman, come too quickly.

Strangely enough, it was not until fairly recently that people began thinking that rapid ejaculations was, indeed, a problem. In fact, the famous sex researcher Kinsey believed that rapid ejaculation not only is not a problem but that it is actually "natural" in the healthy male. The reasons for this are rather complicated, but they were bolstered, in part, by the finding in Kinsey's 1948 research that 75 percent of all males ejaculated within two minutes of the time the penis entered the vagina, and that many men ejaculated within twenty seconds.

Of course, knowing that many other men may have problems with ejaculation, or even knowing that this may be "natural," is probably little comfort to the person who is experiencing the problem. Indeed, rapid ejaculations are frustrating because they make men feel so inadequate and foolish. The problem seems impossible to control, difficult to understand, and downright embarrassing; if you have it, you've probably tried all sorts of methods to delay your ejaculation. You might have tried pinching yourself, biting your lips, putting cream on your penis to deaden the feelings, and thinking about anything but your own pleasure during sexual activity. But nothing works. And the popular literature often chimes in to call men with the problem of rapid ejaculations immature, insensitive to women's needs, and incapable of providing "normal sexual services" to a woman. Your sex life seems to be a disaster. As a result of all this, we wouldn't be surprised if you began avoiding sex more and more (or, if you're attempting to distract yourself, enjoying it less and less). And the more you avoid it, the more likely it is that the next time you do give it a try, you will ejaculate even more quickly than you did before.

DEFINING THE PROBLEM

Actually, there are two general types of ejaculation problems. The first is what has been referred to as rapid or premature ejaculation—that is, ejaculations that come too quickly. The second is what might be called delayed ejaculations—ejaculations that either take too long or don't come at all.

The first of these problems—rapid ejaculations—is by far the most common of the two. In fact, it is the most common male sexual problem. Most sex therapists and researchers have attempted to come up with some kind of quantitative definition of this problem—for example, premature ejaculation is when the male comes within two minutes or ten minutes or twenty minutes or before five thrusts, and so on. Others define the problem in terms of the man's ability or inability to satisfy the women (talk about performance pressure!) a certain percentage of the time in intercourse.

But we believe that most of these definitions are inadequate, if not premature. In the first place, these definitions ignore the range of actual types of rapid ejaculations. Some men come in their pants, before any genital contact, or with only minimal contact. Some men ejaculate before intercourse while playing with a partner; some ejaculate immediately with certain types of stimulation (e.g., oral); some ejaculate just before or just after entry into the vagina. Some men ejaculate after five minutes of thrusting within the vagina; one man we know of ejaculated after some thirty-five minutes of thrusting, but who, since his partner hadn't achieved orgasm yet, considered himself a premature ejaculator.

These last-mentioned situations, and the fact that such a broad range of situations give rise to the charge of premature ejaculation, give a clue to the second reason why we think most quantitative definitions are inadequate. Most don't take into account the feelings and perceptions of the two people involved. More than many sexual problems, those associated with ejaculation become problems only when one or both partners in sexual activity *feel* that a problem exists. In one couple we know of, both the man and the woman come to orgasm within thirty seconds 90 percent of the time. Although this form of sexual compatibility is rare and is certainly not a goal most of us would want to aim for, it does illustrate the drawbacks to most quantitative definitions of ejaculation problems. Neither of the people in that couple considers the man to be a premature ejaculator.

So, if all of the above is true, how *would* we define the problem in which the man or his partner believes that the man comes too quickly?

We believe that the problem can best be defined in terms of the control or lack of control that the male has over his ejaculations. That is, we want to include both what actually happens and how you feel about it. We are interested in helping you achieve as much voluntary control as possible over your ejaculations. Thus, both types of problems associated with ejaculations can be included in this definition. The first, involving rapid ejaculations, involves inadequate ejaculatory control: By the time you really are aware that you're about to ejaculate, it's too late. The second, delayed ejaculation, we see as a problem of overcontrol: you may feel stimulated but unable to ejaculate at all—or, perhaps, unable to ejaculate except under certain conditions or not until a much longer time has passed than you or your partner desires. This is a rarer form of problem. The Treat Yourself program for the problem of overcontrol will be presented following the program for inadequate control.

Now, we don't mean to suggest with our definitions that everyone can—or should—have complete control over his or her body and every sexual function every time. Nor do we mean to suggest that just because you don't have complete control you have a problem (especially if you and your partner are content). What we do mean is that if you're not satisfied, we'd like to help you develop the kind of control that, in most instances, lets you determine roughly when you ejaculate.

Thus, by the time you are finished with this chapter, we hope, you will be able to last a long time if you want to do that (and you can decide how long is long) and to come pretty quickly if that's what you want to do.

PRELIMINARY STEPS FOR BOTH PROBLEMS

As we do for all of the other problems covered in this book, we hope that you'll begin by reading the preliminary material in Parts 1, 2, and 3, especially Chapter 5, "Common Problems of Men." This will give you a feel for what is to come—setting goals, developing contacts, proceeding in a step-by-step way, and so on.

We also think that it's a good idea to see a physician (a urologist) before you start the program. Although ejaculation problems are rarely caused by physical problems, some conditions in your genitourinary tract, such as an infection or an overly tight foreskin, might require medical attention in order to enhance the results of your Treat Yourself program.

Pinpoint Your Problem

Reread Chapter 8 to help you pinpoint your problem. In particular, there are several specific questions you can ask yourself:

1. Do you have different kinds of control in different activities—for example, masturbation versus intercourse?
2. Has your ability either to delay ejaculation or to come quickly changed recently or over the years?
3. Can you achieve adequate control with some partners but not with others?
4. Do you have different kinds of control in different places or situations?
5. Do you have different patterns of control with new partners from the ones you had with old partners?
6. Does your pattern of control change depending on how you feel?
7. Does your pattern of control change depending on what you've done prior to sexual activity—for example, worked too hard, or drunk or eaten too much?

Once you've answered some of these questions, you might already have a clearer idea of what to do. Some problems simply may require changes in certain situations—for example, getting more rest, drinking a little less before sex, or engaging in sex in a place where you are entirely comfortable. (It's possible that a pattern of lack of ejaculatory control can begin when a good deal of sexual activity takes place in a location where one or both partners fear being discovered—by the children, for example.) However, if some answers to these questions still don't provide a clear clue as to what to do, read on.

Try Talking

We know we talk a lot about talking. It's just that the anguish of many sexual problems is shared by a partner, and we believe that the partner has the right to know what's going on. Perhaps even more importantly, talking it over with your partner—outside of the sexual situation—may provide the motivation for both of you to continue in the program. And although we'll suggest a program for you to work on by yourself if you don't have a regular partner, the basic Treat Yourself program involves two people—you and your partner. We think that this can be the most satisfying and the most successful way of proceeding. Sharing the responsibilities of the program, reading the material together, and working together can provide a kind of closeness that may surprise you.

Use Contracts

Be sure to set up contracts for each step of these exercises, whether you are working with your partner or working alone. In particular, don't forget to specify and use, if necessary, your distress signal (make sure that your partner knows it beforehand). Also, build in rewards to help motivate you as you go, and to make the program more enjoyable.

Exercise Your Sex Muscles

Review Chapter 12, "Getting In Touch with Your Body." In particular, practice the exercises for strengthening your sex muscles, the PC and BC muscles. This doesn't help in all situations, although it probably will be especially helpful if your problem is delayed or overcontrolled ejaculation. It also may help you attain slightly greater control over your ejaculations. Master these exercises before you start the formal part of the program.

Now, if you've done all of the above, you're ready to begin one of the Treat Yourself programs to enhance your ejaculatory control.

INADEQUATE EJACULATORY CONTROL: LACK OF STAYING POWER

Just as there is no real agreement on the definition of this problem, there is little consensus on what causes it. One common line of thought is that lack of ejaculatory control comes about because some men never learn to be aware of the sensations that occur just prior to orgasm. This may be a result of early experiences with sex, whether they involved inter-course or masturbation, situations that carried the risk of dis-covery, thus hastening the need for a rapid ejaculation. If a man's sexual experiences were learned in such an atmosphere, with an emphasis on ejaculating as soon as possible, it is not surprising that he never became able to be aware of the fact that he was about to come.

Whether or not this explanation applies to everyone, it does illustrate the goal that the Treat Yourself program will attempt to achieve with you: teaching you to be aware of the sensations that immediately precede ejaculation and, based on that awareness, to learn to control ejaculation. Mastering this principle of control is really crucial and, to say the least, very helpful. We say this with a great deal of confidence because, of all the male sexual problems that sex therapists typically see, the one that they have had the most success in is training people to delay their ejaculations. Though for years "prema-ture ejaculation" was a most difficult problem to treat, recent scientific advances have produced a treatment that can work in almost all cases.

The Program for You and Your Partner

There are several steps you might want to take before getting into the full Treat Yourself program to increase your staying power.

292

HOW LONG?

Time yourself. Get a rough idea of how long it takes you from the point when you begin sex play to the point of ejaculation. If you can insert your penis into your partner's vagina and thrust for a few minutes, then maybe the two of you should talk this over a little bit. It may be less that you come too quickly and more that the sex play that you and your partner engage in isn't adequately preparing your partner. In other words, maybe the pressure you feel to bring your partner to orgasm during actual intercourse, and the guilt you experience when you can't, because you come too quickly, could both be alleviated by taking a little more time for both of you to prepare her. In this way, you may not need a special program at all.

CHECK THE CONDITIONS

Follow through on the questions we suggested earlier in this chapter. If you find certain patterns in your ejaculatory habits, see if some of these can be altered prior to (or instead of) beginning the program. For example, if you're always concerned that one of the kids will pop in when you're having sex, try motel therapy for a weekend. Or, even more simply, try putting a lock on your door. Or, just teach your kids that you expect privacy when your door is closed.

CONCENTRATE ON WHAT YOU DO

A number of your own activities might be changed, thus leading to better control of your ejaculations. We'll describe a few of these. All have been found helpful by some men (though certainly not by all), and you might give them a try.

1. Relax. Try some of the relaxation exercises described in Chapter 11. When you're tense, it's almost inevitable that you'll come more quickly. You might even try to breathe in a different way during intercourse. Breathe out strongly when you thrust forward and inhale and relax the buttocks before returning.

2. Change Movements. Some people have found it very helpful to change the patterns of their thrusting after penetration. Keep track of what you do. If, typically, you thrust forward as deeply as you can after penetration and maintain an up-and-down thrusting motion, try a different motion, like gently moving in a relaxed circular motion. This can be very arousing for your partner too.

3. Change Position. Do you always use the man-on-top position? If so, try another. We especially recommend the woman-on-top position in this situation because it both allows the woman more control of the motion and allows the man to relax his muscles and thus delay ejaculation.

4. Do It More. If you've been avoiding sex because you come too quickly, you probably already realize that this just produces even more arousal and hence quicker ejaculations the next time you try it. Instead of avoiding it, try something like motel therapy (or, at least, increasing frequency at home). In particular, it's a good idea to relax, prepare yourselves for some fun, and then get to it. Even if the first effort produces an ejaculation that comes too quickly—and it almost surely will— try it again as soon after that as you can. Stimulate each other in any way that is acceptable to both of you. Then try intercourse again. If the man can be brought to ejaculate two or three separate times, it's almost certain that, by the third time, ejaculation will occur more slowly. This might even be the case if you increase the frequency of your sexual activities from, say, once or twice a week to every day. The more the better. Taking off the pressure for performance, engaging in a wide range of pleasurable sexual activities, and doing these things on a repeated basis just might do the trick.

But if none of these suggestions works, then you're ready for the formal Treat Yourself program.

Increasing Staying Power with a Partner

Assuming that you and your partner are ready to go to work, talk things over. As we've said before, although these programs can be—and we hope are—lots of fun, they can also be a little frustrating. Neither partner is likely to be completely fulfilled at the beginning. So try to hold off on expecting too much too soon. Set an agreement between the two of you, using a contract from Chapter 10, that you'll be willing to try the program as spelled out in this book and to limit your expectations to just that. It may take a little short-term sacrifice for one or both of you, but we're sure that a lot of long-term happiness will take its place. Read the material in the chapters in Part 3. Again, if the two of you are in the habit of blaming each other, try to hold off. None of these problems is anybody's fault.

If you haven't already done it, pinpoint your problems, using the guidelines in Chapter 8. Then, establish your goals as we suggest in Chapter 10. Discuss the idea that, even though you are going to be concentrating on *increasing* awareness of the ejaculation-and-orgasm cycle, you'll be doing this by slowing down, by proceeding gradually, and by not rushing into a situation, such as one involving intercourse, that requires a high degree of performance from the male.

STEP 1: EROTIC PLEASURE 1

This is particularly important for men who ejaculate even before intromission (inserting the penis into the vagina). Start off with Erotic Pleasure 1—erotic massage without genital contact. The purposes of this are: first, to help relax the man in a nonperformance situation, and, second, to gradually increase his awareness of erotic sensations. (Don't forget that you can take turns doing this to each other.) Remember that at this stage, no genital contact is involved. What *is* involved is a beginning to slow down, a concentrating on sensations, and a selecting of a time and place for pleasuring.

Sam and Betty had been going together for some two years and engaging in sexual relations since their second date. But the frequency of their sexual activity had been decreasing steadily because of Sam's problem. Sam said that it was simple: "I'm a premature ejaculator." It seems that when Sam and Betty started having sexual relations, Sam would come in his underwear after heavy petting. He thought at first that it was just the newness of the situation. But even over time, the farthest they ever got was penetration and two or three thrusts. Then Sam would ejaculate.

Betty was understanding. She would do whatever she could to help, like suggesting that Sam think of something else when they made love. But it was no use. Nothing worked. After he ejaculated, Sam would manually help Betty have an orgasm. But he was so frustrated by now that often he didn't even want to try sex.

Sam and Betty knew that they'd have to do something. So they started out by trying some of the suggestions presented earlier in this chapter. Although Sam was at least able to delay his ejaculation until intromission, he still couldn't control his ejaculation after inserting his penis into Betty's vagina. So they signed their first contract, in which they agreed to go for a week without attempting intercourse.

STEP 2: EROTIC PLEASURE 2—
AWARENESS OF SENSATIONS PRIOR TO EJACULATION

Once you're able to engage in Erotic Pleasure 1 for at least thirty minutes without ejaculating, you're ready for Erotic Pleasure 2. This refers to erotic massage with genital contact. In this stage, don't use any lubricants.

If your problem is not one involving erections, then it's likely that you will be able to achieve erection fairly rapidly. It's also quite likely that you will ejaculate before you want to.

That's okay—if it happens, it happens. But when it does, we want you to be aware of some very important things. As you're lying back, relaxing, with your partner gently massaging your body, attend to the sensations in your body as she approaches and then begins to stimulate the genital regions. In particular, pay close attention to the following:

□ Your breathing patterns.
□ The tightening in your scrotal sac.
□ The way your body tenses up.
□ The way there is a contraction or tightening in your anus.
□ Swelling in your genitals.
□ Your thoughts and fantasies.

What you are looking for here is what we earlier called the sensations that occur just before ejaculation. All of the above will likely change in those moments before ejaculation, and you want to be aware of those changes before ejaculation. Then, if you become aware, you can learn to avoid what is called the moment of "ejaculatory inevitability"—the point at which it is impossible to delay ejaculation because the process has already begun.

If you're having some problems concentrating on these sensations, make sure that you're not paying too much attention to your partner. If this sounds a little cold, we hope that it's something you'll talk over with her. That is, as long as the two of you give each other permission that it's all right for the man to focus solely on himself for a time, then it may be easier to proceed. Also, we hope that you'll be doing this as a sharing process by starting off with affection—some hugs and kisses, talking, and giving your partner her turn at receiving pleasuring.

Of course, you or your partner may become bored or frustrated with this process, and it's up to the two of you to talk this out and be sure that you are sharing.

> Sam and Betty eagerly moved into this stage. But after a few days of Erotic Pleasure 2, Betty confessed to being frustrated by the process. So they wrote their second contract as follows: "We will spend the next four days practicing Erotic Pleasure 2 at least twice per day. We agree to tell each other if we are frustrated or bored with what is going on. If either of us is bored or frustrated, the other agrees to try to meet that person's needs at the moment, whether it means taking a break from pleasuring and doing something else or helping the partner achieve orgasm."

Again, the goal of this stage of the program is to help the male achieve awareness of the onset of this ejaculatory process. Once this is achieved, you can move to either one of the next stages.

STEP 3: STOP–START

The goal here is to use the male's awareness of the urge to ejaculate and to communicate this to the partner. Continue step 2, pleasuring, massaging, and teasing. If the partner is willing, she can gently massage his stomach and inner thighs, play with the testicles, and encourage a high level of arousal. Gently massage the penis until your partner has an erection and then continue with this manual stimulation of the penis.

In the meantime, the man should be relaxing but paying careful attention to all the sensations that we listed before. As soon as you note some changes in any of them, or as soon as you feel the slightest urge toward ejaculation, tell your partner that she should immediately stop massaging your penis. In fact, she should stop stimulating you completely. In a few seconds, the urge to ejaculate will let up. Then, the partner should resume stimulating the man. Continue this several times. If you happen to come during this exercise, don't worry. Think of it as a chance to learn more about the sensations premonitory to ejaculation.

You might want to take note of a couple of other points. First, you shouldn't use any lubricants in this phase. Second, you and your partner can assume any position you like— whatever is comfortable. The position shown in Figure 17-1 is

Figure 17-1.

Figure 17-2.

Figure 17-3.

one that has been found to be very successful, but it is not necessary to use that position if you prefer another. Third, remember that you do *not* want to distract yourself from what's going on. Stay with the experience of your coming ejaculation so that you can be aware of its approach.

The goal at this stage of the program is to aim for at least fifteen minutes of stimulation with no more than two or three "stops." If you find yourself needing more stops, take a little more time between stops prior to your partner's beginning stimulation again.

STEP 3A: THE SQUEEZE TECHNIQUE

If the stop–start technique isn't working well enough for you, if you are not satisfied with it, or if you simply want to try a variation, the squeeze technique has been found highly successful in delaying ejaculations.

Go through the Erotic Pleasure 2 exercises, again without lubricants, just as described above. When you feel the first signs of impending ejaculation, instead of having your partner stop stimulating you, she can try the squeeze. Instead of just stopping, she places her thumb on the underside of the penis just below the glans or head and her first and second fingers on the other side, with the forefinger on the coronal ridge and the middle finger just below this on the shaft. Then, she should squeeze hard for ten or fifteen seconds or until the urge to ejaculate begins to subside. Figure 17-2 shows how the hand should be positioned.

Now this takes a little practice. Many women are afraid that they will hurt their partner and so they won't exert enough pressure. You might want to place your fingers over hers and show her first how hard she can squeeze without hurting you. (You may both be surprised.) Regardless, practice a few times before you have the urge to ejaculate, and your partner will be that much more skilled in this technique.

Another type of squeeze technique is also possible (see Figure 17-3). Instead of squeezing the tip of the penis, squeeze it at the base, with the thumb at the underside, just above the scrotal sac, and the other fingers on the other side of the penile shaft. This, too, will stop the ejaculatory reflex. It will also make the squeeze technique a little easier to use in a later step when you're employing it during intercourse.

With either type of squeeze, you'll probably make a few mistakes. (As a matter of fact, during the first couple of sessions in which you use the squeeze, the woman should use the squeeze pretty much on an arbitrary basis, employing it after the man has a firm erection and not necessarily waiting until the man signals. This will add even more control to the ejaculatory process.) If you squeeze too late and the ejaculation is inevitable, stop squeezing and try to enjoy the ejaculation. It really takes some practice and some communicating between both partners to get this technique down pat. Make sure that you both understand when to apply it. For example, some people use a single word, such as "Now," as a signal to the woman. Others prefer to just use a tap on the hand. Just make sure that you're both using the same signal.

Keep up the squeeze technique, as with the stop–start, until you can last for at least fifteen minutes with no more than two or three squeezes. And don't forget that you still want to offer your partner some of the fun of pleasuring at some mutually agreed-upon point during each session.

Sam and Betty selected the squeeze technique. At first, Betty couldn't get the hang of it. She alternated between feelings of embarrassment and feelings of fear that she would hurt Sam. They practiced the squeeze for two days until Betty really felt comfortable using it. But after that, she rapidly gained in confidence and soon, as Sam said, became "the best squeezer in town." Their contract at this stage stated: "We agree to attempt to spend at least one hour per day in pleasuring exercises with Betty using the squeeze technique to help Sam control his ejaculations. We agree to refrain from attempting intercourse. However, Sam agrees to help Betty reach orgasm at least once during each session. Also, we both agree that, if he has not ejaculated during the session, Betty will bring Sam to orgasm at the end of the session by masturbating him."

STEP 4: STOP–START WITH LUBRICANT ADDED
This is an easy one. Using either the stop–start procedure

299

or one of the squeeze techniques, ask your partner to add the use of a lubricant—one of the ones we've suggested previously, such as "K-Y Lubricating Jelly" or "Transi-Lube." The idea here is to come closer and closer to what it will be like when you actually engage in intercourse. If you and your partner enjoy or don't mind oral sex, try it. It can be very, very stimulating.

Now, the goal, as you can probably see, is to increase the amount of stimulation but to use either the stop–start or the squeeze technique in order to prevent ejaculation. With increasing stimulation, it may be increasingly difficult. But don't get too discouraged if you should come when you don't want to. Just remember to continue paying careful attention to how aroused you become and to the sensations associated with that. Pay particular attention to how you feel when you feel the ejaculation approaching so that you can signal your partner. With continued practice, you'll make it.

You're ready to move to the next step when you can last for fifteen minutes of manual or oral stimulation—without needing the stop–start or squeeze techniques.

STEP 5: PENETRATION—NO MOVEMENT

If you're getting a little tired, bored, or frustrated with all these steps, try to relax. This step, once successfully accomplished, means that you're just about home.

In essence, what we want you to try is intercourse—but without thrusting and without moving around. We still want you to pay careful attention to the sensations that you feel prior to ejaculation.

Begin by having your partner stimulate you—manually or orally—until you have an erection. Try lying on your back relaxing; enjoy the sensations as your partner plays with you. You can also be stroking and stimulating your partner during this time. Your partner should then sit on or between your legs, facing you, with your penis near her vagina; she should continue to tease you, making sure that you maintain your erection. At this point, it's a good idea to let your partner rub your penis around her vaginal area—just so that you're used to this sensation. If you feel that you're about to ejaculate, tell her, and she can apply the stop–start or the squeeze technique. Take your time; take as long as you need to feel confident in your ability to control your ejaculation. When you are ready, your partner should move herself forward, with her hand still holding your erect penis and, with as little movement of the erect penis as possible, guide herself onto the penis. If you need lubrication, go ahead and use it. But first consider your

300

partner's natural lubrication. By stimulating her prior to insertion, you'll make her ready for easier insertion of your penis.

When the penis has completely entered the vagina, the two of you should remain still—no thrusting or moving. Your partner can support her weight by placing her knees along the sides of your body. Now, pay careful attention to the sensations of your penis's being in her vagina. (By the way, if just lying and sitting there looking at each other seems a little silly, well, just enjoy it. Laugh and have a good time.) If you feel the sensations that warn you that you are about to ejaculate, tell your partner. She can then lift herself completely off your penis to stop the stimulation, or partly off to use the squeeze technique, applying pressure to stop your ejaculation. (It's especially easy to use the squeeze at the base of the penis. In fact, it can be applied with the penis still in the vagina.)

This exercise has been called the "quiet vagina." The point is to become used to intercourse gradually, beginning with this process of little or no movement. But, of course, even the quiet vagina can be very stimulating. So if you don't apply the squeeze in time, or if she can't get off in time, and you do ejaculate, just go ahead and enjoy it. This is by no means a failure, and it is especially common the first few times that you try this. But attending to the sensations might allow you to be a little more aware of the approaching ejaculation next time.

If you find that you are ejaculating each time that you try, you may want to back off a little. Return to the previous step, and make sure that you've really mastered it. Then, when you are ready, spend more time having your partner rub your penis around her vagina; in fact, do this for a couple of sessions without any attempt at penetration. Then try it again.

You should try this step several times, until you can maintain your penis in her vagina for roughly fifteen minutes without the need for a stop–start or a squeeze. By the way, it's also quite possible that you'll begin to lose your erection while your penis is still in her vagina. If so, ask your partner to move gently, enough to make your erection firm once again, and then to hold still again.

> Sam wanted to rocket ahead at this point. He felt ready and sure that he could hold his own. But the first time he and Betty tried intercourse, Sam insisted on being on top. He came immediately upon penetration. Betty tried to avoid saying "I told you so." Instead, she convinced Sam of the need to slow down, and they wrote it up as a contract: "Sam and Betty agree to slow down and to let Betty gently rub Sam's penis around her vagina without trying intercourse. Once Sam can handle this for ten minutes without ejaculating, Betty will assume the woman-on-

top position and move Sam's penis into her vagina. Both Sam and Betty agree not to move in this position unless Sam loses his erection fades or unless one gets a cramp. Once Sam can stay in this position for fifteen minutes without coming, we will do it three more times for fifteen minutes each to make sure that Sam can make it."

STEP 6: PENETRATION WITH THRUSTING

You're now ready, as they say, to go all the way. In fact, this step is the same as the last one, with one very big exception. Go through the entire Step-5 procedure, beginning with manual stimulation, woman on top, your partner inserting your penis into her vagina. Now for the exception. Your partner should begin moving—slowly—and with your feedback. Explain to her that the focus at this point is still on your awareness of your ejaculation response, and encourage her not to move too quickly too soon. If you feel yourself beginning to come before you want to, tell your partner. She should stop moving. If that's not enough, she should partly remove herself from your penis and perhaps use the squeeze. Continue this—only the partner moving—until you can last for fifteen minutes. Then proceed to the point where both of you move slowly. Enjoy yourselves. Concentrate on the sensations. If you need to stop or use the squeeze, by all means, use it. Continue this—both of you moving slowly—until you can last for another fifteen minutes.

The last part of this step is to start picking up the pace, both of you moving more quickly and in any way that will enhance your arousal. Use the stop–start or squeeze (just ask your partner to raise herself a little and squeeze at the base of your penis) if you feel your ejaculation coming too soon. Keep this up until—in this position, woman on top—you are both moving as you like it, and until you can last fifteen minutes.

> Betty and Sam decided that they didn't need a written contract for this part of the exercise. They did agree orally not to move too quickly and to be sure to employ the squeeze if Sam was coming too quickly. By the second day of this step, they were moving just as they wanted, with Betty on top but with each giving full pleasure to the other. Sam was so proud of himself. By the second day, he had lasted for twelve minutes, and then, because he and Betty agreed, he had let himself go. It was quite an experience for both of them.

STEP 7: TRY OTHER POSITIONS

By now, you're home free. The last thing you want to try, though, is intercourse in other positions. It might be a good idea to proceed as in step 6, and then, once the penis is inserted with the woman on top, to gently roll over on your sides and to continue intercourse in the side-by-side position. This will move you gradually from the position with the least amount of effort for the male to a position requiring greater effort and, possibly, more stimulation.

Probably the last position to try is with the man on top. This one is the most difficult for ejaculatory control, and you can attempt this one when you're able to last for several minutes in the other positions.

This series of exercises could extend anywhere from two to twelve weeks until you're able to last more or less as long as you want to. It's probably a good idea to use booster sessions—say, once a week—following the completion of all of these steps. So, once a week, or maybe every four or five attempts at intercourse, do a stop–start or squeeze exercise. You may not have perfect control every time for the next couple of months, so these booster sessions can help to ensure that what you've accomplished in the original series of exercises lasts. Don't worry if you come too quickly a couple of times. (For example, a lot of tension about some problem might affect your ejaculatory control. So either avoid sex at those moments or discuss it openly with your partner in order to get her cooperation in delaying ejaculation.) Try a stop–start or squeeze the next time and you'll probably be back on the beam.

By the way, just because you've been able to increase your staying power, this doesn't mean that every sexual encounter has to be delayed just to see how long you can last. You and your partner might decide that a "quickie" seems just right at one point or another. So, go ahead. What we hope is that now you'll be able to choose the length of time you want to last. And we also hope that you and your partner, in making that decision, will enjoy sex more than ever.

Increasing Staying Power Without a Partner

Jerry, at age 24, was ready to swear off sex. He dated a lot and had "gone to bed" with several women, but usually he was so turned on that he came before he actually began intercourse. It wasn't long before he was attempting to avoid sex altogether. He was not seeing anybody on a regular basis; certainly he had no regular sex partner. Jerry had heard that, for his problem, if you didn't have a partner, there was very little that could be done. It was depressing, to say the least.

Luckily, Jerry is wrong. In fact, there is a Treat Yourself

303

program for men who haven't developed satisfactory ejaculatory control, but who have no partners to help them. This program proceeds pretty much the way the program for men *with* partners goes, and it can be just as successful.

In fact, the basic principles and procedures for doing it yourself are pretty much the same as those used with a partner. The critical points involve learning to attend carefully to your arousal cycle—especially the feelings and sensations that occur prior to ejaculation. Then, you learn to develop control by stopping stimulation prior to ejaculation. The key difference between these exercises and those in the previous section is that all of these exercises are done alone, using self-stimulation.

A few basic guidelines before starting the program:

1. Try to do these exercises at least three to five times a week, with each "session" lasting fifteen to thirty minutes.

2. Try to avoid sex with a partner during the period. It could undermine what you're attempting to teach yourself. If you do get sexually involved with someone during this period, it would probably be best to attempt to avoid intercourse, which is the situation that leads most quickly to rapid ejaculation.

3. Read Chapter 13 (the sections on fantasies and self-stimulation). The exercises in this chapter are based on the one described there, and that preliminary reading should help you to get going here.

4. Follow through on all the assessment and goal-setting described in Chapter 9. Even though you're the only one involved in the program (at least, initially), making it as systematic as possible is bound to be a big help.

STEP 1: SELF-STIMULATION USING STOP–START
If you've read the previous sections, you're probably ready for what's going to come now. Basically, what you're going to do now is use self-stimulation to develop your awareness of the sensations that occur just before ejaculation.

In Chapter 13, we presented some ideas about self-stimulation, and about how you can use fantasies in that process. After reviewing that chapter, set aside several periods during the week that will give you the time and privacy you need for this exercise. Give yourself about one half hour per session. Using whatever techniques you have developed for self-stimulation, and without using lubrication, begin to stimulate yourself. However, try to use fantasies as little as possible;

if necessary, use them only to help you begin (we'll explain why in step 3). Concentrate as fully as possible on your penis and on the sensations involved in sexual arousal. We can't emphasize this point enough. If you used fantasies to help you develop your erection, try to shut them off so that you can focus completely on the sensations in your penis. In other words, try to use the fantasies only to help the initial arousal process. Be aware of the increasing excitement you feel as you become more aroused. Notice both the specific physical sensations—for example, tightening of the scrotal sac—and the feelings. As you feel the signs that warn you of an impending ejaculation, stop stimulating yourself. If you've stopped in time, the urge to ejaculate will begin to diminish; this could take anywhere from fifteen seconds to a couple of minutes. It's also likely that your erection will be lost—either partially or completely. Don't worry. It's all part of the process.

Now, it's very common that the first attempts at stopping in this exercise aren't in time and that you do have an ejaculation. Again, don't worry. But we do suggest that you not wait until the last few seconds. Use the stop–start technique well before the ejaculation is inevitable and at any point in the process when you're feeling aroused. You'll soon learn the point when you should stop stimulating yourself in order to delay the ejaculation.

Once you stop the ejaculation, rest for a while, and begin to stimulate yourself again. If you come right away, you probably haven't taken sufficient time to let the ejaculatory urge subside. So rest a little longer, and then try it again. Of course, the more ejaculations you have during a particular session, the weaker will be your urge to ejaculate. So, if you notice that you can hold off much more easily at the end of a session than at the beginning (i.e., if you do experience any ejaculation), it's a little more important to stop the ejaculation right when you begin these self-stimulation exercises, because they would probably be most similar to the situation you would face during intercourse. That is, you would be very unlikely to have ejaculated right before sexual intercourse.

The goal in this exercise is for you to last for fifteen to twenty minutes of steady self-stimulation (with an erection, of course) without ejaculation. By the end of this exercise, this fifteen minutes should not require any stop–starts, although when you're just beginning, it's likely that two or three or even more stop–starts will be necessary. This may take only one or two sessions; it may take several. Either way, though, be sure that you are completely aware of all of the sensations that signal that an ejaculation is coming.

STEP 1A. SELF-STIMULATION WITH THE SQUEEZE TECHNIQUE

Although we think it's more effective and somewhat easier to use stop–start when stimulating yourself, if you have proceeded with stop–start and find that it's not working as you would like, you might want to try the squeeze technique.

Begin to stimulate yourself. At a point of excitement prior to the point of ejaculatory inevitability, stop self-stimulation and apply the squeeze. Do this in the same way and in the same places as in the earlier section describing how your partner should apply the squeeze. But there's one major exception: Whether you are applying the squeeze at the head of the penis or at the base, the hands will be reversed, because you and not your partner, are applying the squeeze. Thus, your thumb will be at the top of the penis with your second and third fingers applying pressure just under the glans. At the base, your thumb will be applying pressure at the top and your second and third fingers at the underside.

Follow through with this exercise just as you would with the stop–start until you can last for fifteen to twenty minutes without ejaculating.

STEP 2: SELF-STIMULATION WITH LUBRICATION

Doing either the stop–start or the squeeze, go through exactly the same exercise as in Step 1, except this time use lubrication when you're stimulating yourself. Again, as we described earlier, this is likely to provide even more stimulation, because it is somewhat closer to what you would experience with your penis in a lubricated vagina. Therefore, it may be a slightly more difficult step in the process. But remember that the point of all of these exercises is to move on a graduated basis from easier to more difficult steps. Adding lubricant simply represents the next, more difficult step.

The goal here is also to last for ten to twenty minutes without ejaculating and without needing a stop–start or a squeeze. You may find that this step takes less time to accomplish successfully than the first one because you've already developed considerable control. Fine. But you may find that it takes as much time as the first step because of the increased stimulation due to the lubricant. That's fine too. Either way, the goal will eventually be achieved. When it is, you're ready to move on.

STEP 3. SELF-STIMULATION WITH FANTASY

You've probably been wondering now what's going to happen when you eventually try sex with a partner. It's a pretty logical question: "How can learning to control my ejaculations

306

when I'm stimulating myself help me to control them in intercourse?" This step is designed to help you do just that.

Remember, in step 1, that we suggested that you try not to engage in too much fantasizing other than the minimal necessary to begin the arousal process? Well, the main reason for this is that the use of fantasies is the best way for making the transition from self-stimulation to having sex with someone else. Thus, the use of fantasies about sex with a partner to develop control while stimulating yourself is the best preparation for actually having control when you do engage in sex with a partner.

Use some of the ideas about fantasies presented in Chapter 13. Prepare for this exercise by thinking in advance about some fantasies that really turn you on. Then begin the self-stimulation exercises—without using lubricants. When a high level of excitement is reached, apply the stop–start or the squeeze, just as you did in the previous steps.

As you become successful in stopping your ejaculations while using this erotic fantasy, and if the fantasy didn't follow the steps that you might follow in a sexual encounter with a partner, begin using a fantasy involving sex with a partner. Really try to get into it. Imagine the entire process, from just thinking about sex to touches, kissing, stroking, genital play, and intercourse. Stimulate yourself to these fantasies, applying stop–start or the squeeze in order to prevent ejaculation. Be prepared for any number of things. You may or may not get through the fantasies all the way to sexual intercourse. (If you don't, pick up at that point during the next session if you can.) You may have more difficulty at some points than at others— for example, fantasizing about the actual thrusting in intercourse, which will probably be accompanied by some degree of thrusting of the pelvis while you are stimulating yourself. With increasing practice, though, you are likely to overcome this problem.

If, however, one particular fantasy does lead to more difficulty than others, try using stop–start a little earlier than you otherwise might have. You can make this fantasy central to the exercise (that is, when you stimulate yourself, use this fantasy more than the others). Then, apply stop–start or the squeeze well before you need to; rest; begin self-stimulation; apply stop–start; and follow the sequence until you are comfortable enough with the scene to apply stop–start or the squeeze at progressively later points.

Remember, even though you're using fantasies, to also try to focus on the sensations accompanying the self-stimulation. If you forget to attend to your arousal level and

307

happen to ejaculate, just try to concentrate a little earlier next time. If you lose the arousing fantasy—say, by drifting into something else—just get back to it. This could happen several times during any session. Also, don't rush through the process. You want to go carefully and slowly through every phase of sexual activity with a partner. For the parts that are the most arousing, stay with them until you have complete control.

When you have good control using the basic fantasy that you have used to this point, make some changes in the fantasy. Imagine even more arousing partners or activities. Apply stop–start or the squeeze as necessary. The goal here is to last for fifteen to twenty minutes of self-stimulation without applying stop–start or the squeeze, while fantasizing the sexual activities that are the most exciting to you.

STEP 4: SELF-STIMULATION WITH FANTASY AND LUBRICANT
Since lubrication can provide even more stimulation, repeat step 3, this time using lubricant. The goal is to last fifteen to twenty minutes using the most erotic fantasies and using lubrication while stimulating yourself.

STEP 5: TRANSFER TO A REAL PARTNER
The following example shows the results:

Jerry went through the entire process up to this point. He had a few "setbacks," especially when he began fantasizing the most erotic situations. When he did this, he forgot to pay attention to the sensations of coming ejaculations, and it took three sessions before he mastered the art of erotic fantasizing while focusing on his penis. But, by slowing down and practicing, he eventually was ready to get to "the real thing." But he was skeptical. In fact, he was plain scared that none of this would work with a partner. Jerry and Bobbi, a woman he had been dating for some five weeks, but with whom he had never attempted intercourse because of his fears of coming too soon, tried the basic steps outlined below. They went gradually through each one, and they needed only two sessions together before they achieved mutually satisfying intercourse. From then on, Jerry was on his way.

First, decide on who your next partner will be. This is particularly important. If you select a woman with whom you have difficulty communicating, you're adding to the possibility that there will be some problem in transferring from self-stimulation to sex with a partner.

Second, discuss with your partner what you have been trying to accomplish. Explain that you need her cooperation, that it will soon make sex more enjoyable for both of you, and that it can actually be fun. If your partner seems uncomfortable or is unwilling, you have several options. You can proceed with her anyhow. We don't recommend this, but it's possible that the self-stimulation exercises you've mastered up to this point may be enough. Your second option is to explain things more clearly, especially by asking your partner to read the relevant parts of this book. The final option is to find a new partner.

Third, go slowly. Ask your partner if it would be all right if the two of you didn't engage in intercourse for your first few encounters. Instead, engage in the whole range of sex play, excluding intercourse. (Be sure to provide for your partner what she needs in order to be satisfied.) Focus carefully on your penis and on the sensations associated with ejaculations. Make adjustments early. In other words, ask your partner to "take a break" for a few minutes if your arousal level becomes too high. Just stop what you're doing until the urge to ejaculate subsides, just as you would using the stop–start. But stop *before* you really need to at first. During the breaks, you can still have a good time, we hope, by enjoying each other's company. You should just focus a little less on the sexual activities during these breaks. Of course, if you goof a little and you do ejaculate, it's no big thing. Enjoy it. Next time, try to stop that particular activity before you get to the point of ejaculatory inevitability.

Fourth, as you are increasingly comfortable about the control you have over your ejaculations, you can begin increasing stimulation. You might even ask your partner to manually stimulate you (first without and then with lubricants) and practice stop–start until you have firm control.

Fifth, you can attempt intercourse once all of the above has resulted in firm control. If you feel extremely excited before insertion, try to hold off a little (say, by relaxing for a short while) before you insert your penis. Once your penis is inserted, move slowly or not at all to begin with. Gradually increase the amount of movement while focusing on the sensations in your penis. If you feel an ejaculation coming before you want to, slow down. Try to hold off on all movements until the urge subsides.

Sixth, make sure that you're checking out each step as you go. Communicate with your partner all the way. Don't rush. If you're having a problem, figure out what it is and either go back a step or stay with that activity until you've mastered it. If a small adjustment in your partner's activity will help (for example, a change in the way she moves her body), ask for it. Don't worry if everything doesn't work out immediately. Look at how far you've come already. Just move a little more slowly, go back to earlier steps if you have to, make sure that you have control, and then move ahead.

Seventh, as you have increased control, slowly change positions and movements, practicing as we've suggested here until you've achieved the kind of control that you want in each situation. With practice and patience, you'll soon be relaxed and comfortable enough to maintain your control so that you and your partner can enjoy sex the way, and as long as, you really want to.

LASTING TOO LONG: EJACULATORY OVERCONTROL

A somewhat less common but certainly no less frustrating problem than coming too soon is called ejaculatory overcontrol. (Some therapists call this delayed or retarded ejaculation.) As a man gets older, he may just naturally take longer to come. But with younger men, this problem may appear in many forms. It could mean that the man can ejaculate with only certain kinds of stimulation, often manual or oral stimulation, and that he cannot ejaculate in the vagina. It could mean that the man cannot ejaculate in the vagina without excessively long and vigorous thrusting, to the point where both partners are so exhausted that they cannot enjoy the experience. It could mean that the man can only ejaculate when he is alone and stimulating himself. And it could also mean that the man cannot ejaculate at all.

It's not completely clear how this problem comes about. There could be any number of experiences that could lead to ejaculatory overcontrol. Sometimes this problem reflects a low level of arousal, one strong enough to bring about an erection but insufficient to bring about orgasm. But our description of the term reflects what is thought to be a common thread in many such problems—overcontrol. Where this is a problem, it is found that the man has difficulty, simply speaking, in giving up control. In other words, he "holds back." Although we certainly don't view this a voluntary act, exerting control in this way may help some men to avoid anxiety. You can think of this in contrast to erection problems where anxiety appears to "control" the man to the point of preventing erections.

For cases involving ejaculatory overcontrol, the man does have firm erections (if not, view the problem as an erection problem and review Chapter 18 first) and does feel sexual arousal. But he cannot ejaculate when and/or where he wants to. Because the inability to let go is central to this problem, the whole Treat Yourself strategy involves *distraction*; the man's thoughts are focused *away* from whatever it is that leads to the excessive control and, in a particularly relaxing environment, onto thoughts and fantasies that will allow him to ejaculate more readily.

Steps in the Program for Overcontrol

Before you go any further, make sure that you've completed the steps at the beginning of this chapter regarding Preliminary Steps for Ejaculatory Problems. This is particularly important because you might find, as an example, that you have difficulty in ejaculating only in certain situations or with certain people. Then, instead of a Treat Yourself program, you may only need to make adjustments in those situations in order to find some improvement. For example, you might try motel therapy (see Chapter 7)—that is, having sex in certain places that are particularly arousing, or having sex in anxiety-free circumstances (not right after a hard day at work) in which there are fewer inhibitions.

You might not have thought of this before, but there is a great deal of similarity between your problem (ejaculatory overcontrol) and the problems of women's having difficulty in experiencing orgasms. Indeed, some sex therapists consider both problems to be "orgasmic problems," and they treat both in similar ways. Of course, we're well aware of the differences between men and women. But the fact that overcontrol and certain inhibitions about "letting go" in sex seem pertinent in both situations lead us to suggest the first step:

STEP 1: REVIEW CHAPTER 15

This is the chapter dealing with women's orgasm problems. Your problem with ejaculatory overcontrol will be treated in essentially the same way, using many of the same exercises. In fact, you can almost use the Treat Yourself program in Chapter 15 on a step-by-step basis to help relieve some of the anxiety and inhibitions that you may be feeling and to help your ejaculation problems. Because this is so, we're only going to summarize some of the key steps for treating yourself in this chapter. This way, you can use both chapters to guide your program.

311

STEP 2: REVIEW CHAPTER 11

In Chapter 11, we've presented a basic program for teaching yourself to relax. Practice these exercises so that you will be comfortable when you proceed with the following steps.

STEP 3: REVIEW CHAPTER 13

Fantasies are going to be an important part in your Treat Yourself program. Take another look at this chapter, and get ready for using some of your favorite fantasies or other distractions to help yourself loosen up and turn on.

STEP 4: COMBINE FANTASIES AND SELF-STIMULATION

The basic purpose of this step is to teach you to stimulate yourself and to ejaculate as quickly as possible. Think about the fantasies that you enjoy most. Make them erotic ones. Then use self-stimulation and try to ejaculate as quickly as possible. It's a good idea to hold off from any attempts at intercourse during this period, and also to avoid attempting to ejaculate for a few days prior to this exercise so that the urge will be stronger. If you're still not coming as quickly as you'd like, you might try using erotic literature to help stimulate your fantasies. This is the *distraction* we were mentioning a little earlier. We think you'll find that the combination of relaxation and distraction speeds up your ejaculations considerably.

Step 4a: Erotic Pleasure 1. If you're going at this with your partner right from the start, you can begin with Erotic Pleasure 1 (or erotic massage without intercourse). Read Chapter 14. You and your partner can start stimulating each other—but without touching your genitals and without attempting intercourse. Relax, try to let those inhibitions slip away, and let the urge to ejaculate build up.

Step 4b: Erotic Pleasure 2. When you've completed the above exercise to the point where you feel relaxed and relatively stimulated, take the next step. Ask your partner to follow through with genital play, as we've illustrated in this and in earlier chapters. Use whatever fantasies or erotic thoughts you find particularly arousing. Don't focus on your penis; rather, distract yourself in any way you can. You might ask your partner to stimulate you in the ways that you find most arousing—using lubricant, orally, or in other ways. (For example, some men find it particularly arousing to have a partner rub her breasts gently along the penis, or to guide the penis in and out between her breasts.) Use your fantasies and let go. Let your partner bring you to orgasm as often and as quickly as you and she can. (This requires some open and clear communication in advance as to what you're trying to accomplish.)

Step 4c: Desensitization—If You Need It. Your problem might be that you can stimulate yourself to ejaculation but when you and a specific partner are having intercourse you cannot ejaculate. You, therefore, might have to set up a specific series of exercises that teach you to stimulate yourself to ejaculation while "desensitizing" yourself to not being able to ejaculate with your partner next to you. Carefully explain this to your partner. It's neither person's fault, so try to avoid hurting each other's feelings with this one.

It is possible that you may be able to achieve satisfactory orgasms when you're alone, but not when you're with your partner. This step helps you to bridge the gap by teaching yourself to ejaculate at a good distance from your partner and progressively coming closer, until you are together when you ejaculate. We know that this may be a difficult step for some people, but it's worth a try.

Stimulate yourself to ejaculation somewhere in the house or apartment, perhaps while your partner is in another room. It might be a little tough at first, especially if you're thinking about the fact that your partner knows that you're stimulating yourself. But keep at it. Use whatever distracting fantasies help. Then, move somewhat closer to your partner the next time, perhaps to the next room. Stimulate yourself to ejaculation. The next step might be opening the door to the room (say, while you are in the bathroom and your partner is in the bedroom) while you're stimulating yourself. The next steps involve being in the same room, first without and then with her watching you. The final step might involve your stimulating yourself to ejaculation while you are next to your partner, with her touching you. Then, freed of the need to "hold back" in her presence, you can move to the step involving your partner's manually or orally stimulating you to ejaculation.

STEP 5: THE BRIDGE

Once your partner is stimulating you adequately to bring you to ejaculation within a period of time that is satisfactory to you (or your own masturbation is doing that), have your partner stimulate you to the point of orgasm using lubricants (and whichever of your own fantasies turn you on). Just prior to ejaculation, have her continue to stimulate your penis with her hand as you insert your penis in her vagina. Keep thrusting with her hand on the base of your penis until just prior to orgasm. Then signal her to remove her hand (a word or touch agreed upon in advance will do) and continue thrusting until you ejaculate in her vagina. The goal here is to gradually make the point of entry earlier and earlier. Once you can consistently enter her vagina and come in a satisfactory period of time, move the period of entry gradually back to the point where you can cut down on the need for manual or oral stimulation.

There are two positions that make this process a little easier—man on top and side-by-side. Rear entry or woman on top are also possible (see the illustrations in Chapter 20), although, particularly in the latter, this is least demanding for the male and therefore least likely to produce more rapid ejaculations.

STEP 6: SWITCHING FANTASIES

During this entire process, you may or may not have been using erotic fantasies or erotic literature to help arouse and distract you. Once you begin the actual act of intercourse, and just prior to ejaculation, switch your fantasies to those involving sex with your partner. Gradually increase the length of time prior to ejaculation that you fantasize about having sex with her. The goal is to have these fantasies assume all the erotic arousal that the other fantasies previously had, so that ejaculation and sexual arousal become more and more related to your usual pattern of sex.

If you have problems with ejaculating after entering your partner's vagina, you may have to back off a step and make sure that you are adequately aroused prior to entry. Don't worry if you can't seem to ejaculate. At that point, you may just want to withdraw and ask your partner to stimulate you manually or orally to orgasm. (Don't forget to return the favor.) One couple who had this problem went back to step 4. The man would read a particularly arousing magazine while his wife stimulated him to orgasm. A few magazines and orgasms later, they made the switch to intercourse with some ease.

If you find the arousal building up along with the urge to ejaculate but then find yourself wondering how long it will be until you ejaculate or whether or not ejaculation will be a good one, try to postpone the ejaculation that particular time. If you are involved in intercourse, remove your penis from your partner's vagina (of course, explain to your partner) and stop the stimulation. Try again later when you are not thinking about your ejaculation and how well you are doing (the "spectator role") but are distracted and simply enjoying yourself.

It's strange how difficult it often is to enjoy ourselves in situations that are supposed to be joyful. But, again, with practice and patience, and with an understanding partner, you can increase your timing and joy in sex, and, we hope, also increase the intimacy you share with your partner.

314

Eighteen

Problems with Erections

If you have a problem getting an erection when you want to get one or keeping it after you've got it, we've got good news for you. The problem will probably disappear all by itself.

That's the truth. Most men, at one time or another, have problems with erections. As we explained in Chapter 5, fatigue, preoccupation with other things, drinking too much, being nervous about something—all these and a hundred other things can create problems with erections. Luckily, most erection problems caused by temporary fears or anxieties are temporary, and they usually straighten themselves out without the need for a special Treat Yourself program.

"Okay," you say, "that's great. But how long do I have to wait? I've been having problems getting an erection for months now."

Well, maybe that *is* a horse of a different color. We said that *most* problems with erections are temporary. They may come and go, depending on the circumstances. Although the man and the woman will undoubtedly be distressed about the problem, when the circumstances change, then satisfactory sexual functioning is likely to return.

So the real question is: What if satisfactory sexual functioning doesn't return? In other words, if the problem has continued long enough to concern you or your partner, if it even seems to be getting worse rather than better, or if you're increasingly tense and uptight when you try to make love or even when you think about it, then it is probably time for you to begin to Treat Yourself.

LET'S CALL IT WHAT IT IS

Dan went to see a therapist, complaining that he was impotent. "Nobody's impotent," was the therapist's response. Dan gave him a dirty look. "Try and tell my wife that!" he exclaimed.

Well, the truth is that that therapist was right. No one is impotent. *Impotence* is a vague term that refers to a set of related, but specific, problems. All of them involve problems in either achieving or maintaining an erection when it's wanted. And having that kind of problem is a lot different from telling yourself, or from being told, that "you're impotent." The term *impotence* implies a complete failure of sexual power and that you're weak or helpless—that you can't make it as a man.

Well, forget it. We don't mean to suggest that not being able to get an erection isn't a problem. If you've ever been faced with it, you know that it is. The frustrations and grief that it can bring can be overwhelming. But what we *are* trying to suggest is that a beginning step in dealing with the problem is to start viewing it differently. It has nothing to do with your manliness; it has nothing to do with a failure of your sexual drive. What it has to do with, specifically, is the fact that you may have partial or nonexistent erections when you want to have a firm erection. These are behaviors, not conditions or illnesses that should rule your life. Most importantly, these are behaviors that can be changed.

Of course, you want to be sure that what you label a problem *is* a problem. For example, as men get older, they may not be able to get an erection as often, as firmly, or perhaps as quickly as they used to. The cure is simple: Don't try harder, and don't view yourself as losing your manhood or as being impotent. Instead, try to relax, don't force the issue, enjoy yourself with what you have, and take a little more time and rest between your attempts at intercourse.

316

As we mentioned in Chapter 5, most erection problems, some 90 percent or more, are related to tension and stress—that is, to psychological and social pressures rather than to physical problems. But it wouldn't hurt to see a physician—your family doctor or internist, or perhaps a urologist (a doctor who specializes in problems in the genitourinary tract)—just to have him check you out to make sure that there's nothing wrong physically. Let's face it, though; you have probably thought about that yourself. Maybe you didn't go because you're too embarrassed. But you'd be surprised: Your physician has heard it all. He probably won't even blink an eye when you tell him. Be sure that you tell the doctor the whole story so that he will give the right tests. And once you can rule out possible physical causes, you can approach the Treat Yourself program with just that much more confidence. If you really don't want to see your doctor first, you could try a Treat Yourself program. For many problems involving erections, this program will do the trick. If not, you can see your doctor at a later date. (If you can get an erection at any time—for example, when you stimulate yourself, when you wake up in the morning, when you're asleep—then the problem is probably not physical.)

So far, then, you've decided to stop thinking about yourself as "impotent." Instead, you can think of yourself as suffering from an occasional or frequent behavioral problem. Once you think of the problem this way, we hope you'll realize that it doesn't mean there's anything wrong with you as a man. Also, when you identify a problem as a specific behavior in this way, it means that it's just that much easier to come up with specific ways of changing it. That holds true when the problem involves erections, as well as when it involves any of the other problems discussed in this book.

There are several things you might try to help yourself, or that you and your partner can try together, before you start a formal Treat Yourself program.

You're Not the Only One

Reread Chapter 5, "Common Problems of Men." You should get the idea from that chapter that you are not alone. Almost all men have problems with erections at one time or another. Too much alcohol, some type of stress or pressure: All people are exposed to these or similar problems, and for many men, the result is a temporary decrease in the ability to achieve an erection. So, believe us that it's nothing new, and that you're not the only one who encounters the problem from time to time.

Don't Fight; Switch

You probably have a better understanding now of the way erection problems can be caused by tension—due to anything from jet lag to job problems. This means that you might have to rethink a little bit about where and when the problem occurs. If you and your sex partner have developed pretty good lines of communication, talk it over with her. From this discussion, you both might get a better idea of the events that precede erection problems. If the day has been a particularly rough one, and if you feel tense or exhausted, you might just want to enjoy each other's company rather than attempting intercourse. How about just lying in each other's arms for a while before saying goodnight? The idea here is to be able to recognize the times and situations when you're feeling uptight or anxious. You don't *always* have to have intercourse to enjoy sex. And you don't *have* to have an erection. Sex, as we've defined it, and as we hope you experience it, can mean a lot more than erections and orgasms.

Motel Therapy
and Other Variations on a Theme

You might want to try changing the time and place you typically attempt to make love. You might have fallen into patterns— days, times, positions, and places—that simply are no longer arousing. Can sex be boring? It certainly can if you're in too much of a pattern. One of the most exciting, stimulating changes is to try going to a motel, even for just one night. You'll be amazed at how "sexy" you will both feel. Maybe a little variety in positions for love-making will help. Try having sex in the morning, when you're rested and more relaxed, rather than late at night, when you're not. Take a look at Chapter 20 for some suggestions of what to do when sex is boring.

The Spice of Life

You might also want to introduce a little more erotica into your lives. "Dirty" books and magazines and maybe even some X-rated movies (you can buy them by the 8-millimeter reel or view them at your local X-rated theater) might add some spice to your love life. But don't force your partner to view them if she doesn't get turned on. On the other hand, you might enjoy them even more together. At the least, this erotica might give you a couple of new ideas for love-making or some hot topics for discussion.

Inappropriate Places

That's right. Try some heavy petting with your partner in places where you can't possibly have intercourse, such as in a movie theater or in a bus. You won't be able to attempt intercourse, but you might find yourself getting erections, which will restore your confidence.

Think of Something Else

If you can't get an erection, does it mean that you have to give up sex altogether? *No way*. If you're having a problem inserting your penis into her vagina, stop trying for a while. Remember that you want to avoid being preoccupied with your sexual "performance." Instead, just try to enjoy all the other things we've talked about—holding your partner close, enjoying the body contact, rubbing each other's bodies, and employing other parts of your body—hands, tongue, and/or lips—to stimulate her. Remember that soft penises have feelings too. It's possible that when you take your mind off trying to achieve an erection and just plain enjoy these other sexual activities, your erection will return on its own.

Make Sure That the Conditions Are Right

A basic rule for good, satisfying sex is that it shouldn't be forced. You should really only have sex when you (and your partner) feel like it. People often feel pressured into having sex even when they're not aroused or when they are preoccupied with other things. And the more frequently this happens, the more difficult it is to enjoy sex. In fact, this alone may be enough to produce erection problems in some men.

Communicate with your partner about how you feel and about how ready you are for making love. Select a time and a place when you and she will feel right, feel good, feel relaxed, and feel comfortable. When you're both in the mood and when the time is right, sex will be much more pleasurable.

319

Make Sure That You're Turned On.

Most men aren't self-starters. They can't will an erection. There are times, of course, when you get an erection just by looking at something or at someone—say, a sexy movie or pictures. But most of the time, men need stimulation—specific help in getting it up. As we mentioned in Chapter 5, men can't operate on the basis that they are always adolescents, when the problem often is keeping yourself from being overstimulated and walking around with an erection all the time.

Here's where a little help from a friend would be most welcome. Some men operate on the basis of the myth that the woman needs to be aroused by stroking and by oral and manual stimulation of the genitals, whereas men don't need to be. Nothing could be further from the truth. Both men and women may need specific, direct stimulation in order to become fully sexually aroused.

Talk it over with your partner. Use the communication guidelines from Chapter 9. Read this chapter and Chapter 5 together. Let your partner know what you want and need (we hope that your partner will tell you what she wants and needs, too). Although genital sex surely isn't the total goal of sexuality, you probably will need some genital stimulation in order to get and maintain an erection for intercourse. Use some of the exercises in Chapter 14. Your partner will probably need to apply direct manual (by hand) or oral (by mouth) stimulation to your penis to help you achieve and maintain an erection some of the time. Once both of you realize that, things may go a lot more smoothly.

If None of These Works

Try not to be discouraged if these efforts don't work. Because really, they were only preliminary suggestions. Many of the pressures causing your erection problems might be rather obvious and even simple enough to respond to relatively simple solutions. But the inability to achieve success using these ideas only means that we have to be moving to the next step.

OVERCOMING ERECTION PROBLEMS WITH A PARTNER

There is one key idea in Treating Yourself for problems with erections: Try to decrease any anxiety or fears that may occur prior to and during the love-making. In order to achieve a satisfactory erection, the man must feel relatively comfortable and able to abandon himself to the sexual experience. Hence, all of the activities described above are designed to explore the factors that may be causing the anxiety and to change the sexual situation to eliminate those factors so that satisfactory love-making can occur.

As you remember, one of the major causes of erection problems is what we call "performance anxiety": the fears and concerns that arise out of your feeling that you have to perform well sexually—that you must be a sexual athlete. One typical cycle involving erection problems goes something like this: For one reason or another, perhaps being overtired or maybe having drunk a little too much, the man can't get an erection one time. The next time, he tries harder and harder, paying attention only to the fact that he must "get it up." Soon, the anxiety caused by this leads to a continuing inability to get an erection. Every time he attempts intercourse, he gets increasingly anxious about whether or not he will be able to "perform." The very fact that he is thinking and worrying about erections prevents them from just happening. Soon the man begins to avoid sex altogether for fear that he will appear to be a fool, a weakling, or an inadequate man. It's a vicious circle because avoiding sex doesn't help either. He just gets that much more anxious when he does try the next time.

This performance anxiety also explains the very common problem of the man's losing his erection just as he attempts to insert his penis into his partner's vagina. This is the point where his performance anxiety is greatest, because he thinks that unless he finishes the sex act completely, he will not perform as a man "should."

Thus, the key to the more intensive Treat Yourself program is the idea of moving gradually but systematically from sexual situations in which there are no demands for performance from the man—that is, no need to develop an erection—to situations in which he will be able to obtain an erection and enjoy intercourse without anxiety.

Getting Ready

If you have a problem in obtaining erections, don't try to cure it just by reading this chapter. This chapter builds on the basic program that was spelled out earlier in this book. So start by reading Parts 1, 2, and 3. Concentrate particularly on Part 3, because the basic program for treating your own sexual problems is spelled out there. You're going to be using most of these procedures: sexual-arousal training, relaxation training, contracts, and graduated assignments.

The entire program works much better if you have a regular partner with whom you can share this experience. Many of the exercises call for two people to arouse each other sexually. So read the book with your partner; discuss all the procedures with her so that both of you understand each step. (If a regular partner is not available, we will offer a program for you at the end of this chapter.) It's important for you and your partner to *fully* discuss this problem with each other. (Here's where those good lines of communication count.) Try to avoid blaming each other. An inability to obtain erections is nobody's fault, and mutual blame only makes the problem worse.

USE CONTRACTS

Review Chapter 10 (the part about contracting). Be sure to use a contract for each major step of the program. Don't forget to build in rewards as you successfully complete different phases of the program. Also, establish an agreement between you and your partner as to what distress signal you'll be using. Since overcoming anxiety is an important goal in this program, you will want to be especially sensitive to the appearance of anxiety. If it does appear, use your distress signal, and return to the previous step until you're comfortable.

Set your goals as we suggested in Chapter 10. Discuss frankly the fact that achieving and maintaining an erection requires a situation that, at first, is completely free of demand for the man. This means some sacrifice on the part of the woman. It means that she will have to participate in the sexual situation with her partner without placing any demand on him that he "perform"—that is, achieve an erection. It means assuring and reassuring him of her cooperation. It means that she should encourage him to continue to engage in sexual activity on a regular basis as, together, they implement the steps of this program.

We want to emphasize that, for the woman in this situation (and for the man in other situations described in this book), the short-term sacrifices that one may have to make should be paid back a hundred-fold once the sexual problem has been overcome. That is, with your encouragement and cooperation, whatever stress you may feel in helping your partner at this early stage will be well worth it. When the two of you begin to enjoy the ultimate result—*mutual* sexual satisfaction—you'll know that it was all worthwhile. But don't get discouraged; the problem won't go away overnight. However, through mutual cooperation, the problem will in time disappear.

322

PINPOINT YOUR PROBLEM

Together, go over Chapter 8, which will help you to pin-point the nature of the problem and when and where it occurs, changes in the problem, and so on. Fill out the sex inventory in that chapter. If your assessment points to any particular problem that you can easily change (e.g., you might realize that the problem only occurs at certain times or places), make those changes.

RELAX

If your assessment indicates that you're a pretty tense person, use one of the relaxation procedures described in Chapter 11. This is an effective way of lessening the tension you might feel even before you enter the actual sexual situation. We suggest the abdominal-breathing exercises and the deep-muscle-relaxation exercise. Using these, you will not only be able to relax yourself in general, but you will be able to relax yourself before you engage in any of the exercises in this program. And this will help you to be that much more success-ful.

NO PERFORMANCE

Finally, make an agreement between you and your part-ner to "leave your orgasms and erections on the shelf." From now until step 4 of the actual program described below, there will be no attempts at intercourse. (We can hear you now: "That's no problem. I can't get it up anyway.") As you will see, though, there will be plenty of opportunity for mutually satisfy-ing sexual activities.

Okay. Now you're all set. If what we describe below seems awfully simple, well, it is. But it's taken a lot of research to point the way to these "simple" solutions. Plan to do three to four sessions a week if possible, saving thirty to forty-five minutes per day for the session, at a time when you both can relax and not be interrupted. If you've followed the instruc-tions up to now, here's what you can do to straighten out your erection problems.

STEP 1: EROTIC PLEASURE 1

A little erotic pleasure may go a long way in treating your erection problem. Erotic Pleasure, as you'll recall from Chapter 14, involves the technique of pleasuring or sensate focus. As a first step, you'll be engaging in the use of erotic massage with-out genital contact. Make sure that you take turns in doing it to each other. Such pleasuring can and should be very satisfying to both partners. Here's where the two of you should sign your first contract, as described in Chapter 10.

> Charles and Ruth had suffered through the problem of Charles's inability to obtain an erection for some three months. The problem had started one night when Charles had had too much to drink. Instead of shrugging it off, Charles started to doubt his manhood and resolved to try harder next time. He became so preoccupied with performing successfully on subsequent occasions that the problem got worse rather than better. Charles and Ruth tried hard to overcome it, but nothing seemed to work. Their attempt at treating themselves systematically according to the principles described here was almost a last resort.
>
> They followed all the procedures described in this book up to the point of this chapter. Then they wrote their first contract on Erotic Pleasure: "We agree to spend at least one hour a night for at least five of the next seven nights in learning and practicing Erotic Pleasure 1. We agree that there will be no genital contact for Charles. We agree also to tell each other just what we like and what we are experiencing during pleasuring. Furthermore, Ruth agrees not to ask, verbally or nonverbally, for any other types of sexual activity from Charles. If we follow through on this part of the program, we will go out to dinner and a movie."
>
> Charles later confided to Ruth that he felt tremendously relieved by the fact that they could just lie there and enjoy each other without his worrying about getting an erection. "As a matter of fact," he said, "I was so damned worried about *your* getting an orgasm that I couldn't even function myself." Both Charles and Ruth reported that, relieved of the pressure to perform, both felt more sensual, more alive—"more tingly," as Ruth described it.

We hope that you'll enjoy this exercise. It's a way of becoming more sensual, more intimate, and more sexual.

Lie in a relaxed position. Let your partner's hands lightly stroke you all over. Pay attention to how it feels when she strokes you like this. Pay attention also to the fact that you can really enjoy this type of stimulation without having to worry about—or get—an erection.

Continue with this exercise for the whole first week. Or, continue until both of you are completely comfortable with each other (use your distress signal if you're not) and with this type of gentle, teasing stroking of the body.

STEP 2: EROTIC PLEASURE 2—ERECTION WITHOUT ORGASM

The next step, once pleasuring without genital contact has progressed to the point where both of you feel relaxed and comfortable with it, is to move to the next sensate-focus exercise described in Chapter 14, Erotic Pleasure 2. We might call this "advanced teasing." The purpose of this exercise is to help the man to achieve an erection in an erotic nondemanding situation. This serves to relieve the sexual activity of whatever tension and anxiety have been associated with it. This exercise is an extension of Erotic Pleasure 1; now, the entire body is included in pleasuring. Don't use lubricants or your mouth. Stick to a dry hand for now. However, the genitals should not be the *only* focus; remember that sensuality can include any and all parts of the body.

This exercise includes gentle stimulation of the genitals in order to produce arousal, in this case erection. But during Erotic Pleasure 2, the goal is to keep the man with erection problems from experiencing any anxiety. So, please, try not to worry about whether you are getting an erection. Don't be a "spectator," and don't worry about "how hard it is." Crazy as it may sound, the best time to get an erection is when you're not thinking about it. Get used to your partner's touching your penis when it's soft as well as when it's hard.

If you're still not completely aroused, try to use erotic fantasies, as we suggested in Chapter 13. Think of images that really turn you on; lie back and close your eyes.

Under relaxed but stimulating conditions, an erection will usually appear. But don't get frightened if the erection disappears. Erections may come and go during sexual activity, even for men without erection problems. So don't worry; it will return. Also, since you and your partner are taking turns giving and receiving pleasure, this coming and going is completely expectable. As a matter of fact, you deliberately want to lose your erection, regain it through stimulation, lose it, and regain it again. (The procedures below will help you to do this.) This will increase your confidence in the fact that you *can* achieve an erection readily.

But just achieving an erection is not the full goal here. Maintaining the erection is important too. There are several ways this is accomplished.

One, of course, is just by continuing the gentle stimulation of the penis. But sometimes—many times, in fact—continuing stimulation will produce arousal sufficient to lead to orgasm. But because we're moving gradually here, we don't want to rush it. So when orgasm approaches, there are two ways to avoid it. (Both of these procedures are described in more detail and illustrated in Chapter 17, which deals with problems in ejaculation. The procedures form the basis for a major part of that program.)

The first is called the *stop–start technique*. When the man feels an orgasm approaching, he simply tells his partner to stop stimulating. She removes her hand from his penis until the urge to ejaculate subsides. (If you ejaculate, don't worry; enjoy it. Just try to stop a little earlier next time.) Probably the erection will diminish as well. Once the urge is gone, gentle stimulation of the penis will bring the erection back.

The second procedure is called *the squeeze technique.* Instead of removing her hand from the penis, the partner will squeeze the penis to stop ejaculation. Properly applied, the squeeze is not uncomfortable. Just follow the instructions in Chapter 17. Have your partner place her thumb on the part of the underside of the penis just below the glans, and her first and second fingers on the opposite side of the penis (this procedure is illustrated in Chapter 17 [Figure 17-2]). Tell her to apply firm pressure for about ten to fifteen seconds (or maybe a little longer if necessary) and then to release. The urge to ejaculate should diminish. So will most of your erection. But erections lost in this way will also return rapidly upon gentle stimulation. This technique can be practiced three to five times over each of the next few encounters. If you're worried about discomfort, let your experience be your guide here. Tell your partner if it hurts. (Don't try this technique without an erection or it really may hurt.) You might even want to place your hand over hers to show her how hard to squeeze.

Don't rush through this step. When you have been able to maintain an erection for fifteen minutes using stop–start or the squeeze only two or three times, and when you can do this three sessions in a row, you're ready to move on.

> Charles and Ruth wrote a contract for this step that read in part: "We agree to engage for the next week in any sexual activity that we mutually choose. However, we also agree to stop short of orgasms by telling each other when we are approaching it, and we agree not to attempt intercourse."

STEP 3: ERECTION WITHOUT ORGASM:
ADD LUBRICANT AND ADDITIONAL STIMULATION

Once you're able to achieve and maintain an erection during step 2, you are ready to add increasing stimulation in order to get as close as possible to the sensations that you might experience during intercourse. Any number of activities can be used, including the applying of a lubricant, oral (mouth–genital) stimulation—if, as we discussed earlier, this is agreeable to both parties—or even mutual pleasuring while you both are fully clothed, if this is particularly arousing to either or both partners. This discussion of what turns each other on, as described previously, will, if you've been following this program, have already taken place. But that doesn't mean that you should now stop talking. Tell each other what feels good during sensate focus. Let's face it: Who wants somebody rubbing your elbow if that doesn't turn you on?

It might get pretty frustrating for both parties to keep approaching, but not achieving, orgasm over and over again. Thus, the surest way of telling whether you are ready for the next step is your own impatience. If you've been consistently successful in achieving and maintaining an erection during steps 2 and 3, and if you feel very comfortable and secure with your ability to achieve erections, we agree: You're ready for some relief.

STEP 4: ORGASM WITHOUT INTERCOURSE

Once you're confident in your ability to have an erection, it's an easy step to the achievement of orgasm. Use everything you have learned—all the erotic play; oral or manual stimulation; sensate focus and massage; and, if you want, erotic fantasies. Let yourself go. For both partners, do exactly what you did in steps 1, 2, and 3, but agree specifically that you may reach orgasm if you desire. Again, this is orgasm without the penis's entering the vagina.

Many people enter this stage with excitement and pleasure at finally being able to achieve orgasm. So it generally flows naturally from the preceding step. As with previous and subsequent steps, this should be a very enjoyable step. Relax, continue to share with each other the feelings that you are experiencing, and continue the full body massage of Erotic Pleasure. If, for some reason, you experience tension or perhaps lose your erection consistently, return to the previous two steps. Then you can build back up to this step. When you've been able to consistently achieve erections and then orgasms, both without intercourse, over a period of from five to seven days, then you are ready for the next step.

STEP 5: PENETRATION WITHOUT ORGASM

If you feel that you'd really like to "go all the way," try to be patient. We think that you're probably about ready to. But you haven't jumped into anything yet without practicing it first, and we don't think that you should start now. So what you're really doing in this step is practicing intercourse. You might call this a pre-intercourse course.

Once again, engage in the same kind of erotic play that you did in steps 1, 2, and 3. But instead of manually or orally stimulating each other to orgasm, when your erection is firm, you may enter the woman for a short while. Now the trick here is to penetrate the vagina, but to remain still and enjoy the sensations. Don't try thrusting or moving around to enhance the sensations. If you feel that you are coming to orgasm, withdraw your penis and ejaculate outside the vagina, just as you did in step 4. Once you've mastered this, you may penetrate and try thrusting or moving around a little. Either you or your partner may engage in this movement. Undoubtedly, this will increase the sexual arousal, but once again, withdraw prior to orgasm and ejaculate outside your partner's vagina.

There are two ways to attempt this penetration. You can select one based on your and your partner's preferences, and particularly on the basis of which one brings about the least anxiety in the man.

The first position is what is called the "nondemand" position because it creates the least pressure (or demand) on the man. In this position, the woman is on the top and is "in charge." As the man is lying on his back, the woman should place herself either straddling his legs or between his legs, kneeling or sitting facing him (if you would be more comfortable, she can sit or kneel by your side rather than between your legs). The woman should continue stimulating the man's penis, and when the erection is good and firm, and when she is also aroused and lubricated, without any movement from the man, she can lower herself onto the man's penis as she guides his penis into her vagina (see Figure 18-1). The woman can then try

Figure 18-1.

Figure 18-2.

a few slow, gentle thrusts and then withdraw herself from the penis by moving up and off it, supporting herself with her knees or feet placed by the man's side. At the same time, she should continue to stimulate the man's penis by hand. Be sure not to thrust too vigorously, because we still don't want the man to have an orgasm inside the woman's vagina. For now, we just want to show him that he can keep his erection during intercourse.

We usually recommend this position because, as we said, it requires the least effort and may therefore produce the least tension in the man.

On the other hand, if the man is mainly or only used to the man-on-top position, starting a new position now may create additional anxiety. So if you're more comfortable with the man on top, use that position (see Figure 18-2). In this position, the man can be in control of entering and thrusting. But, as with the above position, he should thrust only minimally and then withdraw while the woman continues to stimulate his penis by hand.

Choose one of these positions and begin to practice. Remember that in both, ejaculation should occur only outside of the vagina. If you want to delay ejaculation, try the stop–start or squeeze techniques described in step 2. Also, if you feel up to it, it is a good idea to try both positions—the female as well as the male on top. This will increase the range of your experience, and it will also increase your confidence as you are able to maintain your erection.

In some ways, this can be a pretty tough step for both you and your partner. In the first place, this is your first attempt at penetration since the program started. So don't be surprised if a couple of your tries end in failures. But look how far you've come! So if you run into problems, just ease up; don't press too hard. Go back to steps 1 or 2 and continue pleasuring each other without the demand for penetration. But if you approach this step gradually and have carefully followed the preceding steps, then eventually this one will be readily accomplished. Nevertheless, build some "outs" into your contract. That is, if you feel yourself losing your erection or don't feel comfortable or aroused, withdraw and continue pleasuring each other. If you want to, do this to orgasm through manual or oral means.

As we mentioned earlier, for some men the greatest anxiety comes just at the moment of insertion. If this is true for you, and you happen to lose your erection, don't panic. You can either go back to step 4 and work your way up again, or you can ask your partner to stimulate you manually until you have an erection. Apply lots of artificial lubricant before you try penetration. You'll find insertion much easier, even without a full erection.

A second frustration is not being able to move fast enough. You'll probably want to ejaculate in your partner's vagina almost right away. And your partner will want to move toward orgasm with you inside her. We can't say that we blame either of you. But you're almost there, and it will probably be that much easier to achieve complete success if you move at this pace.

What happens if you accidentally ejaculate inside your partner? Well, nothing, really. Enjoy it. But next time you try to penetrate, stick to this program of reaching ejaculation only outside your partner's vagina at this stage.

> Charles and Ruth wrote up their contract for this step as follows: "We agree to have Charles try to penetrate Ruth. After pleasuring each other thoroughly and when we are both fully aroused, Charles will assume the man-on-top position and penetrate Ruth. If Charles feels himself coming to ejaculation, he will withdraw and ejaculate outside Ruth's vagina. After three successful penetrations, Charles will be allowed to attempt some thrusting. But again, he will ejaculate only outside of Ruth. After Charles withdraws his penis, we will continue to engage in sexual-pleasuring activities until we have both experienced orgasms. If, at any time, Charles feels uncomfortable or begins to lose his erection, he will use his distress signal and withdraw from Ruth's vagina, and we will continue our love-making without penetration."

STEP 6: INTERCOURSE: PENETRATION WITH ORGASM
If you've lasted this long, you can't fail. The last step is simply a continuation of the previous one. Engage in all of the first four steps in order and penetrate your partner in either the

330

man- or woman-above position. Either or both of you may begin thrusting, and you may continue until you ejaculate inside your partner's vagina. You *will* enjoy this experience. That's an order.

Actually, as you can see, all of these steps follow logically, one from another. Thus, this last step should be an easy and natural progression from the previous one. But you should be certain to build in all of the safeguards mentioned above. For the woman, the possible frustration of not achieving full sexual satisfaction because of your concern with not putting too much pressure on the man has to last a little longer now. But the woman should try to do everything possible to stimulate and reassure the man at this point, and she should not press for intercourse and orgasm if the man doesn't feel quite ready. It may seem a little hard on the woman at this point, maybe a little selfish. But if you've been going along with the program this far, it's almost over now.

As for the man, if you feel uncomfortable or lose your erection, just do what you did previously. Withdraw from the vagina and continue pleasuring, if you like, to orgasm outside of the vagina. Also, if your partner is not satisfied by these activities, use your pleasuring procedures to bring her to orgasm after you've ejaculated.

In addition to your partner's encouragement, we suggest using any device you like to maintain your arousal. This includes erotic literature, your own fantasies, or any of the different techniques and positions that you've found arousing in the past. Move at your own pace. With success so close at hand, there's no need to rush things.

Continue this step for the whole week, at least until you've completely regained your confidence. Of course, we hope that you and your partner will be using all the techniques of Erotic Pleasure 1 and 2 to arouse each other from now on—not just for the program.

Is this "cure" permanent? That's difficult to say. Few things in life are permanent. What we *can* say, though, is that once you are consistently achieving firm and satisfactory erections, and once both you and your partner are regularly achieving satisfying sexual relations, then that old saying comes into force: Success breeds success. The more satisfied you are with your sexual activities, the less likely you are to have problems. But if future problems do occur, you know what to do. You can start your own sex program once again, using the exercises and techniques you've already mastered.

Remember Charles and Ruth? After three months of no intercourse because Charles could not achieve an erection, they engaged in a self-help program that lasted four weeks. Four

331

weeks! They achieved a satisfactory sexual relationship almost immediately. In fact, they reported an *enhanced* sexual relationship because of all that they had learned. Eight months after they had finished the program, they were still going strong.

OVERCOMING ERECTION PROBLEMS WITHOUT A REGULAR PARTNER

As you know, most of the exercises described above involve a man and his partner's engaging in mutually satisfying sexual activities. So if you're afflicted with erection problems, but you don't have a permanent (or maybe even a temporary) partner, you're probably kind of depressed right now. But cheer up. There are several things you can do—all by yourself—to Treat Yourself.

But, let's make no bones about it. At some point in the process, you'll have to find a partner so that you can put into practice what you've learned. We'll leave that part up to you. But we assume that, if you have an erection problem, it has occurred at least once with a partner—that is, you've probably had an experience with someone else, discouraging as it may have been.

> Walter is a twenty-four-year-old man whose first sexual experience with a woman occurred when he was nineteen. Like those of many young men, Walter's first experience was with a prostitute. It was a disaster. Walter was nervous in the first place, and the surroundings were unfamiliar to him; that made him even more uncomfortable. He was able to achieve an erection with manual and oral stimulation, but when he attempted penetration, he lost his erection. The prostitute teased him about it: "What's the matter, baby—aren't you man enough?" Walter became engaged at age twenty-one and had tried to have intercourse with his fiancée, but he had tried so hard to obtain an erection that he couldn't manage it. With each succeeding attempt, Walter became increasingly anxious, to the point where he dreaded even the thought of making love. Worse yet, what Walter's fiancée thought was "sexual incompatibility" led her to break off the engagement.

Start with a Review

Even if you're working on a problem on your own, you will still be going through many of the basics described in Part 3 of this book. Read those chapters so that you'll be able to move right through the exercises. In particular, you'll be using contracts (that's right, contracts with yourself), relaxation exercises, and a self-stimulation program such as the one described in Chapter 13. In particular, read the part of this chapter on overcoming erection problems *with* a partner. All of these things apply to you too.

STEP 1: RELAXATION TRAINING

Train yourself in the deep-muscle-relaxation exercises in Chapter 11. Practice these until you've got them down pat. Spend as many days as you need with these exercises. We suggest practicing fifteen or twenty minutes, twice a day. You can even use these exercises to relax you before going to bed.

Try this variation. Evaluate yourself on the anxiety scale in Chapter 11, especially when you fantasize about sexual intercourse. After you've mastered the deep-muscle-relaxation exercises, try the same fantasy again and see whether the anxiety is continuing at the same level when you are deeply relaxed. Try this exercise—relaxing yourself and then imagining yourself engaging in intercourse—once or twice a day for two weeks. Keep evaluating yourself on your anxiety scale. If your anxiety begins to drop, you can even start imagining yourself in high-anxiety–producing situations, such as losing your erection just before you attempt intercourse. Do this only when you are deeply relaxed. Keep track of your anxiety, and if it continues to go down on the scale, continue doing this exercise until your anxiety reaches a level that is satisfactory to you.

STEP 2: THE SELF-STIMULATION PROGRAM
WITHOUT ORGASM

Review the material in Chapter 13 on the use of fantasies and self-stimulation. The goal here is to turn yourself on. You want to be able to relax, to enjoy in your own body, to think about erotic fantasies, and then, gradually, to help yourself attain an erection. For this step, though, don't go too far. Learn to get turned on and give yourself an erection, but try not to ejaculate. Use the stop–start or the squeeze techniques from Chapter 17 in order to prevent the ejaculation.

Practice this step until you can maintain an erection for at least five minutes during three sessions in a row.

Walter developed a contract with himself in which he committed himself to engaging in a program of self-stimulation to enhance his sensuality and arousal and to ensure that, in fact, he could actually sustain an erection. The contract was built around several stages of self-stimulation that were similar to the steps one might engage in with a partner. As a reward, Walter promised that he would go see a new display of computers as soon as he finished the first three days of the program.

Walter's first step was to involve himself in any activity that had previously been stimulating to him. Walter chose seeing an adult movie and then fantasizing about it. When he came home, he engaged in a self-stimulation massage, using the fantasies about the women in the movies. At first, he would lie in bed, gently stroking his body; then he stimulated himself, using a light lubricant. But, as he specified in his contract, Walter would not allow himself to ejaculate; he used the squeeze approach to stop impending ejaculation.

STEP 3: SELF-STIMULATION WHILE LOSING AND REGAINING ERECTIONS

This step is really a variation of step 2. The goal here is to bring yourself to an erection, to stop stimulating yourself, to think about something nonsexual, and to lose your erection (use the squeeze technique if you have to). Then, when your erection is gone, start the self-stimulation again in order to achieve an erection. The goal here is to illustrate to yourself that you *can* lose and then regain an erection—in fact, that you can do this several times in a thirty-minute session.

When you are stimulating yourself, use erotic fantasies or any reading material that you find erotic. Then, the switch to nonerotic fantasies and back again will be all that much more dramatic. If you have any problem regaining your erection, make sure that all of the conditions are suitable to relaxing, soothing sexual activity. Check to see that your fantasies or reading material are indeed erotic for you. If none of this works, take a break or try again the next day.

With this exercise, you should be able to lose and regain your erection three to five times per session for three sessions.

STEP 4: SELF-STIMULATION TO ORGASM

Follow through with the same self-stimulation program you used in step 3. This time, allow yourself to reach orgasm. Use a lubricant to add greater stimulation. Repeat this step at least once over the next three or four sessions.

Walter would explore his body in front of the mirror, watching himself as he touched his "sensitive" spots. He now began to stimulate himself to orgasm. As Walter recalled, "By the end of the first week of the program, I was so turned on that achieving an erection was simple. Allowing myself to ejaculate after that was easy and a real treat." Walter practiced self-stimulation to orgasm for some two weeks, gradually extending the period of time during which he could maintain the erection. At this point, he would use any fantasies to enhance his arousal that he wanted, including the fantasy of a sexual encounter with a particularly attractive young woman in the building in which he worked. In addition, during the last week, Walter was particularly careful to imagine that he was actually engaging in intercourse with a firm erection as he stimulated himself to orgasm.

STEP 5: SELF-STIMULATION WITH PARTNER FANTASY

Before you actually try intercourse with a partner, we suggest that you go through the process in your imagination first. If you have a particular person in mind, use self-stimulation while you fantasize the entire sexual experience, from the first touch, to undressing, to seeing each other nude, to stroking each other, to stimulating each other's genitals, and through penetration to orgasm. Try to bring yourself to orgasm using self-stimulation at the point when you reach orgasm in your fantasy with your partner.

If you have any trouble getting an erection at first, you might want to begin by using the erotic fantasies or the reading material that you had been using previously. Once you have an erection, you can switch the fantasy to one that involves your partner. Gradually, you should try to decrease the period of time that you need to fantasize using the erotic literature, until you can use the fantasy of your partner from beginning to end.

We suggest that you stay with this step unless you can go through the whole process using fantasies of your partner at least two or three times.

STEP 6: ADD A PARTNER IN REAL LIFE

The last step, of course, is to be able to have successful intercourse with your partner. But we don't suggest that you jump into this, either. In fact, the best idea here would be to go through all of the steps we suggested in the first part of this chapter when we described a program for men who have partners willing to participate. This undoubtedly means that you will have to communicate with your partner about what it is that you're trying to accomplish. We believe that discretion is the better part of valor. It's a lot better to suffer a little embarrassment by discussing the problem with your partner in advance than to chance a lot more embarrassment later because you moved too fast and weren't quite ready. Given the fact that you've already been through the self-stimulation steps, it's likely that this part of the program will proceed much more quickly than it would have if you were just starting anew with your partner.

The next stage of Walter's program, once he was confident that he would be able to obtain and hold an erection, was to find a partner to complete the process. As luck would have it, he began to date the young woman at work. Walter knew that he would have to approach things gradually. On the third date, they ended up in his date's apartment, where Walter, with great difficulty at first, described the Treat Yourself program he had been working on. Her positive response was extremely encouraging. He and his date engaged in some heavy necking, and Walter used with her many of the Erotic Pleasure exercises that he had developed in his own self-help program. Both the date and Walter were highly aroused. On their next date, they repeated this step and they also manually stimulated each other to orgasm. Walter had no trouble maintaining his erection. On the next two dates, since Walter had promised himself and his partner had agreed not to attempt intercourse for at least four of these sexual encounters, Walter and his partner continued to stimulate each other manually and orally with erotic massage to orgasm. The date seemed not to mind at all. As a matter of fact, she told Walter that all of the erotic play had left her more turned on than she had ever been before.

The last stage of the program came easily for Walter and his new partner. On their next date, they just naturally went from pleasuring each other to intercourse. It was an erotic and rewarding experience for both of them, because each was at a peak of arousal just prior to penetration.

When last heard from, Walter was engaged to this young woman and enjoying a "fantastic love life" with no recurrence whatsoever of his erection problem.

If you have had a problem with erections, and if you have followed either of the above programs—with or without a regular partner—you're probably functioning sexually the way you want to by now. But don't forget what you learned. All of these techniques of love-making can be used over and over again, and you can develop your own variations of them in order to permanently enhance the joys of your sex life.

Nineteen
When Sex Is Distasteful

Ron was very upset. His wife wanted more sex than he did. Frankly, he just didn't like it as much as she did.

Claudia really hoped that her boyfriend would stimulate her clitoris with his tongue. He thought that that was the most awful thing he could imagine.

Bill and Linda fought like cats and dogs about whether they should leave the lights on or off when they made love. She was turned on by the sights of their nude bodies. He claimed that he was shy and preferred to make love in the dark.

Larry wanted to try anal intercourse. Kathy couldn't help thinking that he must be sick to want to try something like that. "Next thing I know," she shouted at him once, "you'll be wanting to stick it in my ear!"

"He wants me to wear a garter belt and stockings when we make love," Annette said. "I must really turn him off if he needs that in order to turn on."

There is so much about sex that can produce pleasure and joy. There is so much that is "right" about sex—that can lead to positive enjoyable experiences for all of us. There is so much about sex that can help us to keep our intimate relationships and make them even stronger. Yes, there is so much that is

337

good about sex that it really is a shame that many of us don't feel free enough to enjoy it more.

We've talked about this several times before, particularly in Part 1. In any number of ways, our society puts limits on the kinds of sex that we are "supposed to" have. There are even laws in some states that make certain sexual practices illegal, even when they occur between two loving adults in the privacy of their own homes. Many public and religious leaders often try to get rid of any sexual activity that they personally don't approve of or are personally uncomfortable with. It is no wonder, then, that with all of this political, religious, and social pressure, some of us feel uncomfortable about expressing ourselves sexually.

Feelings of guilt about very common sexual practices are not unusual in our society. Parents, affected by what they've learned from religious and political leaders, pass on this doubtful "wisdom" to their children: We are very often told that "sex is dirty." Certainly, this is evident from the way we speak in hushed terms—or not at all—about sex, and how we call words describing sexual activity some of our "filthiest" swear words. It's evident also from what we read frequently in the newspapers about one particular group's being harassed or arrested because of their sexual activities. How many of us, as children, were told to stop or had our hands slapped if we were found stimulating ourselves or even just touching our genitals? ("Good boys and girls don't do that.")

Yes, it really seems that our society often robs us of some of the most rewarding, pleasant, and satisfying experiences known to human beings, all because of some outmoded ideas about what is right and what is good. It's always useful to ask, "Right for whom? Good for what?"

Given all this pressure, who really suffers the most? We believe that it is you—and we—because what finally happens with all these negative messages is that we develop a set of inhibitions, a set of ideas and feelings that certain types of sexual expression are bad, perhaps even evil. And there we are with these sexual inhibitions—blocks that keep us from enjoying our sexuality in ways that we might otherwise find very fulfilling.

We most often see these inhibitions in the sexual activities that we find distasteful. We are usually not even aware of how we decided that one or another specific sexual activity is distasteful; we just know that we don't like it. In fact, that sexual activity may have become so distasteful to us that we find it disgusting or repulsive. It is so offensive that we think of people who engage in it or who want to engage in it as sick or as "perverts."

338

Now, we are not talking about activities in which someone gets hurt, either physically or emotionally. Nor are we talking about sexual activities in which one person is forced by another to do something that he or she doesn't really want to do. And we certainly aren't suggesting that everyone should try or even like everything. We're all different and have a right to like or not like whatever we want to.

We are talking, instead, about the broad range of sexual activities that consenting adults participate in without any physical or emotional harm whatsoever. We are talking about sexual activities that both partners can enjoy.

Now, as we said before, when we regard a particular sexual activity as distasteful and as something to avoid, we may not even realize why we feel that way. We may have heard something long ago from a parent or in church. We can't recall specifically what it was, but it has nevertheless left its mark. We may have some vague moral objections, or we may even simply suffer from a lack of experience with or knowledge about that sexual activity. And you know that new things are often scary.

But, for whatever reason, we are left with the feeling, in varying degrees of intensity, that the activity is distasteful—that we don't want to engage in it. The types of sexual activities that *someone* considers distasteful are many. We'll mention only a few; you probably know of many more that you or someone else considers distasteful and to be avoided. For example, think of these for starters:

- Any position for intercourse other than that with the male on top.
- Self-stimulation.
- Anal intercourse.
- Oral sex.
- Sex too often.
- Touching your partner's genitals with your hand.
- Making love with the lights on.
- Making love with the lights off.
- Making love anywhere but in bed.
- Making love in or out of the covers.
- Making love with most of your clothes on.
- Making love in the nude.
- Making love.

This list could go on and on.

If you want to, make your own list of the sexual activities that you find distasteful. Put a check mark in front of the ac-

339

tivities that you think or know your partner might want you to try. Now, put a little circle in front of the activities that *you'd* like to try but feel too uncomfortable to try. Have your partner go through the same procedure. Use the questionnaires in Chapter 8 to guide you in this.

THIS PROGRAM IS FOR YOU, IF . . .

How do you decide if a program to help you try something that you find distasteful is really for you? Put another way, just because something is distasteful, does that mean that you "should" force yourself to go through a Treat Yourself program to get yourself to like it or to find it less distasteful, even if you don't want to?

We have pretty strong feelings about this. Quite simply, we don't believe that anybody should be forced into doing anything sexually that he or she doesn't want to do. This means that if you're going to do a Treat Yourself program to try to make some sexual activities less distasteful because you *have* to do it—somebody is pressuring you—or because you think you "should"—that it's the "right" way to be—then maybe this part of the program is not for you. Ideally, the person working on a program to decrease discomfort or distaste with some sexual activity is the person who really wants to try a particular activity but is somehow a little too uncomfortable to do so.

We said that that would be the *ideal* situation. Unfortunately, things don't often work out in ideal ways in real life. Just as one example, we realize that when your partner gets turned on by some activity and you don't, and he or she wants you to, the situation often doesn't end with a simple "no," and that's it. Any number of things could happen. The whole thing may never even get openly discussed. You know what he or she wants and your partner knows that you know, but you never talk about it. Little tensions and maybe even arguments develop. Or, you may talk about it, but one of you gets so upset at the other that he or she is accused of not loving, or being loved by, the other. Other activities can be affected. The whole problem can escalate from a difference in preferences over a specific sexual activity to a major crisis in your relationship.

So we realize that there may be a number of pressures on you to try to change, and that some of these pressures may even be so subtle that you haven't yet recognized them clearly. But you somehow sense that they are there.

340

Unfortunately, we have no real solution for this problem. Again, we believe that no one should be forced, tricked, or cajoled into sexual activities that he or she doesn't want to participate in. But obviously, that doesn't solve your problem. Beyond our concern that at least you should try to discuss this with your partner in a soothing, relaxing atmosphere without calling each other names or thinking all sorts of horrible things about each other, the final decision is up to you. It's your choice.

But let's try to present the problem in a slightly different light.

We believe that sex is one of the great pleasures of life. We also believe that most inhibitions about or prohibitions against specific types of sexual activity are undesirable. This is because they deprive you of a form of sexual expression that you might find extremely satisfying or, at least, acceptable and extremely satisfying to your partner. In other words, there are a lot of truly enjoyable and exciting sexual activities available that you might be labeling as distasteful or "wrong," but that could prove to greatly enhance your sex life and to be very fulfilling.

But obviously, in many parts of our lives, we consider certain things to be distasteful, impossible, or somehow undesirable. And with many of those things, we actually decide to keep them that way. That is the key. We really want you to be able to make as free and clear a choice as possible.

We are always making choices and decisions about our lives, whether this means small decisions about what to have for dinner or major decisions about our careers or our families. Whether or not you will engage in a particular sexual activity is simply one more of the decisions you can make if you want.

Now, precisely because there are so many sexual activities and variations, it is unlikely that you will be able, or want, to try them all. But if there are one or two activities that you're curious about or that your partner and you may want to try, then you have the option here of making that decision to try them. After all, the absolutely worst thing that could happen is that you try it, experience it, don't like it, and decide not to continue doing it.

We believe that any sexual activity is okay if both people consent to it and if neither is hurt by it or prevented from fulfilling his or her needs. The most "normal" thing about sex is that so many people do so many things. Variations and differences in sexual activity are what's normal. (By the way, this doesn't mean that if you prefer one and only one type of sexual activity or position, that you're not normal; that's okay too.)

So there you have it. The decision is up to you as to

whether you explore something new and different or whether you don't. Again, we wouldn't want to urge you into doing something that you don't want to do. Your guilt or the tension you feel about doing it may be worse than the pressure you're getting for not doing it.

But if you or your partner would like to try a new sexual experience, and you're just not sure how to go about it, read on. We'll move you slowly, carefully, and, we hope, sensitively toward that experience. After all, giving it a try for a while will probably give you the best information of all—your own experience—about whether you want to continue doing it.

THE GENERAL APPROACH
TO DISTASTEFUL SEX

If you've read everything in this book up to this chapter, then you probably have the idea about how to go about working on a sex problem. You work gradually and slowly but surely toward overcoming your fears or inhibitions and toward increasing your comfort with the sexual activity. You also work toward making that activity more desirable, more of a turn-on. You move toward your desired goal in small steps so that you don't jump into anything that produces too much anxiety. And the reasons you do all this are clear: You do it this way because *it works*. Thousands of people have been helped in often dramatic ways by programs such as those described in this book.

The approach to decreasing the distastefulness of certain sexual activities is very similar to the step-by-step exercises described in this book for other sexual problems. All that really changes is the nature of the problem or the specific sexual activity.

For starters, be sure to read the rest of the book, especially Parts 2 and 3. We'll be using exercises from these parts, and it's a good idea to be ready for these in advance. In fact, we urge that you and your partner read these together. Not only will it help you to be prepared, but it may help both of you see that sex problems are no one's "fault"—certainly not yours or your partner's. They do happen, though, no matter what the reason is. Knowing the reason or, for that matter, blaming yourself or your partner won't change that. But by using the types of programs we have described in this book, you can change your behavior.

The following are some of the basic ingredients of a program for helping you to decrease the distastefulness of a particular sexual activity.

Use Contracts

Review Chapter 10 (the part on contracts). By now you are probably aware that contracts are important in our Treat Yourself programs. They ensure that you both know where you are going and how you will get there. They are particularly important when working with distasteful sex, because this can be such a touchy area between you and your partner.

Take particular care to make use of rewards. Don't forget that one of you is working toward something that he or she may not like at all. You will deserve the rewards. The rewards will make it easier to keep up your motivation to try.

Also, be sure to be clear about what your distress signal is and how it will be used. Since there may be several times during this program when you or your partner experiences some discomfort, the distress signal may be used more here than in most of the Treat Yourself programs. Now, the distress signal doesn't mean that one of you is chicken or the other one a jerk. All it means is that one of you is a little uncomfortable with what you're doing, and that it's better to go back to an earlier step, practice that until you're comfortable, perhaps add a relaxation exercise, and then move ahead.

Relax

The relaxation exercises presented in Chapter 11 are particularly important here. As you probably know, just thinking of the sexual activity that you find distasteful can produce anxiety, let alone actually trying it. Increasing your comfort with that activity calls for a direct attack on those anxieties.

Here's how to use relaxation exercises for any Treat Yourself program in order to overcome your discomfort with some sexual activity. First, think about the sexual activity in as much detail as you can. Evaluate the level of your anxiety on the anxiety scale in Chapter 11. Then, while not imagining that particular sexual activity, begin the exercises from Chapter 11; first learn deep abdominal breathing and then deep muscle relaxation. Spend as much time as you need to until you can relax yourself all over within a couple of minutes.

You can use these muscle-relaxation exercises at several points in the program. You can use them when you think about

343

the sexual activity that you're uncomfortable with in order to overcome the anxiety. You can use them to prepare yourself when you are starting each step in the Treat Yourself program. And you can use them during the program if you feel some anxiety coming on. Just use your distress signal, take a break, and use the deep-abdominal-breathing and -muscle relaxation exercises to make yourself more comfortable.

Communication and Negotiation

This is another aspect of the program that takes on special importance when one partner clearly feels uncomfortable about a sexual activity that the other partner wants to try. Read Chapter 9 (on communication) and Chapter 10 (on negotiating to set up a contract). You're going to have to do a lot of talking—without hostility—about what it is that you'd like to try and about how you're going to go about it without putting on pressure. A little later, we'll give you an example of a negotiation program involving increasing the frequency of sexual activity.

Gradual Slow Steps

With all of the Treat Yourself programs, moving from step to step is important. When trying to decrease your inhibitions, it's crucial. What you want to do is move from small step to small step, with each step leading to the next one. You definitely don't want to move too quickly, because that could lead to too much pressure. You start with something easy and nonthreatening, move patiently and gradually toward intermediate steps, and eventually engage in the sexual activity that was distasteful, but you will only be doing it once your discomfort has decreased. Don't move too far too fast.

NEGOTIATING TO CHANGE
THE FREQUENCY
OF SEXUAL ACTIVITY

As we suggested earlier, there are any number of activities that could benefit from negotiations between you and your partner. Since the negotiation process involves the same general principles no matter what the activity, we'll just illustrate one

344

common problem and how you might be able to negotiate some changes in it. Use these same negotiation principles no matter what the activity is that you're working on.

One of the commonest problems that many couples face is that one wants to have sex more than the other (or, of course, vice versa—that one wants it less). The couple may love each other a great deal, but the fact that there's a difference in what each wants can produce a lot of tension. For example, they'll study the statistics on what the so-called "average" couple does and then bombard the partner if the figures agree with their point of view. ("See, the 'average' couple does it 2.3 times a week, and we only do it 2.1 times. Why don't you love me?") Let's face it, though—averages mean nothing for individuals. They may provide information to researchers about large groups of people, but they are of little help to us individually.

At any rate, considerable strain and tension can develop over this problem. So don't wait; negotiate.

Step 1

Be clear about what you want. If you want to increase or decrease the frequency of your sexual activity, try to be clear about how often you think would be about right for you. You might even jot down on a piece of paper how often you think would be right for you. Ask your partner to do the same. Don't show each other the figures yet.

By the way, in thinking about what the problem is, be sure that you don't mistake one problem for another. A common mistake in differences about frequency of sex is that the real problem is that sex is too boring, not that one partner wants it less. If this is the case with you, maybe you should be trying the Treat Yourself program in Chapter 20 on what to do when sex is boring rather than trying to negotiate changes in frequency.

Step 2

Think about how your partner might feel. There are any number of ways you can do this. You might just put yourself in his or her position and try to imagine what it would feel like to want sex either more or less (the opposite of what you want). Try to imagine the frustrations involved in the other person's position. Later, you can ask your partner to put himself or herself in your shoes and to think about what it feels like to want what you want. At this point, though, don't discuss this out loud. You'll do that later. Right now, you're only getting ready for negotiations by figuring out how your partner might feel.

Step 3

Be prepared to compromise. Be ready to give a little. If frequency is the issue, you might think about a figure between what you and your partner want. For example, if she wants sex about five times a week and you want it about once a week, three times a week might be a figure to shoot for. Or, you might want to compromise on types of sex. You might offer to engage in some particular sex activity that your partner really enjoys, and in return, your partner can offer not to demand that you engage in sex so frequently.

Step 4

Set the stage. When you're getting ready to negotiate, don't do it at the wrong time, just before falling asleep in bed, when your partner is grumpy, and so on. Make sure that you both are relaxed and comfortable.

Step 5

Let your partner know exactly what you want. Be as specific as you can. Also, ask your partner to be clear and specific as well.

Step 6

Find out how your partner feels. Of course, be clear about how you feel—the frustrations or desires you feel. Then, both of you exchange roles and try to put yourselves in each other's shoes. (This is where you talk about what you were thinking in Step 2.) You might be surprised and learn a lot about yourself and your partner this way.

Step 7

Don't blame each other. Try not to get into accusations and counter-accusations. That will not help.

Step 8

Give to get. This is a particularly important step when negotiating problems. Please don't expect your partner to merely give in completely to your point of view without any compromise solutions. And we hope that your partner won't expect that from you.

There are several ways that you and your partner can give to get. We've already suggested a couple above—for example, in negotiating frequency of sex, use a figure in between what you and your partner want, or exchange one type of sexual activity for a change in frequency. In addition, what you might do is compromise on the types of sexual activity. We've tried to illustrate throughout this book that sex doesn't always have to involve intercourse. There are fantastic experiences and great sensations you can experience without it. As part of the compromise, instead of intercourse on a particular night, you might simply try the Erotic Pleasure 1 exercises described in Chapter 14. Lie together, stroke each other's bodies, give back massages and so on. Thus, part of the compromise might be, on one night, to substitute this type of sensuality for intercourse.

Step 9

Formalize your agreement. When you and your partner decide, be clear about what the decision is. You might want to write it down on a piece of paper. Also, you might want to leave room for renegotiation. Try out your new arrangement for a month or so. Then, agree with each other that you will evaluate how well things are going at that point and possibly renegotiate a new or different agreement.

Step 10

Leave room for flexibility. If you both agree to have sex twice a week, give yourself the options of increasing or decreasing that in any given week if you both feel like it. Imagine how ridiculous it would be if, after having sex two times in one week, and you both felt like it one more time, one partner said, "Sorry, we agreed to twice a week and we have to stick with it. We have two more days to wait until the week is up. Then we can start over again." The point here, though, is that you both should want it and agree to it.

As we said above, almost everybody thinks of some sexual activity, or activities, as distasteful. We can't provide a program to deal with each. (When the problem is that all sexual activity is distasteful, we suggest following the program in Chapter 15 that deals with arousal and orgasm. Although the program there is specifically for women, men can use it also just by making minor changes in a few of the steps and by reviewing the section in Chapter 17 on ejaculatory overcontrol.) But, as we did with the negotiation example, we can choose one sexual activity—oral sex—and use it as an example of a program to help you to overcome your distaste about a particular sexual activity. We'll include all of the steps you would use, no matter what problems you're working on. In large part, only the problem changes.

Actually, for one reason or another, oral sex is found to be distasteful by many people (although others find it to be a very stimulating and most desirable sexual activity). At any rate, oral sex—mouth-to-genital contact—can be a very pleasant activity. If you or your partner would like to try oral sex and the other person is uncomfortable about it but willing to try this program, then go ahead and give the program a try.

Step 1

Read through all the steps with your partner. Then go back, start over, and practice them, one at a time, for thirty to forty-five minutes each—or longer, if you both agree.

Step 2

Go through all the preliminary steps that we described earlier in this chapter. Negotiate your mutual goals. Communicate about what you each want. Establish a contract. Learn the relaxation exercises and practice them before you begin any of the later steps of this program. Set the scene—select a quiet time and place when you are both relaxed and have little chance of being interrupted.

By the way, one of the less obvious reasons that we recommend that you and your partner be relaxed and communicate more extensively is that research shows that the longer people know each other (and are more comfortable with each other), the more willing they are to try different variations in sexual activity—oral sex included. So, even if you don't try this program now, there's a possibility that, over the years, you and your partner might both feel more comfortable with each other and eventually try this or other forms of sexual activity that might seem distasteful now.

Step 3

Use good personal hygiene. Although this is always important, pay particular attention to cleanliness here. Make sure that both of you wash and rinse your genital areas.

Step 4: Erotic Pleasure 1

Use the Erotic Pleasure 1 exercise described in Chapter 14. This should be a relaxing and enjoyable experience. Don't push ahead any further with this until you are both really enjoying the sensuousness of this step. Once you are comfortable with Erotic Pleasure 1, add the following variations:

1. Select some part of your partner's body—other than the genitals—and kiss it. Begin to let the tip of your tongue run along the skin. When you're comfortable with that, lick the skin in that place only. If you selected a spot that you can gently suck, such as a finger, go ahead and suck lightly on it. If you care to, nibble very gently on that part of your partner's body with your teeth. Be careful not to use too much pressure.

2. Do this kissing, licking, and sucking exercise with other parts of your partner's body, but not yet with the genitals. Your partner should also do this to you if you so desire. At some point, do this with at least one finger.

3. Go through the Erotic Pleasure 1 steps using your mouth and tongue. Find the sensitive but nongenital parts of your partner's body and gently lick them. In particular, you might want to kiss and tickle the inner parts of the thighs. This will gradually bring you closer to the genital area and will get you used to using your mouth there without actually having to attempt mouth–genital contact.

4. Continue this exercise for as many sessions as you need to in order to feel completely comfortable.

Step 5: Erotic Pleasure 2

Just as you did with Erotic Pleasure 1, go through the Erotic Pleasure 2 exercises, as described in Chapter 14. Spend most of your time in nongenital contact, moving gradually and playfully toward genital contact. Go from light and gentle stimulation of the breasts and move gradually to stimulating the genitals with your hand.

1. Once you've explored your partner's body thoroughly with your hands, begin to use your mouth. Follow through with oral contacts to the nongenital parts of the body just as you did with Erotic Pleasure 1.

2. Move your mouth slowly along your partner's body from the navel area up to your partner's chest and breasts. Gently lick each breast. Suck very lightly on one nipple, then on the other. Watch how the nipples stand erect.

3. Be very sensitive to your partner's distress signal. If one partner uses the distress signal, use relaxation exercises and go back to the previous step until you are both comfortable.

4. Ask for and give feedback to each other. Find out how your partner is feeling about each step.

5. Proceed with your eyes open or closed, as you see fit.

6. Use your hands to gently explore your partner's genital area. Be in a comfortable position, perhaps sitting to the side of your partner and, if you prefer, moving later to sit between his or her legs. Then slowly move your mouth down from the chest or breasts along the abdominal area and across the navel. You might want to use the tip of your tongue to outline the genital area.

7. For your first oral–genital contact, simply brush your lips along, or kiss, the genital area. On men, kiss or lightly touch his penis with your lips. Do this on any part of the penis. For women, the man can lightly kiss or brush his mouth over the whole genital area, perhaps kissing the mons pubis or outer lips first.

8. For some people, the easiest way to approach this step is to shower or bathe together as in Figure 19-1, washing off each other's genitals. Then, assured that they are clean, you can simply move to stroking and kissing each other's genitals, either in the tub or when you're drying off.

9. You might want to end this step by finishing the session at that point, perhaps showering again, having a drink or a cup of coffee together, and discussing how the program is going so far.

Figure 19-1.

Step 6

Now you can increase the intensity and the length of time you spend in mouth–genital contact. Start by exploring your partner's body the way you did before. Don't just jump to mouth–genital contact. Get used to each other and to the closeness you are experiencing. Share your feelings with each other as you proceed. It's up to you to teach each other about each other, including what you like and find stimulating and what you don't like.

When you are ready to once again begin stimulating your partner's genitals with your mouth, proceed as you did before. First, lightly kiss the genital area. Brush up and down with your lips. Explore as much of the genitals with your lips as you can.

1. Explore with the tip of your tongue. Move slowly; get used to the idea. (If you're having a rough time, you might want to keep your eyes closed and imagine that you're exploring a lollipop or an orange with your mouth.) If *your partner is a man*, simply run the tip of your tongue along his penis from its base to the tip. You might also want to do this with his scrotum. If *your partner is a woman*, move the tip of your tongue around

351

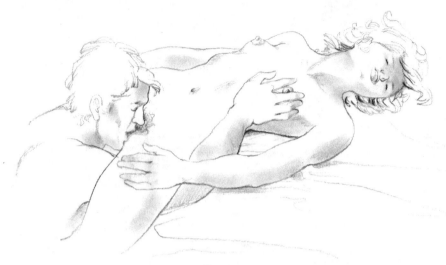

Figure 19-2.

her outer lips. Then, parting them with your fingers, let your tongue explore the inner inner lips (see Figure 19-2). Move up to kiss the vaginal entrance and then the clitoris. Be very gentle. Explore the clitoris with the tip of your tongue. Carefully, run your tongue around the clitoris. If your partner uses her distress signal because the clitoris is too sensitive, move back down to the vaginal entrance and inner lips and gently lick those with your tongue.

2. Be sure that you do not do any pelvic thrusting while your partner is exploring your genitals with his or her mouth. This could really disturb your partner; he or she may fear that you are about to have an orgasm when he or she is unprepared or that it will be hard to breathe.

3. While you are stimulating your partner's genitals with your mouth, you may want to stroke the inner thighs lightly with your hands.

4. Move from oral stimulation of the genitals to oral stimulation of the surrounding areas, such as the inner thighs or the abdomen.

5. When you are both fairly comfortable with this step, you can finish the session. You can relax now and talk about how it is going for each of you, both when you are giving and receiving pleasure. Repeat this step one or two more times.

Step 7

Believe it or not, you've actually moved past the crucial part of this program. If you've gotten this far, you've already given and experienced (if you're changing roles with your partner) oral sex. We hope that you are increasingly comfortable with this activity and maybe even enjoying it. The rest is all gravy.

When you begin this step, again move through the above steps until you are stimulating your partner's genitals with your mouth. Now you can increase the variety and intensity of what you do.

1. When men are being pleasured: You might lick the entire penis as though it were an ice cream cone. Lick his scrotum. Take the tip of his penis into your mouth as in Figure 19-3. Use your tongue to give stimulation. If you want to, you can move more of his penis into your mouth so that the tip is farther in. You should keep control here; if it goes too far down, then simply remove it. You can keep your hands on his penis and gently stroke it at the same time. Move your head and mouth up and down the penis, stimulating it with your tongue at the same time. In particular, use your tongue to lick and rub the underside of the head of the penis. Breathe through your nose so that you won't have to stop.

Discuss in advance with your partner whether he wants to come this way, and especially whether you want him to. If he wants to and you do not want him to, you can always bring him to the point of ejaculation that way and then, at his signal that ejaculation is coming, remove your mouth and help him with your hand. If you don't want him to come in your mouth, we

Figure 19-3.

hope that he recognizes that you are not rejecting him as a man or a lover, and that you'll both talk it over.

If you do want to have him ejaculate in your mouth, let him guide you as to the pressure and rhythm he prefers. When he ejaculates, you can either swallow it (the ejaculate is harmless; in fact, it's largely protein), let it run out of your mouth while he's ejaculating, or just spit it out. You might want to dilute the taste of his ejaculate by accumulating saliva in your mouth or by taking and holding water or some other liquid in your mouth just before he ejaculates.

Two additional points: If you read Chapter 13, you'll remember that sometimes, well before ejaculation, a little liquid appears at the tip of the male's penis. This is not ejaculate but is a sign of arousal, and it can be wiped or licked off. (By the way, don't worry about the possibility of your partner's urinating when his penis is erect in your mouth. Men's systems don't work that way. Men have valves that shut off the possibility of a urine flow when their penises are erect.)

The second point to be aware of is that you might want to help your partner have an orgasm *before* you try oral stimulation. After he's washed off, you can proceed with oral–genital stimulation with less chance of an immediate ejaculation.

2. When women are being pleasured: Once you have begun the process of stimulating her genital area with your tongue, you can intensify your attention to the parts of her genitals that she finds most stimulating. Let her be the guide; she can lead you with words or move your head with her hands.

Try licking the area around and within the vaginal entrance. Penetrate the vaginal entrance with your tongue and lick the walls. Then, move up to the clitoris. Make a circle around the clitoris with your tongue. Then, rub your tongue up and down it. Remember that it is very sensitive, so take your guidance from your partner.

Discuss in advance whether she would like to have an orgasm with you stimulating her with your tongue. If so, gently lead up to it. Use just the tip of your tongue; then use the flat part of your tongue. Let her guide you with her hands. Gently move the clitoris with your lips. Lick the entire clitoral area with the flat part of your tongue. Use increasing pressure (as long as she is enjoying it). Find the rhythm that is most pleasurable and arousing for her. Maintain that rhythm for as long as you can, until she reaches orgasm or until you want to stop. If you tire, continue with other forms of stimulation until you can return to oral stimulation. We suggest that you not hold your breath while doing this form of stimulation because you will have to

keep coming up for air, thereby breaking the rhythm and pos-
sibily decreasing the level of stimulation for your partner.

3. When you're finished, give yourselves a reward, as we
discussed in the first part of this chapter. Talk over the
experience—what you enjoyed about it, the discomforts and
anxieties it may have caused, and what each of you can do in
order to ensure that both of you are receiving as much pleasure as possible from it.

Step 8

Experiment with different types of stimulation techniques. You
might try putting the penis farther into your mouth, or you
might try to extend your tongue farther into her vaginal entrance. Or, try alternating oral stimulation of each other: First
one gives, and then the other gives.

Experiment also with different pressures and rhythms. For
example, you might try movement solely guided by your partner (him or her thrusting) and compare that with movement
solely guided by you (movement of your head and tongue).

Step 9

If you want to proceed one step further, it would probably be
to oral–genital stimulation of both of you at the same time.
This is popularly called "69."

A good position for this is with each of you lying on your
sides, facing opposite ends. This gives both of you equal control. You can each use your partner's under thighs as a pillow
for your head. If the male wants to open his partner up further,
he can just put his arm in the underside of her knee. One
person on top of the other is okay, too, as in Figure 19-4, but
one of you might get a stiff neck.

You can try this mutual oral–genital stimulation, if both of
you are willing, and vary the kinds of stimulation you provide
each other. For example, both of you can provide intense
stimulation at the same time, or just one and then the other
partner can provide intense stimulation.

Any way you approach this, go at it in the same way you
would with any other exercise—slowly, gradually, moving
through the steps we described above, providing feedback to
each other, and proceeding only with the consent of both of
you.

355

Figure 19-4.

This program for becoming comfortable with oral–genital stimulation was presented as an example of overcoming some aspect of sex that is distasteful to one or both of you. You can use these principles for other sexual activities as well. Just remember these suggestions: Move from step to step in a way that will maximize the amount of comfort your partner feels, and try not to move too quickly, because that could ruin the entire program by increasing rather than decreasing the anxiety or discomfort that your partner feels.

Although we've presented this program for your use, we hope that you won't feel pressured to use it. We still believe that a program such as this should be used only when neither partner is forced into it. We want joy in sex to increase for both of you. We don't want to increase one person's joy at the expense of the other's. After all, there are lots of sexual activities that you can enjoy, and you don't have to use them all in order to feel satisfied and fulfilled.

Twenty

When Sex
Leaves You Cold:
Overcoming Boredom

Sex is supposed to be exciting. It's supposed to be something that everybody looks forward to and enjoys whenever it occurs. That's what sex is *supposed* to be, but for many people, much of the time, it isn't. People often experience sex as rather dull, routine, and uninspiring. They have sex because they consider it their duty and because their partners expect it. Many people avoid it whenever they can.

One of the most common problems associated with sex is the lack of interest in it. Yet it is one of the least discussed sexual problems. It is often a very well hidden problem. People who experience lack of interest in their sexual relationships often feel too embarrassed to discuss it with their partners. They feel that they should enjoy sex, and if they don't, they feel that it reflects badly either on them, on their partners, and, perhaps, on both. Many people who lack interest in sex believe, often rightly, that it is too devastating to tell a partner, "Now don't get me wrong; I like you and all that, but you just don't turn me on, I really don't have sexual desire for you, and I don't get much out of our sex life. I'd really prefer just watching TV." That's difficult to say and even more painful to hear.

So, the problem often goes undiscussed, and the partners

have sex as a kind of ritual, with one or both getting little out of it. Or perhaps they think up excuses whenever they can in order to avoid sex: "I've got a headache," "I'm too tired," or "I guess I've got too much on my mind"—when the real reason is "I don't enjoy sex with you."

Of course, most people, even in "ideal" sexual relationships, don't *always* want to have sex. There are times when they *are* tired, or distracted, or, for some reason, just don't *feel* like having sex. As we said earlier, we all have our "conditions" for wanting sex. Very few men are horny all the time, and very few women are juicy all the time. And that's fine. You shouldn't *have to* have sex when you're not interested, any more than you should have to eat when you're not hungry. However, if one or both partners constantly reject the sexual advances of the other, or if one or both rarely feel much sexual desire for the other, or if one or both are just plain bored, then a more basic problem may exist, requiring the efforts of both to do something about it. The longer the problem goes undiscussed and untreated, the more difficult it becomes to do something about it. Furthermore, if the problem is not confronted, it may well show up in other forms, including lack of arousal, erection problems, and lack of orgasms.

In this chapter, we will review some of the common sources of lack of desire and suggest some things that you and your partner, if you have one, can do about it.

CAUSES OF LACK OF INTEREST IN SEX

If sex is so inherently pleasurable, why shouldn't two people who are available to each other turn each other on? Can it be that they don't love each other?

As we have said at regular intervals throughout this book, a loving relationship goes a long way toward making sexual relationships much more rewarding, but it doesn't *guarantee* a stimulating sexual relationship. Even two people who are very much in love with each other may not—from time to time, or even frequently—find each other sexually arousing. This can be difficult for a partner to believe: "If you *really* loved me, you'd want to go to bed with me!" The reasons for a lack of interest in sex are as varied as the people who are involved, and these reasons can be simple and easy to overcome or complex and hard to get at. We'll list some of the more common barriers to sexual desire, as well as some causes of boring sex.

358

Lack of Interest or Skill
in Meeting a Partner's Sexual Needs

If one partner has never learned or really doesn't care what specific sexual activities the other finds pleasurable or distasteful, his or her partner will eventually turn off to the other's sexual overtures. This problem is obviously compounded when the partners don't clearly tell each other, by words or by actions, what they want or don't want. In Chapter 19, we discussed negotiating procedures for when sex is distasteful; we discussed sexual communication in Chapter 9. These chapters can give you ideas about how to avoid making sex a regular exercise in frustration.

Excessive Demands for Sexual Satisfaction

A sexual encounter is most enjoyable when both partners experience more or less strong yearnings for each other. There are many occasions, of course, when one partner is more interested in sex than the other. If there is a wealth of good feelings between the two, then the decision about whether to have sex (or perhaps some compromise like just cuddling) will be negotiated. However, if one partner feels constantly rejected by the other, and if one partner feels regularly pressured by his or her partner to have sex, then eventually sex may be seen as giving in rather than as a mutually enjoyable coupling: "It seems he's always got his hands on me" or "I feel like hiding whenever I see 'that' look in her eyes."

In these sorts of situations, unfortunately, the "hungry" partners may be using their sexual advances as a means of getting reassurance that they are loved or are sexually desirable to their partner—the sex itself being much less important. The more they are rebuffed, therefore, the more they are going to want it. That could be trouble.

With the growth of the feminist movement, it may well be the woman who is more interested in sex than the man. If his male image is challenged (remember, a man is supposed to always be ready), he may be too threatened to refuse, so he may give in, resent it, and not enjoy it—or not give enjoyment to his partner.

Fear of Letting Loose

Many men and women grow to adulthood with a fear of sex or of really letting down their defenses when they're having sex.

They may be afraid of the emotional commitment implied by an intense erotic response. Others may have feelings coming from their early anti-sex training that intense erotic responses to their partners would somehow demean them. ("Sex is dirty.") With these attitudes, sex becomes tolerable only if carried out with restraint. Such a passionless approach can lead to a very dull sex life. Perhaps there is a lesson to be learned from Woody Allen's somewhat overstated observation that "sex *is* dirty, if you do it right."

Rigid inhibitions against enjoying sexual intimacy can be at the core of one or both partners' losing sexual desire for the other. If you just can't allow yourself to let go with your partner, you might want to try some of the exercises suggested in Chapters 15 and 19.

Just Plain Boredom

Lord Chesterfield had three things to say about sex: "The pleasure is momentary, the position ridiculous, and the expense damnable." Anyone who shares his view may not get much pleasure out of sex. If a person thinks that sexual acts are silly, that variety is obscene, and that orgasm is the only goal, then, over the years, sex really can become a drag—and certainly not worth "the expense."

Sex can be exciting, fun, and interesting even for couples who have been sharing a bed for decades. But too often, couples evolve a routine pattern for their sexual contacts that lacks variety and becomes little more than a more or less successful form of mutual masturbation. One or both partners resist breaking the pattern or experimenting, perhaps fearing that that will be interpreted as a put-down for the partner or too much of a risk for themselves. And so it goes, month after month, year after year. Even pizza gets dull if that's all you ever have.

Breaking out of habitual patterns of sexual activities that have become boring *does* take effort. It also takes the willingness of both partners to explore changes in their sexual patterns that may have become comfortable and safe, if not particularly satisfying. For example, just for starters, both of you might start sleeping in the nude if you haven't been doing this already. Just this small step might add a little new spice to your sex life. As we said in Chapter 7, lying together naked is a lot more stimulating than lying together in woolen pajamas.

So, if you and your partner (if you have one) want to get

more life into your sexual relationship, talk it over, shake hands, and come out creative.

In the following sections, we will offer some suggestions that might help you to use your own imagination and self-awareness to get and give more pleasure in your love-making. Remember, sex researchers tell us that many couples often continue their sexual activities into their seventies and eighties. If you live that long, you might as well enjoy it.

We'll first offer some general suggestions and exercises for experimenting with new approaches. These approaches may be used as supplements to your sexual activities if you already have a basically sound sexual relationship. We will also suggest some basic variations in positions for intercourse and their pros and cons, so that you and your partner can consider the possibility of adding variety to your sex life and better meeting your needs and desires.

A NEW LOOK AT YOUR SEXUAL ACTIVITIES

If you have been going through the exercises in this book, you have already done a great deal to break the habits that can make sex boring. Let's review a couple of suggestions from previous chapters.

Check It Out with Your Partner

Any attempt to breathe new life into your sexual relationship will, of course, require the involvement—preferably the enthusiastic involvement—of your partner. As we said at the beginning of this chapter, any comment from you that implies that your partner doesn't turn you on (or never did) is difficult to make—and is probably harmful to do. So let's consider some more positive and potentially successful ways of getting your partner's cooperation.

First, reread Chapter 9, which discusses talking about sex, and attempt to follow through with some of the suggestions from that chapter. If you feel that there is a warm, positive atmosphere in your discussions, you can explore your partner's willingness to attempt some changes in the pattern of your sexual activities. Talk about your affection for your partner and your wish to enhance the way you express it, and emphasize that you want to add to what already exists between

361

you. There's no need to imply criticism or dissatisfaction in what has gone before; what you would like is to *add* to your relationship in order to get more out of it. Use the negotiation steps described in Chapter 10 and illustrated in Chapter 19 if you have to.

Use Your Fantasies

As a point of departure, go back to the exercises that you did in Chapter 13 on enjoying your fantasies. As we said, many fantasies fall flat, are impractical, or are downright messy when translated into real life. But perhaps your fantasies can give you some ideas of new directions that you can take in your sexual activities. What ideas do you get from your fantasies—or from your partner's—that you can use? Have you suggested or can you suggest to your partner trying some of these?

Of course, an element of surprise can enhance sexual activities. Can you think of anything from your fantasies that you can inject as an unexpected turn-on for your partner? It needn't be something major—perhaps a colored light in the bedside lamp, a body oil with your partner's favorite fragrance, a lubricant with an unexpected flavor, or some provocative undergarment in which to begin your love-play. Of course, there's always the danger that the surprise may create more laughter than eroticism. But even so, a little laughter can go a long way toward enhancing love-making and breaking through boredom.

Now let's look at some more specific ways in which you might go about getting more arousal and less boredom into your sexual activities.

IT'S THE LITTLE THINGS
YOU DO TOGETHER

Felix and Miriam had been married for eighteen years. They enjoyed each other sexually, with no particular complaints. Usually, at bedtime, one or the other would give a signal if they wanted to have sex. Felix would then brush his teeth, undress, and get into bed. Then Miriam would go into the bathroom, check or install whatever contraceptive she was using at the time, undress, and join Felix in bed. One night Felix caught a glimpse of Miriam in her panties while she was standing in front of the bathroom mirror. The sight of Miriam in her panties was a real turn-on for Felix. With some embarrassment, he asked Miriam to leave her panties on when she came to bed. She did and they both had a fine time as he removed them as part of their love-play. When they were done, Miriam shyly asked Felix if next time he would mind wearing his briefs to bed. It really turned her on when she saw him in his shorts.

It doesn't take much to add a lot of excitement to a sexual encounter. Books such as *The Sensuous Woman, The Sensuous Man, The Joy of Sex,* and *More Joy of Sex* are packed with ideas. Trying one or more of them doesn't have to be over-planned to the point of being mechanical. You don't need a big production; it can be something spontaneous that just comes over you when you're with your partner.

Nowhere does the saying, "different strokes for different folks" hold more true than in bed. If you and your partner like it, or if you are at least willing to try it, then do it. Perhaps it's just undressing each other, having sex with your clothes on (well, mostly), or discovering a "new" part of your lover's body. Or it could be feeding each other cheese, grapes, or smoked oysters, or sipping wine in bed.

Such ideas are intended to provide spice to a sound sexual relationship. However, like any spice, they won't camouflage the basic problems of a poor relationship. If your sexual problem involves more than boredom, it might be wise to work on your basic relationship before you move into activities that are fairly exotic.

Not all people like all spices. We are certainly not recommending that you try all of them. You should pick and choose. Some of the ideas will appeal to you, some will leave you cold, and some will be downright distasteful. Experiment with any that sound at least acceptable. You might like them. If not, there's nothing much lost.

Other Orifices, Other Appendages

There are many openings, junctures, and other parts of your body that can be stimulated by many parts of your partner's body, and vice versa. The combinations are almost limitless. A penis can be placed between the woman's breasts or between her thighs, approaching her from either the front or the rear. Some men and women enjoy placing the underside of the penis against the vulva, with the upper end against the clitoris, and rubbing against each other. This can even be an enjoyable form of stimulation when the man doesn't have an erection. Remember, soft penises have feelings too!

Sexual activities involving the anus turn some people on and repel others. Some states consider anal intercourse (as

363

well as oral intercourse) illegal. So watch it. Some women experience intense pleasure from it, and many men enjoy the
snug fit. However, there are a number of problems with anal
intercourse in addition to the aesthetic consideration. First attempts for some women, and all attempts by others, can be
quite painful. If you have hemorrhoids, forget it. Cleanliness is
important. Germs and organisms that are natural inhabitants of
the anus can do much harm if they enter the man's urethra or
are transferred by the penis to the vagina after anal intercourse. If you make the switch from anal to vaginal intercourse
(which is particularly tempting in a rear-entry position), wash
carefully first.

The best position for trying anal intercourse, at least for
the first (if not the last) time, is with the woman kneeling and
the man entering from the rear. He should coat his penis with a
thick lubricant, such as "K-Y" or a lubricating cream (the anus
has little natural lubrication), and press *gently* against her anus
(this assumes that he has an erection). She should try to relax
and press back gently against the penis. As she opens, he proceeds in slowly, getting only the head in and then stopping,
moving the penis around slightly. Proceed slowly and at a pace
dictated by the woman's receptiveness. Unlike that in vaginal
intercourse, major stimulation should come on the slow withdrawal of the penis rather than on the thrust. In this position,
the man can also stimulate the woman's clitoris, breasts, and
body with his hands. She can reach back and stroke the man's
scrotum and perineum and perhaps guide the tempo and
depth of the thrusting with her hand.

The anus of many men and women is a very sensitive area
and can be stimulated in a number of ways during love-making
other than by trying anal intercourse. You can stroke your
partner's anus with your fingertips or with a mechanical vibrator. Some men and women experience a pleasant charge
from having a well-greased finger thrust gently into their anus
just at the moment of orgasm. The thrustee may enjoy the
sensation of feeling the contractions of orgasms or ejaculation
inside his partner's anus. But check it out; unexpected penetration of the anus may be painful, harmful, and, to say the
least, unwelcome.

Oral sex (using the mouth to stimulate the penis, clitoris,
vulva, and other parts of the partner's body) is much more
common than anal sex. It is also painless and less likely to
cause disease than anal sex.

The mouth and tongue are very sensitive and are therefore capable of receiving as well as giving much pleasure. Kissing can be an intimate regular part of pleasuring and can go on
through all face-to-face intercourse.

A man can bring a woman to orgasm by stimulating the area around the clitoris with his tongue and lips. Women differ as to what areas are most sensitive, as well as to the pressure, tempo, and type of stimulation they like best. If she doesn't tell you, ask her what she likes.

Similarly, a man and his partner may both enjoy her stimulating his penis, testicles, and surrounding areas with her tongue and lips. Whether he likes being sucked, licked, or nibbled varies from man to man and from time to time, so talk it over. If you and your partner agree, you can continue to stimulate your partner's penis by mouth, either as a way of merely arousing him or of bringing him all the way to orgasm. There is no harm in swallowing the ejaculate, if you like.

Oral sex *can* be painful if done in the wrong way (watch those teeth), and it can be distasteful to some people (see Chapter 19 for more details on how to try oral sex). So be sure that you have mutual interest and cooperation.

And don't forget that there are numerous other areas of men's and women's bodies in addition to their genitals that are enjoyable to stimulate or to have stimulated with the partner's mouth. Many people enjoy licking or being licked on the nipples (both men and women, as in Figure 20-1), in the ears, or in a variety of other places. Let your curiosity be your guide.

Figure 20-1.

Other Stimulants

Most of your sexual arousal comes from touching and being touched by your partner's body and from sexual and affectionate thoughts and fantasies. But how about aphrodisiacs?

Well, there are no known substances that are effective in turning people on. Some consciousness-altering drugs such as marijuana, can enhance sensations and distort time perceptions in a way that some people feel gives greater pleasure to their sexual activities. But these drugs are often either illegal, unsafe, or both.

Although alcoholic drinks will not create sexual arousal, they can be useful in enhancing sexual pleasure by reducing sexual inhibitions. On the other hand, too much alcohol can make erection difficult or impossible, dull the senses, and quite possibly put you to sleep. So if you're going to use alcohol before or during sexual activities, try to find the right amount—enough to reduce inhibitions, but not so much as to impair your physical capabilities.

Other Than Naked

Most relatively well-educated middle-class Americans have sex naked. Other people consider it unnecessary, silly, or embarrassing to take their clothes off for sex (see Figure 20-2). Although nakedness does make it much easier to see and reach all parts of your partner's anatomy, there is much to recommend the use of clothes as part of sexual stimulation. If you

Figure 20-2.

haven't tried it already, go through the process of undressing your partner—feel free to ask for help with complicated buckles, snaps, and hooks. Ask your partner what items of clothing, such as bras, jockey shorts, gauze pants, stockings and garter belts, jock straps, and negligees, really turn him or her on. Wear them. See what it's like to have intercourse wearing some of these items.

If you have the time, resources, and motivation, you can even get into costumes that fit your erotic fantasies—western gear, Roman togas (converted bed sheets will do), or what have you.

Unfortunately, sometimes one partner thinks that the other is kooky or weird if he or she admits to enjoying the partner's wearing a particular article of clothing. Not only can this present difficulties in communication, but the sexual experience can suffer as well.

Perhaps the concern in such a situation is that the partner is turned on only by the article of clothing and not by the person wearing it. In such cases, try talking about it. It's really possible that this will open up new vistas of pleasure for both of you. It really has nothing to do with what your partner thinks of you as a person. He or she simply gets more turned on when you're wearing a particular article of clothing, and your partner may even be able to make love more skillfully or passionately when you wear it. If it turns you or your partner on, and if it doesn't hurt or damage either of you in any way, then this process of sharing may move both of you to greater heights of sexual enjoyment.

Other Places and Other Times

Your bed at night is probably the most usual, convenient, and private place and time for having sex. But you may occasionally want to change the time and locale of your sexual encounters. Again, let your fantasies or imagination be your guide to varying the circumstances for having sex. Too often, the time and place people have sex is determined more by habit—right after Johnny Carson's show, three times a week, on the good old king- or queen-size bed—than by a deliberate decision about what would be most enjoyable. Routine has its advantages. There's security in familiar places and habitual patterns. If they work, that's fine. But occasional departures in time and place can provide an enjoyable pinch of spice to a steady but bland diet.

Sexual activities generally occur at night. Anthropologists suggest that our primitive ancestors chose to have sex in the dark because they tended to be relatively defenseless and thus vulnerable to attack while in the throes of sexual passion, and that the dark protected them from their enemies. Such attacks are now relatively rare. So, except for the pressures of work and the demands of little children, there is no real need to limit one's sexual activities to the nighttime or to the dark. Seeing your partner can be very erotic. In fact, many people find that sex early in the morning, when they are rested from a good night's sleep, can lead to a leisurely and pleasurable sexual contact. There is hardly a time of the day that hasn't something to recommend itself. And unexpected occasions can often provide an erotic opportunity for a "quickie"—maybe while you're dressing to go out for dinner and have a few spare minutes. Or late Sunday morning after reading the funny papers in bed. Although we generally recommend slow, leisurely, gentle sexual encounters, the occasional "quickie" with minimal preliminary pleasuring and a fast pace of intercourse can be a stimulating special event.

And, of course, there are almost no limitations—except local public-decency ordinances—to exciting places to have sex. We have mentioned earlier the advantages of motel therapy to launch a new beginning in your sexual relationship. Masters and Johnson discovered that the fact that couples stayed in a hotel in St. Louis while receiving their therapy added to the stimulation for revising their sexual patterns. If you can get away to a hotel or motel overnight from time to time, even in your own town or city, it can give you a great erotic boost. Certainly, getting away from the job, the kids (we know you love them—but . . .), and calls from your mother-in-law (we know you love her, too—but . . .) can reduce the distractions that keep you from relaxing in your sexual relationship.

However, the new surroundings themselves often add to the eroticism of a stay in a motel. Somehow the setting adds something special to your activities, even if you've been married twenty years.

If you can't afford motel therapy, remember that lots of the best sexual places in life are free. You might try the back seat of the family car at a drive-in movie—or parked in a more discrete place, such as your own garage, if necessary. Consider the woods (watch out for poison ivy), your living-room couch, the kitchen floor, or a borrowed tent in your backyard. Or try whatever your budget, imagination, and modesty will allow.

Having sex in a shower or bath can be a highly erotic experience. If you prefer showering before or after intercourse, why not include your partner? Running water can be quite stimulating. You can use the opportunity for mutual arousal, soaping and massaging the soapy water all over each other's bodies (don't forget the genitals). It's an excellent opportunity, and excuse, to explore new areas.

Intercourse might be difficult in a shower or bath, unless you're a good contortionist and don't mind some knobs and faucets sticking into your ribs. You'd have much more flexibility in a swimming pool or on a private beach—remember that sexy scene in *From Here to Eternity*?

One other idea about place—and this one costs nothing and is more comfortable than a bathtub and more private and available than a beach or swimming pool. Since your bedroom has probably been the setting for most of your sexual activities for years, try making it look different as a symbol of a change in your routine. At the very least, move your bed to a different wall, rearrange the furniture, and put up a new picture or more colorful drapes. Your bedroom is not only the place you sleep—it's also important as the place you make love. Make it look like a good setting for it.

OTHER POSITIONS

Position is *not* everything in sexual intercourse, but alternative positions can add variety to your sexual life.

People often make one of two mistakes about positions for intercourse. One extreme is the belief that there is only one "natural" position for sex—with the man above the woman—and that all other positions are just novelties and are perhaps a bit bizarre. The other extreme is that there are an infinite number of positions and that well-adjusted people should switch regularly from one to another.

Our position on positions is that both of these ideas are unrealistic.

Most people usually develop one or two positions that they use regularly, and as long as both partners find the positions comfortable, pleasurable, and not boring, that's just fine. However, if the position is chosen solely on the basis of tradition or for the pleasure of one partner while the other is limited in his or her satisfaction, then intercourse can become not only boring but an unpleasant mechanical experience as well.

One way of bringing desire back into a lackluster sex life is to be experimental and innovative in the ways you have intercourse. There are no "right" ways for you to have inter-

369

course. What matters is what positions work best for you and your partner.

According to some old stereotypes about sex, "foreplay" was essentially for the woman, to get her aroused and ready, if not eager, for the penis to enter her vagina. Intercourse was essentially for the man, so that he could bring about his own orgasm. Thus, the man on top of the woman has become the most commonly used position—he's in control, his penis is able to penetrate deeply and is not likely to slip out of his partner's vagina, and his body is tensed in such a way that he is most likely to have an intense orgasm. Incidentally, in this position the man's semen is most likely to move toward the woman's cervix, making this position also effective for conception.

However, the position does restrict the woman's ability to move around very much. Many women feel that their sexual satisfaction is limited when they are only a passive recipient of their partner's thrusting. The woman must be able to be an active and full participant in intercourse. Even if the male-above position is satisfying to the woman as well as to the man, its exclusive use can limit the possibility of sexual enjoyment for both partners. Satisfying intercourse often requires variety as well as meeting the mutual need and desires of both partners.

In the following pages, we will discuss the male-above position, as well as three other basic positions for sexual intercourse. (There are, of course, many other positions, but most are variations on these basic four.) Although we are going to suggest that you try each of the four positions, we are not suggesting that you make all or any of them regular parts of your sexual life. This section is not intended as a field manual of erotic positions for sexual acrobats. We know that many people will find one or more of these positions uncomfortable, aesthetically displeasing, and/or even silly. Some positions may not be practical in view of your relative body builds. (Very small women don't usually do well underneath very big men.) The reason we suggest that you try them, if you haven't already, is so that you may have an experience with the variety of intercourse positions that are available to you. Trying these positions, along with your own modifications, will give you the opportunity to explore how well each meets your and your partner's preferences and physical needs. Thus, you will have several possible options to diversify and expand your sexual activities and to avoid sexual boredom.

Each time, begin with the Erotic Pleasure exercises from Chapter 14, and when you are both ready, move into one of the positions. The transition from mutual pleasuring into intercourse should be a natural, flowing progression and not an abrupt change.

Points to Remember About Intercourse

Several points that apply to all positions in intercourse should be kept in mind. Discuss these points with your partner before you begin the intercourse position exercises that follow.

1. Intercourse is more than a mechanical act to produce orgasms.

2. Intercourse should flow naturally from the mutual pleasuring that precedes it, and it should generally begin only when you are both aroused and ready.

3. Intercourse is not the end of a sexual interaction but should usually lead to a quiet period of unwinding and expressing affection to each other after orgasm.

4. Intercourse should usually be a slow, gentle, rhythmic activity in which both you and your partner have a role in determining the pace. Exceptions such as "quickies" or play that may be rough, quick, or jerky may be mutually agreed-upon enjoyable diversions.

5. Both partners should be equally involved in choosing positions, activities, and timing, although you may choose to take turns in taking the lead.

6. It is important to learn and to communicate to your partner your own needs and preferences in intercourse and to understand his or hers.

7. Although both partners will usually seek and enjoy orgasms in intercourse, it is not useful to have orgasms as your primary focus or goal in intercourse. Intercourse that doesn't lead to orgasms for one or both partners can be a loving, enjoyable, and nonfrustrating experience. One partner should never try to force the other partner to pursue an elusive orgasm.

8. From time to time, you, your partner, or both of you may choose to have orgasm from some activity beside intercourse, such as mouth–genital stimulation. If it's acceptable to both of you, this can be a perfectly satisfying alternative. If you so choose, you can also have intercourse before or after one or both of you have orgasm from other sources. Intercourse need not always be the climax to sexual encounters.

Discussing Positions with Your Partner

Before you start focusing on experimentation with sexual positions, it's a good idea to set aside some time to discuss your and your partner's feelings about intercourse in general, and about positions for intercourse in particular. Do you feel that your patterns for intercourse have not been pleasing to you? Does intercourse generally occur too early in your love-making? Do you feel pressured into intercourse when you would prefer other forms of sexual activities? Do you feel pressured from your partner to have an orgasm, or more than one, when you have intercourse? Do you feel that intercourse has become a purely orgasm-oriented activity, and that it has lost (or never had) a focus on mutual pleasuring? If you answered "yes" to any of these questions, you might discuss ways in which you can help each other to relax and enjoy intercourse without being preoccupied either with having orgasms or with giving them to your partner.

As you try each of the four basic positions for intercourse that follow, discuss with your partner your reaction to the position, what you like about it, and what you don't like about it. Feel free to suggest modifications on each of the positions, modifications that would better meet your needs and wishes.

There are, of course, several other "basic positions" that you might enjoy besides the ones we discuss here: standing, sitting, upside down, and backwards—any position in which the penis gets inside the vagina and is comfortable and pleasing for one or both of you is fine. Try them. The worst that could happen is that you may find yourselves with an occasional ache or that you will end up, we hope, with a good laugh.

But we suggest that you start by trying each of these positions. They are the ones that are most likely to give you pleasure and that require the least acrobatic skills. They are arranged in a recommended sequence, so go from one to the next in order, either in one love-making session or in several sessions—just as you choose. Remember, however, the use of "distress signals," which we talked about in Chapter 7. If any of the positions is uncomfortable or unpleasant for you, do not hesitate to let your partner know right away, and either go on to the next position or go back to the previous one. As for the rejected position, check it off to experience. You *don't* have to like or use any position that you find unpleasant. Also, go ahead and give yourself one of the built-in rewards that we described in Chapter 7 for each new position you try or for modifications you have invented. You'll have earned it.

Position One: Man Above

We'll start with the position that most people in the United States use most of the time, the one in which the man lies above the woman. It's as American as apple pie. And, like apple pie, most of us like it and know it well. And even though you will try the peach and rhubarb pies that we'll suggest shortly, and although you might use them from time to time, you may still find yourself regularly coming back to apple.

There are a number of reasons why people choose this position so often. One is, of course, that many people have been taught the myth that it's the only way you're *supposed* to have intercourse. However, there are a number of *good* reasons that make this position so popular. It makes it easy to get the penis in the vagina and keep it in. Many men and women enjoy the deep penetration that is possible in this position. It gives considerable control to the man for the angle, depth, and rhythm of intercourse. Finally, many couples prefer face-to-face positions, in which both partners can look at each other's reactions, talk easily, and kiss during intercourse.

Even though you may be old pros at this position, we'd like you to start with it. Sometimes looking carefully at a position you use regularly can give you a new appreciation of it as well as permit some alterations in how you use it. If you and your partner have used this position, you can begin by talking over what you like about it and what problems you have in using it.

As in all practice sessions with these exercises, remember what we have told you about preliminary give-to-get pleasuring. Don't rush into intercourse; wait until you are both aroused and are ready to make a smooth transition into intercourse.

When you are both ready, the woman should move into a comfortable position on her back, making sure that she allows plenty of head room from the headboard or wall for her partner—especially if he is much taller than she. Better to situate yourself well now than require an awkward move later. The woman should have her knees raised and her legs spread. Some couples find that penetration is better if the woman places a pillow under her buttocks. See if it helps.

The man then places himself above the woman, supporting much of his weight on his elbows and knees. Too much weight on the woman can make her more concerned with suffocation than with enjoying intercourse. On the other hand, some men become so concerned with being a burden on their partners that they hardly touch the woman except at the pelvis.

Try to avoid either extreme. Make contact with more of your body than just the pelvic area if you both decide you'd like to. Although in this position the male has more control over the thrusting movements, the more room he gives his partner, the more she can share in guiding the action.

Once you are both comfortable, there is no need to rush into putting the penis into the vagina unless passion is overwhelming one or both of you. See what pleasuring you can give each other in this position before intercourse. Since the man's use of his hands may be limited by the position, the woman can take the lead in stroking him, or perhaps she can take his penis in her hands and use it to stroke the area around her vulva.

When you're both ready, the woman should place the penis at the opening of her vagina. Then the man slowly slides it in, moving slowly and gently in short strokes. Try to reserve your deep penetration for later, concentrating now on a shallow penetration of an inch or two.

Both partners should focus on the variety of sensations they experience. You can whisper feedback to each other in between kisses if you so choose.

The man and the woman can now concentrate on slowly increasing both the depth of the penetration and the tempo of the thrusting. But remember, despite any temptation to the contrary, to keep the thrusts slow, gentle, and smooth.

As the man approaches ejaculation, he can inform his partner that he is near that point. At that point, deeper and more rapid thrusting will likely enhance his—and his partner's—enjoyment of the sensations of ejaculation. Both should now concentrate on the sensation each receives from the ejaculation.

The woman may have already had one or more orgasms. If she hasn't, she can ask the man to delay his orgasm or she can reach orgasm—or not, as she chooses—after he reaches his. She can do so either from continued rhythmic pressure in intercourse or from manual or other stimulation after he withdraws.

The man should, after ejaculation, remain in the position and stay connected for a while if it is possible and comfortable. (The penises of some men become too sensitive to continue contact for a while after ejaculation.) Concentrate on the sensations you are both experiencing in your genitals and in the rest of your body after orgasm. You may want to describe these feelings to each other as you continue to stroke and kiss each other and hold each other gently.

From time to time in the future, you may want to experiment with various modifications of this basic man-on-top position. The woman may try raising her legs high, perhaps wrapping them around her partner's waist; or, if she's particularly agile, arching her knees over the man's shoulders, as in Figure 20-3; or stretching her legs out straight with the man's legs either between hers or, if your physique and endowment permit it, with the man's legs straddling the woman's. Try whatever modifications you can come up with that suit your tastes and your bodies.

Position Two: Side by Side

In this position, the man and woman lie on their sides facing each other. It is the favorite position of many couples, once they figure out how to get into it. In this position, neither partner is putting weight on the other. Each partner has easy access to stroke his or her partner's bodies and genital areas, at least with the arm they are not lying on. Each partner also has an equal opportunity to set the pace, angle, and depth of pene-

Figure 20-3.

tration. It is a good position for couples in which one partner is much taller than the other, and for couples who want to remain connected and perhaps go to sleep right after orgasm.

Again, begin your experimenting with this position by talking about any experiences you have had with it. When you're ready, after mutual pleasuring, you can move into it in either of two ways: (1) You can begin with the man-above position, with the penis already inserted in the vagina. The man places his weight on his left elbow and knee and the woman pulls her right upper leg and thigh up while they both gently roll over to the man's left side and the woman's right side. Her leg should be pulled up to a comfortable angle, with the left side of the man's waist resting on her right inner thigh. (2) You can also get into this position by having the woman lying on her back, but with her body angled somewhat to her right and her right leg against the bed with her knee angled upward. The man arranges himself on his left side with his left side against her right inner thigh in such a way that his penis finds itself in the neighborhood of his partner's vagina. The woman then places her left leg over his right hip.

The position may take a while to get used to, and it may take a little effort to angle the penis into the vagina. But take our word for it: It works.

While in this position, you can take turns setting the tempo and the depth of the thrust. You can also take advantage of the relative freedom of your hands to explore and stroke your partner's breasts, nipples, testicles, perineum, arms, thighs, and whatever. Look into each other's faces and exchange reactions about your feelings.

There are many variations you can try in this position. The woman may place her lower leg straight and parallel to the man's bottom leg rather than keeping it under him. Or you can reverse the sides you lie on, as in Figure 20-4, depending on who's right-handed and who's left-handed. (You are particularly fortunate in this position if one of you is right-handed and one is left-handed.) See what is most comfortable and pleasurable for you.

Position Three: Woman Above

In this position, the woman straddles or lies above the man. Many couples feel uncomfortable about this position because it violates the tradition that the man is "supposed" to be on top in sex. According to the folklore, he's supposed to be in charge, whereas the woman is supposed to be the passive

Figure 20-4.

partner. In contrast, this position gives the woman the opportunity to be quite active and to take the lead in the pace, angle, tempo, and depth of the thrusting. It also gives the man the opportunity to enjoy being relatively passive and to be the receiver of the pleasure that his partner gives him. Thus, the man can learn as much about his sexuality as the woman can. There is nothing "unmasculine" about that, any more than it's unfeminine for the woman to enjoy expressing her sexuality to the fullest. So trying out this position is not only an opportunity to enjoy a variation in intercourse patterns, but it is a good test of your attitudes about the sexual roles of men and women as well.

In previous chapters in Part 4, we have pointed out the advantages of this position for such sexual problems as lack of orgasms in women and lack of ejaculatory control in men. The position is also particularly good for women who are much smaller than their partners, or for those who are in advanced stages of pregnancy.

Once again, start by discussing any experiences and feelings about this position. See if either of you senses any threat to your masculinity or femininity by using this position. Try to make your transition from mutual pleasuring or from your previous position smoothly.

The man should get himself comfortable on the bed. The woman straddles over him with her knees on the bed on either side of his hips. She can either continue to kneel above him or recline with her body over his, with her legs stretched out beside his.

As in previous positions, you need not initiate intercourse immediately but can continue to pleasure each other. For example, with the woman's pelvis right above the man's, she can place the underside of his penis along her vulva and against her clitoral area. She can then move slowly back and forth in a rocking motion and enjoy the stimulation of his penis and scrotum against her genitals. Do this gently, though. You don't want to put much weight on the man's scrotum and testes.

When you are both ready, the woman can gently grasp the penis and guide it into her vagina, regulating the angle and depth of penetration. Remember to go slowly. Start with shallow penetration, determining the depth of penetration by how much the woman rises up on her knees. Penetration will be smoother if the woman puts herself at a 45° angle to the man rather than sitting straight up (see Figure 20-5).

Meanwhile, the man's hands are free to caress the woman's body, including her breasts and the area around her clitoris and vulva.

The woman can take advantage of her flexibility in this

Figure 20-5.

position to experiment with various angles of penetration, with the depth of the penetration, and with the tempo of intercourse. She can try rocking motions, straight up and down motions, circular motions, or a combination of any of these. Although the man need not remain still during all this, at least initially he should let the woman take the lead, and he should give her feedback on how her various movements feel. He may well find that he is much better able to control the timing of his orgasm in this position. At the same time, her thrusting and his manual stimulation of her genitals help the woman to have hers.

As in the other positions, there are a number of possible variations. Once connected, the man can draw up his knees, with the woman leaning back against them. Or she can straddle the man while he sits on a high stool, on a rocking chair, or even in the back seat of a car.

Position Four: Man Behind Woman

In this position, the man enters the woman from behind, generally with his belly pressed against her buttocks. It is the last basic position that we suggest because so many people feel uncomfortable with it. It is often confused with anal intercourse because the man is behind the woman. However, anal intercourse, as we described it earlier, involves placing the penis inside the woman's anus. In this section, we're talking about a form of penis-in-vagina intercourse that many couples find enjoyable.

The position is also disliked by some because it is not a face-to-face position (unless you're willing to risk a neckache); obviously this position makes looking at each other's faces during intercourse difficult. However, there are a number of advantages to this position. Some couples prefer the "fit" of the penis in the vagina in this position, which is essentially upside down from the other positions. Some enjoy the contact of the man's belly against the woman's buttocks. Further, the man is able to caress many areas of the woman's body during intercourse and has a particularly unobstructed access to her clitoris. It is a good position for a heavy or pregnant woman—her belly won't get in the way.

As you approach this position, do as you have done before: Discuss your experiences and reactions to the position. If you have qualms about it, bring them out.

This position requires more of a break from usual pleasuring positions, but make the transition as smoothly as you can when you're both aroused and ready to go. There are several basic variations on this position, but we'll start with one of the easier ones.

Once you've both become aroused using the Erotic Pleasure exercises, the woman positions herself on her belly with her legs stretched in a V and her head and chest on a pillow. The man kneels between her legs and guides her as she raises her buttocks by inching up on her knees. The man raises or lowers himself and guides the woman's pelvis until her vulva is on a level with his penis. He guides his penis in slightly. He can then either lean forward on his knuckles or hands or continue to kneel on his knees as he proceeds with slow, rhythmic thrusting (see Figure 20-6).

In a more-restful version of this position, both the man and the woman lie on their same sides with the man lying behind the woman. When his penis is settled near her vagina, and when they get into a comfortable position, he inserts his penis. One or both may have to move an upper leg around to get everything to fit just right.

This position may be awkward at first, so take your time and remember to start with slow, regular thrusting, holding off from heavy thrusting until you are well into it. Because of the angle of penetration, the woman may be much more sensitive to deep penetration in this position than in the others. The

Figure 20-6.

woman can share the timing and nature of the thrusting by her own pelvic motions. The man can also stimulate the woman's breasts, stomach, and clitoris while in this position. The stimulation of the clitoral area may be particularly important, because there is no clitoral contact with the top of the man's penis or his pubic area in this position.

After orgasm in this position, you may want to move into a position in which you can more easily embrace and face each other.

A number of variations of this position are possible, whether you try lying down, kneeling, or standing up, or a variation with the woman kneeling on the floor and leaning over the bed, or standing up and leaning over the back of a chair. Use your inventiveness.

AFTER THE ORGASMS ARE OVER

Most couples will usually continue intercourse until the man, at least, has ejaculated. The woman may or may not have had one or more orgasm. If she hasn't, she may or may not still feel the need for one. If she does, she should let her partner know. If she says that she doesn't feel the need for an orgasm, the man shouldn't force it out of guilt or out of his need to prove his sexual competence. If the position used and the man's softening penis allow it, and if the man is not too sensitive after orgasm and the woman requests it, you can stay connected while you move against each other in a manner that the woman considers likely to bring about orgasm (e.g., the pubic bone of the man pressing against the woman's clitoris). If this doesn't work, then the man can try to bring the woman to orgasm by hand, or she can do it herself if she chooses.

You've tried the basic positions and your own variations. Some you liked; some you didn't. And one or both of you have had an orgasm. What now? Many beautiful sexual encounters are spoiled by an abrupt ending, with one partner turning over and going to sleep or the other making a mad dash for the shower. We hope that your experience is not like that described in an old toast:

Here's to love's sweet repose;
Belly to belly, toes to toes;
One quick moment of sheer delight,
Then back to back for the rest of the night.

Love-making doesn't end with an orgasm. As we noted in Chapter 12, perhaps the most important phase in a sexual encounter is the evaluation. What occurs after orgasms can have a great effect on how we later feel about the sexual experience.

After the orgasms, you can, if you choose, wipe any semen and vaginal secretions off your bodies with tissues or a damp towel that you cleverly put by the bed before you started. Then, relax into each other's arms in a comfortable position in which you can look at, stroke, and hold each other as best fits your mood. Talk over your feelings and remember to emphasize any positives. Feel free to play with each other in a relaxed way now that the sexual tension has discharged. Enjoy each other. If you become aroused again, fine. But don't feel that you have to begin intercourse all over again. Remember that most men can only handle one good firm erection and orgasm at a sexual encounter. There's no need to try out for endurance records. However, occasionally you might want to try to see, as a kind of game, how many orgasms you can have. (After one such game, an acquaintance of the authors' bought her husband a license frame for his car with the inscription "Three Times! Once!") But the purpose of your touching after intercourse is to have an exchange of affection and relaxation, often described as an "afterglow"; you need not get started all over again.

A final word about your thoughts as you lie back together and reflect on the sexual activities you have just completed. There are, we imagine, a few human beings who always have sensational sexual encounters with volcanic orgasms and totally joyful feelings every time they have sex. But they are rare. Most of us imperfect beings—no matter how many books we read and courses we take—still have occasional sexual experiences that are dull and unexciting. That's just part of being human. These occasional fizzles only become a major problem when we interpret them as disasters and push ourselves to make every single sexual encounter a momentous event. There are no sexual Olympics. We hope that you will take your sexual doldrums in stride and, in fact, turn them into positives by developing the capacity to laugh at your near misses. Remember, there's always next time.

As long as you are open with your partner, and as long as you share a willingness to experiment and communicate with each other, you have the capacity to grow together sexually for a long, long time.

Epilogue

We wish that our Treat Yourself programs could help everyone who tries to use them. However, we sadly realize that some readers may not be able to get all the help they need from this book. If that has been your experience, and if you've followed the procedures in this book the way we suggested they be used, but you still feel the problems are there, you may choose to seek outside help.

There are, of course, middle roads between treating yourself and getting professional help. For example, you may want to talk your problems over with a close friend or relative. Choose one who you feel is sensitive, warm, and understanding. Of course, your partner may well be your best resource with whom to talk over what is bothering you. And the answers to the questions and checklists in Chapter 8, "Knowing Your Sexuality," may be a good place to begin.

However, if there is no friend or relative available, or if it is not practical to talk with them, or if you have already tried talking with them and your problems persist, then it may be time to seek professional help for your concerns.

Choosing a therapist is an important but difficult process. You will want to make sure that you choose a competent therapist—and one you can afford.

Unfortunately, sex therapy is a relatively new area. There still aren't that many competent sex therapists around. Most states don't license sex therapists, and since almost anyone can, and often does, call him- or herself a sex therapist, there is always the risk of finding yourself pouring money into worthless therapy. Be especially suspicious of sex therapists who advertise sure-fire quick cures for all problems.

The majority of qualified sex therapists are people from the fields of psychiatry, psychology, social work, or pastoral counseling who have had additional specific training in sex therapy. However, don't assume that every physician, social worker, psychologist, or minister has the ability to provide these services. They don't. Unfortunately, until recently, most medical schools, departments of psychology, schools of social work, and seminaries provided very little training for their students in helping people with sex-related problems.

How, then, can you find a decent sex therapist? Here are several ways you can go about it.

1. If you live near a university, contact its department of psychiatry, psychology, or social work and ask to be directed to some local private practitioners who specialize in sex therapy. These universities might even run training programs of their own at which you might receive competent, supervised services at fees lower than those you would usually pay to a private practitioner.

2. If there is a city, county, or state mental-health clinic, or a family-service agency, ask the staff there if they provide sex therapy. If they don't, ask them to recommend someone.

3. If you would prefer a private practitioner, you can try checking with your local medical association, state psychological association, or association of social workers to get their recommendations. Be sure to ask for someone who specializes in sex therapy.

4. Another excellent resource for getting the names of sex therapists in your area is the American Association of Sex Educators, Counselors and Therapists (AASECT), which is the only national organization that certifies sex therapists and counselors. You can get a list of certified sex therapists and counselors throughout the nation by sending $2.00 to AASECT, 5010 Wisconsin Ave., N.W., Suite 304, Washington, D.C. 20016.

5. Finally, one of the best resources for the names of effective sex therapists is from satisfied customers. Ask people you trust and respect whether they know of any satisfied customers of sex therapists.

Whatever method you use to find a therapist, feel free to be a careful shopper. Remember that you will be paying good money for your therapist's services and that you have the right to know whether they're the right therapist for you. Ask about their qualifications, their training certifications, and their licensing. Make sure that they have specific training in sex therapy. After you've described your problem to them, ask what their approach to problems like yours is, what will be expected of you, and how long they anticipate it will take to get some results.

Be direct about what you see as your problems and what you hope to get out of therapy. Ask whether the therapist feels that your goals are reasonable and attainable. It's quite possible that the therapist will present to you a somewhat different viewpoint on your problem from your own. If so, that's fine— as long as it makes sense to you. But remember that you're the boss. Your therapist is working for you to help you on your problem. If you don't think that they can help you, find someone else.

However, don't avoid your problem by going through a succession of therapists. If you want to get helped, you will have to work at your therapy, and you will have to carry out any reasonable suggestions your therapist offers.

Remember: We all have the capacity to change and improve our sexual behavior.

Well, there you have it.

We particularly hope that you've enjoyed the book. We hope even more that you've not only read it and enjoyed it but that you've *used* it. The Treat Yourself programs presented in this book can work if you'll give them half a chance. All we ask is that you try to follow carefully the guidelines we've presented.

Now, as we said, it may be that not everybody who reads this book will be helped, or that the help won't always be 100 percent successful. Nobody can guarantee success. But thousands of people have benefited from programs just like these, and we are confident that you have more than just a fighting chance when you use one of the Treat Yourself programs.

There are millions of people in this country who are suffering from one or more of the sexual problems discussed in this book, who are unhappy about some aspects of their sex lives, or who just want more out of their sex lives. If only a small percentage of these people have been able to resolve their sex problems or enhance their sex lives by using this book, we'd be overjoyed and would feel that it was all worthwhile.

We particularly hope that the person who benefited most from this book was you.

Suggestions for Further Reading

If you would like to go deeper into one or more of the topics discussed in this book, we'd like to help you on that, too. Following, then, is a list of books on several topics related to the ones we've discussed in this book. Although there may be dozens of books for each topic, we've tried to pick representative ones so that you will know which is the best in each area.

General Information on Human Sexuality

These books provide a range of information dealing with human sexuality in general, with anatomy and physiology, and with information on sexual attitudes and behavior.

Brecher, R., and E. Brecher. *An Analysis of Human Sexual Response*. New York: Bantam, 1966.

Ellis, A. *Encyclopedia of Sexual Behavior*. New York: Aronson, 1973.

Gagnon, J. *Human Sexualities*. New York: Scott, Foresman & Co., 1977.

Haeberle, E. J. *The Sex Atlas*. New York: Seabury, 1978.

Hyde, J. S. *Understanding Human Sexuality*. New York: McGraw-Hill, 1979.

Hunt, M. *Sexual Behavior in the 1970s*. Chicago: Playboy Press, 1974.

Katchadourian, H. A., and D. T. Lunde. *Fundamentals of Human Sexuality*. New York: Holt, Rinehart and Winston, 1975.

———. *Biological Aspects of Human Sexuality*. New York: Holt, Rinehart and Winston, 1972.

Masters, W. H., and V. E. Johnson. *Human Sexual Response*. Boston: Little, Brown & Co., 1966.

McCary, J. L. *Human Sexuality*. New York: Van Nostrand Co., 1973. (Also available in a "Brief Edition," Van Nostrand Co., 1973.)

———. *Sexual Myths and Fallacies*. New York: Van Nostrand Co., 1971.

Otto, H. A., and R. Otto. *Total Sex*. New York: Wyden, 1972.

Schulz, D. A. *Human Sexuality*. Englewood Cliffs, N.J.: Prentice-Hall, Inc., 1979.

Sex Therapy

These books are about the best the sex-therapy field has to offer at this point. Although most of these are written for professionals, in these books you'll find detailed information, including the research, about the procedures we've described in this book.

Annon, J. *The Behavioral Treatment of Sexual Problems, Volume 1—Brief Therapy*. Honolulu. Enabling Systems, 1974.

———. *The Behavioral Treatment of Sexual Problems, Volume 2—Intensive Therapy*. Honolulu: Enabling Systems, 1975.

Ayres, T., et al. *SAR Guide for a Better Sex Life*. San Francisco: National Sex Forum, 1975.

Fischer, J., and H. L. Gochros. *Handbook of Behavior Therapy with Sexual Problems, Volume 1—General Procedures*. New York: Pergamon, 1977.

———. *Handbook of Behavior Therapy with Sexual Problems, Volume 2—Approaches to Specific Problems*. New York: Pergamon, 1977.

Kaplan, H. S. *The New Sex Therapy*. New York: Brunner/ Mazel, 1975.

Lehrman, H. *Masters and Johnson Explained*. Chicago: Playboy Press, 1970.

LoPiccolo, J., and L. LoPiccolo. *Handbook of Sex Therapy*. New York: Plenum, 1978.

Masters, W. H., and V. E. Johnson. *Human Sexual Inadequacy*. Boston: Little, Brown & Co., 1970.

Male Sexuality

These books describe male sexuality, both in general and from the more specific viewpoints of suggestions for dealing with specific problems. We recommend them as reading for both men and women.

Farrell, W. *The Liberated Man*. New York: Random House, 1974.

Feigen-Fasteau, M. *The Male Machine*. New York: McGraw-Hill, 1974.

Goldberg, H. *The Hazards of Being Male*. New York: Nash, 1976.

Zilbergeld, B. *Male Sexuality: A Guide to Sexual Fulfillment*. Boston: Little, Brown & Co., 1978.

Female Sexuality

These books describe female sexuality, both in general and from the more specific viewpoints of suggestions for dealing with specific problems. We recommend them as reading for both men and women.

Barbach, L. *For Yourself: The Fulfillment of Female Sexuality*. New York: Doubleday, 1975.

Boston Women's Health Collective. *Our Bodies, Ourselves: A Book By and For Women*. New York: Simon & Schuster, 1973.

Heiman, J.; LoPiccolo, L.; and J. LoPiccolo. *Becoming Orgasmic: A Sexual Growth Program for Women*. Englewood Cliffs, N.J.: Prentice-Hall, Inc., 1976.

Millett, K. *Sexual Politics*. New York: Avon, 1971.

Schaefer, L. *Women & Sex*. New York: Pantheon, 1973.

Relaxation

Although there have been several books written recently about how to relax, these are some of the best.

Benson, H. *The Relaxation Response*. New York: Avon, 1976.

Rosen, Gerald. *The Relaxation Book*. Englewood Cliffs, N.J.: Prentice-Hall, Inc., 1977.

Walker, C. Eugene. *Learn to Relax: 13 Ways to Reduce Tension*. Englewood Cliffs, N.J.: Prentice-Hall, Inc., 1976.

Fantasy and So Forth

These are books and magazines that you can use to help you use your fantasies to enhance your sex life.

Anicar, T. *Secret Sex: Male Erotic Fantasies*. New York: New American Library, 1976.

Chartham, R. *The Sensuous Couple*. New York: Ballantine, 1971.

Comfort, A. *The Joy of Sex: A Gourmet Guide to Lovemaking*. New York: Crown Publishers, 1972.

Friday, N. *My Secret Garden: Women's Sexual Fantasies*. New York: Trident, 1973.

"J." *The Sensuous Woman*. New York: Lyle Stuart, 1969.

Kronhausen, P., and E. Kronhausen. *Erotic Fantasies*. New York: Grove Press, 1969.

"M." *The Sensuous Man*. New York: Lyle Stuart, 1971.

Magazines: *Playboy, Playgirl, Viva, Penthouse*.

Massage

These are books that you can use to help you get even more out of your Erotic Pleasure exercises.

Downing, G. *The Massage Book*. New York: Random House, 1972.

Gunther, B. *Sense Relaxation Below Your Mind: A Book of Experiments in Being Alive*. New York: Pocket Books, 1973.

Inkeles, G., and M. Todris. *The Art of Sensual Massage*. San Francisco: Straight Arrow Books, 1972.

Whelan, S., and R. Cochrane. *The Art of Erotic Massage*. New York: Signet, 1972.

Young, C. *Massage: The Touching Way to Sensual Health*. New York: Bantam, 1975.

Sex and Medical Problems

These books might help if you have a physical or medical problem and you don't know where to go or what to do.

Blackford, B. *Sex and Disability*. New York: Van Nostrand, 1978.

Woods, N. F. (ed.). *Human Sexuality in Health and Illness*. St. Louis: Mosby, 1975.

Sex and Aging

These books are for people who feel that they're too old for sex, and for those who want to help convince them that they are not.

Butler, R., and M. Lewis. *Sex After Sixty*. New York: Harper & Row, 1976.

Rubin, I. *Sexual Life After Sixty*. New York: Signet, 1965.

Index

395